The Faith and Fortunes of France's Huguenots, 1600–85

The Faith and Fortunes of France's Huguenots, 1600–85

PHILIP BENEDICT

Ashgate

Aldershot • Burlington USA • Singapore • Sydney

Published by
Ashgate Publishing Limited
Gower House
Croft Road
Aldershot
Hants GU11 3HR
England

Ashgate Publishing Company
131 Main Street
Burlington
Vermont 05401–5600
USA

Ashgate website: http://www.ashgate.com

British Library Cataloguing in Publication Data

Benedict, Philip.
   The Faith and Fortunes of France's Huguenots, 1600–85.
   (St Andrews Studies in Reformation History)
   1. Huguenots—France—History—17th century.
   I. Title.
   284.5'09944'09032

Library of Congress Control Number: 00–108824

ISBN 0 7546 0225 7

This book is printed on acid free paper

Typeset in Sabon by J.L. & G.A. Wheatley Design, Aldershot
Printed and bound in Great Britain by MPG Books Ltd, Bodmin, Cornwall

Contents

St Andrews Studies in Reformation History

List of Figures and Maps

Figures

Maps

List of Tables

Acknowledgements

Nine of the essays in this volume have been previously published in slightly different form or are also scheduled for concurrent publication. A condensed version of Chapter 1 first appeared in French in Bernard Chevalier and Robert Sauzet, eds, *Les Réformes, enracinement socio-culturel* (Editions de La Maisnie, 1985). Chapter 2 was published as *The Huguenot Population of France, 1600–1685: The Demographic Fate and Customs of a Religious Minority*, Transactions of the American Philosophical Society, vol. 81, Part 5 (1991), which includes an extensive statistical apparatus omitted here. A slightly less complete version of Chapter 4 was published in French in *Annales: Economies, Sociétés, Civilisations* (1985). Chapter 7 appeared in *Le livre religieux et ses pratiques/Der Umgang mit dem religiösen Buch* (Vandenhoeck & Ruprecht, 1991), Chapter 8 in the *Bulletin de la société de l'Histoire du Protestantisme Français*, vol. 146 (2000), pp. 335–66, and Chapter 9 in Ole Peter Grell and Bob Scribner, eds, *Tolerance and Intolerance in the European Reformation* (Cambridge University Press, 1996). Chapter 10 is slated for impending publication in Raymond Mentzer and Andrew Spicer, eds, *Society and Culture in the Huguenot World, 1559–1665* (Cambridge University Press). Chapters 3 and 5 initially appeared in *Past and Present*, nos 109 (November 1985), pp. 100–17 and 152 (August 1966), pp. 46–78, and are reprinted here with permission of the Past and Present Society, 175 Banbury Road, Oxford, England, which possesses the world copyright. I would like to thank all of these publishers and journals for their kind permission to reprint these works.

In preparing the essays for this collection, I have occasionally restored passages cut from the original publication, removed passages that unnecessarily duplicated points made in other essays, corrected errors, and ventured minor stylistic improvements. Although I have generally resisted the temptation to rework the footnotes in order to acknowledge publications that have appeared since each essay first appeared, believing it best that they convey the state of the question at the time each one was written, I have updated citations of previously unpublished works and incorporated a few new details where these bear directly on specific assertions. The tables in Chapter 2 also incorporate new information kindly brought to my attention by Jean-Luc Tulot and Bernard Appy. I would like to thank both of these individuals for furnishing me with this information.

In sharing demographic data about one or more Reformed church with me, these two join many others who displayed similar generosity as I was researching the first version of Chapter 2. Jean-Pierre Bardet, Jean-Noël Biraben, Jean-Louis Calbat, Jacques Frayssenge, Yves Gueneau, Gregory Hanlon, Isabelle Michalkiewicz, Brigitte Maillard and Denis Vatinel all deserve reiterated thanks for their generosity in this regard. Dozens of friends and colleagues also offered suggestions and comments that were helpful in the preparation of one or another of these essays. I can only thank them all collectively and hope that they will not be too offended if I note the particularly important assistance of Ann Blair, Natalie Zemon Davis, Peter Dear, J.H. Elliott, Marc Forster, Stephen Innes, Matt Kadane, Elisabeth Labrousse, Naomi Lamoreaux, Giovanni Levi, Burr Litchfield, Anthony Molho, Jeffrey Muller, Silvia Panichi, Theodore K. Rabb, Joan Richards, Bernard Roussel, Alden Speare and Gerald Strauss. The research for these essays took me to dozens of French archives, libraries, and *mairies*, to whose directors and staff I likewise wish to express my gratitude. I recall with particular fondness the exceptional generosity shown me at the Archives Municipales de Metz, the Archives Départementales of the Charente, the Hérault, the Moselle and the Orne, and the Bibliothèque de la Société de l'Histoire du Protestantisme Français. Fundamental institutional support for these essays came from Brown University through its U.T.R.A. programme, which enabled me to employ four exceptionally able undergraduate research assistants whose work was essential to chapters in this volume: Nathan Drake, Lisa Gamble, Kathleen Garland and Michael Sheehan. I am also deeply grateful for institutional assistance from the Institute for Advanced Study in Princeton, where several of these essays were first researched and written. Finally, I would like to thank Andrew Pettegree for facilitating the publication of this volume and Matt Kadane and Lynda Tavares for help with the preparation of the manuscript.

Abbreviations

A.C.	Archives Communales (followed by locality)
A.D.	Archives Départementales (followed by department)
A.D.H.	Archives Départementales de l'Hérault, Montpellier
A.D.M.	Archives Départementales de la Moselle, Metz
A.D.O.	Archives Départementales de l'Orne, Alençon
A.N.	Archives Nationales
Annales: E.S.C.	*Annales: Economies, Sociétés, Civilisations*
A.R.	*Archiv für Reformationsgeschichte*
Arsenal	Bibliothèque de l'Arsenal (Paris)
B.N.	Bibliothèque Nationale (Paris)
B.P.F.	Bibliothèque de la Société de l'Histoire du Protestantisme Français (Paris)
B.S.H.P.F.	*Bulletin de la Société de l'Histoire du Protestantisme Français*
Benoist	Elie Benoist, *Histoire de l'Edit de Nantes* (5 vols, Delft, 1694–5)
Haag	E. and E. Haag, *La France protestante* (10 vols, Paris, 1846–58)
H.E.B.	*Histoire ecclesiastique de Bretagne, depuis le Réformation jusqu'à l'édit de Nantes*, ed. Benjamin Vaurigaud (Paris, 1851)
H.G.	'Histoire généalogique de Philippe Le Noir Pasteur de l'Eglise Réformée de Blaine composée par lui-même', *Cahiers du Centre de Généalogie Protestante* 26 (1989), 1308–28; 27 (1989), 1364–82; 28 (1989) 1422–40; 29 (1990), 15–23
L.D.S. film	Microfilm in the collection of the Genealogical Society of Utah
R.H.M.C.	*Revue d'Histoire Moderne et Contemporaine*

Introduction

The essays collected here represent a series of explorations in the social and religious history of France's Huguenots between the Edict of Nantes and its Revocation. They are explorations in the sense that they investigate aspects of the history of this minority of roughly one million people that had been little studied when I began this research: how the community evolved numerically and sociologically in the face of ever-intensifying pressure to return to the Catholic church; the nature of Huguenot identity; the religious psychology, cultural practices and mental world of the group and its members. The essays are also explorations in the sense that they investigate the utility of a range of sources and methods that have been little used by historians interested in the long-term consequences of the European Reformations. *Post-mortem* inventories form the basis for studies of Protestant and Catholic reading practices and visual culture; parish register evidence is used to determine marital customs and moral rigour; and marriage contracts are explored to study social mobility, wealth accumulation and patterns of Protestant–Catholic interaction.

When I first turned my attention to seventeenth-century French Protestantism roughly twenty years ago, the questions that guided my curiosity were simple but large ones. I had just completed a study of the Wars of Religion that focused on who became Protestant in the first flush of the Reformation and how the civil wars affected a major provincial city. I next wanted to find out what difference it made that a minority of the population had emerged from the maelstrom of the Religious Wars as adherents of the Reformed faith. How, and how profoundly, did being Calvinist in a preponderantly Catholic country shape their behaviour, outlook and experience?

My research soon gained greater focus as I followed the sociology of urban Reformed churches across the seventeenth century. A generation's worth of study of the social characteristics of those who became Protestant in the 1560s had revealed that the initial converts to the faith were generally a rough cross-section of the urban population. Over the seventeenth century, what might be called a 'mercantilization' of the community occurred. The percentage of merchants among the Reformed increased markedly, and the Huguenots came to exercise a disproportionate influence within important sectors of trade and manufacturing.

The discovery of this pattern naturally led me to wonder if it represented a confirmation of the affinities between Calvinism and capitalism so famously diagnosed by the great German sociologist Max Weber. This is not how most earlier historians of French Protestantism who had noticed the growing Huguenot presence in French trade had explained it. Writing within a historiographic tradition that has long stressed the unjust suffering of the faithful, they argued that this resulted from the discrimination that the Reformed faced in obtaining royal offices or pursuing the learned professions. The main body of scholarship on the European Reformation was also turning away from the issues raised by Weber's famous essay on *The Protestant Ethic and the Spirit of Capitalism*, both because the 'Weber thesis debate' as it had come to be cast had become an increasingly arid scholastic exercise, and because a growing body of scholarship was calling attention to numerous parallels between the Protestant and Catholic Reformations. In place of the older view that depicted Protestantism as the royal road to modernity, most experts increasingly emphasized the ways in which the Catholic and Protestant Reformations resembled one another. Still, the questions raised by the experience of the Huguenots seemed to merit closer examination, especially since new methods of social and cultural history appeared to hold out better prospects of answering the kinds of empirical questions that Weber's ideas provoked. Did the Huguenots display greater inner-worldly asceticism or more of an aptitude for economic success than their Catholic neighbours? Did their religious psychology conform to the picture of Calvinists driven by anxiety over predestination to a rationalized self-monitoring of their ethical behaviour? I found myself launched from a Weberian springboard into research on two fronts: the comparative study of Huguenot and Catholic social and economic mobility, and the investigation of Huguenot religious life.

Many of the essays that follow bear the mark of my engagement with Weberian themes. In light of the recent stress on the parallel consequences of the 'two Reformations', this necessarily had to take the form of controlled comparisons with actually existing Catholic populations. These comparisons often revealed the inadequacies of Weber's arguments. At the end of the process, I none the less remain convinced that his ideas retain considerable heuristic value for students of the European Reformation, even if detailed research often proves them empirically unconvincing, both because they offer a valuable antidote to the tendency to see only the similarities between the various religious families that emerged from the Reformation, and because they oblige the researcher to attend carefully to the potential psychological and behavioural implications of specific theological systems.

As I dug deeper, other questions also presented themselves to my attention. Some were suggested by features of the sources that I encountered. In seeking to determine from probate inventories the books that were most widely disseminated in Huguenot households and thus might have particularly shaped Huguenot religious life, I came across interesting evidence about the kinds of paintings that they owned as well. This prompted an investigation of Protestant and Catholic visual cultures and the popular market for art. Other questions arose from phenomena that my research brought to light. My discovery that many urban Huguenot congregations declined in size over the course of the century prompted a more extensive investigation of the reasons why this might have occurred. This in turn led me to accumulate a great deal of demographic evidence that both shed much light on, and raised new puzzles about, many other aspects of Huguenot behaviour and customs. The frequency with which historians find that new questions are suggested to them in the course of their research is, of course, one of most reassuring evidences for the conviction that what they write is more than simply a projection of their individual interests and 'subject position'. At the same time, historians are also unquestionably products of the times in which they write. Contemporary interest in how multicultural societies can accommodate difference has recently sparked renewed attention to what was formerly cast rather Whiggishly as the 'history of toleration'. My work has not escaped this influence. Recent German discussions of the theme of 'confessionalization' have also inspired me to formulate and confront new questions about the Huguenots and their place in French society.

The methods that I have used to answer these questions draw upon the tools of social history, historical demography, and what the French call 'socio-cultural history'. I came of age intellectually when the 'new social history' was still new, and when French historians were innovating brilliantly in the fields of historical demography, the history of *mentalités*, and the history of the book. I continue to find the techniques developed in these fields powerful tools for bringing to light both hidden patterns of change in the aggregate behaviour of large numbers of individuals and elements of the cultural practices of ordinary people that other sources cannot reveal. The concern to apply these methods to the history of France's Huguenots imposed still another kind of exploration – of archives and libraries across France in search of the kinds of documents required to use these methods that have survived from seventeenth-century communities with important Huguenot populations. Fortunately, the search was not fruitless.

It may also appear from the sequence of the essays in the first two parts of the book that my work has followed the broader trajectory of so much historical investigation in both France and the United States over the past two decades: moving from social history to cultural history, from large-scale statistical projects to micro-historical examinations of 'normal exceptions', and from studying the distribution of cultural artefacts across social categories to studying their appropriation by specific members of these categories. There is undoubtedly a measure of truth to this. In particular, important features of certain later essays were stimulated by Roger Chartier's pathbreaking studies in the history of reading. At the same time, I would stress that all the methods employed here build upon and complement each other. The more detailed case studies would not have been possible until the larger statistical investigations had taught me what was, and was not, typical of Huguenot thought and religious practice. Rather than concluding as I proceeded that newer methods had superseded older ones or that cultural explanations had rendered social ones inadequate, I have consistently moved back and forth between quantitative investigations and case studies, between social history and cultural history. Indeed, my experience of trying to explore a social milieu and cultural world to which it was often difficult to gain access has convinced me of the dangers of the kind of trendspotting found in many historiographic essays and manifestos for new approaches to history. The inevitable tendency of these essays to stigmatize certain methods as outmoded and promote others as the wave of the future can prompt an almost instantaneous withering of fruitful methods of inquiry long before they have reached the point of diminishing returns – witness the sad demise of the quantitative history of the book, which still has a great deal to teach us about which texts were particularly central in past eras and who read them. 'Normal exceptions' simply cannot be recognized without knowing the norm. The force of a cultural system is often best determined by measuring its impact on behaviour through controlled comparison. For these reasons, quantitative and ethnographic methods are ultimately complementary, not contradictory. Likewise, social and cultural history are mutually illuminating specializations, not rival absolutisms competing for explanatory hegemony 'in the final analysis'. The essays that follow are dedicated to illustrating these propositions. They also aspire to suggest that archival prospecting and large-scale statistical investigation, laborious and time-consuming though they may be, need not preclude pleasure and playfulness.

With the benefit of hindsight, I can see that what I have consistently done in these essays is to place the history of the Huguenots within a broader frame of reference than that employed by most previous historians. Up until the recent past, the history of French Protestantism was largely written by French Protestants whose preoccupations were shaped by the faith's problematic and long-contested place within the French national community. From the early martyrologist Jean Crespin to the present, Huguenot historians have particularly emphasized the sufferings and resistance of the faithful. This meta-narrative inevitably foregrounds the sixteenth-century 'struggle for recognition', the Saint Bartholomew's Massacre, the Revocation of the Edict of Nantes, and the eighteenth-century 'desert'. In so far as it brings the years of relative stability under the regime of the Edict of Nantes into view, it orients historians towards the legal and political battles that accompanied the gradual erosion of the rights that the Edict granted the Protestants. A few historians have also explored French Reformed theology during the seventeenth century, notably the important quarrels over the theology of grace sparked by the writings of Moyse Amyraut. The questions that I explore here were suggested to me by my teaching and thinking within an American academic context that draws one's attention to the broader issues in the history of the European Reformation that must be presented in an American classroom. The investigation here of such themes as the Reformation and the book, Calvinism and capitalism, and the strength of confessional identities should make these essays interesting to all those concerned with the Reformation and its long-term consequences, as well as those simply fascinated by the outlook and experience of a group whose history is exceptionally rich in human drama. At the very highest level of generality, they may even speak to some of the largest issues currently debated by historians and social theorists, for at the very moment when Reformation historians turned away from Weber's ideas, believing that they had outlived their usefulness, American social science and historiography took a 'cultural turn' that drew much of its inspiration from that latter-day Weberian, Clifford Geertz. In revealing both Calvinism's force and its limits in shaping the behaviour of its French adherents, I hope that these essays have lessons to impart about the character and determinative power of that great abstraction of our current moment, 'culture'.

PART ONE
Social and Demographic Fortunes

Alençon's Huguenots, 1620–85: The Social Transformations of a Reformed Community

The town of Alençon is well known to students of French Protestantism for its place in the early history of the Reformation. As capital of the *apanage* of the duchess of Alençon, Marguerite of Navarre, the city became a haven for persecuted evangelicals in the early 1530s. Pierre Caroli, a leading member of the reforming circle around Briçonnet in Meaux, served as *curé* of Notre Dame, Alençon's sole intramural parish, between 1530 and 1534. The first French translation of Lorenzo Valla's famous exposure of the forged Donation of Constantine came off an Alençon press, that of Simon Dubois, who also published several of Luther's works and a vernacular New Testament of unquestionably Protestant stamp. Even after the 'conventicules' established in these years were dispersed by royal *commissaires* dispatched to the city following a serious incident of iconoclasm, strong Protestant sentiments survived to resurface following the creation of the first formal Reformed congregation at an unknown date around 1560. In the early 1560s Protestants composed a majority within the city council and *siège présidial*. The town was seized by the Huguenots during the First Civil War in 1562. In 1567 the *bailliage* of Alençon joined those of Caen and Carentan as the only Norman *bailliages* to urge continued toleration of the 'new religion' at the annual assembly of the provincial Estates.[1]

There was far less that was noteworthy about Alençon's Protestant community in the seventeenth century to attract the attention of other than local historians. The city by then had come permanently under direct royal control. The Huguenots no longer dominated the local power structure, although we shall see that they remained important within it during the early years of the century. The history of the town's Reformed

---

1 P. Imbart de le Tour, *Les Origines de la Réforme* (4 vols, Paris, 1905–35), III, 380–82; O. Douen, 'L'imprimeur Simon Dubois et le réformateur Pierre Caroli, 1529–1534', *B.S.H.P.F.* 45 (1896), 200–212; C. Oursel, *Notes pour servir à l'histoire de la Réforme en Normandie au temps de François Ier* (Caen, 1913), pp. 8–9, 29–31, 44–52; Benjamin Robert, *Les débuts du Protestanisme à Alençon* (Alençon, 1937), *passim*; *idem, Alençon Protestant en 1562* (Alençon, 1937); Louis Desgraves; *Répertoire bibliographique des livres imprimés en France au seizième siècle*, (Baden-Baden, 1978–), XXV, 5–16; Maryelise Suffern Lamet, 'Reformation, War and Society in Caen, Lower Normandy: 1558–1610' (unpub. Ph.D. diss., University of Massachusetts, 1978), p. 267.

community is that of the same tightening restrictions and increasing vexations experienced by all other Protestant congregations in the decades leading up to the Revocation – and best recounted by Alençon's pastor Elie Benoist in his *Histoire de l'Edit de Nantes*.

The fates which govern the survival of historical records have decreed, however, that only for the seventeenth century can a social history of Alençonnais Protestantism be attempted. Documents which shed light on Alençon's history in the sixteenth century are so sparse as to leave the contours of the Protestant community in almost total darkness.[2] Beginning in 1616, a continuous series of Huguenot registers of births, marriages and burials becomes available, allowing one to establish for the first time the approximate size of the Reformed community, its numerical evolution over time, and the identity of most of its members.[3] The information in these registers can also be linked with data from the city's notarial records and the numerous lists of masters of different guilds available for scattered years over the seventeenth century, permitting a reconstruction of the evolving occupational profile of the community.[4] Finally, and serendipitously, the Huguenot 'parish' registers and many other local documents shedding light on the Protestant community were scrupulously transcribed in the middle years of this century by the pastor and pioneering historian of the local church, Benjamin Robert, who used them to draw up a remarkable set of genealogies of all local Protestant families. Robert's notes and genealogical registers, now preserved at the Bibliothèque de la Société de l'Histoire du Protestantisme Français, facilitate immeasurably a demographic investigation of the community using the techniques of family reconstruction, while at the same time providing a rich source for study of social mobility over the generations when linked to the available information about occupation and social status.[5]

---

[2] No documents emanating directly from Alençon's Reformed church have survived from the years before 1596, and the city's municipal archives contain nothing from this period other than a few scattered fiscal accounts. Those historians who have attempted to write the history of Alençonnais Protestantism in the sixteenth century have thus been forced to rely on a few judicial investigations and such evidence as is available in the city's notarial records. How sketchy the picture which emerges is, particularly for the period of the Religious Wars, can be seen from the works cited above in note 1.

[3] A.D.O., I, 1–22.

[4] A.D.O., B, Bailliage, Affaires Civiles; E, Tabellionage, Alençon. The notarial records are quite complete for the seventeenth century. Guild lists survive for 41 guilds at one or more points between 1629 and 1694. The purposes for which these lists of guild masters were drawn up is unclear.

[5] Robert's notes had not yet been classified at the time I consulted them. I have checked his transcriptions of the Huguenot registers against the originals and found them to be extremely reliable, although not absolutely devoid of errors of omission or transcription. Unless otherwise indicated, all the information in the pages that follow about the demography and social structure of Alençon's Protestant community will be based on Robert's registers, supplemented by the information in the notarial records and the *bailliage* lists.

This essay seeks to show what the above sources tell us about the social and demographic evolution of Alençon's Reformed congregation over the course of the seventeenth century. In so doing, it has two aims. The first, quite simply, is to offer a contribution to the social history of Protestantism in this era. In the past fifteen years, the history of sixteenth-century French Protestantism has been thoroughly renewed. Despite severe obstacles imposed by scarce and fragmentary sources, a generation of historians beginning with Natalie Zemon Davis and Emmanuel Le Roy Ladurie has managed to provide a far more detailed picture than was previously available of the growth of the Protestant movement, its social contours during its years of peak strength between 1560 and 1568, and its subsequent decline over the course of the Wars of Religion.[6] By contrast, the period of Protestantism's history running from the close of the Religious Wars in 1598 to the Revocation of the Edict of Nantes 87 years later, has been a virtual no-man's-land for scholars. Although a few studies in local journals or the venerable *Bulletin de la Société de l'Histoire du Protestantisme Français* offer some insight into the social structure and demographic behaviour of the Huguenot community during these years, these studies tend to explore their subject in a static fashion and have generally neglected the larger urban congregations which provided so much of the Protestant movement's leadership.[7] In addition to helping fill this gap in our knowledge, this chapter also hopes to suggest how the richer sources available for the seventeenth century can shed valuable light on that central question of French Protestantism's earlier history, the problem of conversion, or, in other words, of who became Protestant in the years of the faith's growth.

---

[6] Davis, 'Strikes and Salvation at Lyons', *A.R.* 56 (1965), 48–64; Le Roy Ladurie, *Les paysans de Languedoc* (Paris, 1966), part 3, ch. 1; Judith Meyer, 'Reformation in La Rochelle: Religious Change, Social Stability, and Political Crisis, 1500–1568' (unpub. Ph.D. diss., University of Iowa, 1977); Lamet, 'Reformation, War and Society in Caen'; David Rosenberg, 'Social Experience and Religious Choice: A Case Study, the Protestant Weavers and Woolcombers of Amiens in the Sixteenth Century' (unpub. Ph.D. diss., Yale University, 1978); Joan Davies, 'Persecution and Protestantism: Toulouse, 1562–1575', *The Historical Journal* 22 (1979), 31–51; David Nicholls, 'Social Change and Early Protestantism in France: Normandy, 1560–62', *European Studies Review* 10 (1980), 279–308; Janine Garrisson-Estèbe, *Protestants du Midi, 1559–1598* (Toulouse, 1980); Philip Benedict, *Rouen during the Wars of Religion* (Cambridge, 1981).

[7] The best recent social study of seventeenth-century Protestantism is unquestionably Yves Gueneau, 'Les Protestants dans le Colloque de Sancerre de 1598 à 1685', *Cahiers d'Archéologie et d'Histoire du Berry* 30–31 (1972). Other significant works include Pierre Bolle, 'Une paroisse réformée du Dauphiné à la veille de la Révocation de l'édit de Nantes: Mens-en-Trièves, 1650–1685', *B.S.H.P.F.* 111 (1965), 109–35, 213–39; Gerard Bollon, 'Minorité broyée et Malthusianisme: Saint-Sylvain-Falaise-Saint-Pierre-sur-Dives au XVIIe siècle', *B.S.H.P.F.* 116 (1970), 489–508; Georges Frêche, 'Contre-Réforme et dragonnades (1610–1798): Pour une orientation statistique de l'histoire du Protestantisme', *B.S.H.P.F.* 119 (1973), 362–83.

Located in the middle of densely populated *bocage* country, seventeenth-century Alençon was an important administrative centre for the southern parts of Lower Normandy, the seat of a *bailliage et siège présidial*, a *vicomté*, a *maitrise des eaux et forêts*, and, after 1636, a *généralité* and *bureau des finances*. The town was also, in the opinion of its *intendant* in 1698, 'one of the most commercially active cities of the province ... for being one lacking a navigable river', a distinction it owed in small part to its ancient linen and woollen industries and in ever larger part to its lace production. This was the city's great growth industry, expanding rapidly in the years after 1630 when a local *fabricante* named Marthe Barbot (a Huguenot) mastered the techniques needed to produce a close imitation of Venetian lace. By century's end, the manufacture of *point de France* employed upwards of 800 women in the city, and the industry's commercial value amounted to 500 000 *livres tournois* per annum.[8]

The Reformed community within this town was substantial by the standards of seventeenth-century French Protestantism, particularly for northern France, but at the point when its contours first become discernible, it was none the less already a clear minority within the city's total population. The first document to yield any indication of the congregation's size is a fragmentary 'Registre de baptesmes adminstrés en l'église Réformée d'Alençon' covering the years 1596–97.[9] It records 71 baptisms in 1596 and 39 in the first eight months of the following year. In these same twenty months, some 378 Catholic babies were baptized in the parish of Notre Dame. No parish registers are extant from this period for the *faubourg* parish of Saint-Pierre-de-Montsort, but baptisms in this parish typically added another 12 per cent to the total number of Catholic baptisms.[10] Judging by the relative number of baptisms celebrated within each confession, then, the Protestants represented 20 per cent of the city's total population as the Wars of Religion drew to a close. Three decades later, when continuous series of baptisms are first available for both religions, the Protestant registers indicated an average of 61.5 baptisms per year from 1625 through 1634, 15.5 per cent of all such ceremonies within the city. The 61.5 baptisms per annum correspond to a total population of perhaps 1500 souls.

---

[8] Louis Duval, ed., *Etat de la Généralité d'Alençon sous Louis XIV* (n.p., 1890), *passim*, esp. pp. 73–6, 121–3. See also G. Despierres, *Histoire du point d'Alençon* (Paris–Alençon, 1886).

[9] B.N., MS Français 15832, fol. 136.

[10] Catholic baptismal registers have survived for the parish of Notre Dame from 1592 to 1599 and 1625 through the end of the century. For Saint-Pierre-de-Monsort, the registers cover the years 1625–34 and 1652–1700. (A.D.O. Registres Paroissiaux, Alençon; A.C. Alençon, 11 E 1–2, 12 E 1–39.) To compare the movement of the Protestant population with that of the city as a whole, I made a simple count of the acts in these registers.

In Lyon and Amiens, the two cities for which the most detailed social studies of sixteenth-century French Protestantism have been carried out, the 'new religion' was emphatically not the faith of a single class; as Natalie Davis concludes, 'The Calvinist movement as a whole drew from rich and poor – from Consular families, notable families, and families of the *menu peuple* – in numbers roughly proportional to their distribution in the population at large.'[11] Less statistically conclusive studies of Grenoble, Montpellier, Rouen, Toulouse, Orléans, Caen and La Rochelle appear to confirm this pattern – or, at any rate, offer no firm reasons to modify it.[12] In seventeenth-century Alençon, the situation was quite different.

Two sets of sources illuminate the social composition of the Reformed church in this era. First, there are the lists of guild masters and of the legal personnel attached to the *vicomté* court, which permit one to calculate with considerable precision the percentage of Protestants within certain social categories. The lists of guild masters are densest in the period 1645–55, when they are available for 32 of the city's *corps de métier*, containing 576 artisans.[13] (See Table 1.1.) Only 34 (5.8 per cent) of these men can be identified as Protestants, well below the faith's total representation within the population at this time. Over half of the Huguenot artisans were clustered in three small guilds with a significant Protestant presence, those of the apothecaries, the dyers and the button-makers, while the

---

[11] Davis, 'Strikes and Salvation', p. 54. See also Rosenberg, 'Social Experience and Religious Choice', p. 21.

[12] Peter France, 'Les Protestants à Grenoble au XVIe siècle', *Cahiers d'Histoire* 7 (1962), 331; Le Roy Ladurie, *Paysans de Languedoc*, pp. 341–4; Benedict, *Rouen*, ch. 3; Lamet, 'Reformation, War, and Society in Caen', ch. 5; Meyer, 'Reformation in La Rochelle', pp. 63–77. Davies, 'Persecution and Protestantism', p. 38, asserts on the basis of lists of suspected Protestants that merchants and the liberal professions were disproportionately represented within Toulouse's Reformed community in the 1560s and 1570s, but these sources consistently reveal a higher percentage of élite Protestants than do the more reliable lists emanating from the Protestant communities themselves. See here Garrison-Estèbe, *Protestants du Midi*, p. 16. Christopher Stocker, 'The Calvinist *Officiers* of Orleans, 1560–1572', *Proceeding of the Sixth Annual Meeting of the Western Society for French History* (Santa Barbara, 1979), pp. 21–3, examines the case of a city in which a slight majority of the *officiers* appears to have been Protestant, but it is not known what the percentage of Huguenots within the total population was. The old but inconclusive debate on precisely this issue in Paul de Félice, 'La réaction catholique à Orléans au lendemain de la première guerre de religion (1563–1565)', *B.S.H.P.F.* 52 (1903), 481–554, esp. 490–91; and Bernard de Lacombe's response, *B.S.H.P.F.* 53 (1904), 173–81, leaves open the possibility that the Huguenots comprised a majority of all the city's inhabitants as well. The great difficulty facing all who would reconstruct Protestantism's social composition in this period is that it is often simply impossible to determine the occupational structure of both a representative sample of the Calvinist population and the larger community from which the converts were drawn.

[13] In all, there were at least 46 guilds in seventeenth-century Alençon. For a few guilds, more than one list of masters has survived from the years 1645–55. Where this is so, I have utilized whichever list contains the highest number of masters.

Table 1.1 Protestants in the *corps de métier* of Alençon, 1645–55

		Total number of masters	Protestants
Textile trades	stocking-makers	17	1
	hatters	13	1
	silkweavers	6	0
	fringemakers (*passementiers*)	38	1
	shearers	7	0
	thread-makers	24	0
	weavers	49	5
		154	8
Food and drink trades	butchers	49	0
	bakers	32	1
	innkeepers	31	1
	vinegar-makers	18	0
		130	2
Leather trades	cobblers	44	0
	shoemakers	25	0
	leather finishers (*mégissiers*)	16	0
	tanners	13	0
	saddle-makers	7	0
		105	0
Metal trades	toolmakers	10	0
	blacksmiths	17	0
	tinkers (*potiers d'étain*)	10	0
	tinkers (*estaimiers*)	4	0
		41	0
Construction trades	masons	14	0
	roofers	11	0
		25	0
Miscellaneous guilds	mercers	28	1
	apothecaries	11	8
	turners	20	2
	buttonmakers	19	9
	locksmiths	13	0
	candle-makers	9	0
	painters–glaziers	6	0
	dyers	5	3
	wax-makers	5	0
	wheelwrights	5	0
		121	23

majority of all guilds did not have a single Protestant master. As Table 1.1 shows, no Protestants at all soled shoes, tanned leather, or made pots and pans in Alençon. Almost none were involved in the food and drink trades. But while the Huguenots were substantially under-represented in the world of the workshop, they were over-represented in the corridors of the Palais de Justice. A 1646 'assise mercuriale', or list of lawyers, notaries and officials attached to the *vicomté*, yields the picture of Protestant strength within the world of law set out in Table 1.2. As can be seen, fully 52 per cent of the barristers, solicitors and notaries were members of the Reformed Church, although the lesser personnel attached to the courts were overwhelmingly Catholic. All three *conseillers assesseurs* of the *vicomté* were also Protestant, although the *vicomté* and his two lieutenants were all Catholic. Huguenots also filled two of the nine seats in the *siège présidial*.[14]

Table 1.2   Protestant representation within the world of the law in Alençon, 1646

	Total	Protestants
Barristers (*avocats*)	31	18
Solicitors (*procureurs*)	20	7
Scribes	4	2
Notaries	8	6
Bailiffs	6	0
Sergeants	19	1

The second approach to the congregation's social composition involves identifying the occupational status of a cross-section of the total Protestant population. For present purposes, the cohort of all fathers whose names appear in the baptismal registers between 1620 and 1629 has been chosen. Unfortunately, occupations cannot be recovered for all of these individuals. The 'parish' registers themselves only note the status of the more prestigious members of the community, and while the notarial records and lists of guild masters permit one to plug many of the gaps left by the registers, by no means all men turn up in these documents. Fully a third of the sample cohort had to be classified 'occupation unknown', most of them in all likelihood journeymen, labourers, or masters of those guilds for which no lists of members have survived from this period.

---

[14] Just twenty years previously, five of the nine positions within the presidial court had been held by Protestants. The A.D.O. possess a *fichier* of all officers in the court. For the *assise mercuriale*: A.D.O., B, Bailliage, affaires civiles, 1646.

Even with this substantial black hole of unknown cases, the élite character of the Reformed community emerges clearly from Table 1.3. As can be seen, lawyers account for fully 12 per cent of the sample cohort (unknown cases included), merchants for 10 per cent, *officiers* for 6 per cent, and doctors and apothecaries for 5 per cent. Another 12 per cent of the sample appear in the sources with the honorifics 'écuyer' or 'sieur' before their name, exercising no known occupation, indicating that they were noblemen, would-be noblemen, or bourgeois living off their *rentes*.[15]

Table 1.3   Occupations of fathers in Alençon's Protestant baptismal registers, 1620–29

Occupation	No.	%
Titled		
'écuyer' (only known 'occupation')	4	2
'écuyer' (all individuals with title)	7	3
'sieur' (only known 'occupation')	26	10
'sieur' (all individuals with title)	40	16
Major *officiers*	14	6
Lesser officials	9	4
Legal personnel	30	12
barristers	20	
solicitors	10	
Medical personnel	13	5
Pastors	2	1
'Bourgeois'	4	2
Merchants	24	10
merchants	23	
mercers	1	
Artisans	36	14
Miscellaneous	5	2
servants & household officials of high nobility	3	
school masters	2	
No occupation available	84	33
Total	251	

[15] In Normandy, the honorific *écuyer* was not exclusively reserved for noblemen as was the case elsewhere. The appellation *sieur* indicated possession of a *seigneurie* but not necessarily noble status. See Jonathan Dewald, *The Formation of a Provincial Nobility: The Magistrates of the Parlement of Rouen, 1499–1610* (Princeton, 1980), pp. 105–6.

In all, at least 48 per cent of the men in the cohort belonged to the ranks of the urban notables (those of the status of merchant or above). Although no occupational census has survived for Alençon, such men typically comprised 20 to 30 per cent of the urban heads of household in an *ancien régime* city.[16]

As Robert already saw, Alençon's Reformed church was 'aristocratic'.[17] Such a finding immediately raises the question: had it always been thus, or did this élite character only come to characterize it during the later years of the Wars of Religion, after many early converts to the Protestant cause had probably returned to the Catholic fold, as so many of their co-religionists elsewhere in Normandy are known to have done?[18] The paucity of information from the sixteenth century makes it impossible to answer this question with certainty, but scattered bits of evidence suggest that the pattern dates back to the early years of the Protestant movement locally and stems from the important role played by the ducal court in the diffusion of the new religion. First of all, other seventeenth-century Huguenot communities whose membership I have analysed do not contain the same disproportionately large number of 'notables'. This category accounts for just 20 per cent of the membership of Rouen's Reformed church in the early seventeenth century, 23 per cent of Montpellier's in the same period, and 26 per cent of Metz's in 1684.[19] The larger urban Reformed churches thus did not generally take on an élite character in the seventeenth century, even those such as Montpellier and Rouen which experienced a substantial

---

[16] The classification schemes used by historians vary so that it is impossible to offer precisely comparable figures on notables as defined here found in other *ancien régime* cities. In seventeenth-century Beauvais, merchants, *officiers*, and the 'bourgeoisie liberale' and 'rentière' accounted for 18 per cent of all heads of households; in early eighteenth-century Grenoble, members of the aristocracy and 'classe moyenne' formed 27 per cent of the population; and in Lyon in 1788, merchants, members of the liberal professions, and 'bourgeois-ecclésiastiques' accounted for 24.5 per cent of the taxpayers assessed for the *capitation*. Pierre Goubert, *Cent mille provinciaux au XVIIe siècle: Beauvais et le Beauvaisis de 1600 à 1730* (Paris, 1968), p. 292; Edmond Esmonin, 'Un recensement de la population de Grenoble en 1725', in *Etudes sur la France des XVIIe et XVIIIe siècles* (Paris, 1964), p. 458; Maurice Garden, *Lyon et les Lyonnais au XVIIIe siècle* (Paris, 1975), p. 134.

[17] Benjamin Robert, *L'Eglise Réformée d'Alençon: Etudes historiques* (Alençon, 1940), p. 30.

[18] On the sharp decline in Protestant strength in Rouen, Le Havre, Caen, Bayeux and Saint-Lô, see Benedict, *Rouen*, pp. 128–37, 251–5. Whether or not this decline was accompanied by changes in the faith's social composition is unknown.

[19] Based on an analysis of all adult males born before 1610 buried in Rouen's Reformed church between 1628 and 1650 (A.D. Seine-Maritime, E, Protestants de Quévilly, Décès); of all residents of Montpellier marrying at that city's Reformed church between 1601 and 1610 (A.C. Montpellier, GG 365–6); and of the detailed 'Extrait et estat général des habitants de la ville de Metz qui font profession de la religion Prétenduë Refformée', *Annuaire de la Société d'Histoire et d'Archéologie de la Lorraine* 3 (1891), 345–75.

wave of defections in the later 1560s and 1570s. It also seems telling that in 1533, a time when Protestantism elsewhere in France was overwhelmingly a 'religion des petits gens', three lawyers, two other notable bourgeois, a merchant, a *grenetier* of the *grenier du sel* and six prominent ecclesiastics turn up among the two score men arrested in Alençon following the local incidents of iconoclasm.[20] Three decades later, several members of the Huguenot majority within the *bailliage et siège présidial* were men who had earlier served in the ducal household.[21] Such evidence suggests that the support given unconventional religious ideas within the circle around Marguerite of Navarre bred a local Protestant movement that was an exception to the typical pattern of early Protestantism as a faith cutting equally across all major elements within the urban population. In this case, at least, the channels of the new faith's diffusion may have exerted an influence over its sociology.

Over the subsequent decades leading up to the Revocation of the Edict of Nantes, Alençon's Protestant community never lost its socially élite character or became anything other than a minority of the city's population. Its numerical and social contours did not remain constant, however. Two highly significant changes occurred: the community shrank steadily in size; and the number of merchants within it rose dramatically, while the contingent of lawyers and *officiers* declined.

The backdrop to these changes was the increasing legal persecution and pressure for conversion that the Protestants experienced over this period. From the energetic public appeals of the controversialists of the first part of the century, to the concerted effort of private proselytization lauched after mid-century by the Congregation for the Propagation of the Faith, to the high-minded bribery of the *caisses de conversion* just before the Revocation, France's Catholics waged an escalating war to save the Huguenots from the error of their ways. In Alençon, the war became particularly intense after 1672. In that year, a Maison des Nouvelles Catholiques was founded to shelter poor Protestant girls wishing to convert against the desires of their family. Five years later came a local chapter of the Congregation for the Propagation of the Faith, one of the many pious works of the duchess of Guise, who retired to Alençon following the death of her husband and spent the last years of her life directing much of her bountiful charity to the task of converting the Huguenots. Meanwhile, the 'application à la rigueur' of the Edict of Nantes introduced by Louis XIV shortly after the beginning of his personal rule hedged the exercise of

---

[20] Robert, *Débuts du Protestantisme à Alençon*, p. 16.
[21] Ibid., p. 24.

the Reformed religion about with increasingly tight surveillance, and a growing current of royal edicts and *arrêts du parlement* restricted Protestant access to an increasing number of occupations. The Parlement of Normandy particularly distinguished itself among the kingdom's *parlements* by its zeal to limit Huguenot opportunities. In 1663 it decreed that no town within the province could have more than one Protestant doctor or surgeon for every fifteen Catholic physicians and barred Huguenots from entering these professions wherever this ratio was exceeded. Within the legal world, royal mistrust of the Protestants had combined with the exclusivism of the leading judicial corporations to make access to office difficult from early on in the century; a 1664 *arrêt* of Rouen's Parlement, later overturned on appeal, tried to ban members of the 'Religion Prétendue Reformée' from becoming barristers as well, and a royal edict of 1681 barred them from the positions of solicitor, bailiff or scribe. Finally, the right of the Protestants to enter the world of the guilds was limited by a 1664 *arrêt du parlement* restricting the number of Huguenot mercers and goldsmiths and a 1669 edict declaring that members of the religion could not form the majority of any guild.[22]

These measures unquestionably contributed to both the decline in Huguenot numbers and the shifts in the community's occupational structure over the decades before the Revocation, but Protestantism's history cannot be reduced simply to a tale of persecution. Close examination of the community's evolution shows that other causes must also be sought to explain the faith's evolution. This is particularly true of its numerical decline.

Figure 1.1, which sets forth the movement of baptisms, marriages and burials celebrated annually in the temple of Alençon, reveals the community's gradual shrinkage. Whereas 656 baptisms were celebrated in the first decade for which figures are available, only 332 were in the ten years just before the Revocation. The decline was particularly sharp after 1669, but it was by no means confined to these years of intensified missionary effort and persecution, for by 1650–59, the number of baptisms had already fallen off 16 per cent to 550.

As Figure 1.2 shows, this decline was not part of a general shrinkage in the city's population. On the contrary, the expansion of lace production and the growth in the ranks of officialdom after 1630 fuelled a 40-year increase in the total number of baptisms celebrated in Alençon, interrupted only by the crises of the Fronde and of 1661–62. The movement of baptisms

[22] Robert, *Les Maisons des Nouveaux et des Nouvelles Catholiques à Alençon avant 1685* (Alençon, 1940), *passim*; A.T. Van Deursen, *Professions et métiers interdits, un aspect de l'histoire de la Révocation de l'édit de Nantes* (Groningen, 1960), *passim*, esp. pp. 118–19, 238, 320, 325; and, more generally, Daniel Ligou, *Le Protestantisme en France de 1598 à 1715* (Paris, 1968), chs 12–13.

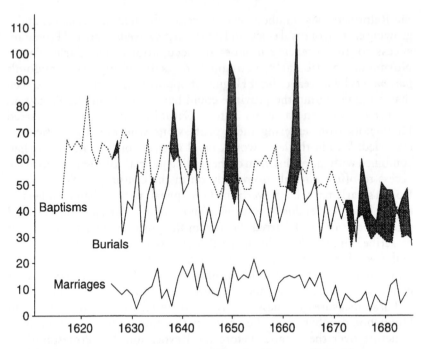

1.1   Reformed baptisms, marriages and burials, Alençon, 1616–85

levelled out after 1670 at about 500 per year (equivalent to a total population in the vicinity of 12 500), but evidence of substantial decline in the population does not appear until the Revocation, when an immediate drop of 10 per cent in the number of baptisms is perceptible.

The overall growth in the city's population before 1685 meant that the Huguenots' relative place within the community declined even more rapidly than their absolute numbers. Where Protestant baptisms had amounted to 15.5 per cent of all baptisms between 1625 and 1634, by 1675–84, they represented just 6.5 per cent of all baptisms.

The marked decline in the number of baptisms visible in Alençon appears to have been typical of many urban Protestant congregations in seventeenth-century France.[23] Discovering the causes of the decline consequently becomes a question of more than purely local interest. It is also a question that takes one directly into some of the most interesting issues in the history of seventeenth-century French Protestantism. Recent studies have unearthed considerable evidence of family limitation practices in the Protestant cantons of eighteenth-century Switzerland, and one author has suggested the presence of such practices among the Norman Huguenots in the

---

[23] See below, Chapter 2, pp. 61–3, 75–80.

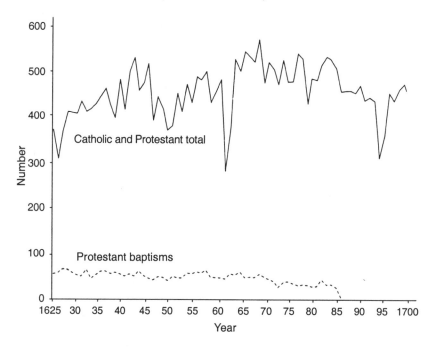

1.2   Total baptisms, Alençon, 1625–1700

seventeenth century, albeit on less than conclusive evidence: a declining ratio of baptisms to marriages.[24] Might the decline in Protestant numbers reflect the precocious utilization of birth control practices among this increasingly beleaguered population? Or might it reflect the spiritual 'lethargy' that certain historians claim to have detected afflicting French Protestantism in this period? In the hands of Pierre Chaunu and Georges Frêche, the faith's numerical evolution has recently been taken as a measure of its spiritual vitality or lack thereof.[25] If a sizeable number of conversions account for the decline in Protestant numbers, the vision of a religion sapped by excessive concessions to the monarchy and *le monde* indeed gains considerable plausibility.

The excellent recent study of conversion in Lyon by Odile Martin has drawn attention to one city in which defections ate substantially into Reformed ranks; this congregation of roughly a thousand members yielded

---

[24] Alfred Perrenoud, 'Malthusianisme et protestantisme: un modèle démographique wéberien', *Annales: E.S.C.* 29 (1974), 975–88; Bollon, 'Minorité broyée et Malthusianisme', p. 498.

[25] Pierre Chaunu, 'Une histoire religieuse sérielle: A propos du diocèse de La Rochelle, 1648–1724, et de quelques exemples normands', *R.H.M.C.* 12 (1965), 5–34; Frêche, 'Contre-Réforme et dragonnades', pp. 362–83.

no less than 568 converts to the Roman church between 1659 and 1685.[26] Conversions were far less numerous in Alençon, even though the Reformed church was no smaller. The records of Alençon's *bailliage* and Maison des Nouveaux Catholiques reveal 116 abjurations between 1661 and 1685, 24 of which involved non-residents. The great majority of these conversions (72 of the 92 cases involving residents) came in the decade immediately before 1685. The median age of those converting before 1685 itself was just eighteen, well below the average age at marriage. These losses would thus have scarcely diminished the child-bearing Protestant population at all. They cannot be considered a major cause of the decline in Huguenot baptisms visible in the decades before 1685.

The relative infrequency of conversions in Alençon can probably be linked to the inbred character of the Norman church. Where Lyon's Reformed congregation was composed primarily of migrants to the great provincial metropolis, just 17 per cent of those Alençon Huguenots married between 1668 and 1684 were born elsewhere, and only 14 per cent wed a non-resident. Family pressure to remain true to the faith of one's ancestors was one of the most powerful forces for confessional loyalty, as is spectacularly shown by several cases before Alençon's *bailliage* court where young people wishing to convert sought relief against parents who beat them or refused to let them out of the house.[27] (It was to shelter potential converts from such pressures that the Catholics felt it necessary to create Maisons des Nouveaux Catholiques and to offer financial compensation to those who converted.) The great majority of Lyon converts, Martin's study shows, were young artisans with few local connections to help them resist the pull of the *convertisseurs*. With many fewer such individuals in Alençon, the lower frequency of conversions is unsurprising.

Although conversion does not appear to have been a major reason why Alençon's Reformed community gradually shrank in size, the detailed dossiers that Robert compiled about those who defected to the Roman church reveal a great deal about the social characteristics of the typical convert, and hence about the phenomenon of conversion in this era. In this inbred community, those who left the church were not particularly likely to be newcomers. All but ten of the 92 inhabitants of Alençon who abjured came from local families with strong roots in the community. Family ties – or the absence thereof – were none the less important in other ways. One or both parents were dead in 23 of 37 cases of individuals who embraced Catholicism as teenagers or young adults. Where one parent was dead, it was the mother in twelve cases of fifteen, suggesting that,

---

[26] Odile Martin, 'Prosélytisme et tolérance à Lyon du milieu du XVIIe siècle à la Révocation de l'édit de Nantes,' *R.H.M.C.* 25 (1978), 306–20.

[27] A.D.O., B, Bailliage, Affaires Civiles, 1664.

despite the image of the Calvinist family governed by a stern patriarch who supervised his children's religious education, the woman of the household may have played the greater role in the process of ideological reproduction. As in Lyon, most converts were young until the year of the Revocation itself. Sixty-one of 82 converts between 1661 and 1684 left the Protestant fold before reaching age 25, with the largest age category being the 15–19 cohort. Adolescents in the process of forging an identity for themselves (the terms are not anachronistic in a seventeenth-century context) were clearly those most open to conversion. A significant number of deathbed conversions also occurred, suggesting the importance of periods of passage more generally. As the Revocation loomed, however, this pattern changed and those of all ages began to break ranks; the converts of the first half of 1685 averaged 39.5 years of age. Women were more likely than men to convert, accounting for 63 per cent of the abjurations. Surprisingly, despite the financial inducements offered by the *caisse de conversion*, the converts did not come disproportionately from the lower occupational strata. On the contrary, they were fairly evenly spread across all social groups, with members of medical and official families being slightly more likely than others to convert. Since these occupational groups were leading targets of the discriminatory legislation of the period, this legislation may have had a modest effect in stimulating conversions. This factor should not be exaggerated, however, for a number of the conversions from within these occupational categories involved teenage girls or deathbed abjurations. Such cases can hardly be ascribed to the convert's desire to obtain or retain a prestigious occupation.

Finally, it deserves noting that, although the total number of conversions in Alençon was not large, the concentration of converts in the 10–24 age category and in the decade just before 1685 meant that within these years as many as one young Protestant adult in ten may have been won over to Catholicism. During these years, the community must undoubtedly have felt that its youth was under siege. The bitterness subsequently expressed by Elie Benoist about the way in which Catholic missionary efforts struck at the heart of the Protestant family is unsurprising in light of these figures.[28]

Did Protestant efforts to limit the number of their children in the face of these pressures account for the shrinkage of the Huguenot community? Although contemporary sociologists have noted that fertility is often lower among minority groups facing discrimination,[29] the evidence provided by

---

[28] Benoist, III, 285. Catholic clergymen likewise expressed bitterness at the ways in which Protestant parents sought to remove children of theirs inclined to convert from the influence of priests who had gained their trust. A.N., TT 230 (17), piece 11, testimony of Jacques Bernard.

[29] Calvin Goldscheider and Peter R. Uhlenberg, 'Minority Group Status and Fertility', *American Journal of Sociology* 74 (1969), 360–72.

family reconstitution offers little evidence that this factor was important in accounting for the decline in size in Alençon's congregation either.

Since the techniques of family reconstitution depend upon knowing the birth dates of those women married within a certain group and then being able to follow the women over the full course of their child-bearing years, and since the registers of Alençon's Protestant church only exist for the years 1616–85, it has been possible to compute full demographic statistics only for couples married between 1635 and 1661, a sample that yields 84 'type I' couples whose fertility can be followed across the full duration of their reproductive partnership.[30] Table 1.4 presents the results of these calculations alongside comparable statistics concerning nearby Catholic populations and the Genevan bourgeoisie of the eighteenth century, a group known to have controlled its fertility. None of the tell-tale signs of family limitation appear among Alençon's Huguenots. Women marrying young did not cease bearing children substantially earlier than those married later in life. The spacing between births did not increase abnormally as women neared their last child. Age-specific fertility was quite high, the reflection of a prosperous urban population that was not consciously controlling fertility.

These calculations, of course, only concern those married before 1661; the possibility remains that the difficult last years before the Revocation saw the Huguenots begin to limit family size. This hypothesis is harder to test, but it too seems unlikely. A highly atypical group of 33 type I families married after 1661 can be reconstituted, but because the Huguenot registers end in 1685, nearly all of these involve spouses married late in life or couples broken by an early death. To supplement such a skewed sample, all cases of couples whose child-rearing career was interrupted by the Revocation have been added. Such a sample obviously cannot be used to calculate age at last birth, but it does reveal birth intervals that were even shorter than those found in the pre-1661 cohort. (See Table 1.5.) Although the fertile Huguenot couples remaining in Alençon had children with the same or greater frequency than the couples of their parents' generation, the ratio of baptisms to marriages none the less declined from 4.64 : 1 in 1626–60 to 4.39 : 1 in 1661–85. What appears to have happened in the year immediately preceding the Revocation is that a certain number of young Protestants either converted to Catholicism or fled abroad after marrying in the city, producing not only the declining ratio of baptisms

---

[30] Those unfamiliar with the technical aspects of historical demography will find a good discussion of the technique of family reconstitution in Etienne Gautier and Louis Henry's classic *La population de Crulai, paroisse normande. Etude historique* (Paris, 1958). The technical procedures are further amplified in Michel Fleury and Louis Henry, *Nouveau manuel de dépouillement et d'exploitation de l'état civil ancien* (Paris, 1965) and Henry, *Manuel de démographie historique* (Geneva, 1967).

Table 1.4 Reproductive behaviour and fertility of Huguenot couples
married in Alençon, 1635–61

Mean age at last birth (women surviving to age 45)

		Comparable figures	
		Genevan bourgeoisie	Tourouvre-au-Perche
Age at marriage			
15–19	38.0 (n=4)	30.9	38.4
20–24	38.1 (n=15)	33.3	40.2
25–29	39.1 (n=15)	37.4	40.0
30–34	42.3 (n=15)	38.8	39.8

Age-specific fertility

Age at marriage	15–19	20–24	25–29	30–34	35–39	40–44
15–19 (n=15)	(0.297)	0.514	0.406	0.347	(0.169)	(0.125)
20–24 (n=31)	–	0.590	0.385	0.335	0.296	0.128
25–29 (n=19)	–	–	0.489	0.446	0.328	0.179
30–34 (n=13)	–	–	–	(0.543)	0.773	(0.300)
35–39 (n=5)	–	–	–	–	(0.413)	
All ages (n=83)	(0.297)	0.549	0.411	0.391	0.384	0.179
Comparable figures, all ages:						
Paris Basin	0.375	0.465	0.431	0.383	0.307	0.157
Bayeux, 1640–1700	0.333	0.414	0.404	0.381	0.367	0.070
Geneva bourgeoisie	0.383	0.450	0.434	0.308	0.181	0.078

Mean intervals between births
(families of 6 or more children, in months)

	1–2	2–3	3–4	4–5	5–6	6–7	ante-penult.	penult.	last
	17.2	22.4	23.4	25.1	21.8	26.2	22.6	27.8	32.1
Comparable figures:									
Geneva bourgeoisie	20.0	20.0	20.7	23.5			25.0	30.9	40.7
Crulai	22.4	25.3	27.2	28.6			28.7	30.9	33.0

Sources for comparisons: Alfred Perrenoud, 'Variables sociales en démographie
urbaine: l'exemple de Genève au XVIIIe siècle', in *Démographie urbaine, XVe–
XXe siècle* (Lyon, 1977), pp. 154, 160–61; Hubert Charbonneau, *Tourouvre-au-
Perche aux XVIIe et XVIIIe siècles: Etude de démographie historique* (Paris, 1970),
p. 141; Jacques Dupâquier, *La population rurale du Bassin parisien à l'époque de
Louis XIV* (Paris, 1979), pp. 353–5; Gautier and Henry, *Crulai*, p. 141.

Table 1.5   Mean interval between births among Alençon's Protestants, two generations compared

	1–2	2–3	3–4	4–5	5–6	6–7
Cohort married 1635–60	17.2	22.4	23.4	25.1	21.8	26.2
Cohort married 1661–85	18.1	17.3	22.6	18.2	20.0	21.0
Number of cases 1661–85	(35)	(35)	(28)	(20)	(18)	(14)

to marriages mistakenly regarded as evidence of family limitation, but also an ageing community characterized by the regular excess of deaths over births visible in Figure 1.1.

We are still no closer to explaining most of the shrinkage of the Huguenot community, particularly relative to Alençon's Catholic population. Two causes remain. First, comparison of the age at first marriage among Protestants and Catholics reveals that the former tended to marry later in life, whether because of difficulties they encountered in establishing themselves in a profession or because of their inner-worldly asceticism. The Protestant marriage registers indicate a median age at first marriage of 28.8 years for men and 26.5 for women in the period 1668–85, whereas a sample of Catholic marriages from the years 1674–84 yields figures of 25.8 for the men and 24.2 for the women. These differences do not stem merely from the élite social composition of the Protestant community. Comparison of Catholic and Protestant notables even reveals a slightly wider gap in the average age at first marriage. With Huguenot women marrying later than their Catholic neighbours, the total number of children born to them over their child-bearing years would obviously have been lower.

A second, still more important cause of the declining Huguenot presence in Alençon lies in the domain of migration into and out of the city. *Ancien régime* cities, it is clear from all studies, were characterized by a constant flow of people through them. Immigration is easy to measure on the basis of local sources that reveal the place of origin of those experiencing a certain life event within the city. Thus the registers of Alençon's municipal hospital reveal that 49 per cent of those who died in this institution between 1678 and 1692 were born outside the city.[31] Mapping the locality of origin of these immigrants reveals that, as in most French cities of comparable size, the great majority came from the surrounding vicinity – over two-thirds from within 25 km of the city. This densely populated area contained tens of thousands of inhabitants but

---

[31] A.C. Alençon, 3 E 1.

just two small Reformed churches.[32] Hardly surprisingly, the flow of immigrants into the city was disproportionately Catholic; whereas just 17 per cent of Alençon's Protestant residents married in the temple were born outside the city, 36 per cent of those married in the large Catholic parish of Notre Dame between 1674 and 1678 were likewise born outside the city. While those moving into the city were overwhelmingly Catholic, there is no reason to believe that the members of Alençon's Huguenot community were any less likely than their Catholic neighbours to seek opportunities elsewhere and emigrate. On the contrary, they may have been more inclined to do so, since studies have shown that merchants and members of the legal professions were particularly likely to move from one city to another over their lifetimes, and Alençon's Protestant community was disproportionately composed of such individuals.[33] More than anything else, migration patterns into and out of the city probably lie at the heart of the gradual numerical decline of this substantial urban congregation in an overwhelmingly Catholic hinterland.

At the same time that the size of Alençon's Reformed community shrank by close to half, its social composition also changed significantly. Already a church of notables in the early decades of the seventeenth century, it became still more of one as the century progressed. Lawyers and royal officials became less numerous, while the number of merchants expanded. Indeed, by the eve of the Revocation this community, that accounted for just 6.5 per cent of the city's total population, provided upwards of a quarter of its leading merchants.

Table 1.6 sets out these shifts in the social composition of the community. As can be seen, those holding offices of some sort dropped from 10 to 5 per cent of fathers whose children were baptized in the temple between the 1620s and the 1670s, while lawyers fell from 12 to 5 per cent. Conversely, those bearing the honorifics écuyer or sieur rose from 19 to 35 per cent, and merchants shot up from 10 to 30 per cent. Only one élite group of significance remained roughly stable, the medical professions, and here doctors and surgeons gave way to apothecaries. Overall, those whom we might classify as notables climbed from the already high 48 per cent to a striking 68 per cent.

---

[32] For population densities, see Jacques Dupâquier, *Statistiques démographiques du Bassin parisien, 1636–1720* (Paris, 1977), pp. 31, 656. For the Protestant population A.N., TT 230 (17); Samuel Mours, *Essai sommaire de géographie du protestantisme réformé français au XVIIe siècle* (Paris, 1966), pp. 14–15.

[33] Jean-Pierre Bardet, 'Problèmes d'un bilan urbain: comment l'établir en l'absence de recensement. L'exemple de Rouen au XVIIIe siècle', *Bulletin de la Société d'Histoire Moderne* (1981), 23.

Table 1.6   Occupations of fathers in Alençon's Protestant baptismal
registers, 1620–29 to 1670–79

	1620–29		1645–54		1670–79	
	No.	%	No.	%	No.	%
Titled						
écuyer (only known 'occupation')	4	2	10	5	8	6
écuyer (all individuals with title)	7	3	12	6	9	6
sieur (only known 'occupation')	26	10	17	9	22	15
sieur (all individuals with title)	40	16	30	15	42	29
Major officiers	14	6	4	2	3	2
Lesser officials	9	4	12	6	4	3
Legal personnel	30	12	21	11	7	5
barristers	20		16		6	
solicitors	10		5		1	
Medical personnel	13	5	11	6	10	7
doctors	5		5		0	
surgeons	5		2		1	
apothecaries	3		4		9	
Pastors	2	1	3	2	3	3
'Bourgeois'	4	2	0		0	
Merchants	24	10	42	21	44	30
merchants	23		37		35	
mercers	1		5		9	
Artisans	36	14	26	13	11	8
Miscellaneous	5	2	0		3	2
No occupation available	84	33	51	25	30	20
Total	251		197		145	

The surviving guild lists confirm the disproportionate place that the
Huguenots came to occupy within the world of local commerce. Protestants
accounted for five of nineteen linen merchants in 1676 and ten of seventeen
merchant-drapers in 1673. The mercers' guild expanded particularly
dramatically over the middle years of the century, perhaps in tandem with
the growth of the lace industry. As Table 1.7 shows, the number of
Huguenots within this group grew more rapidly yet – this, significantly,
despite restrictive legislation aimed at keeping Protestants out of this trade.

Within the lace industry itself, Protestants accounted for 12 per cent of all town-dwellers involved in the trade, but they bulked far larger among the entrepreneurs who dominated this overwhelmingly feminine industry. Of the 29 wealthiest *marchandes* or *fabricantes de point* as measured by the size of their dowries in their marriage contracts, twelve were Protestant. Of the eight richest of all, five were Protestant. The mean Protestant dowry amounted to 1657 *livres*; the mean Catholic dowry to 561 *livres*.[34]

Table 1.7   Protestants within the Mercers' Guild in Alençon, 1647–73

	1647	1661	1673
Total number of masters	28	43*	69**
Protestants	1	7	16

*one name is illegible.
** two names are illegible.

Meanwhile, the figures from several *assises mercuriales* confirm the Protestants' growing exclusion from the bar. (See Table 1.8.) Where the Huguenots accounted for 49 per cent of all barristers and solicitors in 1646, they occupied just 15 per cent of the same posts in 1682. The organization of the *assises mercuriales* by seniority reveals the total exclusion of Huguenots from the bar in the years just before the Revocation. Of the last thirteen barristers admitted prior to 1682, not one was Protestant.

Table 1.8   Protestants in the Alençon *assises mercuriales*, 1646 and 1682

	1646		1682	
	Total	Protestants	Total	Protestants
Barristers	31	18	23	5
Solicitors	20	7	18	1
Scribes	4	2	4	0
Notaries	8	6	6	0
Bailiffs	6	0	12	0
Sergeants	19	1	12	0

---

[34] All statistics concerning the lace industry are calculated from the biographical dictionary of lacemakers in Despierres, *Histoire du point*, pp. 181–272.

The shift in membership within Alençon's Reformed community from law and office toward trade was hardly unique to this city. I have been able to trace similar trends within the Protestant congregations of Rouen and Montpellier, and the important role played by the Huguenots within French commerce by 1685 has been remarked upon by observers from the Venetian ambassador onward.[35] This 'mercantilization' of the Protestant community would appear to be a striking example of the Weberian affinity between Calvinism and capitalism, but this is not how French historians of Protestantism have usually explained it. They have instead emphasized the obvious alternative explanation of Huguenot economic success, namely that it was a function of persecution. As Charles Weiss wrote: 'Excluded gradually from positions at court and virtually all civilian offices, they found themselves in the happy situation of being unable to impoverish themselves through luxury and idleness. Forced to devote themselves to agriculture, commerce, and industry, they compensated themselves richly.'[36]

The Alençon evidence seems at first glance to confirm this view, for it reveals a concurrent rise in the number of merchants and decline in the number of royal officials and lawyers. Robert's genealogies demonstrate, however, that the descendants of those families excluded from offices or the bar were not those who swelled the ranks of Protestant merchants. If one traces the descendants of those holding important offices or serving in the bar in the 1620s (see Table 1.9), it emerges that by far the largest group among them became not merchants but bourgeois, *sieurs de*, or *écuyers* with no other known occupation. In other words, they became *rentiers*. Far from saving the Huguenots from idleness, exclusion from office pushed them toward it, and no Protestant sense of calling held them back. Many other descendants of this group continued in the world of the law or entered medicine. One chose the military. Except among the descendants of solicitors, the lowest-status group among them, just three entered trade.

Tracing the ancestors of the merchants who made up so large a percentage of the Protestant community by the 1670s likewise reveals that few of them were descended from individuals who exercised the kinds of trades closed off to the Huguenots. (See Table 1.10.) A majority of the

---

[35] *Officiers* and *hommes de loi* formed 5 per cent and merchants 11 per cent of all adult males whose burial is noted in the records of Rouen's Reformed church between 1628 and 1650. Among fathers of children baptized between 1670 and 1674, the former groups comprised 3 per cent and merchants 19 per cent. Calculations derived from the vital records of the church, A.D. Seine-Maritime, E Protestants de Quevilly. For Montpellier, see below, Chapter 3, p. 143. On the place of the Huguenots in French trade, see Scoville, *Persecution*, pp. 133–9.

[36] Quoted in Samuel Mours, *Le Protestantisme en France au XVIIe siècle* (Paris, 1967), p. 129.

Table 1.9   Descendants of Protestant royal officials and legal personnel in Alençon

Descendants of high royal officials

Sons	barrister	2	*grenetier au grenier de sel*	1
	bourgeois	2	ship captain	1
	écuyer	1	medical doctor	1
	sieur de	1	apothecary	1
	draper	1		
Grandsons	none traceable locally			

Descendants of barristers

Sons	*sieur de*	11	bourgeois	1
	écuyer	4	medical doctor	1
	barrister	4	merchant	1
	conseiller du roi	1	linen dyer	1
Grandsons	*sieur de*	1	military officer	1
	bourgeois	1		

Descendants of solicitors

Sons	*sieur de*	6	notary	1
	merchant	5	apothecary	1
	solicitor	3	bourgeois	1
	écuyer	1		
Grandsons	merchant	2	barrister	1
	bourgeois	1		

Table 1.10   Ancestors of Protestant merchants in Alençon

	Father's occupation	Grandfather's occupation
Merchant	17	6
Unknown	10	8
Sieur de	6*	2
Legal personnel	5	5
Artisan	5	4
Apothecary or other medical personnel	2	2

*4 known to have exercised another occupation as well.

merchants in this period can be determined to have been the sons of either merchants or artisans. Many of the ten cases of fathers whose occupation is unknown may also have been from artisan ranks. By contrast, one finds just five merchants whose fathers worked in the world of the law courts: two sons of solicitors, two sons of notaries, and one son of a scribe. Looking back to the preceding generation, the picture remains essentially the same, with artisans, merchants and unknown cases accounting for 67 per cent of all grandparents, and the group of those exercising a legal profession once again composed of scribes, notaries and solicitors. Surprisingly, the fathers of all but three of the 44 known Protestant merchants active in the 1670s appear themselves in the records of Alençon's church. The group of merchants was thus homegrown. The growing Protestant domination of local trade was not the work of immigrants bringing capital or skills into Alençon from outside.

The conclusions that emerge from this exercise in genealogy are clear. With rare exceptions, the sons and grandsons of Alençon's many Protestant lawyers and royal officials of the 1620s did not become merchants if they could not, or chose not to, follow their fathers' footsteps. They behaved in ways consistent with the general mores of *ancien régime* society, becoming *rentiers* or entering other trades less tainted by the demeaning stain of labour. The many merchants of the 1670s were similarly descended from good mercantile stock, from families engaged in other occupations of similar prestige, or from artisan ranks. To say this is not to say that the growing place of the workshop and the counting house within the Reformed community owed nothing to the barriers preventing Protestants from purchasing offices or entering the bar. These barriers may have deterred bright young merchants' sons from pursuing such careers, although in the segmented bourgeoisie of the *ancien régime* the movement of individuals from mercantile families into the law was less common that is often supposed.[37] A full exploration of Protestantism's mercantilization would require far more space than is available here and take us well outside the walls of Alençon, but the evidence presented here certainly suggests that the explanation of Huguenot economic success provided by Ernst Troeltsch and Max Weber may deserve a more thorough hearing than it has received so far from students of French Protestantism.

---

[37] Bernard Quilliet, 'La situation sociale des avocats du Parlement de Paris à l'époque de la Renaissance (1480–1560)', in José Luis Alonso Hernandez et al., *Espace, idéologie et société au XVIe siècle* (Grenoble, 1975), pp. 127–9; Lenard R. Berlanstein, *The Barristers of Toulouse in the Eighteenth Century* (Baltimore, 1975), p. 35. Both of these studies indicate that only about one lawyer in ten was a merchant's son.

This brief statistical sketch of an urban Reformed congregation in seventeenth-century France has revealed some significant findings. Although the upheavals of the Wars of Religion gave way after 1598 to three generations of uninterrupted legal toleration, the Huguenot community did not cease to evolve. Alençon's Protestants generally resisted the efforts of their would-be converters, but the congregation could not withstand the eroding effects of migration and so declined in size. This numerical decline occurred despite high Protestant fertility. Calvin's followers do not appear to have pioneered the practice of family limitation in seventeenth-century France. The social composition of the congregation likewise changed over three generations, with the percentage of merchants increasing dramatically and the number of lawyers and royal officials declining. Surprisingly, these concurrent developments were largely separate, suggesting that while the second of them was clearly the result of opportunities being closed to the Huguenots, the first may have resulted from superior commercial aptitude as well as mounting persecution. Finally, the social and numerical evolution of Alençon's Protestant community appears to have been typical of other French urban congregations in this period. Its initial social composition was decidedly atypical, however. From the first moment when its makeup can be reconstructed with some precision onward, it comprised a disproportionate number of members drawn from the urban élite. This, it would appear, was a legacy of the original support given the movement in the court of Alençon's duchess Marguerite of Navarre. In thus retouching existing generalizations while revealing or corroborating others, this essay reminds us of the complexities of the link between religion and society in the *ancien régime*, while offering hope that the search for larger patterns is not necessarily condemned to failure by the multiplicity of local cases.

CHAPTER TWO

The Huguenot Population of France, 1600–85

Prologue

During his travels in France between 1676 and 1678, John Locke, that concerned Protestant, frequently asked the people he met about the situation of the local Huguenot community. The entries in his diary show a particular interest in possible changes in the number of Protestants. Thus, an entry of February 1676 notes about the Huguenots of Montpellier: 'they and the papist laity live togeather friendly enough in these parts. They sometimes get and sometimes loose proselytes. ... The number of Protestants in these latter years neither increases nor decreases much.' Another entry offers an even more optimistic view of the recent fate of the city's Huguenots: 'They tell me that the number of Protestants within these twenty or thirty last years are manifestly increased, and doe dayly.'[1]

Locke's interest in the numerical evolution of the Protestant community that made him something of a pioneer in the study of Huguenot demography is readily understandable. In many southern French towns with a substantial Protestant population, the local *consulat* was divided between Huguenots and Catholics according to a numerical formula roughly linked to each confession's strength. Here, changes in the relative size of the two communities were matters of immediate political import, so much so that after Montauban's population was decimated by the terrible plague of 1653, the city's ministers wrote to their fellow pastors throughout the country urging them to encourage young people in their congregation to move to Montauban. Only thus could efforts by 'our adversaries' to fill the void with Catholic immigrants be forestalled.[2] Even where the political stakes were not so pressing, to know how many Huguenots lived within a given part of France was – and still is – to begin to understand their place within that region. To know whether this minority grew or shrank over the course of the period which ran from the Edict of Nantes to its Revocation, and to understand the causes for any changes in the size of different Protestant communities, are to begin to probe the faith's vitality and its ability to withstand the growing pressure

---

[1] John Lough, ed., *Locke's Travels in France 1675–1679* (Cambridge, 1953), pp. 28, 41.

[2] B.N., Ms Nouvelles Acquisitions Françaises 22702, fols 15–16, Verdier to Paul Ferry, 3 January 1654.

toward religious conformity exerted by a resurgent Catholic church and an increasingly powerful state. Most broadly of all, to determine the numerical fate of this one post-Reformation confessional community is to add to our understanding of the tenacity and character of confessional attachment within the larger universe of European states within which the religious upheavals of the sixteenth century gave rise to a measure of religious toleration and pluralism. In brief, establishing the Huguenot community's numerical evolution is a necessary prologue to any more detailed investigation of its experience in this period, as well as a contribution in its own right to the study of confessional attachment in the century following the Reformation.

Locke did not just ask about the number of Protestants. He was also curious about their religious practice and moral behaviour, especially whether or not they could truly be said to be the 'Reformed'. Here, his informants were more pessimistic. 'Mr. Bertheau told me that there was little piety or religion among their people and that the lives of the Reformed was no better than that of the Papists', one entry notes. Echoes another, 'The Protestants live not better than the Papists.'[3]

Although Locke did not use the techniques of historical demography in investigating the comparative morality of Protestants and Catholics, that other, funnier historical demographer *avant la lettre*, François Rabelais, had already realized a century earlier that parish registers could be used to determine how closely people cleaved to the teachings of the church. 'In the baptismal register of Thouars', notes Pantagruel, 'the number of children is greater in October and November than in the other ten months of the year; and so by retrospective computation we find that they must all have been made, conceived, and engendered in Lent.'[4] Of course, the significance of this (miscalculated) observation was not easy to decipher. Pantagruel and Friar John disagreed as to whether the more numerous conceptions resulted from the kinds of food consumed during Lent, which stimulated sexual activity, or from the preaching of the season, which shamed husbands into abandoning their maidservants and returning to their wives. Whatever the difficulties in determining the meaning of the patterns thus revealed, modern historical demographers have followed these *doctes* in realizing that the statistical tendencies which can be deduced from parish register investigations bring to light otherwise unobservable patterns of social and religious behaviour. Not only does the seasonal movement of baptisms and marriages illuminate the extent to which people adhered to, or broke, the Catholic church's calendar of Lenten and Advent

---

[3] Lough, ed., *Locke's Travels*, pp. 28, 94.

[4] François Rabelais, *The Histories of Gargantua and Pantagruel*, trans. J.M. Cohen (Harmondsworth, 1955), Book V, ch. 29, p. 673.

prohibitions. Rates of illegitimate births and premarital conceptions can indicate how strictly standards of sexual morality were followed, while the length of time people waited before having their infants baptized after birth sheds light on prevalent attitudes toward the sacrament of baptism. The sober statistics of historical demography provide a valuable complement to the study of religious history.[5]

The questions which Locke asked of his hosts in France define the two goals of this study. Its primary aim has been to assemble the surviving information that can be used to trace reliably the numerical evolution of France's Calvinist minority between 1600 and 1685. Section 1 analyses the pattern of change brought to light by this evidence. In the course of gathering this information, it was also possible to accumulate material that sheds interesting light on aspects of Huguenot piety and behaviour, the focus of Section 2.

Like many historical investigations, this one took shape only gradually, and some explanation of its genesis may help readers understand the extent of the information it presents. When I began research on the social history of seventeenth-century French Calvinism, I had no intention of carrying out an extended demographic investigation. Both the authoritative opinion of Samuel Mours and some acquaintance with the experience of the Protestant congregation I knew best, that of Rouen, led me to believe that after the often violent fluctuations in size experienced by many Huguenot communities over the course of the later sixteenth century, the years from 1600 to 1685 formed a period of calm during which the Protestant population evolved along lines essentially similar to those of France as a whole. Exceptions might exist, notably the dramatic fate of La Rochelle brought to light by Louis Perouas, but this was surely an extraordinary case, tied to that city's tragic experience during the siege of 1628–29.[6]

As I began to explore the changing sociological composition of several large urban congregations, I discovered that my original presuppositions were wrong. To take the case of Montpellier, it turned out that Locke had not been misinformed; the number of Huguenots there remained remarkably stable from the 1640s through the 1670s. But this was at a level close to 30 per cent lower than that of the first decade of the seventeenth century, for the number of Protestants living in the city had been substantially reduced by siege during the revolt of 1621–22 and by

5 As has been strongly argued by E. William Monter, 'Historical Demography and Religious History in Sixteenth-Century Geneva', *Journal of Interdisciplinary History* 9 (1979), 399–427.

6 Perouas, 'Sur la démographie rochelaise', *Annales: E.S.C.* 16 (1961), 1131–40.

plague in 1629. Meanwhile, Montpellier's total population had grown significantly from the time of Henry IV to that of Louis XIV, with the result that while the Huguenots formed 60 per cent of the city's inhabitants in the 1610s, they were reduced to a minority of 30 per cent by the 1660s. Most of the other urban communities I first looked at experienced a comparable, if often more gradual, decline in size.

As I discovered more and more such cases of decline among the communities I studied, I grew increasingly curious. Was the phenomenon of diminishing numbers confined to the congregations located in larger cities, or was it more generally typical of the fate of Protestant communities over the course of this period? Was it sharper in certain regions of the country than in others? And what accounted for it? Was this a confirmation of the 'lethargy' and 'spiritual sickness' which certain distinguished historians of French Protestantism have diagnosed as afflicting the cause in this period? Or were there simpler political or demographic causes?

At this point, I began to investigate Huguenot demography seriously, working in two directions. First, I carried out a detailed study of a single community which experienced a significant decline in size, using the techniques of family reconstitution in order to probe in depth the causes of decline. I chose Alençon for this purpose, since the time-consuming process of reconstituting its Protestant families was greatly facilitated by the existence of an excellent set of genealogies for all its Huguenot inhabitants.[7] Second, I sought to accumulate aggregate data about the evolution of enough different Protestant communities throughout France so that the overall movement of the Huguenot population and its chief regional variations could be traced with some reliability from 1600 to 1685. This latter ambition gradually expanded into an effort to incorporate into the study the data contained in all surviving sets of Huguenot vital records covering a long stretch of the seventeenth century. Two events facilitated this expansion of the project's goals. First, Jean-Noël Biraben of the Institut National d'Etudes Démographiques kindly agreed to share with me information about a significant number of churches that he had accumulated in the course of his reconstruction of the movement of France's total population from the first widespread establishment of parish registration through 1670.[8] Second, the publication of an inventory

---

[7] These genealogies were drawn up by the pastor and local historian Benjamin Robert, and are now conserved along with the rest of his notes at the B.P.F.

[8] Biraben and I initially envisaged the joint publication of our results but with time recognized that the differences of our aims and timetables precluded this. I owe Dr Biraben a great debt of gratitude, as I do all of the many other *chercheurs* who kindly communicated to me information they had gathered about individual congregations. The full extent of my debts may be seen from the appendix of the original version of this study, published in the *Transactions of the American Philosophical Society*, Vol. 81, Part 5, 1991. This appendix

of all known demographic sources concerning France's Huguenot population revealed that our joint efforts had brought us close enough to exhausting the fullest sets of registers that it was conceivable to envisage examining them all.[9]

This study has thus come to be built upon all of the known parish register and census evidence bearing upon the changing size of France's Huguenot population over the course of the period between the Edict of Nantes and its Revocation – specifically, upon census figures or annual totals of baptisms for any Protestant church or community for which such evidence spans forty or more years of the century. It is important to point out that I take France to refer here to that territory under the control of the French crown for the full period 1600–85. Although Reformed congregations also existed in this era in certain other communities located within the modern boundaries of France (e.g., Colmar, Mulhouse, Sainte-Marie-aux-Mines, Sedan and the principality of Orange), and although Louis XIV's annexation of Alsace incorporated an important Lutheran population into the kingdom as well, the history of these communities obeyed a different logic from that of the Reformed churches subject to the control of the Bourbon monarchs throughout the century. Its reconstruction and explanation are best left to local historians of those communities.

While this study is built upon evidence gathered for over six score congregations or localities, it is also important to stress that the extent of the information assembled about each one varies considerably. Reconstructing the secular trend of the Protestant population in the community in question has always been the first priority when gathering data about a given locality. Where time and the sources permitted, such matters as the seasonal movement of marriages, the evolution of the Catholic population in the same community, and (most time-consuming and hence rarest of all) rates of illegitimacy or prenuptial conceptions have also been explored. While the basic sample retained for use in analysing the secular trend of the Protestant population concerns 120 localities, the discussion of certain issues rests upon just two to two dozen cases.

However extensive the archival base upon which it rests, a national survey such as this, based upon the often summary exploitation of a restricted group of sources, necessarily has one further limitation. The

---

provides full bibliographic references, year-by-year figures, and a brief discussion of the state of the evidence for each locality examined in this study. Readers interested in further details about particular churches are referred to this version of the study, which also provides many figures and tables eliminated in this reprinting.

[9] Gildas Bernard, *Les familles protestantes en France, XVIe siècle–1792. Guide des recherches biographiques et généalogiques* (Paris, 1987).

methods employed here can provide a sound basis for generalizations about the aggregate experience of the group being studied. As will be seen, they bring to light numerous hitherto unsuspected regional variations in its destiny and behaviour. They can even suggest some of the causes of the trends they uncover. Often, however, they raise as many questions as they answer. Time and again, in carrying out the research for this project, I have had to suppress the urge to settle down in an individual archive or region in order to do the extensive digging necessary to explain some intriguing trend or pattern brought to light by the evidence, lest this project take even longer to complete than it already has. Time and again, in consequence, it has been possible for me to do no more here than offer hypothetical explanations for important phenomena brought to light and to urge more research on the topic. It is increasingly apparent that great regional variations characterized both the sociology of seventeenth-century French Protestantism and the patterns of coexistence and confessional identity formation which governed Catholic–Protestant relations in this period. This national investigation is offered in the hope that it can help to stimulate more of the detailed local studies of individual Protestant communities and of the relations between their members and their Catholic neighbours that are so desperately needed to illuminate these variations, as well as to highlight those regions where such studies might be particularly fruitful.[10] When more such studies have been carried out, not only the explanations offered here, but indeed many of the findings themselves, may look very different.

1. A declining minority

The size and distribution of France's Protestant minority, c. 1660–70

Any examination of Huguenot numbers in the seventeenth century must begin from the work of Samuel Mours. In a series of books and articles culminating in his *Essai sommaire de géographie du protestantisme réformé français au XVIIe siècle* of 1966, this dedicated pastor-historian drew together the information contained in the scattered surviving regional censuses of Protestantism, the immense and highly uneven monographic literature on the local history of the religion, and a few original baptismal registers in order to build up, case by case and region by region, the best picture of Protestantism's numerical strength and geographic distribution

---

10 One particularly important study was under way when this chapter was first written and has since been completed: Gregory Hanlon, *Confession and Community in Seventeenth-Century France: Catholic and Protestant Coexistence in Aquitaine* (Philadelphia, 1993).

available to date.[11] Earlier estimates of Huguenot numbers had ranged as high as two million. Mours's patient investigation showed that a figure on the order of 850 000 was far more probable. His breakdown of Protestantism's strength by region also highlighted the most striking characteristics of the cause's geographic dispersion: the clustering of over four-fifths of the country's Huguenots within the crescent of provinces running from Dauphiné across Languedoc and Guyenne and up the west coast into Poitou; and the disproportionately urban nature of the faith, especially in the northern half of the kingdom. Even though Mours appears to have used rather unsystematic criteria to classify different communities by size and character, his figures suggest that over 40 per cent of the Huguenot population of this latter portion of France lived in towns, whereas the percentage of the country's total population living in communities of two thousand inhabitants or more around 1700 stood between 15 and 19 per cent.[12] Mours's estimates, his 1958 work makes clear, apply to the period 1660–70, years for which evidence about the strength of the faith in different regions is abundant, but before the increasingly harsh measures of discrimination leading up to the Revocation had begun to take their toll on the size of the Protestant community.[13]

Mours's work represents a monument of modest and patient scholarship, but subsequent investigations of Protestantism's strength within certain regions have indicated that his figures may still exaggerate slightly the size of the community to which he was so attached. This is particularly true of his estimates for those regions where he had to build up his figures on a case-by-case basis. Thus, after a very careful review of all the evidence

---

[11] Mours, 'Essai d'évaluation de la population protestante réformée aux XVIIe et XVIIIe siècles', *B.S.H.P. F.* 103 (1958), 1–24; reprinted in *Les Eglises réformées en France: Tableaux et cartes* (Paris–Strasbourg, 1958), pp. 157–68; 'Essai sommaire de géographie du protestantisme réformé français au XVIIe siècle', *B.S.H.P.F.* 111 (1965), 303–21; CXII (1966), 19–36, also separately published (Paris, 1966).

[12] Jacques Dupâquier, *La population française aux XVIIe et XVIIIe siècles* (Paris, 1979), p. 40; Dupâquier, ed., *Histoire de la population française*, II *De la Renaissance à 1789* (Paris, 1988), p. 87; and Philip Benedict, 'Was the Eighteenth Century an Era of Urbanization in France?' *Journal of Interdisciplinary History* 21 (1990), 196, 211, all provide estimates of the percentage of the population living in communities of two thousand or more inhabitants. Deciding just what attributes qualified a locality as a city is, of course, one of the most delicate problems facing students of *ancien régime* French society. While claiming, 'nous prenons le mot ville dans son acceptation la plus large, y comprenant des petites villes, telles que Sainte-Foy, en Guyenne; Anduze, en Cévennes; Die, en Dauphiné' (*Essai sommaire*, p. 40), Mours none the less does not appear to have bestowed urban status on other localities of roughly equal size which contemporaries also considered cities, such as Barbézieux and Cognac.

[13] Mours, *Les Eglises réformées de France*, p. 158.

available about the vast *province synodal* of Orléanais–Berry, Yves Gueneau arrived at a figure of between 10 750 and 11 400 Protestants within this region, where Mours had suggested 15 500.[14] A similar investigation of the colloquy of Moyen-Poitou yielded an estimate of 40 000 souls, where Mours had placed the number at 50 000.[15] By no means are all Mours's figures equally inflated. For much of the Midi he was able to rely on the censuses of Protestants drawn up by the local authorities in many regions after 1661, and a comparison of his figures with the original sources indicates that he usually, although not always, respected the accuracy of these documents, which are unquestionably the best available sources for this purpose. A thorough review of Mours's sources and of the corrections of his figures which have been offered since their publication yields the revised estimates set forth in Table 2.1, which also modify his figures to make them refer to France's boundaries of 1610 and to a more systematic division of the communities within which the Protestant churches were located according to their total size.[16] As can be seen, a more accurate approximation of the total number of Protestants living within these confines in the years 1660–70 might place the figure at just under 800 000 people. These revised figures offer us a starting point for the backward extrapolation of the Huguenot population and a context for judging how representative is the sample of congregations on which this study rests.

---

[14] Gueneau, 'Protestants du Centre 1598–1685' (unpub. *thèse de troisième cycle*, Université François Rabelais de Tours, 1982), pp. 103–29.

[15] André Benoist, 'Les populations rurales du "Moyen-Poitou Protestant" de 1640 à 1789' (unpub. *thèse de troisième cycle*, Université de Poitiers, 1983), p. 469.

[16] In classifying churches or localities according to size, I have placed those churches or censuses which encompassed people inhabiting a wide geographic area in the category of community from which the majority of those concerned were drawn. Although contemporaries considered many localities of less than 2000 inhabitants to be cities, I have chosen a population of 2000 as the cut-off point to define cities for the sake of simplicity. Population estimates of community size have been drawn from a wide range of sources, most notably Jacques Dupâquier, *Statistiques démographiques du Bassin Parisien 1636–1720* (Paris, 1977); Paul Bairoch, Jean Batou and Pierre Chèvre, *La population des villes européennes de 800 à 1850/The Population of European Cities from 800 to 1850* (Geneva, 1988); René Le Mée, 'Population agglomérée et population éparse au début du XIXe siècle', *Annales de Démographie Historique*, 1971, 467–94, extrapolated backward on the basis of eighteenth-century trends in the urban population of the region as set forth in Benedict, 'Was the Eighteenth Century an Era of Urbanization?' and the parish register information examined in the course of this study. It goes without saying that the classification decisions contain a risk of error. Most particularly Anduze, Alès and Uzès, which have been placed here in the category of small towns, all fell very near the cut-off point of 5000 inhabitants and may have exceeded it for at least part of the period in question. Recalculating all statistics with these cities placed in the larger rather than the smaller category introduces only minor changes into the results.

Table 2.1   The Reformed population of France, c. 1660–70

Synod	Number of churches	Total Protestant population	Cities of 5000+ inhabs	Cities of 2–5000 inhabs	Rural population
Six northern synods					
Ile-de-France–					
Champagne–Picardy[1]	47	51 000[2]	21 650	4 500	24 850
Normandy	43	42 200[2]	21 000	2 400	18 800
Brittany	11	2 600[3]	1 300	300	1 000
Anjou–Maine–Touraine	21	10 200[2]	5 525	600	4 075
Orléanais-Berry	23	11 500[4]	2 500	5 000	4 000
Burgundy	26	17 000	1 800	1 200	14 000
Total	171	134 500	53 775	14 000	66 725
Ten southern synods					
Poitou	49	77 500[5]	11 000	2 000	64 500
Saintonge–Aunis–					
Angoumois	60	93 500[6]	16 000	7 500	70 000
Basse-Guyenne	72	97 000[7]	14 000	5 000	78 000
Béarn	46	25 000[8]		6 500	18 500
Haut-Languedoc–					
Haute-Guyenne	64	80 000	15 500	7 500	57 000
Bas-Languedoc	63	81 000[9]	16 500	12 000	52 500
Cévennes	59	74 000[10]		18 000	56 000
Vivarais	29	48 000		3 500	44 500
Provence	12	8 000[9]	400	400	7 200
Dauphiné[11]	71	78 000	4 500	7 000	66 500
Total	525	662 000	77 900	69 400	514 700
Grand total	696	796 500	131 675	83 400	581 425

Note: These estimates refer to the Reformed population living within France's borders of 1610.

[1] Plus Metz and Pays Messin.

[2] Comparison of certain of Mours's estimates of the size of individual churches with the size suggested by the number of baptisms celebrated within them indicates that he overestimated their ranks. His estimate has been reduced accordingly.

[3] Revised estimates kindly provided by the local historian Jean-Luc Tulot.

[4] Accepting the corrections of Gueneau.

[5] Accepting the corrections of Benoist for Moyen Poitou and using the average of Mours's estimates for the province's other two *colloques*, rather than the higher number.

[6] Figures for the *colloque* of Aunis corrected on the basis of Louis Perouas, *Le diocèse de la Rochelle de 1648 à 1724: Sociologie et pastorale* (Paris, 1964), esp. pp. 130–33.

[7] Modified in light of Lucile Bourrachot, 'Démographie et société dans les documents ecclésiastiques du diocèse d'Agen au XVIIe siècle', *Annales du Midi* 76 (1964), 215–22.

[8] Splitting the difference between the two censuses of Béarn's Protestant population in 1665, rather than accepting the higher estimates provided by the Reformed church itself. On these, see pp. 88–9.

[9] Mours's estimate of 1956, which seems more accurate when checked against his sources than his subsequent evaluation.

[10] Figures for the *colloque* of Saint-Germain-de-Calberte corrected on the basis of J.R. Armogathe, 'Le diocése de Mende au 17me siècle. Perspectives d'histoire religieuse', *Revue du Gévaudan* n.s., 17 (1971), 92.

[11] Excluding the principality of Orange but including the Valcluson.

Source: Mours, *Essai sommaire*, p. 41, modified as indicated in notes.

The sources and the sample

Two kinds of sources exist which enable one to trace the movement of the Protestant population within given localities between the promulgation of the Edict of Nantes and its Revocation. The first, censuses or other enumerations of Protestant households within a certain area, offers the most convenient, and probably also the most accurate, gauge of the size of individual Huguenot congregations. Such documents are fairly abundant for the years after 1661, when central government surveillance of what the authorities termed the 'Religion Prétendue Réformée' (R.P.R.) intensified. Except for the closely watched towns and regions close to France's eastern border, however, it is uncommon for such estimates to have survived from the earlier part of the century. It is more uncommon still for several such estimates to have survived for a single community at widely spaced dates between 1600 and 1685. For this reason, it has been possible to rely here on census information for only a handful of localities.

By contrast, Protestant vital records provide a far more widely available gauge to the changes which might have occurred in the size of individual Protestant communities between 1600 and 1685. The very first national synod of the French Reformed church, held in 1559, decreed that all congregations of the newly established church should maintain a record of the baptisms and marriages celebrated within them, and the obligation to note burials as well was added in 1584. Although some churches were clearly delinquent about maintaining such registers, although many were lost when the Revocation precipitated the dispersion of the papers belonging to the Reformed churches, and although others have succumbed to the vicissitudes which winnow with time the availability of all historical documents, a large corpus of such registers none the less exists today in France's national, departmental and communal archives and in private hands or libraries in France, Switzerland and even South Carolina.[17] If these documents are particularly abundant for the years after 1667, when royal legislation dictated new standards for maintaining all parish registers in the kingdom and required copies to be turned over annually to the king's officials, no less than 126 sets of registers stretch back for thirty years or more before 1667 and span, albeit often with lacunae, at least four decades of the century. Two other good sets of such registers were destroyed during the Second World War, but the number of acts in them

---

[17] Bernard, *Les familles protestantes*, now provides a full guide to these registers. For their history, see B. Faucher, 'Les registres de l'état civil protestant en France depuis le XVIe siécle jusqu'à nos jours', *Bibliothèque de l'Ecole des Chartes* 84 (1923), 304–46; Jacques Fromental, *La Réforme en Bourgogne aux XVIe et XVIIe siècles* (Paris, 1968), p. 113.

was fortunately counted by scholars who worked before that time. The number of acts in still another lost set can be reconstructed from tables in the community's Catholic parish registers.[18]

Occasionally kept in the same volume as the minutes of the church's consistorial deliberations, these registers were typically maintained by either the pastor or a lay member of the consistory, often on the basis of 'billets' or 'cartelz' which the interested parties or designated officials turned over to them following the celebration of a baptism, marriage or burial.[19] Marginal notations occasionally betray the imprint of Protestant theology and devotional practice. Thus, Bellême's register begins with citations of the biblical passages relating to baptism, while the keeper of Saint-Jean-du-Gard's register implored, 'May God guide my hand.'[20] An elder of Rochechouart, a congregation troubled by both internal conflicts and the hostility of the local seigneur, included a passionate prayer for the survival and concord of his church, while the cover of Fraissinet's register is graced by moralizing verses that combine a range of injunctions – use your time well, speak and deal honestly, don't forget your friends, be a convivial host – which neatly confound overly simple interpretations of Protestant ethics.[21] Not all of the marginalia are religious in character. The doodling pen of Jean de Castorret of Lagor, the Cassius Clay/Muhammad Ali of scribes, could not refrain from recording, amid elaborate curlicues, 'My first time when I wanted to write, I wrote as sweetly as a fly.'[22]

Despite the provisions of the national synods, burial registration is manifestly incomplete or entirely non-existent in the great majority of registers before 1667, and it is not uncommon for these registers to omit marriages as well. Although this diminishes the potential of many sets of Protestant vital records as sources for calculating sophisticated demographic statistics, the copious series of baptisms still offer an acceptable source for tracing fluctuations over time in the Protestant population, since changes in the level of baptisms offer a rough guide to the overall trend of the population as a whole – so long as fertility rates or the ratio between births and baptisms did not change markedly over time (possibilities that will be explored in the sections to follow), and so long as the baptisms were recorded continuously and scrupulously.

---

18 Full references to the sources consulted are provided in the appendix of the original version. The registers destroyed in the Second World War were those of Caen and Saint-Lô, while Loudun's registers must be reconstructed from tables in the city's Catholic registers.

19 This can be inferred from marginal comments within the registers themselves.

20 A.D.O., I, 43; A.C. Saint-Jean-du-Gard, GG 20. Similar sentiments in A.C. Montpellier, GG 321, 'A Dieu seul sage soit honneur et gloire en siecles des siecles'; 'Louange a Dieu'.

21 A.D. Haute-Vienne, Etat civil protestant, Rochechouart, 2nd register; B.P.F., MS 422.

22 A.D. Pyrénées-Atlantiques, 4 E 301.

The best-maintained of the Huguenot 'parish' registers are unquestionably among the richest and most informative sets of all such records from this early period of the French *état civil*, and the reconstitution of Alençon's population suggests that baptisms within that church were recorded with care. None the less, in reading through certain of the baptismal registers, it is difficult to avoid the suspicion that acts have been overlooked or omitted. In certain cases, it is clear that the normal pattern of celebrating baptisms was interrupted for stretches of several months or even years at a time because of the absence of a pastor. Often in such cases, baptisms were performed at irregular intervals by ministers visiting from nearby localities. Still, we would expect the number of baptisms to be abnormally low in these years since more children would die before they were able to receive the sacrament. Since my goal in this study has been less to achieve a year-by-year count of the number of vital events occurring among France's Huguenots than to assemble the best evidence possible about the overall size of different Protestant congregations at different eras, such years have been omitted from consideration in the calculations which follow.

In other cases, negligent record keeping produced longer periods of deficient registration. Some scribes were considerate enough of future generations to note shortcomings, as did the elder of Saujon who wrote in the margin of his register, 'Those hereafter interested in seeking the names of the children baptized ... since I was received as elder and elected to keep the present baptismal paper shall remain advised that several parties received the sacrament of baptism without being registered for lack of having ... delivered note of their names and of the said children in conformity with the order.'[23] Cases such as these have naturally been eliminated from consideration here for the length of the period for which registration appears incomplete. So too have registers characterized by abnormally large fluctuations in the number of acts from year to year where these fluctuations cannot confidently be ascribed to normal demographic events or political perturbations. But what is one to do with registers of smaller churches where the number of acts fluctuates sharply from year to year (something which may simply be a function of their size rather than any deficiencies in registration), or with registers which contain large gaps between acts without the movement of the dates suggesting that registration ceased for a certain period of time? I must admit that I have not been able to develop a hard and fast set of criteria which could be consistently applied to determine deficient registers. Instead, I have tried to remain suitably vigilant about the quality of the registers examined,

---

[23] A.C. Saujon, état civil, culte réformé, fol. 217. Similar explanations of defective or missing registration in A.D. Landes, 1 J 468; L.D.S. film 687553 (A.C. Lasalle, GG 13).

without being so exigent as to rule out potentially significant information every time the least suspicion about the quality of registration arose. The reliability of certain sets of figures retained for this study is unquestionably less great than that of others.

Beyond these problems in assessing the completeness of individual registers – problems which, it must be admitted, are typical of any study based upon the parish registers of this era – the Huguenot baptismal registers also pose one special problem of interpretation which rarely arises when dealing with other contemporaneous vital records: that of fluctuating boundaries. The limits of most parishes in seventeenth-century Europe were fixed by centuries-old custom and rarely altered. France's Reformed temples, on the other hand, often attracted worshippers from well beyond the immediate locality in which they were located and not infrequently saw a change in the area from which they recruited their members, either as annex churches were created nearby, or, as happened with increasing frequency after 1661, as neighbouring temples were closed down for being in violation of the terms of the Edict of Nantes interpreted *à la rigueur*.

Faced with this problem of shifting church boundaries, historians seeking to aggregate information about many such churches can choose one of two courses of action. They may either try to make the data about each church refer to a stable geographic area, by introducing appropriate corrections, or they may accept all the evidence in the raw state in which it has come down to us and assume that in aggregating the information, the cases where the number of baptisms has swelled over time because a nearby temple was closed are counterbalanced by others where the series of acts ends because it comes from a temple that was itself closed and where the number of subsequent baptisms may consequently be reckoned as zero. The former course is unquestionably preferable. It makes each individual church or locality an illuminating unit of analysis, while at the same time enabling one to skirt the necessity of determining, for each gap in a church's records, whether the church was closed during the years for which the registers are deficient or whether the gaps derive from the subsequent loss of its records, something which frequently cannot be done on the basis of the surviving evidence. But this methodological choice does mean that one must be able to detect and correct for any changes which might have occurred in the catchment area of the churches studied.

In most cases, this is not difficult. Many of the registers note, at least intermittently, the place of residence of the families bringing their children to be baptized. Where this information indicates that people from a certain locality suddenly began to attend services at a temple which they had not previously frequented, the acts concerning these newcomers can be eliminated so that all figures continue to refer to a fixed geographic area.

Where the registers fail to note the parish of residence, striking changes in the number of acts from one year to the next can still serve as a warning that the church's boundaries may have changed. In these cases, histories of Protestantism in the region or the published lists of Reformed churches which existed at different dates in the century often clarify whether or not these changes indeed stemmed from fluctuations in the church's boundaries.[24] Once it has been determined that this was indeed the case, a comparison of the level of baptisms for the five-year periods before and after the neighbouring church opened or closed can provide an approximate indication of the magnitude of the change in the number of baptisms induced by this event. The figures can then be corrected accordingly. In certain cases, however, it is simply impossible to determine an accurate correction factor for boundary changes known to have occurred. Such cases have been eliminated from consideration here. Of course, the possibility remains that certain boundary changes may also have gone undetected, particularly in the case of registers which do not record the place of residence of those bringing their children to baptism.

Once all registers marked by apparently deficient registration or uncertain boundary changes have been eliminated from consideration, apparently reliable evidence remains about a sample of 120 geographic entities, or roughly 17 per cent of the total number of churches in existence around 1660.[25] Map 2.1 indicates the location of these communities. As can be seen, the sample communities are scattered across the breadth of the country with the exception of the northern and central Massif Central and the Breton peninsula, where Protestantism never took deep root. Every one of the sixteen *provinces synodaux* into which the French Reformed churches were grouped is represented by at least one church, as are 51 of the 61 *colloques* into which the churches were further subdivided.[26]

---

[24] In tracing the fate of different churches, I have relied especially upon the lists of the Protestant churches existing in 1603, 1620 and 1626, and of those closed between 1656 and 1685 in Haag, I, 269–73, 315–34, 378–81; on P. Gachon, *Quelques préliminaires de la Révocation de l'Edit de Nantes en Languedoc (1661–1685)* (Toulouse, 1899); and on the lists of churches sending delegates to provincial synods of the Reformed church to be found in the records of these synodal assemblies, most notably the Auzière collection of the B.P.F.

[25] The percentage is approximate and the term 'geographic entities' used advisedly, since not all of the entities analysed are similar in nature. Most of the evidence concerns individual churches, which of course recruited members from more than a single locality. In certain cases, the analysis bears only upon a stable sub-unit of the full geographic region served by a given church. Where the available evidence is composed of census data, the figures refer to the population living within a given bailliage or town. Finally, in two cases (Metz and Saint-Quentin-Lehaucourt), I have analysed separately the rural and urban dwellers of a single church.

[26] The *colloques* which are not represented in the sample are those of the Pays de Gex, Bas Poitou, Saint-Jean-d'Angély, Haut Agenais, Vic-Bihl, Oloron, Haut Quercy, Pays de Foix, Baronnies and Valcluson.

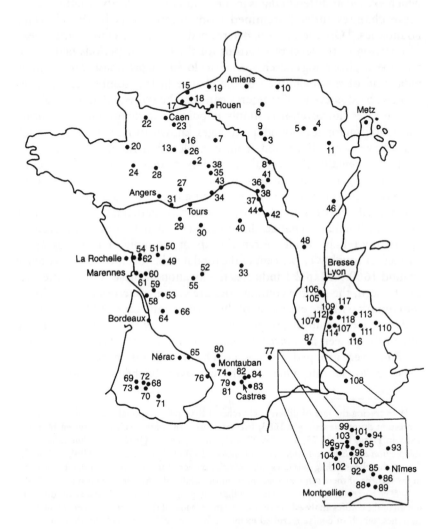

Map 2.1 Congregations and localities with reliable data about the long-term movement of the Protestant population

Key

Localities arranged by synod.
The numbers refer to the map on the facing page.

Ile-de-France–Champagne–Picardy
Amiens
2 Authon-du-Perche
3 Chalandos
4 Châlons-sur-Marne
5 Chaltrait
6 Compiègne
7 Fontaine-sous-Prémont
8 Landreville
9 Meaux-Nanteuil
10 Saint-Quentin-
Lehaucourt
11 Wassy
(Metz)

Normandy
13 Alençon
Caen
15 Fécamp
16 Laigle
17 Le Havre
18 Lintot
19 Luneray
20 Pontorson-Cormeray
Rouen
22 Saint-Lô
23 Saint-Pierre-sur-Dives

Brittany
24 Vitré

Anjou–Touraine–Maine
Angers
26 Bellême
27 Château-du-Loir
28 Laval
29 Loudun
30 Preuilly-sur-Claise
31 Saumur
Tours

Orléanais–Berry
33 Aubusson
34 Blois
35 Châteaudun
36 Châtillon-sur-Loing
37 Châtillon-sur-Loire
38 Dangeau
39 Gien
40 Issoudun
41 La Celle-Saint-Cyr-Dollot

42 La Charité
43 Mer
44 Sancerre

Burgundy
Bailliage de Bresse
46 Is-sur-Tille
Lyon
48 Paray-le-Monial

Poitou
49 Chef-Boutonne
50 La-Mothe-Saint-Héray-
Exoudun
51 Mougon
52 Rochechouart

Aunis–Saintonge–Angoumous
53 Barbézieux
54 Dompierre-Bourgneuf
55 La Rochefoucauld
La Rochelle
Marennes
58 Mortagne-sur-Gironde
59 Pons
60 Saint-Jean-d'Angle
61 Saint-Just
62 Salles

Basse-Guyenne
Bordeaux
64 Coutras
65 Layrac
66 Mussidan
Nérac

Béarn
68 Arthez
69 Bellocq
70 Lagor
71 Nay
72 Orthez
73 Salies

*Haute-Guyenne–
Haut-Languedoc*
74 Briatexte
Castres
76 Mas-Grenier
77 Millau
Montauban
79 Puylaurens

80 Réalville-Albias
81 Revel
82 Roquecourbe
83 Saint-Amans
84 Vabre

Bas-Languedoc
85 Aigues-Vives
86 Codognan
87 Les Vans
88 Lunel
89 Marsillargues
Montpellier
Nîmes
92 Sommières
93 Uzès

Cévennes
94 Alés
95 Anduze
96 Aulas
97 Lasalle
98 Monoblet
99 Saint-Etienne-Vallée-
Française
100 Saint-Hippolyte-
du-Fort
101 Saint-Jean-du-Gard
102 Saint-Laurent-le-Minier
103 Soudorgues
104 Suméne

Vivarais
105 Annonay
106 Boulieu
107 Privas

Provence
108 Lourmarin

Dauphiné
109 Beaumont-lès-Valence
110 Embrun
111 Gap
112 Loriol
113 Mens-en-Trièves
114 Montélimar
115 Montjoux
116 Orpierre
117 Pont-en-Royans
118 Vercheny

Despite the extensive geographic spread of this evidence, the surviving evidence does not constitute a perfect sample of the universe of Protestant churches existing in the seventeenth century. At least three biases can be detected. First, and most important, records of urban congregations are considerably more likely to have come down to us than those of rural churches; the survival rate for rural baptismal records is particularly poor in the Midi and Centre–West. As a result, the sample contains 46 per cent of the churches located in the larger cities of northern France, 36 per cent of those in its smaller cities, and 20 per cent of its rural churches, while for the Midi and Centre–West the comparable figures are 38, 38 and 9 per cent respectively. Since urban–rural and North–South differences were highly significant, the analysis to follow will examine the churches of each broad community type and region separately before combining the results obtained in a manner which accords due weight to the relative importance of each category.

Second, the sample is particularly thin on evidence about certain smaller regions of Protestant strength, most notably the Pays de Gex, the heartland of the Protestant Vivarais around the valley of the Ardèche, and the entire synod of Basse-Guyenne. To judge by the broader regional patterns which will emerge in the subsequent pages, it seems unlikely that this substantially skews the results obtained, but readers should keep this pattern in mind in evaluating the evidence presented.

Finally, as might be expected, there is a clear tendency toward disproportionate survival of records from the larger and more important churches within each category. Assuming that the total population of the churches in the sample can be estimated by multiplying the number of baptisms in the urban and small town churches by 25, the number of baptisms in the rural churches by 30, and the number of families or hearths in census data by 4.5 – all standard assumptions about this period that will be used throughout this study – it can be computed that fully 25 per cent of the estimated total Protestant population of 1660–70 lived in the sample localities, even though these represented only 17 per cent of the number of churches existing at the time. The increased likelihood of survival of records from the larger churches introduces a degree of bias into the sample, for the largest congregations tended to experience a greater decline in size over the course of the period analysed here than did the smaller ones. The sample will thus exaggerate slightly the extent of Protestantism's decline over these years. The extent of this distortion is small.[27]

---

[27] The extent of the distortion may be estimated by introducing a correction factor into the back-projection of the total Protestant population that accords the churches of below average size within each category sufficient additional weight so that the average size of the sample churches becomes equal to the average size of all churches within each category. Such a correction reduces the unweighted estimate of the total Protestant population *c.* 1600–10 by 1.4 per cent.

Precocious 'Malthusianism'?

As has already been suggested, the method which our sources oblige us to adopt to trace changes in the size of many congregations, that of following the movement of baptisms within them, is reliable only if the ratio between the number of baptisms and the total membership of these churches remained relatively constant over time. Some investigation of possible changes in this ratio is thus clearly necessary before we turn to look at the movement of baptisms in our sample communities. This means seeing first of all whether or not the Huguenots began to practise birth control on a large scale in this period, for if they did, this would sharply depress the number of acts in the baptismal registers even in the absence of any drop in the total Protestant population.

Reason certainly exists to suspect that France's Protestants might have begun to control their fertility in the seventeenth century. Jean-Pierre Bardet has recently shown conclusively that French town-dwellers began to practise family limitation on a significant scale from the end of the century onward, while Alfred Perrenoud has demonstrated that Protestant regions of Switzerland were more precocious than Catholic ones in adopting such practices in early modern times, a development which he attributes to the Reformers' more positive evaluation of marital sexuality, which in their estimation need not aim strictly at procreation.[28] Furthermore, sociologists of contemporary societies have observed that religious minorities who are objects of discrimination often have fewer children than their neighbours of the dominant faith.[29] Indeed, one local study of a Norman Protestant community, finding a declining ratio of baptisms to marriages in the years before 1685, has already suggested that the Huguenots began to limit family size as the Revocation approached.[30]

The best evidence, however, indicates clearly that France's Huguenots were not pioneers in birth control. In his massive study of the Rouennais population, Bardet examined the behaviour of that city's sizeable Protestant minority and found only a slight difference in fertility between Protestants and Catholics. The typical couple married between 1640 and 1669 within the Roman church could expect to bear 7.32 children over the course of a

---

[28] Bardet, *Rouen*, I, 263–88; Perrenoud, 'Malthusianisme et protestantisme: un modèle démographique wéberien', *Annales: E.S.C.* 29 (1974), 975–88. For more on the views of the leading Protestant theologians and their relationship to earlier Catholic teachings about sex, see James Brundage, *Law, Sex and Christian Society in Medieval Europe* (Chicago, 1988), pp. 447–53, 551–3, 555–7

[29] Calvin Goldscheider and Peter R. Uhlenberg, 'Minority Group Status and Fertility', *American Journal of Sociology* 74 (1969), 360–72.

[30] Gérard Bollon, 'Minorité broyée et Malthusianisme: Saint-Sylvain–Falaise–Saint-Pierre-sur-Dives au XVIIe siècle', *B.S.H.P.F.* 116 (1970), 489–508.

life together unbroken by the death of either partner before age 45. The comparable figure for Protestants married between 1640 and 1685 was 7.14. By way of comparison, the probable number of offspring of a Catholic couple married in the middle of the eighteenth century, when birth control practices had spread, was just 5.44 children.[31] Similarly, Brigitte Maillard's reconstitution of Tours's Protestant families finds extremely high age-specific fertility rates and very short intervals between the birth of successive children into the 1670s.[32] My own family reconstitution study of Alençon's Protestant community, an élite urban congregation, likewise reveals none of the signs historical demographers have developed to detect the practise of family limitation within marriage, even in the period after 1661, when royal policy toward the Huguenots became harsher and Bollon suggests that birth control practises began to spread as a consequence. Since it is known that family limitation began to be widely practised far earlier in France's cities than in the surrounding countryside, and that Normandy was a region of particularly precocious 'Malthusianism', the lack of evidence of birth control practises within these congregations argues powerfully against the hypothesis that any decline in the baptisms celebrated in the Protestant churches to be examined here might have stemmed from the conscious limitation of marital fertility within this increasingly beleaguered minority group. And yet, a declining ratio of baptisms to marriages can also be detected in both Alençon's and Rouen's Protestant communities in the years before 1685.[33] This appears to have been due to the increase in both emigration and conversion among young couples in prime child-bearing age during the years immediately before the Revocation.[34]

Other factors affecting the level of baptisms

While France's Protestants do not seem to have begun to limit their marital fertility significantly before 1685, other developments can be observed whose effect would have been to alter slightly the relationship between recorded baptisms and the total size of the Huguenot community. The first concerns the changing delay between birth and baptism – a topic

---

31 Bardet, *Rouen*, I, 271 and 276.
32 Maillard, 'Religion et démographie', 550–56.
33 Ratio of baptisms to marriages

	Rouen		Alençon	
	1630–59	5.33:1	1626–60	4.64:1
	1660–85	4.88:1	1661–85	4.39:1

34 See pp. 24–7. Using the records of Châtillon-sur-Loire, Gueneau, 'Protestants du Centre', 244, shows a significant increase in the average age of those receiving burial in the years just before the Revocation.

whose examination also exemplifies how parish register evidence can speak to questions of religious behaviour and practice.

From the late Middle Ages onward, the Catholic church placed great emphasis on the absolute necessity of baptism as a precondition for salvation. Church synods urged the faithful to be sure that the sacrament was administered as quickly as possible after birth, lest newborns die without receiving it and be barred from having their bodies buried in hallowed ground. The extent to which concern about the danger of allowing babies to die unbaptized came to be shared among the faithful is attested by the multiplication of 'sanctuaires à répit', shrines which became celebrated for their power to effect a miraculous resuscitation of stillborn babies long enough for them to receive the sacrament.[35] Early Catholic parish registers that note the date of both birth and baptism generally reveal the majority of newborns to have been baptized within 24 hours, although the sense of urgency was less great in the Midi.[36]

The Reformation, of course, marked a rupture with the Catholic doctrine that baptism was absolutely necessary for salvation. In Protestant dogma, baptism was a token of future mercy and a symbol of initiation into the community, not a *sine qua non* of redemption. According to decisions taken at early national synods of the Reformed church and reiterated consistently thereafter, parents were not to imitate their Catholic neighbours and call upon a clergyman or, in extremis, the wet-nurse to baptize their newborn as soon as possible, but were to wait for a regularly scheduled church assembly to present the infant for the sacrament before the entire congregation. But this was an element of Protestant doctrine which clearly encountered resistance among converts to the new faith, for throughout

---

[35] Jacques Gélis, 'La mort et le salut spirituel du nouveau-né. Essai d'analyse et d'interprétation du "sanctuaire à répit" (XVe–XIXe s.)', *R.H.M.C.* 31 (1984), 361–76; Jeanne Ferté, *La vie religieuse dans les campagnes parisiennes 1622–1695* (Paris, 1962), pp. 294–300; Jacques Toussaert, *Le sentiment religieux en Flandre à la fin du Moyen Age* (Paris, 1963), pp. 90–92.

[36] For studies of seventeenth-century Catholic parish registers that compute the median delay between birth and baptism and reveal a majority of newborns baptized within a day after birth, see Marcel Lachiver, *La population de Meulan du XVIIe au XIXe siècle (vers 1600–1870): Etude de démographie historique* (Paris, 1969), p. 70; Ferté, *Vie religieuse dans les campagnes parisiennes*, p. 300; and Denise Turrel, *Bourg-en-Bresse au 16e siècle: les hommes et la ville* (Paris, 1986), p. 18. Since the great pioneers of demographic studies on the basis of parish register evidence, Louis Henry and Pierre Goubert, both declared that the registers they had looked at showed the overwhelming majority of children baptized almost immediately after birth, it has become so axiomatic within French historical demography that this was the rule that most French local parish register studies do not even compute birth–baptism intervals. But cf. John Bossy, *Christianity in the West 1400–1700* (Oxford, 1985), p. 14, whose suggestion that 'tomorrow would usually do' for baptizing newborns in southern Europe appears to be confirmed by the evidence to be presented in the paragraphs to follow.

the later sixteenth century and into the first third of the seventeenth, local and national synods of the French Reformed church took up issues raised by the requests of parents to allow their newborns to be baptized at times or places other than the twice- or thrice-weekly services at the temple.[37]

While the synodal records testify to the survival of concern about the urgency of baptism, the baptismal registers suggest that, by the seventeenth century, the great majority of Huguenots accepted the church's rules about the sacrament. In my admittedly hasty reading of numerous Protestant baptismal registers, I noticed just one entry which indicates an emergency baptism in violation of the decisions of the national synod: the 'presentation' to Laval's church of a newborn girl of noble parentage who had already been baptized by 'a pastor of the Roman church, in fear for her death'. The alibi offered was that this was the doing of the family's servants.[38] More tellingly, the average delays between birth and baptism that can be calculated from the registers indicate, with just one exception, that by the seventeenth century a broad willingness had taken hold within Protestant ranks to wait a half a week or more before the administration of the sacrament. Over the first two-thirds of the century, furthermore, the trend was to wait longer and longer before baptism.

Only a fraction of all Huguenot baptismal registers note the date of both birth and baptism, and then often for brief periods only. The first register to do so, that of Gien for the years 1570–71 and 1580–81, reveals a median delay of 2.5 days between the two events.[39] Table 2.2 marshals evidence about this question from the reign of Henry IV onward. During the period 1595–1633, the interval most commonly ranged between 4 and 7 days north of a line running from Bordeaux to Lyon and between 5 and 17 days south of that line, although in Niort in 1628 – a time of civil war and thus heightened inter-confessional tension – the majority of the faithful had their newborns baptized within twenty-four hours. By the middle third of the century, the median delay had increased to 3–11 days across northern and central France, to 10–29 days across most of the Midi, and had attained fully 34 days in Saint-Etienne-Vallée-Française, in the upper reaches of the Cévennes. Although information is available for the same church in both of these periods for just four cases, the trend was

---

37 Jean Aymon, *Tous les Synodes Nationales des Eglises Réformées de France* (The Hague, 1710), pp. 19, 446–57; Paul de Félice, *Les Protestants d'autrefois* (3 vols, Paris, 1897–99), I, 182–6; Fromental, *La Réforme en Bourgogne*, p. 91; Janine Garrisson-Estèbe, *Protestants du Midi, 1559–1598* (Toulouse, 1980), pp. 247–8; Gueneau, 'Protestants du Centre', p. 262.

38 André Joubert, *Histoire de l'Eglise réformée de Laval* (Laval, 1889), p. 68. While this was the only such case I encountered, I should stress that my chief concern in working through the baptismal registers was always to count the number of acts quickly and accurately. I did not read every entry closely.

39 B.P.F., Ms 1082 (1). n = 122.

Table 2.2   Intervals between birth and baptism, selected Reformed
churches

	Evidence from 1590–1633	Evidence from 1634–67	Evidence from 1667–85
A. Median delay between birth and baptism			
Amiens	1624–26: 7 days (n = 132)		
Bellême		1639–50: 3 days (n = 117)	
Châlons-s/Marne	1612–15: 5 days (n = 98)	1641–43: 4 days (n = 71)	
Pont-de-Veyle	1604–6: 5 days (n = 97)		
Mougon	1603: 6 days (n = 151)		1677–78: 7 days (n = 148)
Niort	1628: 1 day (n = 104)		
Rochechouart	1605–8: 4 days (n = 104)		
Saujon		1640–41: 11 days (n = 105)	
Anduze	1609–11: 17 days (n = 587)	1656–60: 29 days (n = 786)	1682–83: 7 days (n = 286)
Briatexte	1595–99: 5 days (n = 55)	1654–59: 24 days (n = 44)	
Labastide d'Armagnac	1616–22: 19 days (n = 101)		
Mas-Grenier		1637–41: 10 days (n = 81)	
Mens-en-Trièves	1618–24: 10 days (n = 100)		
Montagnac-sur-Auvignon	1610–40: 8 days (n = 105)		
Montpellier	1613: 7.5 days (n = 357)		
Orpierre		1633–35: 10.5 days (n = 112)	
Saint-Etienne-Vallée-Française		1634–37: 34 days (n = 103)	
B. Percentage of newborns baptized within first week of life			
La Rochelle	1626–30: 86%	1661–65: 61%	1681–84: 90%
Saint-Jean-du-Gard		1663–67: 16%	1681–84: 56%

Sources: La Rochelle – Katherine L.M. Faust, 'A Beleaguered Society: Protestant Families in La Rochelle, 1628–1685' (Ph.D. diss., Northwestern University, 1980), pp. 33, 46; Saint-Jean-du-Gard – Didier Poton, *Saint-Jean-de-Gardonnenque. Une communauté réformée à la veille de la Révocation (1663–1685)* (n.p., 1985), p. 23. All others – as given in the appendix to the first edition.

for the median delay to increase in three of them. Interestingly, a similar willingness to postpone baptism can be detected among the Catholics living in heavily Protestant regions in the later seventeenth century as well. In Marennes, Nérac, Montpellier and Lodève, the median delay between birth and baptism for children born to Catholic parents ranged between 5 and 9 days in the 1660s and 1670s.[40] By contrast, the figure was just two days in such strongholds of Languedocian Catholicism as Carcassonne and Narbonne. The Protestants' more casual attitude toward prompt baptism appears to have been communicated to their Catholic neighbours in regions where the Protestants set the tone.

Then, in the years just before 1685, the trend for the Protestants to wait longer to bring their children for baptism reversed itself, as Louis XIV permitted stronger measures to be taken against the heretics. No matter how much the behaviour of ordinary Catholics might have been modified by the Protestant example, the Huguenots' willingness to postpone the baptism of their newborns for a week or longer appeared to certain devout members of the Roman church to betoken a dismaying lack of concern for the fate of their newborns' souls. In several parts of the country, forcible Catholic baptisms were administered to sickly Huguenot newborns or to infants who had not received a church baptism.[41] To prevent their children from receiving such unwanted baptisms 'à la papaulté', Protestant parents began to bring their infants to the temple for christening far more expeditiously, and Reformed synods even took up once again the issue of whether private baptisms at home might be permissible. As can be seen, the median delay between birth and baptism in Anduze fell to 7 days in 1682–83, where it had attained 29 days in 1656–60. Where more than 20 per cent of all that community's families had waited over two months before having their newborns baptized in this earlier period, less than 1 per cent now did so. Similarly, the percentage of Protestant newborns baptized within a week now rose from 16 to 56 per cent in nearby Saint-Jean-du-Gard, and from 61 to 90 per cent in La Rochelle.

---

40 For Marennes, median delay 9 days 1668 (n = 120; A.C. Marennes, état civil, St Pierre-de-Salles); Nérac median delay 5 days 1671–72 (n = 89; L.D.S. film 730822); Montpellier median delay 7.5 days 1664 (n = 376; A.C. Montpellier, GG 16); Lodève median delay 7 days 1670 (n = 141; Mireille Laget, 'La naissance aux siècles classiques. Pratique des accouchements et attitudes collectives en France au XVIIe et XVIIIe siècles', *Annales: E.S.C.* 32 [1977], 965); Carcassonne median delay 2 days 1684 (n = 131; L.D.S. film 1217814); Narbonne median delay 2 days 1661–66 (n = 106; L.D.S. film 1175673). In Agen, the median delay was 4 days in 1670–72 in the parish of St Caprasy (n = 104; L.D.S. film 786940).

41 Katherine L.M. Faust, 'A Beleaguered Society: Protestant Families in La Rochelle, 1628–1685 (Ph.D. diss., Northwestern University, 1980), pp. 40–51. This valuable dissertation contains a great deal of demographic information.

One might wonder if the fluctuations just revealed concerned exclusively those newborns who appeared healthy and consequently able to survive a wait of several days or weeks before baptism. Perhaps sickly babies were always rushed off to the sacrament at the first available opportunity, even while the ceremony was delayed for more robust ones. Alençon's excellent burial registers show that this may have been the case early in the seventeenth century, but that by the middle of the century it was not so. (See Table 2.3.) Increasingly, the town's Huguenots were willing to see offspring of theirs die without baptism. One result of this, of course, would have been that a small but growing fraction of births would go unrecorded in Protestant registers of baptism. The increase in this percentage observable in Table 2.3 corresponds with what could be deduced from theoretical calculations from the era's demographic rates. Given the high rates of infant mortality prevailing at the time and the particular vulnerability of newborn babies to disease, each additional week of delay between birth and baptism should have added from 1 to 3 per cent to the ranks of those newborns who would be expected to die before baptism.[42] The gradual internalization of a Protestant understanding of baptism revealed by the evidence of birth–baptism delays was thus a development that could have accounted for a decline of one or more percentage points in the number of baptisms recorded in the Reformed church's records between 1600 and 1670, even in the absence of any other changes in the size of the community.

Table 2.3   Recorded cases of burial of unbaptized infants in Alençon, 1626–85

Years	Cases	Cases as percentage of total baptisms
1626–46	3	0.2%
1647–67	13	1.2%
1668–85	5	0.8%

While the tendency to postpone baptism for longer periods of time was an exclusively Protestant phenomenon, broader changes in marriage behaviour that were occurring throughout France in this era would also have reduced with time the ratio of baptisms to total population. Numerous demographic studies have shown a tendency for young people in most, although not all, regions of France to postpone marriage until a slightly

---

42 Calculated on the basis of the mortality rates presented in Lachiver, *La population de Meulan*, p. 197.

later age over the course of the century.[43] Since calculating age at first marriage accurately requires a lengthy process of record linkage, I have explored this question for just one Protestant community, Alençon. (See Table 2.4.) In this city, the increase which occurred was so modest among women that one hesitates to place too much weight on the finding. Nevertheless, the tendency for the age of first marriage to increase among women appears to have been general enough in France in this era for one to suspect that a similar evolution occurred in many Protestant communities in this period, especially when it is recalled that the Huguenots faced increasing difficulties in establishing themselves in many crafts as the century progressed.

Table 2.4   Mean age at first marriage among Alençon's Protestants

	1645–67		1668–85	
	Men	Women	Men	Women
	27.5	25.7	28.8	26.1
Cases	(85)	(125)	(48)	(53)

At the same time, in what was almost certainly a related development, there is evidence that the percentage of women who never married also increased in this period, at least in the towns. Katherine Faust has documented such a trend among the Protestants of La Rochelle, where the percentage of never-married women among those dying at age 40 or above increased from 1.3 per cent in 1636–60 to 6.9 per cent between 1661 and 1683.[44] A similar trend emerges in predominantly Catholic Rouen, and an increase in the number of unmarried female heads of household can be detected in Dijon's tax rolls.[45] Both of these developments, of course, would have had the effect of depressing gross fertility rates.

For three reasons, then, the movement of baptisms over time exaggerates slightly the fall which occurred in France's Huguenot population between 1600 and 1685. The evidence is not extensive enough to permit the calculation of a precise correction factor to compensate for the distortions introduced by such trends.

---

43 The best summary of the evidence is to be found in Jean-Louis Flandrin, *Familles: Parenté, maison, sexualité dans l'ancienne société* (Paris, 1976), p. 183. Cf. Alain Croix, *La Bretagne aux 16e et 17e siècles: La vie, la mort, la foi* (Paris, 1981), p. 194, for a region unaffected by this trend.

44 Faust, 'Beleaguered Society', p. 229.

45 Bardet, *Rouen*, I, 322; James R. Farr, 'Consumers, commerce, and the craftsmen of Dijon: The changing social and economic structure of a provincial capital, 1450–1750', in Philip Benedict, ed., *Cities and Social Change in Early Modern France* (London, 1989), p. 158. Bardet does not analyse the rates of permanent celibacy by confession.

The pattern of decline

Having explored the nature and limitations of the available evidence, it is now time to see what it suggests about the fate of the individual congregations comprising the sample and the movement of France's Huguenot population as a whole between the Edict of Nantes and its Revocation. As already explained, the congregations in the sample have been divided into categories according to their geographic location and the size of the localities from which they drew their members. To make comparisons possible between a large number of churches for which the data often cover quite different years within the period 1600–85, the dates from 1660 to 1670 have been taken as the standard point of reference for all churches. These years are those for which data exist for the largest number of churches. Their use also facilitates comparisons with the overall figures on the Protestant population derived from Mours.

For each church, a base index was computed using the average number of annual baptisms celebrated in those years between 1660 and 1670 for which evidence was available. Where no figures were available for these years but data survive from the decades both preceding and following them, a straight-line method of extrapolation was used to calculate the base index. Where figures were available only for years either preceding or following 1660–70, these figures were extrapolated forward or backward to the base period on the assumption that the church evolved along the same lines as the constellation of nearby congregations closest to it in character and location. In the case of those churches whose evolution is known from censuses rather than the movement of baptisms, the population estimates have been transformed into an approximate level of baptisms using the standard assumptions of 4.5 people per household and a birth rate of 40 per thousand. For each congregation, the base index was then compared against the average number of baptisms per year in the earliest period of the century for which reliable figures have survived in order to measure the community's evolution over the course of the years before 1660–70, and all of the cases within each category have been aggregated to calculate the overall movement of the churches within the category. Similarly, any surviving figures from the 1670s and 1680s have been compared with the base index to calculate the evolution over the last fifteen years of the period of legal toleration. To obtain a rough indication of shorter-term trends within each category before 1660–70, decade-to-decade comparisons have also been made, using figures from all those congregations for which data are available for at least three years of each decade being compared and extrapolating figures for the remaining congregations for which the evidence suffers from larger gaps according to the most probable assumptions about each church's evolution in light of what is known about its history.

Analysed in this fashion, the data reveal significant variations, not only between the churches of northern France and those located in the Midi and Centre–West, but also among those situated within each half of the kingdom. In view of the complexity of the pattern, the evidence will be examined here initially by category and region, before the results obtained are combined to estimate the overall evolution of the Huguenot population.

Northern France   Throughout northern France, the Huguenots generally comprised a small and powerless minority. To be sure, the congregations of certain major provincial cities, notably Metz, Caen and Dieppe, still counted their members in the thousands and comprised a significant fraction of the total city population; a few smaller towns in western France or along the Loire (e.g., Saumur, Loudun, Jargeau) were Huguenot *places de sûreté*; and scattered concentrations of rural Protestants could be found in regions such as Normandy's Pays de Caux, parts of the Blésois, or the formerly Genevan Pays de Gex. For the most part, however, the urban congregations had seen their numbers greatly reduced by persecution and violence from the levels attained during the first flush of Protestant expansion in the 1560s – such proud centres of Huguenot strength during the First Civil War as Lyon and Orléans now housed a thousand Protestants or fewer – while few rural or small town congregations had ever extended their membership much beyond the local nobility or a smattering of small-town craftsmen and professionals. Acutely aware of past atrocities and the present insecurity of their position, the Huguenots of these regions kept a prudent distance from the agitation of their southern co-religionists in the 1620s, seeking above all to live in peace with their Catholic neighbours. Even so, many congregations were shaken by periodic fears of renewed violence against their members, and when civil war broke out again in the south in 1621–22, many Norman ministers thought it prudent to flee to England.[46]

Within such a context, the fate of the churches in this region was to experience a long, gradual decline that accelerated as the Revocation drew nearer. This decline was slightly more marked in the churches located in towns of more than 5000 inhabitants than in those located in smaller towns or rural areas, especially when the movement of the number of

[46] B.P.F., MS 209, provides a particularly vivid echo of the attentiveness of one Protestant minister to the local circulation of news and rumour of all sorts and to the recurring fear of developments which might provoke 'remuments'. Excerpts from this document have been published by A. Galland, 'Un coin de province (Falaise et ses environs) à l'époque de l'Edit de Nantes', *B.S.H.P.F.* 48 (1899), 12–29. On the flight of Protestants to England in 1621–22, see F. de Schickler, *Les Eglises du Réfuge en Angleterre* (3 vols, Paris, 1892), I, 390–91.

Protestants is compared with the broader demographic evolution of the communities in question.

Table 2.5 presents the data about each church in a manner designed to reveal the long-term trend as clearly as possible, while Figure 2.1 combines the data about all of the localities in this category into a weighted index of the decade-by-decade movement of the population. In this, as in all the other categories of churches, the evolution was by no means uniform. As can be seen, the number of Protestants living in one city, Saint-Quentin, increased quite substantially over the course of the century. This was truly a special case, in that Protestantism took only feeble root here during the late 1550s and early 1560s (the great age of the faith's expansion elsewhere in France), no church was 'planted' in the vicinity until 1570, and the foundations for a significant Huguenot community only came with the arrival of a growing stream of textile workers and manufacturers in the seventeenth century from just across the border in the Spanish

Table 2.5   Secular trends: the cities of northern France

	Earliest period for which data available (with dates in question)	1660–70	1670–79	1680–85
Alençon	65 (1616–29)	52	37	31
Amiens	56 (1605–10)	[35]	26	16
Angers	16 (1600–09)	18	15	14
Blois	37 (1600–09)	28	20	16
Caen	229 (1600–11)	119	–	–
Châlons-s/Marne	33 (1600–09)	34	–	28
Châteaudun	24 (1600–09)	12	10	8
Issoudun	17 (1609–14)	18	19	11
Laval	4 (1601–09)	2	1	1
Le Havre	53 (1600–09)	35	36	33
Loudun	110 (1600–08)	63	52	33
Lyon	41 (1601–11)	49	53	50
Metz	299 (1600–09)	187	220	205
Rouen	175 (1600–03)	198	174	153
Saumur	39 (1600–09)	33	28	22
Saint-Lô	64 (1600–09)	42	36	33
Saint-Quentin	233 people (1599)	130 families		'nearly 120' families
Tours	55 (1632—39)	40	43	33
Vitré	23 (1600—09)	19	14	13

All figures represent the average number of baptisms per year in the period in question unless otherwise indicated. Figures in brackets represent extrapolations.

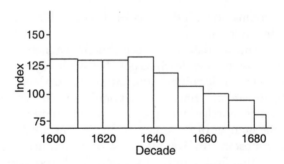

2.1   Cumulative index: northern big cities (1660–69 = 100)

Netherlands.[47] A significant number of other churches also saw their ranks increase or remain stable, at least until the 1630s or 1640s, when a downward trend set in in many of them that appears to coincide with a general *renversement* of the demographic *conjoncture* in these towns. In Lyon, Rouen, Issoudun, Châlons-sur-Marne and Angers, the congregation was in the 1660s as large as, or larger than, it had been at the earliest period in the century for which information is available. In the majority of churches, however, the level of baptisms had declined by this time to a point below its initial level. This fall was particularly marked in Caen, Metz, Loudun and a few of the smallest churches, such as Laval or Châteaudun, all of which witnessed the level of baptisms celebrated within them sink by 38 to 50 per cent between the early years of the century and 1660–70. Overall, the size of these churches fell by 25 per cent between the earliest years of the century for which figures are available in each case and the period 1660–70 (an average span of 57 years). If it is assumed that the 19 cases in the sample represent a random sample of the total universe of churches located in larger northern cities, the standard error for this figure is ± 5 per cent. The decline was concentrated in the last four and a half decades before 1685 and assumed particularly accentuated dimensions in the years just before the Revocation. Between the 1660s and early 1680s, baptismal levels fell a further 19 per cent from their 1660–70 plateau.

Protestantism's numerical decline within this category of localities is even more marked when the ranks of the Reformed are compared to the total population of the cities in question. Table 2.6 sets forth the evidence for those towns in the sample whose general demographic evolution is known. As can be seen, most grew in size, a trend in keeping with the findings of recent studies that reveal that France's cities as a whole grew

---

47 Alfred Daullé, *La Réforme à Saint-Quentin et aux environs du XVIe à la fin du XVIIIe siècle* (Le Cateau, 1905), *passim*.

Table 2.6   Importance of the Huguenot minority within sample cities of known total population: northern France

Alençon		1625–34		1650–59	1675–84
estimated population		9900		11250	12700
per cent Huguenot		15.5		12.2	6.5
Angers	1600–11			1652–63	
estimated population	24 800			31 800	
per cent Huguenot	1.6			1.1	
Blois	1600–09	1620–29	1640–49	1660–69	1680–84
estimated population	16 300	16 200	18 600	16 200	14 800
per cent Huguenot	5.7	5.9	4.7	4.3	2.6
Châteaudun	1600–04			1666–70	
estimated population	7500–8500			7500	
per cent Huguenot	7.5			5.6	
Le Havre				1665	
estimated population				6–7000	
per cent Huguenot				13.5	
Loudun	1603–08		1645–55	1660–69	
estimated population	6500		10 000	8750	
per cent Huguenot	41		21	18	
Lyon		1636		1650–60	1679–88
estimated population		42–49 000		67 500	97 750
per cent Huguenot		2.9		1.8	1.2
Metz		1635			1684
estimated population		19 092			20 710
per cent Huguenot		33			21
Rouen	1600–09	1620–29	1640–49	1660–69	1680–84
estimated population	60 233	73 096	88 953	82 642	69 518
per cent Huguenot	6.2	6.9	6.6	5.8	5.3
Saumur		1611–24			1690–1701
estimated population		9625			10 075
per cent Huguenot		14			
Tours					1675–80
estimated population					46 000
per cent Huguenot					2.2
Vitré	1600–09	1620–29	1640–49	1660–68	
estimated population	8000	8000	9500	9000	
per cent Huguenot	7.2	7.8	6.2	5.3	

Sources for population estimates: Alençon: B.P.F, fonds Robert; A.C. Alençon, 11 E 1–2, 12 E 1–8, 21, 26–39; Angers: François Lebrun, *Les hommes et la mort en Anjou aux XVIIe et XVIIIe siècles: Essai de démographie et de psychologie historiques* (Paris, 1971), p. 162; Blois: baptismal figures kindly furnished by Jean-Noël Biraben; Châteaudun: Marcel Couturier, *Recherches sur les structures sociales de Châteaudun, 1525–1789* (Paris, 1969), pp. 89, 104–5; Le Havre: André Corvisier et al., *Histoire du Havre* (Toulouse, 1983), p. 80; Loudun: A.C. Loudun, GG 184, 187–8, 245; Lyon: Olivier Zeller, *Les recensements lyonnais de 1597 et 1636: démographie historique et géographie sociale* (Lyon, 1983), pp. 331–7; Maurice Garden, *Lyon et les lyonnais au XVIIIe siècle* (Paris, 1970), pp. 31–2; Metz: Jean Rigault, 'La population de Metz au XVIIe siècle: quelques problèmes de démographie', *Annales de l'Est*, 5th ser. 11 (1951), 309; Rouen: Jean-Pierre Bardet, *Rouen aux XVIIe et XVIIIe siècles. Les mutations d'un espace social* (Paris, 1983), II, 34; Saumur: Lebrun, *Les hommes et la mort en Anjou*, p. 159; Tours: Alexandre Giraudet, *Recherches historiques et statistiques sur l'hygiène de la ville de Tours et sur la mouvement de sa population depuis 1632 jusqu'à l'époque actuelle* (Tours, 1853), p. 81; Vitré: Alain Croix, 'La mort quotidienne en Bretagne (1450–1670)', unpublished thèse de doctorat d'état, typed copy conserved at A.D. Ille-et-Vilaine, vol. 5. All estimates of total population derived from baptismal levels have been calculated using a multiplier of 25. Where possible, the percentage of Huguenots has been calculated on the basis of a comparison of the number of Catholic and Protestant baptisms celebrated within the city.

more rapidly than its total population in this era.[48] This increase in the overall population of these cities meant that the Protestants' place as a percentage of the total population declined even more significantly than the absolute number of Huguenots living within them. This table also calls attention to what appears to be a consistent and significant pattern within this category of churches: the larger the percentage of Protestants living within a given city at the beginning of the seventeenth century, the greater the decline in the absolute number of Protestants over the course of the century. As a result of this pattern, the Huguenot minorities of Metz, Loudun or Alençon bulked far smaller within the walls of those towns in the age of Colbert than they had in the time of Sully.

The twelve small-town congregations of northern France experienced slightly less of an aggregate decline in their numbers between the earliest years of the century and 1660–70: 20 per cent, over an average span of just 45 years.[49] The decline was particularly accentuated in the congregations located in western France – Fécamp, Laigle, Bellême and Chateau-du-Loir – and in the erstwhile Loire valley citadel of Sancerre. By contrast, the other small-town churches of the upper Loire valley lost no more than 10 per cent of their numbers over the years before 1660–70, and the same rough stability prevailed within the small churches of Compiègne and Paray-le-Monial. (See Table 2.7.) The cumulative decade-by-decade trend shows that the overall level of baptisms within this category of churches headed gradually and virtually uninterruptedly downward over the course of the century. (See Figure 2.2.) Once again, the decline accelerated in the period just before the Revocation, and baptismal levels in the 1680s were 83 per cent of what they had been in 1660–70. Unfortunately, total population figures are not available for any of these communities, thus ruling out comparison between the general evolution of these communities and the fate of their Huguenot minority.

The nineteen congregations of northern France which have been labelled here as 'rural' (many were located in cities or market towns of fewer than 2000 inhabitants and included among their members a large percentage of artisans or bourgeois) experienced an aggregate decline over the years before 1660–70 that differs little from the preceding two categories – minus 22 per cent for an average period of 52 years.[50] Once again, significant

---

48 Dupâquier et al., *Histoire de la population française*, II, 87–8; Philip Benedict, 'French Cities from the Sixteenth Century to the Revolution: An Overview' in Benedict, ed., *Cities and Social Change*, p. 28.

49 Again assuming that these are a random sample of the total universe of churches located in communities of this size, this figure can be computed also to have a standard error of ±5 per cent.

50 Standard error of this figure as an estimate for the total category of churches: ±3.5 per cent.

Table 2.7   The small towns of northern France

	Earliest period for which data available (with dates in question)	1660–70	1670–79	1680–85
Aubusson	29 (1620–29)	28	26	30
Bellême	16 (1634–39)	7	6	4
Château-du-Loir	2 (1610–19)	1	1	–
Compiègne	9 (1632–39)	8	9	9
Fécamp	24 (1613–19)	15	–	–
Gien	50 (1600–09)	45	37	–
La Charité	2 (1637–42)	4	5	4
Laigle	5 (1602–09)	1	–	–
Mer	65 (1615–24)	61	60	46
Paray-le-Monial	9 (1602–09)	[11]	11	–
Sancerre	85 (1618–22)	56	45	47
Wassy	43 (1626–32)	33	30	29

All figures represent the average number of baptisms per year in the period in question unless otherwise indicated. Figures in brackets represent extrapolations.

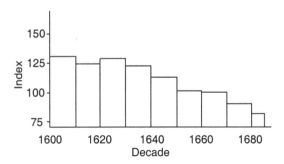

2.2   Cumulative index: northern small towns (1660–69 = 100)

variations emerge from case to case, as can be seen from Table 2.8. While the important churches of Luneray and Meaux-Nanteuil (composed predominantly of *vignerons* and other agricultural workers from the *plat pays* around Meaux and hence classified here as a rural church) and the small ones of Châtillon-sur-Loing and Dangeau grew ever so slightly in size, the number of Protestants fell by a third or more in the Bresse, the Pays Messin, and the little churches of Authon-du-Perche, Pontorson and La Celle-Saint-Cyr-Dollot. Map 2.2 brings to light a clear geographic pattern to the fate of these churches and their small-town cousins. Those located west of Paris, particularly in the region running from Normandy

Table 2.8   The rural congregations of northern France

	Earliest period for which data available (with dates in question)	1660–70	1670–79	1680–85
Authon-du-Perche	13 (1600–09)	8	10	6
Bailliage de Bresse	265 families (1621)	–	–	129 families
Chalandos	13 (1631–39)	12	16	9
Chaltrait	24 (1603–12)	19	19	14
Châtillon-s/Loing	16 (1608–19)	[18]	15	9
Châtillon-s/Loire	70 (1600–10)	64	61	47
Dangeau	8 (1622–29)	11	9	4
Fontaine-Prémont	26 (1618–22)	18	20	24
Is-sur-Tille	47 (1607–16)	39	35	38
La Celle-St-Cyr	8 (1614–21)	5	–	–
Landreville	37 (1620–22)	25	29	–
Lehaucourt	60 (1610–15)	41	35	28
Lintot	237 (1609–19)	177	173	150
Luneray	62 (1624–29)	64	66	–
Meaux-Nanteuil	87 (1600–09)	89	82	63
Metz 'villageois'	122 (1600–09)	70	77	81
Pontorson	10 (1600–09)	4	–	–
Preuilly-sur-Claise	13 (1600–09)	9	9	11
St-Pierre-sur-Dives	6 (1624–32)	5	4	–

All figures represent the average number of baptisms per year in the period in question unless otherwise indicated. Figures in brackets represent extrapolations.

south through the Perche and Maine to the Touraine, appear to have been far more likely to have experienced above average declines than those located in the east and southeast of the Paris Basin. As with the small-town churches, the erosion in the ranks of these congregations appears to have been gradual from the first decade of the century onward. (See Figure 2.3.) Still again, the haemorrhage intensified in the years just before the Revocation. Baptisms among this category of churches in the 1680s stood at 85 per cent of the level of 1660–70.

While the northern urban congregations in the sample drew their members predominantly from growing cities, some of the more important centres of rural Protestantism were located in demographically stagnating or declining regions. The Pays de Caux housed probably the largest concentration of rural Protestants north of the Loire, and two large rural churches represent it within the sample. This appears to have been a region of general population decline, for the level of baptisms in eleven Catholic parishes was 5 per cent lower in the 1660s than at the beginning of the

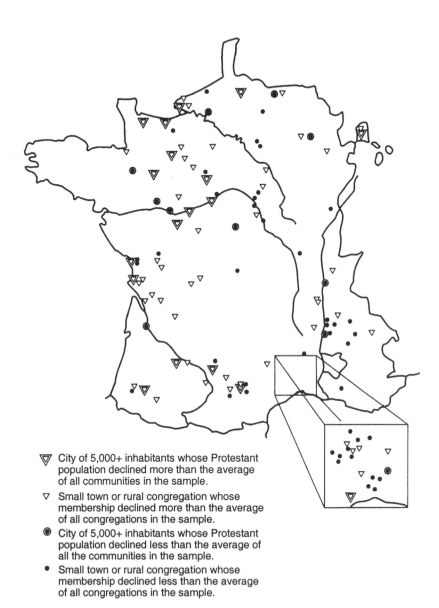

Map 2.2 The pattern of decline of the Protestant population

City of 5,000+ inhabitants whose Protestant population declined more than the average of all communities in the sample.

Small town or rural congregation whose membership declined more than the average of all congregations in the sample.

City of 5,000+ inhabitants whose Protestant population declined less than the average of all the communities in the sample.

Small town or rural congregation whose membership declined less than the average of all congregations in the sample.

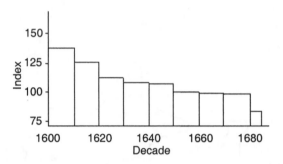

2.3   Cumulative index: northern rural congregation (1660–69 = 100)

century.[51] Similarly, the 'villageois' of the Pays Messin worshipping at Metz and the numerous inhabitants of the rural Vermandois who shared the temple of Lehaucourt with the residents of Saint-Quentin both lived very close to France's borders in regions which suffered considerable devastation during the Thirty Years' War, an event which depressed population levels more generally throughout eastern France.[52] In all four of these cases, which together account for roughly half of all rural baptisms in the sample, some, if not all, of the numerical decline must be attributed to the broader economic and demographic fate of the region, rather than to any decline particular to the Huguenot community. Pending the completion of Biraben's investigation of the movement of France's population as a whole before 1670, it is harder to compare the other rural churches in the sample with the broader demographic evolution of the regions in which they were located, but the work to date about the broad region around Paris suggests only moderate growth during this era.[53] In short, unlike the urban churches,

---

51 Jacques Bottin, *Seigneurs et paysans dans l'ouest du pays de Caux (1540–1650)* (Paris, 1983), Appendix A, 1–10; Jean-Noël Biraben, 'Population et économie en pays de Caux aux XVIe et XVIIe siècles', *Population* 61 (1986), 937–60. Here once again, Dr Biraben was kind enough to furnish me with his raw figures, which supplement those published by Bottin.

52 Charles Abel and F. de Bouteiller, eds, *Journal de Jean Bauchez greffier de Plappeville au dix-septième siècle* (Metz, 1868); Stephane Gaber, *La Lorraine meurtrie* (Nancy, 1979); Marie-José Laperche-Fournel, *La Population du Duché de Lorraine de 1580 à 1720* (Nancy, 1985), p. 106; Dupâquier, *Population rurale du Bassin Parisien*, p. 191; Jean-Noël Biraben and Alain Blum, 'Population Trends in France, 1500 to 1800. Comparison with Other Western and Eastern Countries', unpublished paper, 46th session of the International Statistical Institute, 1987, p. 8.

53 Dupâquier, *Population rurale du Bassin Parisien*, pp. 190–92; Pierre Goubert, *Beauvais et le Beauvaisis de 1600 à 1730: Contribution à l'histoire sociale de la France au XVIIe siècle* (2 vols, Paris, 1960), I, 612–16, II, 50–53; Jean Jacquart, *La crise rurale en Ile-de-France, 1550–1670* (Paris, 1974), pp. 597–609, 680–85; Jean-Marc Moriceau, 'Mariages et foyers paysans aux XVIe et XVIIe siècles: L'exemple des campagnes du sud de Paris', *R.H.M.C.* 28 (1981), 483; Biraben and Blum, 'Population Trends in France, 1500 to 1800', pp. 7–8.

many of the largest rural churches were located in regions whose general demographic vigour was limited.

The patterns revealed in this survey of all three categories of northern churches help to illuminate the causes of these churches' decline. One cause has already been mentioned: the general demographic stagnation or decline of certain regions of important rural Protestant strength. Beyond this, at least four other factors contributed to the erosion of Huguenot numbers.

Emigration abroad was unquestionably the least important of these factors until the years just before the Revocation. While a trickle of emigration may be detected in the direction of such neighbouring Protestant regions as England, Switzerland and the Low Countries over the first six decades of the century, perhaps widening into a thin flow after Louis XIV assumed personal rule in 1661 and began what Lavisse has so aptly labelled his policy of 'persecution sournoise' (it was precisely in 1661 that the French church of Berlin was founded), evidence from the French church of London, long one of the greatest centres of refuge for France's Protestants and hence perhaps the best barometer of long-term trends in emigration, suggests that the outflow was only large enough to maintain the church at a steady size until 1681. Only after that date, when the first *dragonnades* in Poitou provoked a sharp upsurge in emigrants fleeing France, did the number of new members admitted to the church begin to increase. Protestants were also well represented among the merchants and indentured servants who settled the French Antilles in this era, and again the number of Huguenot migrants appears to have increased after 1681. None the less, the total outflow of migrants to both Europe and the Caribbean cannot have amounted to more than a few hundred people per year before the 1680s, a tiny fraction of the total Huguenot population. The majority of the refugees who made the Huguenot exodus from France the largest intra-European mass migration of the era did not leave the country until after the Edict of Nantes was revoked.[54]

---

[54] De Schickler, *Les Eglises du Réfuge en Angleterre*, I, 376, 390–401: II, 8–9, 311; Robin D. Gwynn, 'The Arrival of Huguenot Refugees in England, 1680–1705', *Proceedings of the Huguenot Society of London* 21 (1969), 366–73; Gwynn, *Huguenot Heritage: The History and Contribution of the Huguenots in Britain* (London, 1985), p. 35; Gabriel Debien, 'La société coloniale aux XVIIe et XVIIIe siècles. Les engagés pour les Antilles (1634–1715)', *Revue d'Histoire des Colonies* 37 (1951), 187–90; Jean Orcibal, *Etat présent des recherches sur la répartitition géographique des 'Nouveaux Catholiques' à la fin du XVIIe siècle* (Paris, 1948), pp. 3–4n; Faust, 'Beleaguered Society', p. 361; Janine Garrisson, *L'édit de Nantes et sa Révocation: Histoire d'une intolerance* (Paris, 1985), p. 172; Robert Richard and Denis Vatinel, 'Le consistoire de l'Eglise réformée du Havre au XVIIe siècle: Les pasteurs', *B.S.H.P.F.* 127 (1981), 7–8; Rémy Scheurer, 'Passage accueil et intégration des réfugiés huguenots en Suisse' in M. Magdelaine and R. von Thadden, eds, *Le Réfuge huguenot* (Paris, 1985), pp. 48–9; Jean-Pierre Poussou, 'Mobilité et migrations', in Dupâquier et al., *Histoire de la*

Of equally modest importance in this part of France was the direct impact of political and military events. Two communities in the sample did experience a significant reduction in size as a result of changes in the structure of local authority. A sharp drop visible in the number of baptisms in Sancerre after 1639 stemmed from the acquisition of the county of Sancerre by Henri II de Bourbon, prince of Condé. Although the son and grandson of great Huguenot champions, Condé had been raised a Catholic at the court of Henry IV and was an energetic crusader against any Protestants unfortunate enough to live in territories under his jurisdiction. Following his acquisition of Sancerre, he ordered the local temple closed and sought to have the lion's share of the local tax burden shifted on to the shoulders of the town's Huguenots. The church was only reopened in 1652 in recompense for the loyalty which Sancerre's Protestants demonstrated to the crown during the Fronde, and the number of baptisms celebrated in the subsequent years was less than two-thirds of what it had been before 1640.[55] Similarly, Pontorson, on the border of Normandy and Brittany was a Huguenot *place de sûreté* until 1621, when it was bartered to the king by its commander Gabriel de Montgommery for 100 000 *écus* and a new command. Its temple was closed for a period, and when it reopened five years later in nearby Cormeray, the departure of the duke and his retinue had reduced its ranks to less than half its former size.[56] These, however, represent just two cases out of 50. The distance which the northern Protestants kept from the agitation of their southern co-religionists in the 1620s meant that the overwhelming majority of churches did not suffer the direct impact of these civil wars in the dramatic ways which many more of their southern counterparts did.

---

population française II, 125–30. Not surprisingly, relatively few of those involved in the most importart current of French emigration abroad before 1685, that of labourers and artisans from south-western France in the direction of Catalonia, appear to have come from predominantly Protestant parts of this region. J. Nadal and F. Giralt, *La population catalane de 1553 à 1717: L'immigration française et les autres facteurs de son développement* (Paris, 1960), part 2.

55 Gueneau, 'Protestants du Centre', pp. 415–16. The baptisms attributed to Sancerre between 1641 and 1651 involved inhabitants of the town but were performed at other nearby churches.

56 A. Galland, 'L'ancienne Eglise réformée de Pontorson-Cormeray d'après un registre d'état civil inédit', *B.S.H.P.F.* 58 (1909), 448–63. Saumur's church experienced the consequences of political events in a more attenuated fashion. A Huguenot *place de sûreté* until 1621, it was shaken in that year by battles between soldiers and its large student population and then saw the disgrace of its Protestant governor, the great Duplessis-Mornay, who was replaced by a Catholic. Its baptismal curve reveals a marked trough during the subsequent years. Louis André, *Les sources de l'histoire de France. XVIIe siècle (1610–1715)* (8 vols, Paris, 1913–35), V, 84.

Considerably more important for Protestantism's numerical fate in northern France appears to have been that basic fact of urban life and death in the era, the inability of cities to reproduce themselves naturally. As we have already seen, a far higher percentage of northern France's Protestants lived in cities than did the French population as a whole. This meant that the community was particularly vulnerable to the substantial excess of deaths over births that characterized Europe's larger cities.[57] That this was an important factor in shaping Protestantism's numerical evolution is clearly suggested by the fact that the number of Huguenots declined most sharply and most consistently in those cities within which the Protestants formed a large percentage of the population at the beginning of the century and where the normal flow of migration would not have been expected to bring as many Huguenots into the city as lived there already. Conversely, many of the cities whose Reformed churches managed to maintain their size were ones where the Protestants formed a relatively small percentage of the total population, smaller than that found in the broader regions which fed these cities with immigrants.

The conversion of a certain number of Huguenots to Catholicism formed the fourth cause of the faith's decline. Assessing the importance of conversions in accounting for the thinning Protestant ranks raises an issue with particularly broad implications for the history of the 'petit troupeau' in this period, since perhaps the fundamental force shaping its experience was the mounting pressure to convert. From the public disputations of the first part of the century, to the concerted campaign of private proselytization launched around mid-century by the Congregations for the Propagation of the Faith, to the discriminatory measures restricting Huguenot access to many professions enacted during Louis XIV's personal rule, and finally to the pious bribery of the *caisses de conversion* and straightforward terror tactics of the royal dragoons, France's Catholics waged an escalating campaign to save the Huguenots from the errors of their ways. Faced with this pressure, the Protestant pastorate sought to create a strong sense of attachment to the Reformed cause through preaching and catechetical education that justified Reformed doctrine and

---

[57] The late Allan Sharlin recently questioned the existence of this so-called 'urban graveyard effect': 'Natural Decrease in Early Modern Cities: A Reconsideration', *Past and Present* 78 (1978), 126–38. A spate of rebuttals has convincingly vindicated the traditional wisdom on the basis of family reconstitution evidence. See especially Jean-Pierre Bardet, 'Problèmes d'un bilan urbain: comment l'établir en l'absence de recensement. L'exemple de Rouen au XVIIIe siècle', *Bulletin de la Société d'Histoire Moderne* (1981), 3, 21–9; and Alfred Perrenoud, 'Croissance ou déclin? Les mécanismes du non-renouvellement des populations urbaines', *Histoire, Economie, Société* 1 (1982), 581–601. Bardet calculates that Rouen's eighteenth-century population of 70 000 would have declined to 45 000 in 50 years and 28 000 in a century in the absence of any migration either into or out of the city.

pointed out the errors of papistry. As recent commentators have realized, the extent to which the Protestants resisted the blandishments of the *convertisseurs* is one measure of the vitality of the faith. The amount of movement back and forth between the two religions also sheds light on the rigidity of confessional boundaries and the extent to which the two denominations had become closed, self-recruiting communities by this period.

Direct evidence about the frequency of conversions is often scattered and uneven, but it can be obtained from a variety of sources, most especially lists of abjurations or of new church members. These sorts of records tend to indicate that where the Protestants formed a substantial, stable community, conversions were relatively rare. Where, on the contrary, they formed just a small minority, conversions were significantly more numerous. Thus, in Alençon, the records of the civil courts and the Maison des Nouveaux Catholiques reveal 92 abjurations between 1659 and early 1685.[58] Since, over this same period, the Protestant baptismal registers indicate that the local Huguenot community declined by 500 people or more, and since the majority of the Protestant conversions occurred in the years 1680–84 and involved primarily teenagers, such cases would have accounted for just a small fraction of the decline in the number of baptisms celebrated within this community. In Caen, with its still more important Protestant minority, we also find relatively few conversions. Lists of abjurations from two parish churches reveal 47 between 1654 and 1663, some of them involving outsiders to the city, while the records of the Maison des Nouvelles Catholiques indicate a further 24 between 1658 and 1661; against these must be set 48 known conversions from Catholicism to Protestantism between 1669 and 1680.[59] But in Lyon, where the Huguenots formed a far smaller percentage of the total urban population, and where far more of them were recent immigrants to the city, 568 Protestants are known to have converted between 1659 and the summer of 1685 – this out of a total Reformed population roughly comparable in size to Alençon's and far smaller than Caen's.[60] Robert Sauzet's outstanding study of Catholic proselytization efforts in the diocese of Nîmes similarly reveals that the smaller the percentage of Huguenots in any given community, the higher the rate of conversion, although in this region where the Protestants were in the majority, more Catholics may

---

58 B.P.F., fonds Robert, 'Abjurations'.

59 Galland, *Essai sur l'histoire du Protestantisme à Caen*, pp. 166, 190. Here too a significant increase in the number of conversions is visible after 1680. After averaging eight new entrants per year from 1658 through 1673, the Maison des Nouvelles Catholiques received 24 converts in 1682 and 25 in 1683. Records of two parishes reveal another 50 conversions between 1680 and 1682. Ibid., pp. 190–91.

60 Odile Martin, *La conversion protestante à Lyon (1659–1687)* (Geneva, 1986), pp. 62, 157.

actually have embraced Protestantism than the other way round.[61] Thus, while most of the studies done to date of Catholic efforts to convert the Protestants have shown that the Huguenots were highly resistant to Catholic missionary efforts, these studies have examined primarily regions of considerable Protestant strength, i.e., precisely those regions where the harvest of conversions appears to have been smallest. It seems that conversion was more significant where the Protestants were numerically weak and socially isolated, and that in some regions it did cut into Protestant strength more significantly.

It has not been possible to seek evidence about the number of conversions in every region examined here, nor is it clear that abjuration lists or other surviving church documents are abundant enough to provide more than a very partial tally of all the passages from one religion to another in this period. This is one of the questions that will not be fully understood until painstaking local studies have been executed, tracing large numbers of families and their religious affiliation over several generations. But in light of the evidence just reviewed, it does not seem unreasonable to treat conversion as a residual variable within the context of this study. That is to say, where a decline in Protestant strength cannot be explained by other, more easily discernible factors such as demographic trends in the region as a whole or the direct impact of military or political events, conversion may be accounted a significant cause of decline. If such a procedure is justified, then the rural and small-town congregations of western France emerge as a region where conversion appears to have been particularly important in reducing Huguenot numbers. This impression gains added plausibility when it is remarked that the regions from Lower Normandy through Maine and the Perche into Touraine where we have seen that above-average decline was the norm were also regions where Protestantism was primarily the faith of small, scattered groups, primarily drawn from the ranks of the local seigneurs or educated townsmen.[62] Even if the lesser

---

[61] Robert Sauzet, *Contre-Réforme et Réforme Catholique en Bas-Languedoc: Le diocèse de Nîmes au XVIIe siècle* (Paris, 1979), pp. 166, 178–84, 256–8, 279–90, 360–66, esp. p. 286. Further evidence that conversions were proportionately more numerous where Protestantism was weaker may be found in Gregory Hanlon, *L'univers des gens de bien. Culture et comportements des élites urbaines en Agenais-Condomois au XVIIe siècle* (Bordeaux, 1989), pp. 239–41. In the diocese of La Rochelle, the percentage of Protestants won over to the Roman church annually between 1648 and 1679 was 0.2 per cent. Louis Perouas, *Le diocèse de la Rochelle de 1648 à 1724: Sociologie et pastorale* (Paris, 1964), p. 305. But this study says nothing about conversions in the opposite direction.

[62] Among the churches in western France, the parish registers of Authon-du-Perche, Crocy, Laigle, Bellême, Laval and Preuilly-sur-Claise all provide some indication of the occupational status of their members. Merchants predominate in the first and textile workers in the second, but men accorded the title of seigneur bulk the largest in all of the others. A.N., TT 230 (17) offers further evidence of the importance of aristocratic Protestantism in this region.

nobility did not desert the Protestant cause to the same degree that its greatest aristocratic champions did over the course of the century, regional studies have shown that this was also a group within which attachment to the Protestant cause weakened over time.[63] In the current state of our knowledge, it does not seem possible to weigh conversion's precise importance as a cause of Protestantism's numerical decline relative to the other causes also eroding the strength of the community in these years, but it does seem probable that it was a force of some significance.

Aside from these four forces which combined gradually to erode Protestantism's numerical strength, one possible additional cause must also be mentioned, although more research will be required before it can be confirmed that it was also of significance. Evidence from Alençon reveals that the Protestants married later than did their Catholic neighbours, perhaps because of the greater difficulties they faced in establishing themselves in an occupation. As Table 2.9 shows, the gap was one of greater than two years for both men and women in the years immediately before the Revocation – a period, admittedly, when the situation was particularly unfavourable for the Huguenots because of the numerous discriminatory measures limiting their access to certain trades. Breakdown of the figures according to status shows that these differences cannot be attributed to the élite character of Alençon's Protestant community, since a comparison confined to those couples in which the man was a merchant, lawyer, or member of another high-status group reveals a gap in the average age at first marriage which is even larger.[64] If further local studies

Table 2.9   Age at first marriage in Alençon

	Men	Women	'Notables' only	
	Men	Women	Men	Women
Protestants, 1668–85	28.8	26.5	28.7	25.5
Catholics, 1674–84	25.8	24.4	25.3	22.4

Sources: B.P.F., fonds Robert; A.C. Alençon, 12 E 21–8.

63 In the *élection* of Bayeux, 70 noble family heads (13 per cent of the regional total) were Protestant in 1597, 61 (10 per cent of the regional total) in 1661. Of the noble families of the Beauce won over to Protestantism in the sixteenth century, a quarter of the families that escaped extinction before 1685 converted to Catholicism before that date. James B. Wood, *The Nobility of the Election of Bayeux, 1463–1666: Continuity through Change* (Princeton, 1980), p. 161; Jean-Marie Constant, *Nobles et paysans en Beauce aux XVIème et XVIIème siècles* (Lille: Service de Reproduction des Thèses, 1981), p. 340.

64 The differences found between the two confessions are all statistically significant to at least a 0.02 level of confidence, according to the test for the difference of means.

confirm the existence of such a difference between the two confessions, then the depressing effect of the 'prudential check' on gross Protestant fertility will also have to be added to the list of causes of Protestantism's dwindling place within seventeenth-century France.

The Midi and Centre–West Within the great crescent of Huguenot strength which ran from Poitou to Dauphiné, the Protestants were in a very different situation from their co-religionists north and east of the Loire. In many areas, they formed the majority of the population or faced their Catholic neighbours on terms of equality. Before the 1620s, their control of many strongholds was confirmed through the secret articles of the Edict of Nantes. Here, what Elisabeth Labrousse has called 'des attitudes triomphalistes, assez "XVIe siècle"', reigned for much of the century. But the Protestants' militant response to threats, or perceived threats, to their position, combined with the crown's eagerness to reduce the military danger posed by a large number of fortified garrisons in the hands of an organized minority of uncertain loyalty, gave rise in the 1620s to a series of civil wars which saw the full force of the king's armies brought to bear against the leading Protestant citadels. Far more so than in the north, the numerical evolution of the Huguenot population of the Midi and Centre–West was shaped by the force of these events, especially in the cities.

Figure 2.4 and Table 2.10 set forth the fate of the sample's nine churches of the Midi and Centre–West located in cities of 5000 or more, a group of churches that includes many of the largest and most important congregations in the entire country. As can be seen from the individual graphs of four large churches for which the evidence is particularly complete, the events of the 1620s cut deep swaths through these congregations' ranks. La Rochelle, as might be expected, was especially hard hit. This capital of Huguenot resistance housed about 17000 Protestants in the 1610s, but the terrible siege of 1629 killed close to 10000 people, and, following the port's fall, Protestant immigrants were forbidden to settle in the city and take their place. Only 47 per cent as many baptisms were celebrated in La Rochelle's several Reformed temples in the 1630s as had been in the 1610s, and over the subsequent decades the size of the community continued to shrink. Montauban, whose Protestant community was the country's largest in the 1610s, experienced a somewhat less murderous siege in 1621, but here too the movement of baptisms reveals a deep trough at the time, followed by only partial recovery. Baptisms were just 70 per cent as numerous between 1623 and 1632 as in the 1610s, and again the church continued to shrink in size over the subsequent decades, with the plague of 1653–54 standing out as a second particularly important moment in its diminution. In Montpellier, both the siege of 1621 and the killing plague which swept through much

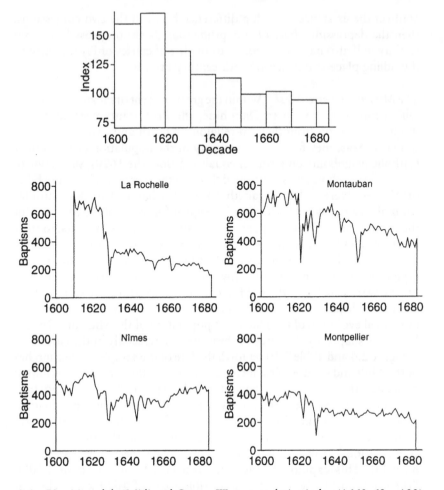

2.4   Big cities of the Midi and Centre–West, cumulative index (1660–69 = 100) and individual cities

of Languedoc in 1629 left deep cuts in the number of baptisms, reducing the total number of baptisms in the 1630s to 65 per cent of the level of the 1610s, while Nîmes, although never directly besieged for an extended period of time like the other three cities, also clearly felt the impact of the fighting in the region in the 1620s, even before being hit by the plague of 1629. Here baptismal levels in the 1630s were 67 per cent of what they had been in the 1610s, but the church's membership would begin to climb again from the 1660s onward, as the city began to experience the dramatic expansion which its enormously successful textile industries would bring it over the late seventeenth and eighteenth centuries.

Table 2.10   The cities of the Midi and Centre–West

	Earliest period for which data available (with dates in question)	1660–70	1670–79	1680–85
Bordeaux	300–400 families (1616)	[72]	75	–
Castres	213 (1620–21)	144	138	127
La Rochelle	671 (1610–19)	234	222	170
Marennes	346 (1636–39)	258	260	–
Montauban	673 (1600–09)	481	412	382
Montélimar	111 (1598–1601)	98	91	70
Montpellier	366 (1600–09)	261	260	222
Nérac	408 (1603–16)	170	161	–
Nîmes	447 (1600–09)	386	436	450

All figures represent the average number of baptisms per year in the period in question unless otherwise indicated. Figures in brackets represent extrapolations.

While the other churches in this category contain gaps in their records which prevent one from following the movement of their Protestant population as continuously as in these leading centres of the cause, several of them also clearly suffered from the events of the 1620s. Much of the dramatic long-term decline in the size of Nérac's church stemmed from this decade, when the city was besieged and subsequently punished for its role in the troubles by having its Chambre des Comptes and Chambre de l'Edit transferred elsewhere.[65] Castres was also besieged in 1621, and the surrounding region was racked by fighting for much of the subsequent decade.[66] Its surviving baptismal records unfortunately begin only in 1620, but the number of acts they record in 1620–21 would never be approached again, while the church's marriage records, which survive from 1609 onward, record just 56 per cent as many weddings between 1631 and 1640 as between 1610 and 1619.[67] Of the big-city churches in

---

[65] Marc Forissier, Nérac, ville royale et huguenote (Nérac, 1941).

[66] M. Estadieu, Notes chronologiques et statistiques pour servir à l'histoire de la ville de Castres (Castres, 1883); idem, Annales du Pays Castrais (Castres, 1893); Jules Cambon de Lavalette, La Chambre de l'Edit de Languedoc (Paris, 1872). This last court sat for most of its existence at Castres, but between 1623 and 1632 and again between 1671 and 1679 was transferred elsewhere.

[67] A.D. Tarn, F 5198bis–5122. The period 1631–40 has been chosen for this comparison in order to eliminate the exceptional number of marriages celebrated in 1630, in compensation for the numerous households broken or marriages delayed during the preceding years. In the years 1664–73, the level of marriages was still 41 per cent below the level of the 1610s. In that same period, the number of baptisms was 33 per cent below the level of the years 1620–21.

the sample, only three show no trace of having borne the brunt of the events of the 1620s: that of Bordeaux, a small church in an overwhelmingly Catholic city which actually expanded in size over the course of the period, thanks presumably to the play of migration patterns; that of Montélimar, which, like all of Dauphiné, escaped the fighting of the 1620s, and which lost only a tenth of its ranks over the course of the years to 1660–70; and that of Marennes, whose records only begin in 1635 and reveal a pattern of decline over the subsequent five decades. Not only did war and plague cut large swaths through many Huguenot congregations in the 1620s, there is also evidence of mass conversion in certain localities.[68]

Taken together, the big-city churches of the Midi and Centre–West experienced a greater aggregate decline in the number of baptisms before 1660–70 than any other category of churches analysed here: minus 36 per cent over an average period of 54 years.[69] As the decade-to-decade index shows, the pre-1670 decline was concentrated almost exclusively between the 1610s and 1630s. Indeed, the fall in the number of baptisms between these decades was equivalent to the total decrease between 1600–09 and 1660–70. In the decades after 1660–70, some further decline set in, but this decline was less marked than in the northern French churches of the same era. The level of baptisms in the 1680s was 90 per cent of the 1660–70 level.

Precisely because the fate of many of these cities was shaped in large measure by what happened to their Huguenot population, the overall population of these cities displayed less of an upward trend than other French cities of comparable size. (See Table 2.11.) La Rochelle, Montauban and Nîmes all needed time to recover from the traumas of the 1620s. The decline in the number of baptisms celebrated in Marennes's Reformed church turns out to have been part of a broader decline in that city's population between 1635 and 1685, one probably linked to the situation of the region's salt trade and the silting up of the nearby port of Brouage. Still, while less expansive than the northern French cities in the sample, these towns did see their aggregate population grow by 14 per cent between the earliest and latest dates for which information is available about each of them. The relative decline in the number of Protestants within these cities' walls was thus even greater than its absolute decline. The causes of this at once relative and absolute decline emerge clearly enough from its

---

68 Catholic documents boast of 300 conversions in and around Montauban, over 800 in Saint-Jean-d'Angély, and 750 in Saint-Antonin between 1622 and 1624. Louis Desgraves, 'Un aspect des controverses entre catholiques et protestants, les récits de conversions (1598–1628)', in *La conversion au XVIIe siècle* (n.p., 1983), pp. 98–101.

69 As a measure of the evolution of this category of churches as a whole, this figure has a standard error of ±1 per cent. If Alès, Anduze and Uzès are classified as well as cities of 5000+, the category's rate of decline falls to 34 ± 1 per cent.

Table 2.11   Importance of the Huguenot minority within sample cities
of known total population: Midi and Centre–West

Bordeaux		<u>1630</u>		<u>1675</u>
estimated population		42 000		49 000
per cent Huguenot		2		4
La Rochelle	<u>1610–19</u>	<u>1631–40</u>	<u>1655–64</u>	<u>1675–84</u>
estimated population	19 500	18 000	18 000	22 500
per cent Huguenot	86	45	35	21
Marennes		<u>1636–40</u>	<u>1660–68</u>	
estimated population		8800	6900	
per cent Huguenot		53	52	
Montauban	<u>1600–09</u>		<u>1650</u>	<u>1677</u>
estimated population	17,000 + small but unknown	18 500		16 700
	number Catholics			
per cent Huguenot	90–99?		70	58
Montpellier		<u>1610–19</u>	<u>1661–65</u>	
estimated population		16 300	21 400	
per cent Huguenot		60	30	
Nîmes	<u>1600–08</u>	<u>1631–40</u>	<u>1655–64</u>	<u>1675–84</u>
estimated population	13 700	12 300	14 000	18 000
per cent Huguenot	83	73	62	62

Note: Certain of the urban population estimates offered here must be taken as
highly approximate. Montauban's Catholic population in 1650 and 1677 is
estimated from baptismal levels concerning those years alone. The Protestant
baptisms in Marennes are divided between the city and the surrounding localities
on the assumption that their distribution in every period in question was the same
as in 1668, when evidence is available about the place of residence of those bringing
their children for baptism to the temple. Sources for population data concerning
the Catholic fraction of the population: Bordeaux: baptismal figures kindly
furnished by Jean-Noël Biraben; La Rochelle: figures estimated from the graph in
Louis Perouas, 'Sur la démographie rochelaise', *Annales: E.S.C.* (1961), 113;
Marennes: A.C. Marennes, état civil, paroisse St-Pierre-de-Salles; Montauban: A.D.
Tarn-et-Garonne, 1 GG 1, 2 GG 1; Montpellier: A.C. Montpellier, GG 5–7, 16;
Nîmes: baptismal figures kindly furnished by Jean-Noël Biraben. The figures may
include some inhabitants living outside the walls of these cities in their surrounding
terroir.

chronology and pattern. Having seen their ranks reduced sharply by the
events of the 1620s, most of these congregations were not able to replenish
their numbers even when their cities began to grow again, because
migratory patterns brought a higher percentage of Catholics into these
cities than had previously lived within them – or, in the case of La Rochelle,
because laws forbade Protestants to settle there. Given what is known

about the factors encouraging or discouraging large numbers of conversions, this was probably a very minor cause of decline within these bastions of Huguenot strength except during the 1620s.

The Reformed churches located in the smaller towns of the Huguenot crescent form an intermediary category between the big city and the rural churches. Since many were also located in Huguenot *places fortes* caught up in the fighting of the 1620s, they shared much of the fate of those churches located in bigger communities. The overall decline in size which they experienced was all the same less dramatic, and it was less thoroughly concentrated between the 1610s and 1630s. At the same time, their evolution displays regional variations similar to those that we shall discover among the rural congregations.

Figure 2.5 and Table 2.12 set out the information about the 17 churches in this size and geographic category. Privas experienced particular horrors during the civil wars. Following its capture by the royal troops in 1629, it was allowed to burn to the ground. Then, in 1664, fearing that the city was becoming repopulated by too many Protestants and might again become a thorn in its side, the crown banished all its inhabitants of the religion prétendue réformée (R.P.R.). Some dared to defy this ban, but the number of Protestant families enumerated by a census of the subsequent year none the less suggests that the total number of Huguenots in the city was less than half what it had been at the beginning of the century.[70] The ranks of Millau's Protestants also fell sharply and enduringly in 1629, and one suspects that these years were also a turning point for the church of Sommières, besieged repeatedly during the decade.[71] Many other churches in this category, however, either held their own (Lunel, Alès),

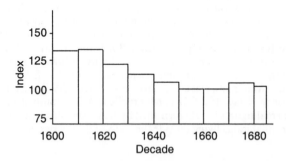

2.5   Cumulative index: small towns of the Midi (1660–69 = 100)

---

[70] Elie Reynier, *Histoire de Privas* (3 vols, Aubenas, 1941–46), I, 187; Alain Molinier, *Stagnations et croissance. Le Vivarais aux XVIIe–XVIIIe siècles* (Paris, 1985), pp. 247–50; A. Lloyd Moote, *Louis XIII, the Just* (Berkeley, 1989), p. 203.

[71] André, *Sources de l'histoire de France*, V, 95, 106, 136.

Table 2.12　The small towns of the Midi and Centre–West

	Earliest period for which data available (with dates in question)	1660–70	1670–79	1680–85
Alès	161 (1606–11)	160	178	–
Anduze	190 (1600–04)	136	133	141
Annonay	94 (1600–07)	48	52	–
Barbézieux	165 (1600–04)	92	72	–
Embrun	19 (1633–39)	14	17	13
Gap	29 (1625–33)	24	27	23
Lunel	53 (1626–29)	52	54	42
Millau	132 (1610–19)	93	87	83
Orthez	[160] (1600–09)	96	–	–
Pons	70 (1596–1600)	52	54	–
Privas	110 (1594–1613)	213 families	–	–
Puylaurens	65 (1632–41)	56	–	47
St-Hippolyte	99 (1600–09)	142	136	–
St-Jean-du-Gard	86 (1624–29)	96	104	95
Salies	111 (1600–07)	91	–	–
Sommières	110 (1626–28)	80	79	96
Uzès	226 (1617–21)	148	167	165

All figures represent the average number of baptisms per year in the period in question unless otherwise indicated. Figures in brackets represent extrapolations.

declined very gradually over the period (Salies, Embrun), or experienced a particularly sharp drop in the earliest years of the century (Annonay, Barbézieux). Some may have grown at the expense of others, for of the three churches located close to one another in the heart of the Protestant Cévennes – Anduze, Saint-Hippolyte and Saint-Jean-du-Gard – the last two increased significantly in size while the first shrank markedly.

Overall, these congregations experienced an aggregate decline of 25 per cent over an average period of 51 years before 1660–70.[72] The fall-off was 35 per cent in those eight churches that were located in *places de sûreté* or towns otherwise controlled militarily by the Protestants in the first decades of the century, versus 15 per cent in the nine communities which did not experience a loss of military privileges over the course of

---

[72] As a measure of the evolution of this category of churches as a whole, this figure has a standard error of ±3 per cent. The figures remain unchanged with Alès, Anduze and Uzès removed from this category of churches.

the century.[73] It was also substantially greater in the Vivarais (minus 58 per cent for 2 churches), Saintonge (minus 39 per cent for 2 churches) and Béarn (minus 31 per cent for 2 churches) than in Dauphiné (minus 21 per cent for 2 churches) and Bas-Languedoc-Cévennes (minus 12 per cent for 7 churches). The decade-to-decade index suggests that two-thirds of this decline was concentrated between the 1610s and 1630s, with the rest coming gradually over the following twenty years. Unlike the preceding categories examined, this group of churches increased in size ever so slightly in the last decades before the Revocation. The level of baptisms in the 1680s was 102 per cent of that of 1660–70. Evidence about the movement of the Catholic population between 1600 and 1685 is rarely available for these towns, but from such evidence as has come to light, it appears that their overall population tended slightly downward over these eight decades.[74]

The same sort of regional differences which can be seen among the small-town congregations emerge even more clearly within the rural churches of the Huguenot crescent. One region, Dauphiné, witnessed an actual increase in the number of baptisms recorded in its rural churches, amounting to 14 per cent between the earliest period for which evidence is available and 1660–70.[75] As can be seen from Table 2.13, this stemmed primarily from the substantial increase in the number of baptisms registered in Mens-en-Trièves, but the trend was upward as well in Beaumont-lès-Valence, while four other congregations reveal stability in the number of

---

[73] The eight small towns under Protestant military control around 1610 were Embrun, Gap, Lunel, Orthez, Pons, Privas, Sommières and Uzès. Haag, X, 257–60, provides a full list of the towns under Huguenot military control.

[74] The fullest evidence exists for Millau, for which Jacques Frayssenge was kind enough to furnish me with annual figures concerning Catholic as well as Protestant baptisms. The city grew very slightly over the course of the period, with the percentage of Protestants declining steadily:

	1610–19	1630–39	1655–64	1675–84
Estimated population	3300 + small number of Catholics	3000	3500	3700
Percentage Huguenot	?	84	72	56

Anduze, Saint-Hippolyte and Saint-Jean-du-Gard were all virtually entirely Huguenot as late as 1663, so the movement of Protestant baptisms in them can be taken as indicating the movement of their total population between the first years of the century and this date. Together, they display no change. In Orthez, Salies and Sommières, for which censuses provide an indication of the percentage of Protestants in 1663–65, the number of Protestant baptisms alone in the early years of the century stood at higher levels than the total number of baptisms suggested by these censuses in the 1660s, so these towns clearly all diminished in size. Sauzet, *Contre-Réforme et Réforme Catholique en Bas-Languedoc*, pp. 394–5; A.N., TT 234 (197). Privas also declined in total size. Molinier, *Stagnations et croissance*, pp. 247–50.

[75] Standard error of this figure as an estimate for all churches in this category: ± 10.5 per cent.

Table 2.13   The rural congregations of the Midi and Centre–West
(Béarn excluded)

	Earliest period for which data available (with dates in question)	1660–70	1670–79	1680–85
Dauphiné				
Beaumont	40 (1613–21)	55	44	55
Loriol	56 (1614–19)	55	54	61
Mens-en-Trièves	42 (1604–07)	71	74	68
Montjoux	8 (1608–16)	8	–	–
Orpierre	47 (1633–39)	[37]	35	–
Pont-en-Royans	31 (1613–19)	30	23	25
Vercheny	12 (1633–39)	[12]	–	12
Provence				
Lourmarin	41 (1600–09)	32	36	33
Vivarais				
Boulieu	11 (1600–09)	3	–	–
Cévennes				
Aulas	88 (1613–17)	79	69	–
Lasalle	52 (1600–08)	64	76	–
Monoblet	44 (1600–09)	32	33	42
St-Etienne-V-F	50 (1600–09)	47	39	47
St-Laurent-Minier	27 (1610–19)	29	35	31
Soudorgues	41 (1619–28)	29	34	30
Sumène	45 (1601–09)	65	54	44
Bas-Languedoc				
Aigues-Vives	23 (1623–33)	27	36	37
Codognan	6 (1600–09)	[8]	9	–
Les Vans	41 (1595–1600)	40	40	36
Marsillargues	55 (1600–09)	47	53	47
Haut-Languedoc–Haute-Guyenne				
Briatexte	15 (1600–12)	10	–	–
Mas-Grenier	22 (1600–09)	8	–	–
Réalville-Albias	49 (1618–21)	56	–	–
Revel	68 (1600–09)	50	43	40
Roquecourbe	50 (1614–19)	33	38	42
Saint-Amans	20 (1603–08)	35	33	–
Vabre	61 (1627–29)	68	64	56
Basse-Guyenne				
Coutras	14 (1600–09)	[10]	–	–
Layrac	36 (1610–19)	11	7	–
Mussidan	23 (1600–09)	12	–	–
Aunis–Saintonge–Angoumois				
Dompierre	11 (1636–39)	19	11	12
La Rochefoucauld	36 (1608–19)	15	–	–
Mortagne	36 (1613–20)	25	–	–
Saint-Jean-d'Angle	51 (1636–39)	30	28	–
Saint-Just	174 (1601–09)	109	91	68
Salles	13 (1602–09)	13	–	–
Poitou				
Chef-Boutonne	43 (1602–09)	28	30	25
La-Mothe-St-Héray	367 (1618–30)	[348]	355	–
Mougon	241 (1600–05)	[167]	171	–
Rochechouart	34 (1600–08)	15	–	–

All figures represent the average number of baptisms per year in the period in question
unless otherwise indicated. Figures in brackets represent extrapolations. The churches
are arranged by synod.

acts between the earliest date for which their registers are available and 1660–70. Only Orpierre declined in size before the 1660s, and even its decrease was modest. Little decline followed in the subsequent decades, for in the 1680s, the level was still 99 per cent of what it had been in 1660–70.

If the evidence is insufficient to generalize about trends in the Vivarais or Provence,[76] the abundant data concerning the greatest single region of concentrated Huguenot strength, that stretching from Montpellier and Nîmes up into the Cévennes, show that here the rural Protestant population remained virtually unchanged beween 1600 and 1685. As the history of the small-town churches located in this region has already indicated, significant shifts did occur in the distribution of the population between different communities in this region. Monoblet and Soudorgues shrank considerably in size, while Lasalle and Sumène grew. But taken together, the eleven rural churches in the synods of Bas Languedoc and the Cévennes saw the number of baptisms celebrated within them drop by just 1 per cent between the earliest dates in the century for which information is available about each and 1660–70, and by a further 1 per cent between that period and the 1680s.[77]

Continuing westward, the synod of Haut-Languedoc–Haute-Guyenne was a region of transition. Despite some variation among them, the four churches located in the rugged hills above Castres – Briatexte, Roquecourbe, Saint-Amans and Vabre – displayed an aggregate growth of 4 per cent to 1660–70, even though they were heavily engaged in the fighting of the 1620s. (Roquecourbe's registers note the death of church members in skirmishes as far afield as Montauban and Lombez.) By contrast, the three churches located slightly farther westward in the plain of the Lauragais and the valleys of the Garonne and Aveyron – Revel, Réalville-Albias and Mas-Grenier – showed an aggregate tendency toward decline. This was especially marked in Mas-Grenier, whose church shrank by more than half over the course of the period to 1660–70. Overall, the seven rural churches of this synod registered a decline of 7 per cent to that decade.[78] The downward trend accelerated in the last decades before the

---

76 It should be stressed that the single rural and two small-town churches of the Vivarais for which evidence survive are all highly atypical of the region as a whole. Both Annonay and Boulieu were located far from the major centres of Protestant strength in this region along the valley of the Ardèche and around Largentière, while Privas's suffering as a result of the civil wars and royal policy was exceptional. Although a sharp drop is visible in the size of all three of these churches, it is probable that most churches located in this region evolved according to a pattern far closer in nature to that which characterized the churches of the nearby Cévennes.

77 Standard error for the change to 1660–70 as an estimate for all churches in this category: ±5.5 per cent.

78 Because of the considerable variation within this category of churches, the standard error of this figure as an estimate for the entire category of churches is a high ±12 per cent.

Revocation, with the level of baptisms in the 1680s falling to 91 per cent of that of 1660–70.

Across the plains and valleys of Aquitaine, Saintonge and Poitou, the rural churches appear to have had even greater difficulties in retaining the faithful. Just three churches represent the synod of Basse-Guyenne in the sample: Coutras, which remained constant in size between 1600 and 1650, Mussidan, which experienced an extended decline amounting to 47 per cent between 1600–09 and 1660–70, and Layrac, which witnessed an even greater extended decline of 69 per cent between 1610–19 and 1660–70. The same significant downward trend appears in Mortagne-sur-Gironde in Saintonge, in La Rochefoucauld in the Angoumois, in Rochechouart on the border between the Limousin and Haut-Poitou, in Saint-Just and Saint-Jean-d'Angle in the *marais salants* near Brouage, and in Mougon and Chef-Boutonne in the great region of rural Protestantism around Niort and Saint-Maixent. The only unquestionable exceptions to the general pattern of decline within this region were two small congregations located in the thinly settled plain of Aunis, Salles and Dompierre-Bourgneuf. As for the registers of the large, adjoining Poitevin churches of La-Mothe-Saint-Héray and Exoudun, these pose an archivistic conundrum. Records of these two churches, which consolidated into one when the temple of Exoudun was closed in 1666, were apparently once kept separately.[79] Today, the Archives Départementales des Deux-Sèvres house four registers kept together in a single *liasse* marked 'La-Mothe-Saint-Héray-Exoudun'. Exasperatingly, none of the three earliest registers bears a title page, nor is the place of residence of those bringing their children to be baptized noted in any of the four registers. Several of them overlap in time, and the acts they contain concern different individuals. If, as seems probable, the earliest registers are those of the two different churches of La-Mothe-Saint-Héray and Exoudun, while the last one, from the 1670s, concerns the two churches merged, then, as Table 2.13 suggests, these two large churches altered little in size between 1618–30 and 1675–77. But this conclusion is decidedly conjectural. Since these two churches were so large, a significant difference in results hangs upon the decision whether to accept this evidence as reliable or not. For that reason, total statistics for the rural churches of the synods of Poitou, Aunis–Saintonge–Angoumois and Basse-Guyenne combined have been calculated twice, once with the figures for these churches included and once with them excluded. The aggregate decline to 1660–70 works out to 26 per cent if they are retained and 37 per cent if they are not.[80] Although records for relatively

---

[79] See Dez, *Histoire des Protestants du Poitou*, pp. 461–2.

[80] Standard error of this figure as an estimate for all churches in this category: ±6 per cent.

few of these churches survive from the 1670s and 1680s, those which do suggest continued, sharp decline in these decades.

From this review of Protestantism's fate across the Midi, it is clear that the cause experienced far greater decline in its ranks in the Centre–West and Aquitaine (although it should be remembered that evidence survives for just a few communities in this latter region) than in Dauphiné and Languedoc. What explains these regional contrasts? Even though preliminary results of Biraben's investigation of the movement of the French population before 1670 suggest that Dauphiné and the Mediterranean and western coasts may have been more buoyant demographically than the interior of Aquitaine,[81] regional variations in the general rate of population growth can provide at best a very partial explanation of the observable phenomena. That greatest heartland of rural Huguenot strength, the Cévennes, seems to have witnessed no population growth at all in this period. Four rural communities located in the most overwhelmingly Protestant part of the region that are represented in the sample, Lasalle, Monoblet, Saint-Etienne-Vallée-Française and Soudorgues, were all still 95 per cent Huguenot or more in the decades just prior to the Revocation.[82] Since the number of baptisms celebrated in their Protestant churches fell slightly over the first six decades of the century, we can conclude that their overall population changed little over this period, just as was the case for the small towns of the region.[83] If the Protestant churches of this area registered less decline than was the norm elsewhere in the Midi, it was thus not because they were located in an area of particular demographic dynamism. On the contrary, this was a region where Protestantism's strength grew relative to Catholicism, even as the overall population of the region remained stable.[84] In the *élection* of Niort, in contrast, the number of *feux* is known to have increased by 7.5 per cent between 1630 and 1685, while the increase was greater still (13 per cent) in the three localities in this administrative unit represented within our sample, Chef-Boutonne, La-Mothe-Saint-Héray and Mougon.[85] Here, the Huguenots were losing ground even as the overall population grew a bit, indicating a genuine failure to retain the allegiance of the faithful.

---

81 Biraben and Blum, 'Population Trends in France, 1500 to 1800', pp. 7–9.

82 Sauzet, *Contre-Réforme et Réforme Catholique en Bas-Languedoc*, pp. 394–5; Jean-Robert Armogathe, 'Missions et conversions dans le diocèse de Mende au dix-septième siècle (1629–1709)', unpub. thèse de l'Ecole Pratique des Hautes Etudes, 1970, p. 9.

83 See above, note 74.

84 An increase in the percentage of Huguenots is visible in the less exclusively Protestant part of the region around Le Vigan. Sauzet, *Contre-Réforme et Réforme Catholique en Bas-Languedoc*, p. 284.

85 Benoist, 'Les populations rurales du "Moyen-Poitou Protestant"', pp. 495, 905–8.

Detailed social histories of the Protestant communities of these regions and of the relations between their members and their Catholic neighbours are still in their infancy, but the work done to date already hints that the extent of interaction and intermarriage between members of the two faiths varied considerably from region to region.[86] One can hypothesize that the boundaries between the two faiths may have been far more porous in Aquitaine and the Centre–West than in Dauphiné or the Cévennes, and that this encouraged more passage from Protestantism to Catholicism in the former regions than in the latter. It may also be that the degree of indoctrination in the basics of the faith was greater among the rural Protestants of the Cévennes and Dauphiné. Or perhaps the strength of aristocratic power in Poitou and the south-west created a seigneurial Protestantism characterized by less tenacious attachment to the cause on the part of ordinary church members than was the case elsewhere in France. Such an interpretation receives support from a remarkable memoir written by an anonymous Catholic observer in 1618 describing the 'Estat de la religion en Poictou'. A general indifference to religious matters prevailed among the common people of the province, the memoir suggests. 'The *sieurs particuliers* of the villages of the so-called Reformed religion constrain their subjects to go to the *presche*, most of them with the stick and the more moderate among them by preventing anybody from holding any office or tenure under their control or that of the townsmen who own holdings from them.' Confessional identity was so weak that 'if one asks the mothers to what religion their daughters belong, they think they are responding civilly by saying that they don't belong to any yet and will be of that of their husband'.[87] Only detailed local studies, especially ones which are explicitly comparative in nature, will unlock the precise keys to the regional differences visible in Protestantism's fate across the Huguenot crescent. The riddle of explaining these differences clearly represents an important and intriguing task for future research.

So far, this survey of Protestantism's evolution in the rural areas of southern France has skirted one region, Béarn. This formerly independent

---

[86] Gabriel Audisio, 'Se marier en Luberon: catholiques et protestants vers 1630', in *Histoire sociale, sensibilités collectives et mentalités. Mélanges R. Mandrou* (Paris, 1985), pp. 243–4.

[87] A.N., TT 262 (8). On the strength of seigneurial institutions in this region of France, see Charles Dugast-Matifeux, ed., *Etat du Poitou sous Louis XIV* (Fontenay-le-Comte, 1865), pp. 93–131 (report of the intendant containing numerous observations about the power and petty tyranny of local noblemen); Pierre Goubert, 'Sociétés rurales françaises du 18e siècle: Vingt paysanneries contrastées, quelques problèmes', in his *Clio parmi les hommes* (Paris–The Hague, 1976), p. 68; Louis Merle, *La métairie et l'évolution agraire de la Gâtine poitevine de la fin du Moyen Age à la Révolution* (Paris, 1958), esp. pp. 63–70; Jacques Peret, *Seigneurs et seigneuries en Gâtine poitevine: Le duché de la Meilleraye, XVIIe–XVIIIe siècles*, Mémoires de la Société des Antiquaires de l'Ouest, 4th ser. XIII (Poitiers, 1976), part II.

principality united to the crown of France on the accession of Henry of Navarre forms a highly special case and boasts unusual documentation. It was the one region of France where the Reformation was imposed from above by an act of state. Between 1570–71 and 1599, under Jeanne d'Albret and her son Henry of Navarre, the mass was abolished and all parishes were required to conform to a Reformed church order. In 1599, the Edict of Fontainebleau provided Béarn's Catholics with their rough counterpart of the Edict of Nantes, once again permitting worship according to the Roman rite in twelve specified localities across the principality and in those parishes whose patrons had remained faithful to the old church. But functioning parishes often revived only slowly, and it was not until several years after Louis XIII made his *chevauchée de Béarn* in 1620 to oversee the enforcement of subsequent edicts ordering the restitution of all church lands seized at the time of the Reformation, that Catholic worship was restored in every parish.[88] Thereafter, the situation of Béarn's Protestants was comparable to that of the other members of the French Reformed church, with whom the Béarnais had affiliated themselves in 1616 in the vain hope that alliance with the main body of French Protestants might slow the process of Catholic restoration.

Béarn thus represents one of the rare cases in European history of a territory which underwent a generation of enforced Protestantization, then saw a regime of toleration established. Only a fraction of the population became convinced Protestants. In 1665, the royal intendant carried out a religious census that indicated that, out of a total population of 129 457, only 21 804 individuals (4869 families) were still Protestant.[89] The local synod of the Reformed church protested that this census undercounted the number of its members and produced a document of its own asserting that the proper number of Protestant families was 6382 – or, assuming

---

[88] Béarn's ecclesiastical legislation may be followed on the basis of Pierre Tucoo-Chala, *Histoire du Béarn* (Paris, 1962), pp. 49–68; and Tucoo-Chala and Christian Desplat, *La Principauté de Béarn* (Pau, 1980), pp. 176–7. The slowness with which the old system of parishes actually revived emerges from such Catholic parish registers as that of Nay (A.C. Nay [conserved at A.D. Pyrénées-Atlantiques], GG 1). Although this was one of the twelve specified localities in which Catholic worship was to be restored under the Edict of Fontainebleau, continuous services were only re-established in 1612. For the first decade after that date, the parish register includes many acts involving inhabitants of nearby communities in which Catholic services had clearly not yet been re-established. Only in 1622 does the register cease noting the place of residence of those bringing their children for baptism, a probable indication that the acts henceforward concern this parish alone.

[89] A.N., TT 234 (197). An excellent guide to all of the regional religious censuses dating from the later seventeenth century has been drawn up by René Mieybegué of the A.D. Pyrénées-Atlantiques.

the same family size, 28 591 individuals.[90] Either way, no more than 17 to 22 per cent of the population was still Protestant.[91] A second official census drawn up in 1682 asserts that the number of Protestants had fallen by that date to 19 455 individuals, out of a total population which now numbered 168 093.[92] Again the Reformed church cried undercounting and responded with a document of its own, claiming 6188 families faithful to the church.[93] Despite the differences between these documents, they agree in suggesting that further decline had occurred in the number of Protestants. On the eve of the Revocation, the Huguenots were thus a weakening minority of less than 20 per cent in a region which had once been entirely Protestant by law.

How had the number of the faithful in this region evolved between the Edict of Fontainebleau and the religious censuses of 1665? The baptismal registers of six churches survive which cover part or all of that period. These churches are not representative of the region as a whole, for all were situated in localities in which Protestantism resisted erosion more successfully than elsewhere. (See Table 2.14.) Still, it does not seem unreasonable to assume that the chronology of the decline registered in these churches between the turn of the century and the 1660s was typical of the region as a whole, even if the extent of that decline was not. As Table 2.14 makes clear, over four-fifths of the decline in the number of baptisms celebrated in these churches took place over the first three decades of the century, when Catholic services were being reestablished throughout the region. As can be seen from the examples of Arthez, Bellocq and Lagor, where the registers are continuous for much or all of the period 1600–30, the years around 1620 witnessed the sharpest fall-off in Protestant baptisms, suggesting that Louis XIII's *chevauchée* was the central event for the revival of Catholicism in these communities, not the Edict of Fontainebleau. Further, slow decline occurred between the 1630s and the 1660s.

If the chronological pattern of decline found among these churches is typical of the region as a whole, the following conclusions thus emerge. First of all, comparison between the level of baptisms in these churches

---

90 B. Vaurigaud, 'Statistique des églises du Béarn vers le milieu du XVIIe siècle', *B.S.H.P.F.* 5 (1857), 1–6. I have eliminated from the total provided by this document the 32 families residing in Saint-Palais, located in Basse-Navarre.

91 As indicated above in Table 2.1, comparison of the two censuses from the mid-1660s with each other and with the estimates of congregation size which one can derive from the Protestant baptismal registers suggests that the truth lies somewhere between the two estimates.

92 B.N., Ms Fonds Français 8248.

93 A. Cadier, 'Les églises réformées du Béarn de 1664 à 1685', *B.S.H.P. F.* 30 (1881), 111.

Table 2.14 Average number of baptisms per decade in six churches of Béarn

Congregation	1580s	1590s	1600s	1610s	1620s	1630s
Arthez			[49.9]	48.4	23.0	19.9
Bellocq	76.8	69.1	73.2	67.8	58.6	38.0
Lagor			45.7	47.6	33.4	30.3
Nay			[40.0]		23.6	18.1
Orthez	168.0		[160.1]			103.0
Salies		113.7	110.9		111.3	106.4
Total			483.8			315.7

Note: Figures in brackets are extrapolations from the nearest available figures. The percentages in the final column refer to all of the communities served by each temple. Since a few of the smaller localities listed in their baptismal register do not appear in the census figures, these percentages contain a margin of error.

around the turn of the century and the total number of baptisms which might be surmised from the combination of the number of Protestant acts and the percentage of Huguenots in these communities around 1665 suggests little growth in the total population of the region between 1600 and 1665. There may even have been some decline. At the time of the Edict of Fontainebleau, Béarn thus certainly housed upwards of 100 000 inhabitants, all of whom, whether they liked it or not, had to be baptized within the Reformed church if they were to receive Christian baptism at all. Once the option of worshipping according to Catholic rites was restored, the majority of the population immediately abandoned the Reformed church. By the 1630s, upwards of three-fifths of Béarn's population was probably back in the Roman fold. Even those families which remained faithful to the Protestant cause then demonstrated less fidelity over subsequent generations than did their co-religionists in most other regions. The number of baptisms declined by a further 12 per cent between the 1630s and 1660s. The rival censuses of 1665 and 1682 reveal still further decline of 4–12 per cent between those dates. Finally, at the Revocation, fewer refugees in both absolute and proportional terms fled Béarn than any other *province synodal* of the French Reformed church, while fidelity was equally rare among those who remained within the kingdom. In 1787, with the restoration of legal toleration, just 4784 Protestants remained in Béarn.[94]

---

[94] Mours, *Les églises reformées en France*, pp. 168–76, esp. p. 172; Tucoo-Chala, *Histoire du Béarn*, p. 76.

Table 2.14 *concluded*

1640s	1650s	1660s	1670s	Percentage Protestant in 1665 according to census of intendant
22.0		20.2	27.6	34
		[33.3]		79
26.6		23.8		40
18.4	16.6	13.1	13.2	35
91.8	86.9	95.8		66
	111.4	90.5		96
Total		276.8		

Was the striking failure of Béarn's magisterial reformation to create an enduring Protestant community the result of difficulties encountered by a small, poor state in implementing the process of religious change and recruiting an effective parish clergy committed to the spread of a new understanding of the gospel? Should it be attributed to pre-existing social arrangements or cultural patterns which made the region particularly resistant to efforts from above to implant Protestantism? Or was the extent to which Protestant ideas took hold among the mass of the Béarnais in one generation no different from the degree to which the new faith took root over the same span of time in other regions where the Reformation was imposed from above on a fairly isolated and overwhelmingly rural area? In the absence of any good study of the process whereby the Reformation was implemented in Béarn – and, for that matter, a dearth of studies of other comparable regions – one can only raise these questions. Clearly, this is another area which invites further research. Clearly, too, the contrast between the withering away of Protestantism in this region and the greater fidelity found elsewhere in France shows the differences in the tenacity with which subsequent generations clung to a minority religion resulting from personal choice and one born of princely decree.

One final set of statistics remains to be calculated for the rural churches of the Midi. This concerns the aggregate evolution of these 44 churches. Together (making no attempt to compensate for the uneven survival of records by synod), they registered a decline of 16 per cent over an average period of 52 years before 1660–70 if La-Mothe-Saint-Héray–Exoudun is included, and 18 per cent if it is excluded. The decade-to-decade index (Figure 2.6) shows a gradual and quite steady decline over the full period 1600–85, interrupted only by some recovery in the 1660s. The level of baptisms in the 1680s was 92 per cent that of 1660–70.

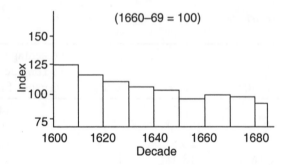

2.6 Cumulative index: rural churches of the Midi and Centre–West

The national trend Having surveyed every region and size category of churches, we are now in a position to estimate with some precision the overall movement of the Protestant population from 1600 to 1685. Table 2.15 takes the revised estimates of the number of Protestants *c.* 1660–70 as its starting point and extrapolates backward from the estimates for each category of churches according to the movement of baptisms within that category over the first six decades of the century. As can be seen, such a procedure suggests that approximately 960 000 ± 35 000 Huguenots lived in the kingdom of France, excluding Béarn, around the end of the reign of Henry IV. When it is recalled that the movement of baptisms exaggerates slightly the extent of decline over these years, it is evident that this figure must be reduced slightly to obtain a truer estimate – perhaps by

Table 2.15 Estimating France's total Protestant population, *c.* 1610, excluding Béarn

Category	A	B	C
N. urban	52 775	133.3 ± 5	70 349 ± 2639
N. small town	14 000	125.6 ± 5	17 578 ± 700
N. rural	67 225	127.7 ± 3.5	85 846 ± 2353
S. urban	77 900	156.2 ± 1	121 716 ± 779
S. small town	62 900	130.1 ± 3	81 821 ± 1887
S. rural	496 200	115.6 ± 5.9	573 393 ± 29 276[a]
		117.9 ± 6	585 142 ± 29 772[b]
Total			950 703 – 962 452 ± 37 634 – 38 130

A – Total Protestant population *c.* 1660–70 (from Table 2.1)
B – Ratio of baptisms at earliest available date to baptisms in base period plus standard error
C – Estimated total Protestant population *c.* 1610
[a] with La-Mothe-Saint-Héray–Exoudun
[b] without La-Mothe-Saint-Héray–Exoudun

an additional 10 000 to 50 000 souls, yielding a final estimate of 930 000 ± 70 000. To these must be added the 100 000–125 000 inhabitants of Béarn, the great majority of whom were still at least nominally Reformed. These results, it might be noted, come remarkably close to the estimate of Protestantism's numerical strength set forth by Jean Gontery in a 1610 sermon in the church of Saint-Etienne-du-Mont in Paris, where the Jesuit father is recorded to have said that the Protestants claim to be 900 000 souls in all of France.[95] Another, more commonly repeated estimate of the number of Huguenots in France around the beginning of the seventeenth century appears to be slightly farther off the mark. This is the assertion that 1.25 million Huguenots lived in France in 1598, a figure purported to derive from a census of Protestants carried out by Henry IV at the time of the Edict of Nantes. No reference to this estimate is known before 1692, and its authenticity seems questionable.[96]

Figure 2.7 sets out the decade-to-decade trend. The same sources that speak of a census of Protestants carried out under Henry IV also claim that the ranks of the cause increased by a third over the subsequent years before Richelieu's arrival in power, but the data examined here offer no evidence of such growth. Many urban congregations may have registered a modest increase in size, but this was more than counterbalanced by the movement of the rural churches, particularly those in Béarn and the

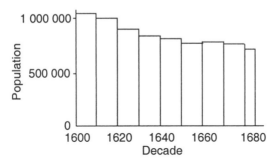

2.7   Estimated total Protestant population of France and Béarn, 1600–85, by decade

---

[95] Pierre de l'Estoile, *Mémoires-Journaux* (12 vols, Paris, 1889–95), X, 337–8, quoted in Jacques Pannier, 'La Réforme dans le Vermandois: l'Eglise de Saint-Quentin', *B.S.H.P.F.* 45 (1896), 232. L'Estoile identifies the Jesuit preacher as 'Gontier', but no Jesuit of that name appears in Henri Fouqueraye's detailed *Histoire de la Compagnie de Jésus en France des origines à la suppression* (5 vols, Paris, 1910–25). Gontery, a central figure among the Jesuits in Paris and an active controversialist, appears to be the correct identification.

[96] 'Un dénombrement des réformés de France en 1598', *B.S.H.P.F.* 1 (1853), 123–4, citing this estimate in Gregorio Leti's 1692 biography of Elizabeth I. This census is also cited in an eighteenth-century copy of the acts of the 1663 provincial synod of Poitou. Nathaniel Weiss, 'Statistique du Protestantisme Français en 1598', *ibid.*, 38 (1889), 551.

Centre–West. The 1620s and 1630s were then the years of the most rapid decline, centred overwhelmingly in the Midi and resulting from the full restoration of Catholicism in Béarn and the disastrous impact of the civil wars and plague upon so many southern centres of Huguenot strength. More gradual decline continued through the 1650s, before the 1660s brought the one decade in which Protestant baptismal levels increased, largely, one supposes, as a result of the country's general recovery from the economic difficulties of the era of the Thirty Years War and the Fronde. As measures of persecution intensified in the final decades before the Revocation, the ranks of the Huguenots began to thin again, with the decline proving particularly marked in the churches of northern France. From the late 1670s onward, in fact, many of the congregations in northern France displayed a condition of permanent demographic crisis, with burials consistently outnumbering baptisms as emigration and conversion both accelerated.[97] But while the minority congregations of the north eroded rapidly in the years of increasing harassment before 1685, Huguenot ranks remained firm in many regions of the Midi where the Protestants were most numerous. The overall decline of the faith in these last years was thus far less marked than the experience of its most visible urban congregations might have led observers to believe. The broadest lesson of Figure 2.7 is thus a surprising one. The number of Huguenots diminished more rapidly in the first half of the seventeenth century than in the decades immediately preceding the Revocation. On the basis of a projection similar to that used to estimate the Protestant population around 1610, one can place the number of Huguenots living in France on the eve of the first great *dragonnades* in 1681 at *c.* 730 000.

In conclusion, the ranks of French Protestantism experienced, between the reign of Henry IV and the arrival of the first dragoons in Poitou, an irregular decline that amounted to slightly under a quarter of the faith's initial strength if one excludes the exceptional region of Béarn, and to just under a third of its strength if one includes it. This decline was particularly marked in the cities, especially those with large Huguenot communities at the beginning of the period. Whether in La Rochelle or Montauban, Metz or Caen, Nérac or Alençon, the percentage of the population represented by the Protestants was far smaller on the eve of the Revocation than it had been eight decades previously. While less marked, the decline was real

---

[97] This phenomenon may be observed in Alençon, Blois, Châtillon-sur-Loire and Dangeau, although it does not appear in Rouen, Mer, Marchenoir and Saint-Sylvain. I found no evidence of a similar phenomenon in any community of the Midi, although I did not examine the movement of burials in every community whose registers I utilized. Those in the Midi for which I did explore this question include Chef-Boutonne, Mens-en-Trièves, Gap, Sommières, Anduze, Roquecourbe and Nérac. Gueneau, 'Protestants du Centre', pp. 243–4; Bollon, 'Minorité broyée et Malthusianisme', p. 501.

enough in the rural areas and small towns as well, especially those located in the western portions of the kingdom. While the Protestants' failure to maintain their ranks in certain regions points to the force of conversion in reducing their numbers in these areas, the restoration of Catholicism within a Béarn which had been only partially Protestantized, the bitter harvest of the revolts of the 1620s, the inability of many of the large urban congregations to reproduce themselves, and the apparent lack of economic and demographic dynamism within such strongholds of rural Protestantism as the Cévennes and the Pays de Caux must all be accounted significant causes of the decline as well. The long, slow erosion of France's Huguenot community between 1600 and 1685 was a complex phenomenon with multiple causes.

2. Demography and *mentalités*

In the effort to know the 'chrétien quelconque d'autrefois', historians of Protestantism must be particularly resourceful. The past generation may have seen the aims and methods of religious history renewed by a concern to reconstruct the beliefs and practices of Europe's ordinary inhabitants, but it is no accident that most of the pathbreaking studies in this enterprise have been devoted to Catholic Europe. Catholicism's abundance of voluntary associations, such as confraternities, and of rituals, such as pilgrimages or anniversary masses for the dead, makes it a religion whose ordinary practice is particularly rich in those gestures of commitment which leave traces for future generations of historians. In de-emphasizing individual ritual gestures and stressing the inward experience of faith, the Reformers created a religion whose practice is far harder for historians peering back across the centuries to seize.

To be sure, certain documents do enable historians of Protestant societies to gain insight into the religious culture of those who lived within them. In those regions where ecclesiastical visitations were regularly performed, the records of these visits provide glimpses into the assiduity of participation in the sacraments and the educational enterprises of the church, even if the encounter between educated urban divines and uncommunicative villagers suspicious of officious outsiders must be interpreted with caution. Spiritual diaries or memoirs often cast a remarkably sharp light on the lives of those believers committed enough to keep such diaries. Consistory or church court records tell of the behaviour of notorious sinners. Still, the limitations of all of these sources are evident.

As the Prologue has already suggested, historical demography can contribute to religious history not simply by illuminating the numerical evolution of a religious group, but also by shedding light on aspects of its behaviour that are difficult, if not impossible, to establish in any other fashion. (Section 1's discussion of the length of time people waited to have their children baptized has already attempted to illustrate this claim.) Furthermore, the great advantage of the statistics derived from parish register sources is that they shed light on the behaviour of the entire community in question, not merely on those who excelled in either piety or detectable misbehaviour. Of course, the findings yielded by such methods have their limitations too. While curves and statistics can reveal how widespread certain forms of behaviour were and how these changed over time, they cannot tell us the meaning of these practices for those who engaged in them. This can only be learned from literary sources, and thus the demographic data need to be set in as rich a context of ethnographic information as possible. For this reason, the evidence unearthed through demographic investigation is best thought of as complementary to approaches to the historical study of religion drawing on the methods of folklore and historical ethnography, methods whose value has become increasingly evident in recent years.[98] While the ethnographic record can document the existence of certain beliefs and practices and tell us how those who held or performed them interpreted them, it rarely indicates just how widely shared these were or precisely when they appeared or disappeared. This is what demographic sources can clarify.[99]

The seasonality of marriage

The related issues of birth and marital seasonality offer particularly interesting insights into the attitudes of the first generations of Protestants toward both the old rituals and rhythms of the Catholic church and certain customary beliefs whose origin must be sought outside the theological systems of either church. The alternation between *temps clos* and *temps ouverts*, between periods of feast and periods of fast, was one of the

---

[98] As in such works as William A. Christian, Jr, *Local Religion in Sixteenth-Century Spain* (Princeton, 1981) and *Apparitions in Late Medieval Spain* (Princeton, 1981); Philippe Joutard, 'Protestantisme populaire et univers magique: le cas cévenol', *Le Monde Alpin et Rhodanien* 5 (1977), 145–71; and Lyndal Roper, ' "Going to Church and Street": Weddings in Reformation Augsburg', *Past and Present* 106 (1985), 62–101.

[99] Marius Hudry, 'Relations sexuelles prénuptiales en Tarentaise et dans le Beaufortin d'après les documents ecclésiastiques', *Le Monde Alpin et Rhodanien* 1 (1974), 95–100, offers an excellent example of an ethnographic study which could have been usefully supplemented by demographic investigation. The author assembles a series of fascinating texts describing the local practice of *albergement* (bundling) and denouncing its consequences for the virtue of the region's young women, but he makes no effort to determine if prenuptial conceptions were in fact particularly numerous in this region, as might easily have been done on the basis of its parish registers.

fundamental rhythms of life in pre-Reformation Europe and, later, those parts of the continent which remained faithful to Rome. One aspect of this was the highly seasonal pattern of marriages. Demographic investigation of the seasonality of marriage has shown considerable regional variations in the times when people were most and least likely to wed, with local customs, the calendar of work, and the dates of important local events, notably hiring fairs, all influencing the frequency of marriage in any given month. Throughout Catholic Europe, however, one constant stands out. Very few marriages were celebrated during the months when the church calendar forbade weddings, that is to say, March (Lent) and December (Advent).

The Reformation, particularly in its Calvinistic variants, marked a rupture with the old prohibitions against marriage during Lent and Advent. Changes in popular practice quickly followed these theological changes in many parts of Protestant Europe. The March and December dips disappear rapidly from Genevan curves of marriage seasonality in the wake of the Reformation there.[100] They are similarly absent in Dutch Reformed churches and in Puritan New England in the seventeenth century.[101] But this disappearance of old patterns of seasonality was not universal in those regions that were made Protestant by law. A respect for the old prohibition of marriage during Lent lived on after the Reformation in Scotland, where the break from this custom came only after 1640, as first the Covenanters and then the Cromwellians stepped up the campaign to instil more thoroughly Reformed behaviour in the faithful.[102] In England, the old church calendar was never explicitly changed with regard to prohibited periods for marriage, although the ban on marriage during Lent and Advent was challenged by Puritan opinion and was not explicitly reiterated in the Elizabethan Canons or the Book of Common Prayer. The

---

100 Alfred Perrenoud, *La population de Genève du XVIe au début du XIXe siècle: étude démographique* (Geneva, 1979), pp. 383–5.

101 G.J. Mentink and A.M. van der Woude, *De demografische entwikkeling te Rotterdam en Cool in de 17e en 18e eeuw* (Rotterdam, 1965), p. 140; van der Woude, *Het Noorderkwartier*, A.A.G. Bijdragen XVI (Wageningen, 1972), 791; David Cressy, 'The Seasonality of Marriage in Old and New England', *Journal of Interdisciplinary History* 16 (1985), 14–15.

102 Gordon Donaldson, *The Scottish Reformation* (Cambridge, 1960), p. 180; Walter Roland Foster, *The Church before the Covenants: The Church of Scotland, 1596–1638* (Edinburgh–London, 1975), pp. 73–4; T.C. Smout, *A History of the Scottish People 1560–1830* (London, 1969), pp. 83–6; L.D.S. films 1040102, 1040126 (parish registers of Dunfermline, county Fife; originals in the New Register House, Edinburgh, Old Parochial Registers 424/1–3). Dunfermline's registers reveal the following monthly indices of marriages:

	J	F	M	A	M	J	J	A	S	O	N	D
1562–90	103	142	18	84	108	159	117	94	54	56	144	125
1600–39	104	127	23	75	99	159	125	106	58	66	135	126
1640–79	86	79	62	83	76	154	114	125	47	78	148	146

transplanted Englishmen of the colonial Tidewater displayed a pronounced tendency to avoid March marriages, while Wrigley and Schofield's figures for England as a whole show sharp troughs in the number of marriages during Lent and Advent during the later sixteenth and early seventeenth centuries. These, however, subsequently diminished in size to 1800, without the Lenten dip ever disappearing. The precise regional and chronological pattern of the increasing rejection of these prohibitions has not yet been explored in a manner which would clarify its causes, but, clearly, it must be linked both to the rise of Puritanism and to the growth of more secular attitudes.[103]

If these comparisons show the interest of seasonal patterns of marriage as an indication of the extent to which Protestant populations in fact broke with traditional Roman practices, what do we find among France's Huguenots? One leading French demographer and historian, citing seventeenth-century evidence from the Sancerrois and Lower Normandy, has argued that the prohibitions against marriage during Lent and Advent were so deeply rooted in the popular mentality that they were even respected by the Protestants, a claim which has subsequently found its way into the textbooks.[104] Yet such fidelity to Catholic custom would seem surprising in a community whose initial members (outside Béarn) had all freely embraced Protestantism and its doctrines. When one looks back to the sixteenth century, besides assembling as much information as possible about the seventeenth, a more complex story emerges. Table 2.16 sets out the information.

Good registers of marriages which date back to the earliest days of formal Reformed churches in France are rare, but they exist for Anduze, Montpellier and Metz.[105] These show that the Protestants quickly began to celebrate marriages during the closed periods. Numerous weddings were performed in all three localities during both Lent and Advent, 1562, and the indices of March marriages for these earliest years (where a figure of 100 would be expected if weddings were distributed evenly across the entire year) suggest only the tiniest hint of any tendency to avoid marriage

---

103 E.A. Wrigley and R.S. Schofield, *The Population History of England 1541–1871* (Cambridge, Mass., 1981), pp. 298–300; Cressy, 'Seasonality of Marriage', pp. 1–2, 20; J. Wickham Legg, *English Church Life from the Restoration to the Tractarian Movement* (London, 1914), pp. 260–61; Keith Thomas, *Religion and the Decline of Magic* (New York, 1971), pp. 620–21.

104 François Lebrun, *La vie conjugale sous l'Ancien Régime* (Paris, 1975), p. 38. See also Cressy, 'Seasonality of Marriage', p. 3; Robert Muchembled, *Société et mentalités dans la France moderne XVIe–XVIIIe siècle* (Paris, 1990), p. 47.

105 A few marriages were also recorded by one of Caen's pastors for the period 1560–63. See C.E. Lart, ed., *The Registers of the Protestant Church at Caen (Normandy)* (Vannes, 1907).

Table 2.16   The seasonal movement of marriages

Locality	Dates	Jan.	Feb.	Mar.	Apr.	May	Jun.	Jul.	Aug.	Sep.	Oct.	Nov.	Dec.	n
1562–68														
Anduze	1562–65	93	110	108	141	86	97	86	79	141	108	59	93	164
Metz	1562–68	152	128	83	94	107	106	111	108	71	72	76	92	805
Montpellier	1562–68	96	115	127	130	121	96	81	114	69	80	84	89	798
1572–99														
Anduze	1572–96	100	82	95	111	104	109	89	109	113	92	100	95	950
St-Etienne-V-F	1574–83	161	92	99	119	115	95	107	46	126	92	79	69	154
2 churches in Béarn*	1573–99	195	253	70	66	92	74	42	30	56	44	105	185	592
Metz	1579–99	171	134	24	126	109	91	106	65	72	63	102	141	1893
Montpellier	1580–89	115	143	98	110	92	112	73	82	90	119	60	108	730

* Bellocq, Orthez

Locality	Dates	Jan.	Feb.	Mar.	Apr.	May	Jun.	Jul.	Aug.	Sep.	Oct.	Nov.	Dec.	n
1600–60														
Alençon	1629–59	100	125	137	97	111	109	105	85	88	88	68	88	414
Anduze	1610–59	120	84	108	146	51	117	82	121	93	112	79	86	644
Annonay	1640–59	143	139	116	115	132	87	53	32	126	58	109	95	223
Barbézieux	1600–35	113	196	151	144	116	93	88	59	37	49	66	94	813
2 churches in Béarn*	1620–68	142	128	92	93	87	88	92	85	82	93	101	117	745
Blois	1600–59	110	144	24	116	67	132	167	97	72	76	123	76	387
Castres	1609–59	124	125	138	139	61	122	88	85	70	68	87	96	1574
Châlons s/Marne	1600–42	129	78	39	120	90	110	126	103	86	106	163	52	366
Loriol	1637–60	69	101	92	178	46	142	84	88	71	126	79	126	308
Marennes	1637–49	123	128	83	91	112	76	114	99	74	82	121	98	736
Marsillargues	1613–54	102	152	109	166	68	155	43	79	87	70	82	95	520
Metz	1600–59	113	159	33	108	106	101	113	107	63	72	93	136	3642
Montpellier	1602–16	94	110	107	156	61	126	72	74	79	95	113	117	906
Mougon	1600–04	158	263	158	100	168	111	71	10	5	15	90	61	231
	1633–59	133	183	55	132	138	114	85	24	26	117	127	74	1478
Nîmes	1625–59	127	125	106	134	61	118	50	71	62	142	105	101	2477
Niort	1622–37	158	151	71	143	94	108	77	54	70	91	59	128	350
Preuilly s/Claise	1600–59	91	133	50	135	50	73	151	131	125	81	83	101	117
Rouen	1631–64	125	157	20	104	127	87	112	75	118	106	104	65	1443
Roquecourbe	1612–59	118	168	128	112	38	142	89	86	40	38	102	144	369
2 churches in Perche†	1600–60	72	119	40	121	125	116	76	109	100	101	112	113	293
Revel	1600–59	111	99	115	143	75	125	122	65	77	89	91	91	820
Tours	1633–59	162	194	46	95	123	103	100	46	103	62	72	100	153
Vabre	1625–49	105	115	122	133	56	115	105	73	61	84	122	112	338
Wassy	1627–59	196	101	116	107	69	95	92	69	107	81	72	92	102

* Lagor, Salies
† Authon-du-Perche, Montgoubert

Locality	Dates	Jan.	Feb.	Mar.	Apr.	May	Jun.	Jul.	Aug.	Sep.	Oct.	Nov.	Dec.	n
1660–84														
Alençon	1660–83	114	102	140	64	150	123	114	62	96	88	75	72	228
Annonay	1660–79	79	141	98	126	128	82	55	110	101	61	120	104	198
Blois	1660–78	185	166	34	87	151	87	118	118	104	17	104	34	70
Castres	1660–84	95	131	105	164	50	117	111	83	85	97	79	87	571
6 churches in Gard*	1668–84	111	120	99	181	31	109	70	72	81	149	102	78	571
Loriol	1661–83	101	73	53	141	75	100	93	88	82	119	123	150	267
Marennes	1669–80	76	155	47	82	106	108	135	110	91	100	116	78	576
Marsillargues	1668–83	104	74	147	158	61	146	31	37	89	98	114	141	192
Montélimar	1660–81	127	170	145	102	99	84	81	67	77	74	91	88	334
Montpellier	1668–80	107	129	97	158	68	114	69	88	80	74	122	100	780
Nérac	1668–80	117	151	56	163	32	150	36	65	88	93	100	157	292
Nîmes	1660–84	102	121	120	153	40	114	64	62	62	133	123	108	2191
Niort	1670–80	175	199	13	86	98	128	120	32	38	169	150	0	551
2 churches in Provence†	1669–84	101	110	151	167	117	150	67	50	104	67	69	50	211
Revel	1660–84	121	119	103	175	36	100	133	127	25	121	75	66	195
Roquecourbe	1660–84	90	126	77	112	26	146	122	96	106	70	119	115	184
Rouen	1665–84	114	126	22	85	129	94	138	76	92	116	117	91	740
Saint-Just	1669–83	110	152	26	98	153	107	136	84	116	75	107	40	408
Tours	1670–78	181	174	68	140	125	59	113	68	47	79	70	79	104
Wassy	1660–84	75	146	66	94	124	189	91	91	34	33	129	132	142

* Alès, Anduze, Lasalle, Monoblet, Sommières, Soudorgues
† Lourmarin, Manosque

during either Lent or Advent, and that for only one of these churches, that of Metz.[106] The rapid Protestant rejection of traditional Catholic practice concerning the *temps clos* in these communities was part of the joyous, aggressive rejection of Catholic interdictions, now seen as the fraudulent inventions of a venal clerisy, that was so typical of this springtime of the French Reformation. There is little respect for tradition here.

During the subsequent nine decades, from 1570 to 1660, significant regional differences appeared. Between 1572 and 1599, the Protestants of the Cévennes continued to display complete indifference to prohibitions about marriage in Lent or Advent, and their co-religionists in Montpellier and Béarn respected them scarcely more.[107] In Metz, however, a clear and very marked tendency to avoid marrying in Lent, although not in Advent, reappeared from 1579 onward; indeed, the fall in the number of March marriages visible in this church between 1579 and 1599 was every bit as pronounced as in Catholic parishes of the era, and from the time of the League through the 1630s, its marriage registers even noted the date of Easter and the resumption of weddings in its aftermath. During the first six decades of the seventeenth century, pronounced respect for the Lenten interdict can also be clearly observed among the Protestants of Châlons-sur-Marne, Rouen, the Perche, Blois, Tours, Preuilly-sur-Claise and, after 1630, Mougon. By contrast, throughout the regions of Huguenot strength from the Vivarais across Languedoc to Béarn – as well as in Barbézieux, Alençon and Wassy – no attention whatsoever continued to be paid to the *temps clos*. Between these two extremes, a modest tendency to avoid March marriages can be observed in Loriol, Marennes and Niort. Only in Rouen and Châlons-sur-Marne were the Advent restrictions much observed.

From the chronology just revealed, it seems clear that, where French Protestants displayed signs of respect for the Catholic prohibitions against marriage during Lent and Advent in the seventeenth century, this was

---

106 The technique for calculating seasonal movements used throughout this study is that outlined in Henry, *Nouveau manuel*, pp. 103–5. Caen's Protestants may have been more hesitant about celebrating marriages during March. Here, just one of 27 recorded weddings for 1560–62 took place in March. Obviously, the number of cases is too small to attach much reliability to these figures.

107 It must be admitted that the case of Béarn poses some difficult problems of interpretation. The number of baptisms celebrated in March there fell well below the level one would expect if marriages were distributed evenly across the year, but the two communities in the sample for which evidence is available for the sixteenth century were characterized by a highly seasonal marriage pattern, in which over half of all weddings took place in winter from December to February. The number of weddings celebrated in April was also well below what one would expect if marriages were distributed evenly across the year. It is consequently hard to know whether the March dip was simply a part of broader seasonal rhythms which governed life in this part of the world or was linked to Lent in some way. It was, in any case, not very pronounced.

rarely if ever the product of uninterrupted fidelity to deeply rooted traditions. Instead, it appears to have been a mark of political insecurity and the desire not to offend Catholic sensibilities. Section 1 has already alluded to the considerable differences which distinguished the behaviour of those Protestants who lived in regions where the faith was pervasive and powerful from that of those who had been made acutely aware of their vulnerability by the events of the recurring civil wars, most especially by the Saint Bartholomew's Massacre.[108] In comparison with certain other aspects of Huguenot behaviour, the Protestants' disregard of traditional interdictions against marriage during Lent or Advent does not appear to have been especially shocking to their Catholic neighbours. Unlike conflicts over the burial place of recent converts or the Protestant refusal to pay the respect which the Catholics considered appropriate when encountering a procession in the street, the celebration of weddings during Lent was not a common cause of the anti-Huguenot *émotions* which punctuated the seventeenth century with some frequency, nor do Catholic peasants appear to have been particularly offended by remarks made in conversation that Lent was merely a human invention.[109] None the less, marrying during Lent did violate Catholic sensibilities, and the Huguenots surely wished to avoid this in those regions where they felt least secure. The geographic pattern of respect for Catholic prohibitions regarding Lent displays a clear correspondence with the regions where the Protestants were numerically most isolated and politically most vulnerable. But this distinction between those churches whose members displayed a tendency to avoid marriage in March and those whose members paid no attention to Lent is not simply the distinction between the churches of northern France and those of the Huguenot crescent. It is noteworthy that the Protestants of Wassy and Alençon dared to disregard the Lenten interdicts – a sign, I would hypothesize, that they felt safer about their local political

---

[108] See pp. 60, 75. For the very different attitudes governing Protestant behaviour in different parts of the country, see also Labrousse, 'La conversion d'un huguenot au catholicisme en 1665', *Revue d'Histoire de l'Eglise de France* 64 (1978), 57; Labrousse, Philippe Joutard, Janine Estèbe and Jean Lecuir, *La Saint-Barthélémy, ou les résonances d'un massacre* (Neuchatel, 1976), pp. 83–6; Philip Benedict, *Rouen during the Wars of Religion* (Cambridge, 1981), pp. 147–50, 242; Sauzet, *Contre-Réforme et Réforme Catholique en Bas-Languedoc*, pp. 190–201, 305–24.

[109] Benoist recounts numerous episodes of anti-Huguenot violence in the seventeenth century. None of these appears to have been provoked by marriages held during prohibited periods. See also *Plaintes des Eglises réformées de France, sur les violences et injustices qui leur sont faites en plusieurs endrois du Royaume* (n.p., 1597); Pierre Blet, *Le clergé de France et la monarchie: Etude sur les Assemblées Générales du Clergé de 1615 à 1666* (2 vols, Rome, 1959), II, 342–88; Marc Venard, 'Le comportement du peuple provençal face au fait protestant au XVIe siècle', in *Cinq siècles de Protestantisme à Marseille et en Provence* (Marseille, 1978), p. 33.

situation than most of their co-religionists of northern France. Equally noteworthy is the appearance of respect for these interdicts in the churches of Poitou and Saintonge after the revolts of the 1620s and their repression.

In 1662, a decision of the Conseil d'Etat made the prohibitions of the Roman church binding on the crown's Protestant subjects as well.[110] Now the Huguenots were legally required to abstain from marrying during Lent and Advent or to obtain a licence if they wished to do so. Combined with the general intensification of persecution during the years of Louis XIV's personal reign, this *arrêt* furthered the Huguenot tendency to respect the Catholic interdicts, but even it failed to generate universal compliance with these rules. Once again the pattern of compliance or non-compliance suggests that this was closely linked to each church's local political situation.

In the provinces of the Centre–West, the authorities were particularly vigilant about enforcing measures directed at the Huguenot population.[111] Here – in La Rochelle, Niort, Saint-Just and Marennes – March and December marriages fell off dramatically.[112] A greater, although by no means universal, respect for the Catholic prohibitions may also be seen in Loriol and Nérac. But the crown's writ still ran considerably weaker in Languedoc. From Castres and Revel to Montpellier and the Cévennes, the number of Protestant marriages celebrated during March was slightly lower than in the preceding or following months after 1662, but remained considerable. In Marsillargues, proportionately more marriages were celebrated during March than previously, while Lourmarin, Manosque, Montélimar and Nîmes were other communities in which the Protestants consistently defied this legislation with apparent impunity. Quite curiously, the frequency of March marriages by Protestants also increased in Blois, Tours and Alençon. When Elie Benoist wrote that the 'Reformez' paid no attention to the 1662 edict, he was reporting accurately the experience of his own church, but his statement cannot be generalized to all of the kingdom's churches.[113] In most northern churches, the drop-off in marriages during March was quite pronounced. But the regulations concerning Advent were far less widely respected here, as was the case throughout the century. It would appear that marriage during Advent was not as offensive to Catholic sensibilities as marriage during Lent, and that the legal prohibition of Advent marriages after 1662 was only enforced in the Centre–West.

---

110 Benoist, III, 479.

111 Ibid., III, 624 and *passim*; Faust, 'Beleaguered Society', p. 14 and *passim*.

112 For La Rochelle, see Faust, 'Beleaguered Society', p. 189. As the author does not provide annual index values, I have not included this case in Table 2.16.

113 Benoist, III, 623–4: 'Comme il [the arrêt of 1662] assujettissoit les Reformez aux loix canoniques, pour lesquelles ils n'ont jamais eu la moindre veneration, ils n'y defererent point; et ils continuerent par tout à benir les mariages en toute saison.'

In sum, in the first flush of the Reformation's implantation in France, the country's Huguenots violated canon law interdictions against March and December marriages with what one presumes to have been calculated insouciance. Following the Saint Bartholomew's Massacre, those living in regions where the faith was least secure recognized that discretion dictated that they ought to respect at least the Lenten interdict, and over the subsequent century more and more communities bowed to this rule, first as their political situation weakened, then as the legal obligation to do so was imposed. Still, even on the eve of the Revocation, the Protestants of large parts of the country continued to feel secure in defying the law on this score.

The examination of the seasonal movement of marriages contains other lessons as well. One of the most striking findings to emerge from the investigation of marriage seasonality in other Protestant countries is that, even where the pattern of marriage tied to the Catholic church calendar disappeared, the triumph of the Reformation did not necessarily involve the rationalization of attitudes toward the seasons that might be expected as a consequence. In many Calvinist regions, other beliefs about the appropriateness or inappropriateness of certain times for marriage took hold instead. Figures from the Low Countries show a pronounced tendency for marriages to cluster in May between 1670 and 1800.[114] For Geneva and the nearby Pays de Vaud, Perrenoud has documented the striking advance of a converse tendency to avoid marrying in May. This *creux de Mai* first appears in Genevan statistics in the 1570s and becomes marked from the turn of the century onward, enduring into the nineteenth century. In the surrounding countryside and in the city of Lausanne, it is already pronounced in the later sixteenth century, when parish registers first become available.[115]

The belief reflected in these Swiss figures, namely that May was an unlucky time for marriages, is well known to demographers and folklorists of France as well. Folklorists have collected numerous proverbs to the effect that May marriages are doomed to be short-lived or to yield sickly or deficient children, if any children at all. Demographers have shown that a tendency to avoid marrying in May spread gradually over the course of the nineteenth century, moving outward from two centres: the Mediterranean coast and the lower Loire valley and nearby Upper Poitou. The *creux de Mai* does not appear, however, in most

---

114 Mentink and ven der Woude, *Rotterdam*, p. 140; van der Woude, *Noorderkwartier*, p. 791; A.J. Schuurman, 'De bevolking van Duiven, 1665–1795: Een historisch-demografische studie', *A.A.G. Bijdragen* 22 (1979), 154. These authors provide no full explanation of this phenomenon.

115 Perrenoud, *Population de Genève*, p. 383–9; *idem*, 'Calendrier du mariage et coutume populaire: Le creux de Mai en Suisse romande,' *Population* 38 (1983), 925–40.

statistics on the seasonality of marriage from the last century of the *ancien régime*.[116]

After reviewing the various explanations which have been proposed to account for this phenomenon, Perrenoud argued that the idea that May was an unlucky time to marry was a widespread and deeply rooted popular belief – very possibly linked to the larger cycle of May *reinages* and courting festivities – which came under attack during the Counter-Reformation as the church sought to enforce its own calendar of prohibitions at the expense of all 'pagan' and 'superstitious' rivals. A provincial council held in Bordeaux in 1624 ordered all clerics in that archdiocese 'to uproot from people's minds the insane and superstitious notion some have not to wish to marry in the month of May, as if the month augured badly for marital fidelity and the prosperity of the marriage'. Only where or when the control of Rome had been rejected, Perrenoud suggests, whether at the Reformation or with the 'dechristianization' of the nineteenth century, could this belief flower. Far from being uncompromisingly hostile to all superstition, then, Calvinism may actually have provided more fertile ground than Counter-Reformation Catholicism for the development of certain beliefs about lucky and unlucky times.[117]

As Table 2.16 makes clear, the Huguenots of much of southern France came to share the aversion to May marriages. A clear *creux de Mai* is visible in communities from Dauphiné across Languedoc to the Agenais in the seventeenth century, appearing in Loriol, the Cévennes, Marsillargues, Montpellier, Castres, Vabre, Roquecourbe, Revel and Nérac. This phenomenon was confined to this region. The *creux de Mai* does not appear in Annonay, Provence, Béarn, or the Centre–West, nor does it make anything other than a single appearance in northern France

---

116 Arnold Van Gennep, *Manuel de folklore francais contemporain* 5 vols (Paris, 1937–47), I, 379–80; Jean Bourgeois, 'Le mariage, coûtume saisonnière: contribution à une étude sociologique de la nuptialité en France', *Population* 1 (1946), 623–42; Jacques Houdaille, 'Un indicateur de pratique religieuse: la célébration saisonnière des mariages avant, pendant et après la Révolution française (1740–1829)', *Population* 33 (1978), 367–79; Nicole Belmont, 'Le joli mois de mai', *L'Histoire* (May, 1978), pp. 16–25; Perrenoud, 'Calendrier du mariage et coûtume populaire', pp. 925–7. Of the many monographs and articles devoted to the historical demography of individual old regime communities or regions, I have encountered only one in which the examination of the seasonal movement of marriages reveals an eighteenth-century *creux de Mai*: Jean-Pierre Poussou, *Bordeaux et le Sud-Ouest au XVIIIe siècle: Croissance économique et attraction urbaine* (Paris, 1983), p. 613 (concerning Sainte-Foy-Tarentaise in Savoy).

117 Perrenoud, 'Calendrier du mariage et coûtume populaire', *passim*, esp. pp. 926–7. In a still unpublished paper, 'The Sacred and Conjugal Sexuality in Sixteenth-Century Lyon', Natalie Zemon Davis links the avoidance of marriage during May to traditional beliefs that women's sexual appetite was at its height in that month. 'Marrying under the sign of such disturbing sexuality', she argues, 'bode ill.' I would like to thank Professor Davis for showing me this paper before publication.

(Blois 1600–1659), an appearance that is in all probability a statistical fluke.

The records of Anduze and Montpellier, which extend back into the sixteenth century, permit us to establish some chronological boundaries to this tendency to avoid marriage during May. (See Table 2.17.) In both communities, the May dip emerges clearly only from the first decades of the seventeenth century onward, although a faint trace of such a pattern may be observed in Montpellier in the 1580s and Anduze in the 1590s. The *creux de Mai* thus represents here, as in Geneva, not the survival of pre-Reformation beliefs, but a new pattern of behaviour that only took hold in these two communities around the turn of the century.

As Table 2.17 also indicates, shunning May marriages was by no means an exclusively Protestant phenomenon in the seventeenth-century Midi. If French demographers of the *ancien régime* have not previously insisted much on the *creux de Mai*, this seems to be simply because so few parish register studies have been devoted to southern France for the period before the eighteenth century. The recent *Histoire de la population française* includes aggregated figures by region combining data about marriage seasonality for three decades between 1580 and 1689 that shows a tendency to avoid May marriages in the Midi and Rhône regions.[118] Soundings in early parish registers across Languedoc and Aquitaine reveal that the aversion to marrying in May was marked among the Catholics of Nîmes, Montpellier, Lunel, Nérac, Castelnaudary, Bordeaux and two villages of the modern department of the Aude – in other words, in both city and countryside and in regions that remained almost entirely faithful to Rome as well as those where the Catholics lived side by side with an important Protestant population.[119] Comparison of Catholic and Protestant behaviour within two confessionally divided cities, Nîmes and Montpellier, suggests

---

118 Dupâquier et al., *Histoire de la population française* II, 297–9.
119   Seasonal movement of marriages: Catholic communities of the Midi

		J	F	M	A	M	J	J	A	S	O	N	D	n
2 parishes of Aude*	1608–89	78	272	23	81	36	202	141	59	72	72	168	19	361
Bordeaux	1660–80	132	254	23	107	33	119	101	79	115	60	181	6	–
Castelnaudary	1630–70	117	252	30	143	22	204	105	54	80	48	154	12	1189
Lunel	1610–67	140	203	36	180	59	142	62	73	64	89	142	23	420
Nérac	1624–82	129	186	35	109	71	124	99	69	131	57	212	0	167

* Barbaira, Bellegarde-du-Razes

Sources: L.D.S. films 1179035 and 1179046 (A.D. Aude 1 E 27 and 1 E 32): M. Sudre, 'Aspects démographiques de la paroisse Saint-Michel de Bordeaux (1660–1680),' *Annales de Démographie Historique* (1974), 239; L.D.S. films 1217818–9 (A.C. Castelnaudary, GG 4, 7, 10, 12, 16, 22, 25, 30, 33, 37), 1179307, 730822 (A.D. Lot-et-Garonne, 4 E 199/18–19). May marriages were also avoided in Lyon in the 1570s and in the Morvan in the seventeenth century. Davis, 'Sacred and Conjugal Sexuality', p. 9; Jacques Houdaille, 'Quatre villages du Morvan 1610–1870', *Population* 42 (1987), 664.

Table 2.17 The appearance and evolution of the *creux de Mai*

	Anduze Protestants				Castres Protestants		
Years	Apr.	May.	Jun.	Years	Apr.	May.	Jun.
1562–79	114	99	97				
1580–96	117	103	113				
1610–23	153	59	130	1609–29	132	74	126
1642–59	138	43	105	1630–59	149	46	117
1660–83	205	30	81	1660–84	164	50	117

Montpellier

	Protestants				Catholics		
Years	Apr.	May.	Jun.	Years	Apr.	May.	Jun.
1562–68	130	121	96				
1580–89	110	92	112				
1602–16	156	61	126				
				1623–28	97	90	144
				1631–49	153	71	140
				1650–69	126	55	135
1668–80	158	68	114	1670–84	138	79	139

Nîmes

	Protestants				Catholics		
Years	Apr.	May.	Jun.	Years	Apr.	May.	Jun.
				1608–20	178	100	133
1625–39	115	73	110	1630–39	134	70	125
1640–59	155	47	127	1640–59	175	58	150
1660–84	153	40	114	1660–84	135	66	117
				1690–99	120	90	91

that the practice may have taken hold slightly earlier among the Huguenots in Montpellier than among their Catholic neighbours and that in both cities it may have begun to weaken slightly earlier among the Catholics than among the Protestants. Still, what is most striking is the parallelism between the behaviour of the two groups.[120] The belief in the unluckiness

---

[120] In interpreting the evidence in Table 2.17, it should be recalled that the 1620s were troubled years in Montpellier and that figures from this decade may reflect atypical patterns. Unfortunately, in the regions for which I have explored this issue, Catholic marriage registers exist for only a few, scattered years before 1600 and are too spotty to enable one to reconstruct the chronology and geography of this practice's spread.

of May marriages was clearly shared by Catholic and Protestant alike in important parts of France in the seventeenth century. Then, the belief weakened. By the 1690s, the *creux de Mai* had disappeared from the seasonal movement of marriages in Nîmes; it is scarcely visible in Bordeaux in 1711–15.[121]

What we are dealing with here is thus a popular belief, embraced by Catholics and Protestants alike, which waxed and waned at several different moments in French history. Is its eighteenth-century declension to be attributed to a successful assault by reforming Catholicism on 'superstition' and rival calendrical systems? One can wonder, since – the Bordeaux example to the contrary notwithstanding – concern with this issue was decidedly muted in synodal statutes from the Midi.[122] The practice may have come and gone for very different reasons, perhaps following a process of spreading enthusiasm sparked by reported events which appeared to confirm the belief, and subsequent disenchantment as such events became rarer, similar to the process governing the cycles in the popularity of healing shrines.[123] Reconstructing the full story of the rise and fall of the *creux de Mai* is another task that requires still more extensive investigation than it has been possible to carry out here.[124] The information assembled in this

---

121 Poussou, *Bordeaux et le Sud-Ouest au XVIIIe siècle*, p. 603.

122 I have examined the following synodal decrees for southern France: *Ordonnances et constitutions synodales decrets et reglemens, donnés au Dioceze de Bordeaux par feux Nosseigneurs le Cardinal de Sourdis, Henry Descoubleau de Sourdis, Henry de Bethune, Archeveques de Bordeaux, Reveus, confirmés et augmentés par Monseigneur Louis d'Anglure de Bourlemont, Archeveque de Bordeaux, Primat d'Aquitaine* (Bordeaux, 1686); *Statuts synodaux du dioces d'Alby, publiez au synode tenu le XXVI May MDCXCV* (Paris, 1695); Simon de Peyronet, *Jus sacrum ecclesiae tolosanae* (Toulouse, 1669); *Statuts et reglemens synodaux du diocèse d'Agen. Leus et publiez depuis l'année 1666 renouvelez et confirmez dans le Synode tenu à Agen les 11 et 12 du mois d'Avril 1673* (Agen, 1673); *Statuts synodaux du diocese d'Alet, Faits depuis l'année 1640 jusque'en 1674* (Paris, 1675); *Ordonnances synodales pour le diocese d'Uzes avec le prosne et autres formulaires necessaires pour l'administration des sacrements* (Nîmes, 1635; another ed. Montpellier, 1654); *Ordonnances synodales du dioceze de Rodez* (Rodez, 1674). Only the synodal statutes of Agen refer to the issue, urging parish curés to seek to abolish 'distinctions de mois et de jours heureux ou mal-heureux pour le mariage' as part of a far broader assault on superstitions. Among the many synodal references to superstition assembled by Jean-Baptiste Thiers in his *Traité des superstitions* (2nd edn, Paris, 1697–1704), denunciation of the belief in lucky or unlucky days or months for marriage appears in the statutes of the diocese of Sens for 1658, of Evreux for 1664, and of Grenoble for 1690. Thiers's own discussion of superstitions regarding time (Part 1, Book 4, ch. 3) makes no reference to the belief that May was an unlucky time for marriage.

123 William A. Christian, Jr, *Person and God in a Spanish Valley* (2nd edn, Princeton, 1989), 50–78, esp. pp. 64–5.

124 Ideally, such an investigation would trace as precisely as possible both the geographic and chronological contours of this phenomenon over time and the sociology of those who either embraced or defied it.

study none the less underscores several larger points of importance. First, the two confessions clearly did not form self-enclosed worlds of belief and practice in seventeenth-century France. New cultural or folkloric elements which arose independently of either theological system could become shared by the faithful of both. Second, it has become increasingly evident in recent years that the image of *méridional* Calvinism as so complete and powerful a system of religious culture that it effaced all competing folk beliefs or cultural practices – a picture encapsulated in the image of *cévenol* women singing psalms to their babies as lullabies – is overdrawn. Reformed synodal records from later seventeenth-century Dauphiné reveal the continued strength of practices which made May a month of maypoles, 'desbauches et insolences', charivaris and 'ranconnements de mariages'. A community of Huguenot refugees in Hesse has preserved to the present day May customs that were once traditional in the uplands of Dauphiné from which the founders of this community emigrated, but have now disappeared from Dauphiné itself.[125] Anduze's consistory records reveal the survival of magical practices and conjuring well into the second half of the seventeenth century, and nineteenth-century folklorists found that *cévenol* Protestants continued to seek remedies against the evil eye then.[126] The spread of the *creux de Mai* throughout Huguenot communities of the Midi provides still more evidence of this coexistence of Calvinism and 'popular culture'.

Lent and conceptions

In addition to the sharp drop in the number of marriages during March and December, the seasonality of demographic events followed the Roman church calendar in a second way, too, in traditional Catholic Europe. A small but clear dip in conceptions is visible during Lent in virtually all the Catholic regions for which the seasonal movement of conceptions has been calculated from a number of cases sufficient to yield reliable results.

Where the decline in marriages during Lent and Advent clearly resulted from the provisions of canon law, the cause of this March dip in conceptions has been the subject of extended debate. Initially, modern demographers tended to attribute the fall in conceptions during March to church teachings

---

125 Pierre Bolle, *Le protestant dauphinois et la république des synodes à la veille de la Révocation* (Lyon, 1985), p. 171; Jean Imbert, 'La Mayence dauphinoise en pays Hessois', *Le Monde Alpin et Rhodanien*, 1 (1974), 185–7.

126 A.C. Anduze (at A.D. Gard), GG 45, fols 116, 315; Joutard, 'Protestantisme populaire et univers magique', pp. 151–5. The Anduze consistory records also testify to the survival of a vigorous and rowdy *abbé de jeunesse* still able in the 1660s to extract its traditional levy upon newly married couples despite repeated attempts to end this practice on the part of both the consistory and the *consulat*.

which discouraged sexual intercourse during Lent. In the early Middle Ages, it was strictly forbidden to make love during Lent. By the close of the Middle Ages, this *necessitas obedientiae* had become a *consilium reverentiae*, but it was still recommended as such by preachers and catechists during the sixteenth and seventeenth centuries.[127] If fewer children were conceived during March, this was because at least a fraction of the Catholic faithful followed these precepts.

But not all historians have been willing to ascribe the fall in conceptions to greater continence during Lent on the part of the Catholic faithful. In an article published in 1974, François Lebrun expressed the most serious doubts.[128] Abstinence from sex during Lent, he noted, was urged neither in the numerous seventeenth-century sets of synodal statutes nor in such influential devotional handbooks of the era as Saint François de Sales's *Introduction à la vie dévote*. Once Jansenism developed, it was awkward for non-Jansenist priests to counsel parishioners to refrain from intercourse during Lent, since one of the rigorist positions of Jansenism which mainline churchmen denounced as erroneous was a revival of the older claim that abstinence was positively required during this period. Furthermore, Lebrun investigated the movement of conceptions in one rural parish whose priest was a committed Jansenist and found no increase in the respect for continence during Lent as a result of this priest's tenure, but rather a decline. Lebrun's arguments were not entirely convincing. His calculation of seasonal fluctuations in the Jansenist parish rested on too few cases to be statistically significant, and he himself cited seventeenth-century texts which instructed priests to exhort their parishioners to continence during times of fast. Furthermore, he offered no alternative explanation that would explain the March dip in conceptions. None the less, his article opened up once again a question that had appeared to be closed.

The most spectacular discovery concerning the March dip in conceptions was recently made by Jean-Pierre Bardet. In his study of Rouen's population, he found that fewer conceptions occurred during Lent not only within the population at large, but also within two sub-populations whom one would hardly expect to show much respect for Catholicism's teachings about sexual continence in Lent: the Protestants, and the mothers of illegitimate children. Only common conditions imposed on all of these groups could account for this pattern, he reasoned. The dip

---

127 Etienne Hélin, 'Opinions de quelques casuistes de la Contre-Réforme sur l'avortement, la contraception et la continence dans le mariage', in Hélène Bergues et al., *La prévention des naissances dans la famille: Ses origines dans les temps modernes* (Paris, 1960), pp. 247–9; Davis, 'Sacred and Conjugal Sexuality', pp. 3–4.

128 Lebrun, 'Démographie et mentalités: Le mouvement des conceptions sous l'Ancien Régime', *Annales de Démographie Historique* (1974), 45–50. See also Pierre Chaunu, *La civilisation de l'Europe des Lumières* (Paris, 1971), p. 132.

must have resulted from temporary sterility provoked by the changes in diet associated with Lent, an explanation proposed by Jacques Dupâquier as well.[129] Since butchers' shops were closed by law during Lent, no town-dweller could avoid the church's ban on eating meat and butter. Of course, it might be wondered if the ordinary *ancien régime* Frenchwoman's diet included enough meat and butter for immediate physiological consequences to follow from being unable to eat these. Still, if the Bardet–Dupâquier interpretation is correct, the March dip in conceptions reflects not voluntary but imposed asceticism. Rabelais would certainly have been pleased to learn of this difference of opinion among modern schoolmen, since the terms of the debate are precisely those which set Pantagruel and Friar John to arguing: do seasonal movements in the number of conceptions around Lent result from changes in diet or in actual sexual behaviour?

Care must be exercised in calculating the seasonal movement of conceptions among the Huguenots. While the standard method for determining this, extrapolating backward nine months from the seasonal movement of baptisms, is acceptable in studies involving communities where the delay between births and baptisms was brief, such techniques can lead to misleading conclusions for communities where parents commonly waited weeks or even months before having their infants christened. A comparison of the movement of births and baptisms in Anduze around mid-century reveals that in certain periods of the year, most notably July and September, the town's Protestant inhabitants waited longer before having their children baptized than in others. Consequently, the seasonal movement of baptisms fails to convey accurately the seasonal movement of births. For most Huguenot congregations, one must patiently note down the precise date of birth for each child to determine the seasonal pattern of conceptions.

This has been done for two communities whose registers regularly note the date of birth as well as of baptism, Anduze and Annonay. The movement of baptisms has also been utilized for four congregations located in parts of France where the typical delay between birth and baptism does not appear to have been long: Niort, Tours, Alençon and Rouen.[130] The results are set forth in Table 2.18. To these cases could be added that of the Brie, studied by Eva Telkès, who found no decline in March conceptions there.[131]

---

129 Bardet, *Rouen* I, 311–16; Dupâquier, *Population rurale du Bassin Parisien*, pp. 325–9, 380–81.

130 The figures for Tours are taken from Maillard, 'Religion et démographie', p. 549.

131 Telkès, 'Les Protestants en Brie au 17ème siècle: Approche démographique et socioéconomique' (unpubl. *mémoire de maitrise*, Université de Paris, 1971), unpaginated. Telkès does not provide the precise monthly figures.

Table 2.18   The seasonal movement of conceptions

Community and dates	No. of cases	O J	N F	D M	J A	F M	M J	A J	M A	J S	J O	A N	S D
						Month of birth or baptism:						
						Month of conception:						
Rouen, 1630–84	–	109	112	98	107	102	110	104	91	85	89	96	97
Alençon, 1620–80	2666	94	101	93	105	118	118	115	95	91	84	87	99
Niort, 1623–36,'70–80	3881	103	95	111	120	128	109	95	92	67	76	93	113
Anduze, 1609–83	6385	113	107	123	113	114	97	90	89	84	86	86	100
Annonay, 1600–64	3368	113	102	106	116	117	106	91	90	85	87	94	93
Tours, 1632–84	–	110	125	85	101	100	103	99	103	87	81	100	106

The results of this exercise just add to the uncertainties involved in seeking to make sense of the March dip in conceptions. As can be seen, the same March dip found in Rouen appears in Alençon and Tours. But in Niort, Anduze and Annonay, as in the Brie, no decline emerges.

If the legal closing of butchers' shops were the key to the March dip in conceptions, then we would expect to find such a dip everywhere among the Huguenots except where they controlled local government or felt that they could defy the regulations banning the sale of meat during Lent. Edicts forbidding meat from being sold or served publicly during Lent were promulgated by the crown in 1549 and 1563, as Protestantism grew in strength in France. They were reiterated locally in certain areas in the seventeenth century after violators were found infringing them, or as part of broader anti-Huguenot campaigns.[132] It is clear, however, that the Huguenots could ignore them with impunity in certain regions of seventeenth-century France. A Dutch traveller noted with some pleasure that a Protestant innkeeper served him meat on a Friday in Pons in 1635, while according to Elie Benoist, it was common for all the rules concerning Catholic fast days to be ignored in those regions where the Huguenots formed a majority of the population and dominated the *consulat*.[133] In light of this, it is not surprising to find no March dip in a Huguenot town such as Anduze or even in Annonay, where the Protestants formed roughly half of the population. But the absence of such a dip in Niort admits of no such explanation, since the Huguenots were in the minority here and the authorities in Poitou seem generally to have been vigilant in their

132 Nicolas Delamare, *Traité de la police* (Paris, 1722), I, 388; Jacques Decanter, 'La vie municipale à Rochechouart de 1639 à 1643', *Bulletin de la Société Archéologique et Historique du Limousin* 95 (1968), 180.

133 Hans Bots, 'Voyages faits par de jeunes hollandais en France. Deux voyages types: Gysbert de With et Nicolas Heinsius', in *La découverte de la France au XVIIe siècle* (Paris, 1980), p. 475; Benoist, III, 23–4, 40.

enforcement of the laws concerning Protestant behaviour. Indeed, according to a complaint of the 1601 provincial synod of Poitou, officials in nearby Saint-Maixent even conducted house-to-house searches on fast days to ensure that the Protestants were not eating meat.[134]

If forced to explain the evidence which has come to light with regard to this question to date, one might argue that the decline in March conceptions within France's Catholic population resulted from the combination of abstinence from sex and dietary changes during Lent, and that those Protestant communities sharing a similar decline were particularly prosperous urban ones within which the legal closure of butchers' shops would have altered members' diets sufficiently to provoke a visible drop in the number of conceptions. But it must be admitted that this explanation is highly speculative. The mysteries of this particular *creux de Mars* continue to defy simple explanation. We have not progressed much beyond Rabelais.

'Paillardise'

A final area where demographic statistics can illuminate the degree of respect accorded moral norms espoused by the churches lies in the area of sexual morality, as revealed by statistics of illegitimate births and premarital conceptions. Few scholars today would pose the question in precisely the same terms as Locke: 'Were the Reformed better than the Papists?' Nor is it possible, after the many recent studies devoted to the history of courtship practices and of bastardy, to view the strength of commitment to religious teachings as the only force controlling levels of illicit sexual activity in early modern Europe. Local customs governing courtship and the degree of sexual intimacy permitted fiancés varied widely from region to region, and these produced significant regional variations in the rates of illegitimate births and prenuptial conceptions. Within the Paris Basin, for instance, illegitimacy rates seem to have been consistently higher in Normandy than anywhere else, and pregnancy out of wedlock does not seem to have brought the shame upon the young couple that it did in the Ile-de-France.[135] Economic conditions also exerted their influence. Illegitimacy rose in periods of economic difficulty, while Segalen hypothesizes that the amount of freedom given young people during courtship was linked to the local distribution of economic power. In regions characterized by considerable

---

134 B.P.F., MS 579 (1), fol. 31.

135 Dupâquier, *Population rurale du Bassin Parisien*, pp. 367–70. See also the important collection of essays edited by Peter Laslett, Karla Oosterveen and Richard M. Smith, *Bastardy and its Comparative History: Studies in the History of Illegitimacy and Marital Nonconformism in Britain, France, Germany, Sweden, North America, Jamaica and Japan* (Cambridge, Mass., 1980).

economic inequality and sharp class lines, free contact between all of the young people of the village posed a threat to maintaining the social order, and customs were more restrictive than in areas where wealth and property were more equally distributed.[136] For all the importance of these forces, however, the influence which the religious climate exercised on sexual behaviour remained considerable. Perhaps the most striking evidence of this is the astoundingly low levels of illegitimacy and of prenuptial conceptions found in Geneva in the generation immediately following the Reformation. An illegitimacy rate of 0.14 per cent and prenuptial conceptions of just 1 per cent are striking confirmation of the reformation of manners in this city which so enchanted godly visitors.[137] It is obvious that figures on illicit sexual activity can tell us something about the actual prevalence of that great concern of Calvinist consistories and Catholic confessors alike, 'paillardise'.

Tables 2.19 and 2.20 set forth information about extramarital sexual conduct within several Huguenot congregations in the seventeenth century. Where figures are available about the Catholic population of the same or nearby communities, these have been provided as well in order to permit comparisons between the two faiths that are affected as little as possible by variations in regional customs.

What emerges from these figures is the remarkable infrequency with which babies were conceived out of wedlock. None of the communities for which information is available here reveals rates of either illegitimate births or premarital conceptions quite as low as late sixteenth-century Geneva – not even Meaux and Chalandos in the virtuous Brie. None the less, all witnessed relatively few such events. Furthermore, wherever comparisons are possible with nearby Catholic populations, the Protestant rates turn out to have been lower. Gregory Hanlon's work on Layrac has shown that such interconfessional comparisons of illegitimacy rates must be interpreted with caution. While Protestant women in Layrac bore fewer illegitimate children than their Catholic counterparts, the town's consistory records contain several cases of men denounced for fornication that are not echoed by entries in the baptismal registers recording the christening of their offspring. This was a region where the Protestants tended to be the more prosperous residents of the chief settlement of the community

---

136 Martine Segalen, *Love and Power in the Peasant Family*, tr. Sarah Matthews (Chicago, 1983), pp. 21–4; David Levine and Keith Wrightson, 'The Social Context of Illegitimacy in Early Modern England', in Laslett et al., *Bastardy and its Comparative History*, pp. 158–75. The link which these last authors identify between peaks of illegitimacy and periods of economic crisis is corroborated as well by French figures for the later years of Louis XIV's reign. Molinier, *Stagnations et croissance*, pp. 369–70; Kathryn Norberg, *Rich and Poor in Grenoble 1600–1814* (Berkeley, 1985), pp. 95–7.

137 Monter, 'Historical Demography and Religious History', pp. 414–16.

Table 2.19   Illegitimacy rates: illegitimate births as percentage of all baptisms

Protestants		Catholics	
Alençon (1620–85)	0.03	Bayeux (17th c.)	1.2
		Tourouvre au Perche (1640–1729)	0.8
Anduze (1642–64)	0.6	Sérignan (1650–80)	0.9
La Rochelle (1625–83)	0.5		
Layrac (1610–74)	0.5	Layrac (17th c.)	1.0
Meaux & Chalandos (17th c.)	0.02	Coulommiers (1670–1790)	0.3
		Argenteuil (1670–95)	0.3
Montjoux	0.9		
Puylaurens (1630–50)	1.2		
Rouen (1631–85)	0.8	Rouen (1670–89)	3.5

Sources: Alençon: B.P.F., fonds Robert; Bayeux, Tourouvre, Coulommiers and Argenteuil: Dupâquier, *Population rurale du Bassin Parisien*, pp. 369–70; Anduze: L.D.S. films 670776–7; Sérignan: Alain Molinier, 'Une paroisse du Bas Languedoc: Sérignan, 1650–1792', *Mémoires de la Société Archéologique de Montpellier* XII (1968), 164; La Rochelle: Faust, 'Beleaguered Society', p. 192; Layrac: Gregory Hanlon, *Confession and Community*, p. 147 (the Catholic figure for this community is given as being 'in the vicinity of one per cent'); Meaux and Chalandos: Telkès, 'Protestants en Brie', n.p.; Montjoux: Jean Sambuc, 'Le registre des protestants de Montjoux (Drôme) 1608–1669 suivi d'une étude sur la famille des seigneurs dudit lieu', *B.S.H.P.F.* CXV (1969), 92; Puylaurens: G.E. de Falguerolles, 'Les paroissiens de l'Eglise réformée à Puylaurens (1630–1650)', *B.S.H.P.F.* CXI (1965), 94; Rouen: Bardet, *Rouen*, II, 176.

and the Catholics the less wealthy inhabitants of the surrounding hamlets, and it was common across France at this time for illegitimate births to be the product of relationships between higher-status men and lower-status women, especially servants. The higher rates of illegitimacy recorded in the Catholic parish registers of the region thus may stem in part from the offspring of such mixed couplings.[138] More generally, as the figures for Alençon remind us, the children of wealthier families seem to have cleaved more tightly to prescribed standards of sexual behaviour than did those of artisan or labourer stock, and part of the observable difference between the Catholic and Protestant figures stems in other cases as well from the frequent position of the Protestants as something of a local economic élite.[139] But this explanation can hardly account for the low rates of

---

138 Hanlon, *Confession and Community*, p. 147.

139 This was especially true in Alençon, La Rochelle and, to a lesser degree, Rouen.

Table 2.20   Premarital conceptions: children born within seven months of their parents' marriage as percentage of all first births

Protestants		Catholics	
Alençon (1640–84)	5	Bayeux (1640–1700)	8
'notables'	4		
non-'notables'	11		
Anduze (1654–65)	4	Sérignan (1650–80)	11
Annonay (1640–70)	3	Bourg-St-Andéol (1662–1715)	15
La Rochelle (1630–83)	4		
Meaux & Chalandos (17th c.)	2	Coulommiers (1670–1790)	4
		Argenteuil (1670–95)	7
Rouen (17th c.)	6	Rouen (17th c.)	10

Sources: Alençon (n = 129): B.P.F., fonds Robert; Bayeux, Coulommiers and Argenteuil: Dupâquier, *Population rurale du Bassin Parisien*, pp. 369–70; Anduze (n = 77): L.D.S. films 670776–7; Sérignan: Molinier, 'Une paroisse du Bas Languedoc', p. 164; Annonay (n = 222): L.D.S. films 1069212–3; Bourg-Saint-Andéol (n = 33): Molinier, *Stagnations et croissance*, p. 362; La Rochelle (n = 1657): Faust, 'Beleaguered Society', p. 192; Meaux and Chalandos (n = 230): Telkès, 'Protestants en Brie', n.p.; Rouen: Bardet, *Rouen*, I, 325 (the caption on this table is in error).

prenuptial conceptions found in either Anduze, where virtually the entire population of the town was Protestant, or Meaux, where the Huguenot community was composed primarily of *vignerons* and other agricultural workers.[140] While it was a staple of Huguenot sermons to deplore the sinfulness of the *troupeau* and to attribute any misfortunes which befell the community to the increasing wickedness of its members, the evidence regarding Protestant sexual behaviour suggests that, within a country and an era generally characterized by remarkably low rates of illegitimate births and premarital conceptions, the Huguenots cleaved a bit more tightly yet than their Catholic neighbours to ruling standards of sexual morality.

Is this to be attributed to the tight consistorial surveillance to which they were subjected? Obtaining a precise idea of just how closely the ministers and elders watched the behaviour of church members is extremely difficult. The national synod of 1579 decreed that 'all offences which are duly admitted and for which amends have been made will be removed from the Consistory Books, except those accompanied by disobedience which have been punished by suspension from the Lord's Supper or Excommunication'.[141] A brief examination of several surviving

---

[140] Telkès, 'Protestants en Brie', unpaginated.
[141] Aymon, *Tous les Synodes Nationales*, p. 141.

seventeenth-century consistorial registers suggests that this rule was not always followed to the letter.[142] In certain years before 1661, for example, Anduze's records note cases that came before the consistory which did not result in suspension from communion.[143] None the less, the majority of consistorial registers from this period appear to record primarily administrative matters concerning the running of the church, decisions about the distribution of charity, and general warnings issued to the congregation about misbehaviour – not investigations of reported individual misdemeanours – without it being clear how fully this represents the entire scope of the consistory's activities. From the Anduze records, it appears that the intensity of disciplinary surveillance did not come close to approaching the sort of institutionalized spying found in the most rigorously controlled Reformed communities. In nearly all the cases of suspected sexual immorality that were taken up by Anduze's consistory, the evidence of wrongdoing would have been known to much of the community; either the woman in question was pregnant, a man was maintaining a 'femme mal vivante' in his house, or a group of young men had attempted to drag a young woman from her house 'aux fins de malverser avec elle'.[144] Once again, however, the secretary of the consistory may have seen fit to put down in writing only those cases which had already created a degree of community scandal. There may also have been a further level of consistorial investigation of private sins that has been forever lost from view. If the cases recorded in Anduze's consistorial register

---

142 I examined the registers of Anduze, 1659–73 (A.C. Anduze at A.D. Gard, GG 45); Niort, 1629–84 (Bibliothèque Municipale de Poitiers, MS dom Fontenau, XXXVII, fols 2–137); and Blois, 1665–77 (Paul de Félice, *La Réforme dans le Blaisois: Documents inédits* [Orleans, 1885; repr. edn, Marseille, 1979]). For other studies which make use of seventeenth-century consistory records, see Hanlon, *Confession and Community*; Solange Bertheau, 'Le consistoire dans les Eglises réformées du Moyen-Poitou au XVIIe siècle', *B.S.H.P.F.* 116 (1970), 527–8; Alfred Leroux, 'L'Eglise réformée de Bordeaux de 1660 à 1670 (d'après le cinquième registre du Consistoire)', *B.S.H.P.F.* 69 (1920), 177–208; J.-P. Hugues, *Histoire de l'Eglise réformée d'Anduze* (Montpellier, 1864), pp. 556ff.

143 After 1661, a new secretary took over. Subsequently, the register not only records no such cases of disciplinary matters which did not lead to suspension from communion; the number of cases noted which did result in this penalty also drops off sharply. Continuing references to people readmitted to the peace of the church suggest that suspensions from communion none the less continued to be handed out. Hanlon also reports loquacious consistory records for Layrac before 1630, 'when a cloak of silence falls over the proceedings of the consistory'.

144 I had hoped to be able to see just how effective consistorial surveillance was by examining whether or not those couples who could be determined through family reconstitution techniques to have engaged in premarital intercourse drew the attention of the consistory. Unfortunately, none of the cases where children were born to couples in Anduze within seven months of their marriage occurred during the years when the register I examined provides details about disciplinary cases.

can be taken to speak for the level of consistorial surveillance throughout France, then the low rates of illegitimate births and premarital conceptions found in the seventeenth-century Huguenot churches must be attributed at least as much to the church members' internalization of values condemning illicit sex, or to the fear of community shame, as to the external pressure of ecclesiastical discipline. Far more research in the consistory records will be needed, however, before any confident statements can be made about this.

Conclusion

Within the historiography of seventeenth-century French Protestantism, itself dominated by historians of Huguenot stock, the chief interpretative debate of the past generation has concerned the vitality of the community in the generations preceding the Revocation of the Edict of Nantes. The debate began when the leading historian of the subject, Emile G. Léonard, broke polemically with the previously reigning *topos* of an innocent and defenceless community unjustly persecuted, in his 1961 *Histoire générale du Protestantisme*. Léonard suggested instead that the Reformed community bore a degree of responsibility for its ultimate fate in the France of Louis XIV, to the extent that it had allowed itself to be weakened internally over the course of the century by too many compromises with the monarchy and *le monde*.[145] This diagnosis appealed to the prophetic streak so pronounced in Pierre Chaunu, who, in a long review essay, extracted from Léonard's work the lesson that the community was 'spiritually sick' until it was saved *in extremis* by 'the beneficial ... revival of persecution'.[146] Most recent work has tended to reject this picture of the Huguenot community in the seventeenth century as unduly pessimistic, but few among the *petit troupeau* of historians who have written about this group have been able to ignore Léonard's ideas.[147]

For historians approaching the history of French Protestantism less out of a desire to come to grips with the strengths and weaknesses of their

---

[145] Léonard, *Histoire général du Protestantisme* (3 vols, Paris, 1961–64), II, 331–50.

[146] Pierre Chaunu, 'Les crises du XVIIe siècle de l'Europe réformée', *Revue Historique* 223 (1965), 36, 59.

[147] See, for instance, Garrisson, *L'édit de Nantes et sa Révocation*; Solange Deyon, *Du loyalisme au refus: Les Protestants français et leur Député Général entre la Fronde et la Révocation* (Lille, 1976); Pierre Bolle et al., *Le Protestantisme en Dauphiné au XVIIe siècle* (n.p., 1983); Elisabeth Labrousse, *'Une foi, une loi, un roi?' La Révocation de l'Edit de Nantes* (Geneva, 1985). Cf. Philippe Joutard, 'The Revocation of the Edict of Nantes: End or Renewal of French Protestantism?', in Menna Prestwich, ed., *International Calvinism 1541–1715* (Cambridge, 1985), pp. 339–68, esp. p. 367.

own tradition than out of a broader interest in the nature of religious life in the post-Reformation era, a different range of questions may seem better suited to illuminating the history of this religious minority. Once a stable situation of religious toleration was established in France, how much movement was there back and forth from one confession to the other? A generation after the initial establishment of Reformed churches in France, how thoroughly had their members internalized the practices and values incarnated in the official theology of the religion? How great were the differences between those regions where the new faith was imposed from above by an act of state and those where it was voluntarily embraced by its adherents? And to what extent did Protestantism and Catholicism form rival, self-enclosed worlds of belief and practice in this bi-confessional polity? Questions such as these, it might be suggested, offer the promise not only of illuminating the Huguenot experience, but also of breaking the history of this relatively small religious minority out of the ghetto to which it still is too often confined, so that it may become more fully integrated into the broader social history of post-Reformation European Protestantism and of what German historians call the 'confessionalization process'.

The information assembled in this study can be seen to speak to both of these *problématiques*. The evidence of Section 1 suggests that, forty years after the initial establishment of Reformed churches, the level of popular attachment to these institutions varied greatly between the one part of France where the religion was imposed from above as an act of state, Béarn, and the rest of the country. In the former region, roughly three-fifths of the population reverted to Roman Catholicism as soon as it was possible to do so, and the ranks of the Protestants continued to dwindle significantly even after this date. Elsewhere in France, the number of Protestants also declined nearly uninterruptedly between the first decade of the seventeenth century and 1685, but the overall drop-off was only in the vicinity of 25 per cent over these eight decades. The decline had multiple causes: a net outflow of converts toward Catholicism, the loss of lives and adherents which accompanied the revolts of the 1620s, the gradual erosion of Protestant strength in many cities due to immigration from a more heavily Catholic rural hinterland, the lack of demographic dynamism in such heartlands of Protestant strength as the Cévennes, and some emigration, accelerating to major proportions only after 1681.

In certain regions, to be sure, the decline in Protestant strength dramatically altered the balance of local power. Such erstwhile Huguenot capitals as La Rochelle and Montpellier came to house a majority of Catholics by the second half of the century. Exclusively Huguenot Montauban saw a significant Catholic element arise within its walls, and the substantial communities of such northern cities as Caen, Alençon and

Metz all shrank markedly in size. Without such changes in these cities' confessional makeup, such royal actions as that of placing Montauban's *consulat* entirely in Catholic hands in 1661 would not have been possible.

None the less, the overall impression that emerges is of a confessional community which successfully retained the attachment of the majority of its members throughout the period running from the Edict of Nantes to its Revocation – although significant regional differences distinguished much of western and south-western France, where the erosion of Protestant strength was not inconsiderable, from other regions of Huguenot strength, where the ranks of the faithful held up much better. The dizzying expansion which Protestantism knew for a brief moment on the eve of the Wars of Religion was halted and reversed by the civil wars and the violence which accompanied them. Once a measure of peace was finally established nearly four decades later, confessional identity had been more or less firmly fixed throughout the kingdom of France properly speaking. The Reformed churches might still win over a few converts. They might lose a few more, particularly in regions such as Aquitaine and Saintonge. Most people, however, continued to identify with what had by now become the faith of their ancestors, despite continuing Catholic missionary efforts and mounting legal pressure to return to the Roman fold. Furthermore, most of the causes of the gradual numerical erosion that did occur within the Protestant ranks are not ones which suggest fundamental weaknesses in the community's institutional fibre, although they do perhaps reflect poorly on the wisdom of political decisions made in the 1620s. It certainly seems exaggerated to suggest that the Protestant community would have died out over the long run had it not been for the reinvigorating shock of the Revocation.

The impression of a well-structured community also emerges from evidence assembled about Huguenot religious comportment. The rapid rejection of prohibitions against Lent and Advent marriages, the steady advance of a Protestant understanding of baptism, and the low rates of extramarital sexual activity all suggest a religious community in which the moral and theological principles articulated by the church leaders were widely shared among the faithful. Such a conclusion, it is worth stressing, could only be reached through the use of statistical methods such as those employed here. The archives of repression, notably consistory records, can indicate the forms of behaviour which the church sought to eliminate, but they can never indicate with certainty how widespread such practices might have been and whether they increased or diminished with time, for the simple reason that one can never be certain whether changes in the number of recorded cases concerning a specific offence indicate alterations in the frequency of the offence or in the amount of attention devoted to it by those doing the repressing. Such records can provide evidence about the persistence of Catholic practices, but they cannot demonstrate their gradual abandonment. A satisfactory history of Protestant religious practice must exploit more than these documents alone.

While commitment to Protestant tenets was widespread, Calvinism was by no means a total ideology. The emergence of the *creux de Mai* in Protestant marital patterns throughout the Midi shows that the members of the faith were at least as receptive as their Catholic neighbours to extra-ecclesiastical cultural beliefs about lucky and unlucky seasons. The reappearance of a tendency to avoid marriages during Lent in many regions shows that, where the Protestants were a relatively small and cowed minority, they accepted certain Catholic rhythms of life rather than risking offence against ingrained religious sensibilities. At the same time, the fact that the Catholic inhabitants of certain heavily Protestant regions also began to postpone the baptism of their children for a week or more shows that other Catholic religious sensibilities were not as deeply ingrained as might previously have been thought. A degree of interpenetration of religious practices clearly occurred between the two confessional groups living side by side in seventeenth-century France. They were not hermetically sealed communities of belief and practice.

Perhaps as important as any of the broader conclusions which can be drawn from this study are the unresolved, and previously unseen, questions to which it calls attention. Was the inability displayed by the rural and small-town congregations of much of western France to resist significant numerical erosion as successfully as their counterparts in Languedoc or Dauphiné the product of different patterns of Protestant–Catholic interaction? Of the force of seigneurial influence in the initial establishment of Reformed churches in the West? Of other salient differences between churches in different regions? Does the rapid falling away from Protestantism once Catholic worship was re-established in Béarn testify to the superficial protestantization inherent in all attempts to impose a Reformation from above on a predominantly rural population, or to particular failings in the way in which the Reformation was implemented in this particular statelet? Why did the population of the Cévennes stagnate in the seventeenth century? Can any persuasive correlations, either positive or negative, be established between the belief in the unluckiness of May marriages and either Calvinism or the Counter-Reformation? As Joseph Schumpeter once wrote, 'We need statistics not only for explaining things, but also in order to know precisely what there is to explain.' In the process of establishing the changing numerical contours of the Protestant community in seventeenth-century France, this study has also tried to suggest some new things to explain. If the social history of French Protestantism in this era is to be invigorated, such new problems may be precisely what is needed.

CHAPTER THREE

Faith, Fortune and Social Structure in Seventeenth-Century Montpellier

In the past few decades, historians of continental Europe, especially of Germany, have articulated the theme of 'confessionalization' and shown its utility for illuminating how western Christendom became split between rival religious families in the wake of the Reformation, and reorganized around fidelity to the increasingly precisely defined statements of orthodoxy that each set forth in its confessions of faith.[1] Twenty years ago, Hans-Christoph Rublack urged historians of this process to add to their research agenda the simple question: 'How "deep" did confessional differentiation cut?'[2] In so far as his appeal has been heard – and we are, in fact, only beginning to understand how such matters as literacy or demographic practices varied across the confessional spectrum – discussion of this question has scarcely engaged with one of the classic questions of Reformation historiography: the degree to which the members of the different post-Reformation churches might have differed from one another in their economic attitudes, behaviour or performance. Earlier historians and social scientists argued with gusto the fine points of what became enshrined in the literature as the 'Weber thesis debate'. The recent social history of the Reformation has accorded little systematic attention to this topic, even though its methods now permit the investigation of the question in ways unknown to earlier generations.

Issues once considered important often cease to inspire scholarly investigation after a time, not because they are fully resolved, but because they come to appear stale, outmoded, politically discreditable, or implausible in the light of other knowledge about the period. To a large extent, that is what has happened to the Weber thesis debate. The view that Protestantism, particularly its Calvinist variants, begat the particularly

---

[1] Ernst W. Zeeden did the most to articulate this theme, especially in his *Die Entstehung der Konfessionen: Grundlagen und Formen der Konfessionsbildung im Zeitalter der Glaubenskämpfe* (Munich, 1965). The prominence it has subsequently attained is attested by such works as Heinz Schilling, ed., *Die reformierte Konfessionalisierung in Deutschland: Das Problem der 'Zweiten Reformation'* (Gütersloh, 1986); Harm Klueting, *Das konfessionelle Zeitalter, 1525–1648* (Stuttgart, 1989); Hans-Christoph Rublack, ed., *Die lutherische Konfessionalisierung in Deutschland* (Gütersloh, 1992).

[2] Hans-Christoph Rublack, 'Konfession als demographischer Faktor?', in Horst Rabe, Hansgeorg Molitor and Hans-Christoph Rublack, eds, *Festgabe für Ernst Walter Zeeden* (Münster, 1976), p. 62.

dynamic or unfettered pursuit of gain was a nineteenth-century common-place even before Weber provided the most famous explanation of why this might have been so in *The Protestant Ethic and the Spirit of Capitalism*. Weber's arguments initially provoked a great deal of fruitful research, especially into the economic ethics of the different churches in the sixteenth and seventeenth centuries. But with time, the debate about his views ossified into an increasingly scholastic exercise, tangled in exegetical disputes about what he really said and generating diminishing returns in terms of original empirical research. In the past generation, the advance of ecumenical attitudes and the new understanding of the devotional practices and social ethos of post-Tridentine Catholicism offered by scholars such as H.O. Evennett, John Bossy and Louis Chatellier led specialists in the history of continental Europe to see that the very assumption that Protestantism stimulated economic success might rest less on reliable evidence than on hostile caricature, derived in Weber's case largely from the *Kulturkampf*.[3] In place of the older contrast between an economically dynamic and modernizing Calvinism and a Catholicism whose adepts 'lived ethically, so to speak, from hand to mouth', the leading German historians of a neo-Weberian persuasion now argue for a transconfessional process of 'social disciplining', sometimes presented in crudely functionalist fashion as the ideological handmaiden of state-building, with comparable economic and political consequences for the 'two Reformations'.[4] This interpretative shift occurred largely independently of any detailed research into the comparative economic behaviour of the members of the different confessions.

---

3 Philippe Besnard, *Protestantisme et capitalisme: la controverse post–wébérienne* (Paris, 1970), pp. 7–8; Jean Bauberot, 'La vision de la Réforme chez les publicistes antiprotestants (fin XIXe–début XXe)', in Philippe Joutard, ed., *Historiographie de la Réforme* (Neuchâtel, 1977), pp. 226–7; Gordon Marshall, *In Search of the Spirit of Capitalism: An Essay on Max Weber's Protestant Ethic Thesis* (New York, 1982), p. 20; Paul Münch, 'The Thesis before Weber: An Archaeology', in Hartmut Lehmann and Guenther Roth, eds, *Weber's Protestant Ethic: Origins, Evidence, Contexts* (Cambridge, 1993), pp. 51–71; H. Outram Evennett, *The Spirit of the Counter-Reformation* (Cambridge, 1968); John Bossy, *Christianity in the West, 1400–1700* (Oxford, 1985); Louis Chatellier, *L'Europe des dévots* (Paris, 1987).

4 Max Weber, *The Protestant Ethic and the Spirit of Capitalism*, trans. Talcott Parsons (New York, 1958), p. 116; Wolfgang Reinhard, 'Gegenreformation als Modernisierung? Prolegomena zu einer Theorie des konfessionellen Zeitalters', *Archiv für Reformationsgeschichte*, 48 (1977), 226–51; Wolfgang Reinhard, 'Zwang zur Konfessionalisierung? Prolegomena zu einer Theorie des konfessionellen Zeitalters', *Zeitschrift für historische Forschung* 10 (1983), 257–77; Heinz Schilling, 'Die Konfessionalisierung im Reich – religiöser und gesellschaftlicher Wandel in Deutschland zwischen 1555 und 1620', *Historische Zeitschrift* 246 (1988), 30–45; Ronald Po-Chia Hsia, *Social Discipline in the Reformation: Central Europe, 1550–1750* (London, 1989); Heinz Schilling, 'Confessional Europe', in Thomas A. Brady, Jr, Heiko A. Oberman and James D. Tracy, eds, *Handbook of European History, 1400–1600: Late Middle Ages, Renaissance and Reformation*, 2 vols (Leiden, 1994–5), II, pp. 641–81.

Of course, grand interpretations of the prominence of the Weber thesis do not vanish overnight from the historical imagination. They continue to inspire comment from researchers starting from other questions who unearth information relevant to them, and they retreat from the scene at an uneven pace among scholars of different national and topical specializations. Thus, several recent historians whose research has illuminated the relative economic position of Protestants and Catholics in multi-confessional German cities of the early modern era have been moved by their findings to comment on the Weber thesis – in directly contradictory fashion. In Oppenheim, Augsburg and Colmar, it has been discovered, the Protestants, both Lutheran and Reformed, were on average wealthier than their Catholic neighbours, although they were also disproportionately represented among the poorest inhabitants of Augsburg. In Oppenheim, furthermore, they also had larger reserves of grain in storage, even when controlled for wealth.[5] In his study of Oppenheim, Peter Zschunke presents these findings as substantiation of the Weber thesis, albeit with the significant modification that Lutheranism was fully as conducive as Calvinism to the development of attitudes favourable to economic success.[6] But his research fails to explore the extent to which the differences in wealth observable between the rival faiths might simply have stemmed from the play of migration in this historically Protestant town, where the majority of Catholics were recent immigrants. This is one of the factors considered crucial by Etienne François in his study of Augsburg. Explicitly rejecting any sort of 'elective affinity between capitalism and Protestantism', François insists instead upon 'indirect and thus largely contingent causes' to account for the Lutherans' greater wealth. Specifically, he highlights the different profile of the two religious communities in the wake of the devastations of the Thirty Years War and confession-specific contrasts in the subsequent pattern of immigration into the city. The overall picture that emerges from his original and deeply researched study is of two religious groups that did not differ markedly from one another in their demographic or economic comportments – indeed, whose members often collaborated economically with one another – but that remained sharply

---

[5] Peter Zschunke, *Konfession und Alltag in Oppenheim: Beiträge zur Geschichte von Bevölkerung und Gesellschaft einer gemischtkonfessionellen Kleinstadt in der Frühen Neuzeit* (Wiesbaden, 1984), pp. 114–25, 267; Bernd Roeck, *Eine Stadt in Krieg und Frieden: Studien zur Geschichte der Reichsstadt Augsburg zwischen Kalenderstreit und Parität*, 2 vols (Göttingen, 1989), II, 890–902; Etienne François, *Protestants et catholiques en Allemagne: identités et pluralisme. Augsbourg, 1648–1806* (Paris, 1993), pp. 96–145; Peter G. Wallace, *Communities and Conflict in Early Modern Colmar, 1575–1730* (Atlantic Highlands, 1995), esp. pp. 62–88, 163–76, 275. All these comparisons draw primarily upon the evidence of tax records.

[6] Zschunke, *Konfession und Alltag in Oppenheim*, pp. 114–25, 267.

separated by the 'invisible frontier' of different confessional identities, memories and conceptions of the other group.[7] But neither author, it must be said, pursued very systematically the reasons for the observed differences, nor did either compare across time the relative wealth mobility of the members of the different religious faiths living in the city he studied.[8]

Historians of Britain and British North America have been understandably slower to assimilate the work on European Catholicism that challenged older assumptions about Protestantism's distinctive modernizing character, while Weberian themes have always been especially prominent in the historiography about Great Britain and New England.[9] It is therefore not surprising that, even as arguments about the importance of Protestantism in making the modern world have largely disappeared from the literature about the Continent, important recent studies of Scotland and Massachusetts reiterate the view that Protestant doctrine contributed significantly to the process of economic development in these regions.[10] Even the most thorough and methodologically sophisticated of these studies seem insular and unconvincing to one familiar with the literature highlighting the similarities between the social ethics and pious praxis of post-Reformation Catholicism and Protestantism on the Continent, for the simple reason that it is virtually impossible to avoid *post hoc ergo propter hoc* logic when dealing with regions overwhelmingly loyal to one church. Perhaps the clearest example of the problems involved in trying to substantiate a Weberian interpretation through a study of these societies is provided by the most systematic and methodologically original of such works, Gordon Marshall's study of Calvinism and the development of capitalism in early modern Scotland, *Presbyteries and Profits*. Marshall is able to demonstrate that the themes and anxieties that Weber diagnosed as characteristic of mature Calvinism – labour in one's calling, asceticism,

---

[7] François, *Protestants et catholiques en Allemagne, passim*, esp. p. 128.

[8] Peter Wallace does offer information of this sort – without, however, making the problem an explicit focus of analysis: Wallace, *Communities and Conflict in Early Modern Colmar*, pp. 76, 171, 257. His evidence shows significant fluctuations over time in the relative average wealth of the members of the rival confessions.

[9] I have traced elsewhere the reception of Weber's ideas in Britain and the United States, as well as among historians of continental Calvinism: Philip Benedict, 'The Historiography of Continental Calvinism', in Lehmann and Roth, eds, *Weber's Protestant Ethic*, pp. 305–25.

[10] T.C. Smout, *A History of the Scottish People, 1560–1830* (London, 1969), ch. 3, esp. pp. 96–100; Gordon Marshall, *Presbyteries and Profits: Calvinism and the Development of Capitalism in Scotland, 1560–1707* (Oxford, 1980); James A. Henretta, 'The Weber Thesis Revisited: The Protestant Ethic and the Reality of Capitalism in Early America', in his *The Origins of American Capitalism: Collected Essays* (Boston, 1991), pp. 35–70 (a highly nuanced argument); Stephen Innes, *Creating the Commonwealth: The Economic Culture of Puritan New England* (New York, 1995).

predestination and the concern for proof of personal election – became more common in Scottish Calvinist preaching as the sixteenth century gave way to the seventeenth. He is able to demonstrate that the behaviour of Scottish entrepreneurs displayed more systematic, calculating and economically rational habits of minds as the seventeenth century advanced. But he is unable to demonstrate any necessary connection between these two developments, largely for want of a non-Calvinist control group.

Given the elements of avoidance, contradiction and variation across national cultures that currently characterize the historiography pertaining to this topic, a direct investigation of possible differences over time in the economic behaviour or performance of Catholics and Protestants living in the same community seems potentially rewarding. Necessarily, such an investigation must be comparative and statistical. If those elements of Protestant – or more specifically of Calvinist – doctrine thought to stimulate inner-worldly asceticism, rational economic calculation, and accumulation actually affected behaviour in the manner postulated by Weber and his disciples, then this should reveal itself through the more successful enrichment of Calvinist than of Catholic families in the same community. Unless such differences can be found within confessionally mixed communities, then Occam's razor ought to be applied to arguments that continue to insist upon the importance of religious factors for the economic history of overwhelmingly Calvinist regions such as Scotland or New England.

This chapter attempts such an investigation, inspired by the conviction that if the old Weberian themes are taken as simple hypotheses to be investigated with the techniques of the now not-so-new social history, they remain a useful starting-point for exploring the question of how deep confessional differences cut in early modern society, as well as a stimulus to valuable archival prospecting. The precise focus will be upon the social structure and wealth of the two major confessional groups within an important provincial town in seventeenth-century France, Montpellier. Changes in the wealth and social composition of these two groups will be followed from 1600 to 1670, the core of the longest uninterrupted period of legal toleration for the 'so-called reformed religion' under the provisions of the Edict of Nantes.

This topic has been virtually unstudied to date, despite the considerable amount of recent research on the French Reformation inspired by the methods and questions of social history, since the overwhelming focus of this work has been on the sociology of the Calvinist movement in its initial phase of growth between 1555 and 1565. How conversion to Protestantism might have been influenced by occupational status, wealth, or literacy has been much explored; how those who embraced the faith subsequently evolved in comparison with their Catholic neighbours far less so. It is known that between the Edict of Nantes in 1598 and its revocation in 1685, the ranks of the Protestant minority declined modestly in numbers, with the largest urban communities often shrinking the most in relative strength simply because city populations in this era did not reproduce themselves naturally and the surrounding countryside rarely contained as many members of the faith. Over this same span, a significant fraction of the high Protestant nobility converted to Catholicism, while the ranks of Protestant office-holders thinned and a growing percentage of members of the faith pursued commercial careers.[11] But whether the increasing legal vexations and limitations with which the Protestants found themselves faced, especially in the years after 1661, led to any slippage in their economic situation, or whether on the contrary they were able to increase their wealth relative to their Catholic neighbours, remains unknown.

Montpellier offers a particularly appropriate locale to investigate this question, for three reasons. First of all, it was a fairly substantial city of roughly average demographic dynamism and considerable economic diversity. With approximately 15 500 inhabitants in 1600 and 22 500 in 1700, it was one of roughly two dozen French provincial towns of what might be called second-level importance, a cut below such provincial giants as Marseilles, Toulouse, or Lyons, but exercising considerable regional influence. It was the second administrative capital of Languedoc, home to the province's sovereign tax-courts and, after 1632, an intendant. The celebrated medical faculty brought its university European renown. Commercially, it was no longer the great hub of Mediterranean trade that it had been in the fourteenth and fifteenth centuries, but it still served as the chief marketplace for the region's wine trade and a centre for the importation and preparation of Mediterranean wool, demand for which grew as Languedoc's textile industries emerged as the kingdom's most dynamic in the late seventeenth and eighteenth centuries. The city's own textile workers produced fustians, woollen blankets and other cloths, while many women made verdigris, a dyestuff valuable enough to be mentioned alongside the pastel of Toulouse in Lodovico Guicciardini's celebrated account of Antwerp's trade at the end of the sixteenth century.[12] This

---

11 Daniel Ligou, *Le protestantisme en France de 1598 à 1715* (Paris, 1968), pp. 192–207; Kathleen L.M. Faust, 'A Beleaguered Society: Protestant Families in La Rochelle, 1628–1685' (Northwestern Univ. Ph.D. thesis, 1980), pp. 118–20; above, Chapters 1 and 2.

12 Lodovico Guicciardini, *The Description of the Low Countreys and of the Provinces thereof*, ed. Thomas Danett (London, 1593, S.T.C. 12463), p. 37; Louis J. Thomas, *Montpellier, ville marchande: histoire économique et sociale de Montpellier des origines à 1870* (Montpellier, [1936]), pp. 128–51; Frederick M. Irvine, 'From Renaissance City to Ancien Régime Capital: Montpellier, c.1500–c.1600', in Philip Benedict, ed., *Cities and Social Change in Early Modern France* (London, 1989), pp. 105–33; Anne Blanchard, 'De Pézenas à Montpellier: transfert d'une ville de souveraineté (XVIIe siècle)', *R.H.M.C.* 12 (1965),

combination of administrative and commercial importance accounts for Montpellier's healthy demographic expansion over the course of the seventeenth century. But its growth was hardly atypical of France's cities in this period. The mean population growth of those towns for which we have reliable demographic estimates at the beginning and end of the century was 42 per cent, only slightly below the figure registered by Montpellier.[13]

Secondly, no other French city of comparable size and socioeconomic diversity was as equally divided between Catholics and Protestants for the full course of the period in question. At the close of the Wars of Religion, the Huguenots formed the slightly more numerous party, accounting for 57–60 per cent of the town's inhabitants.[14] With the renewal of civil war in 1621, they were strong enough to seize control of the city and prohibit Catholic worship, but a two-month siege in 1622 ended in their capitulation and reduced the Protestant population. A devastating plague in 1629 further winnowed the ranks of indigenous town-dwellers. In the years that followed, royal edicts transferred local political dominance to the city's Catholics; a decree of the early 1630s mandated equal representation for each religious group within the city council, and a second measure of 1656 gave the Catholics exclusive control. The demographic balance also swung in the Catholics' favour. Between 1635 and 1639, 62 per cent of those drawing up marriage contracts in the city made arrangements to wed in the Roman church. By the 1660s, seven out of every ten residents were Catholic. But the Huguenots still remained a large minority – larger, in all likelihood, than in any other French city of comparable size except Montauban or Nîmes, both of which had been thoroughly Protestant dominated at the beginning of the century.[15] A city so closely balanced between the two faiths offers a particularly appropriate site for attempting comparisons between significant samples of Protestants and Catholics.

35–49; Arlette Jouanna, 'De la ville marchande à la capitale administrative (XVIe siècle)', in Gérard Cholvy, ed., *Histoire de Montpellier* (Toulouse, 1984), pp. 127–56; Anne Blanchard and Henri Michel, 'De la place forte à la capitale provinciale: des réformes aux lumières', ibid., pp. 157–223; Reed Benhamou, 'The Verdigris Industry in Eighteenth-Century Languedoc: Women's Work, Women's Art', *French Historical Studies* 16 (1989-90), 560–75.

[13] Philip Benedict, 'French Cities from the Sixteenth Century to the Revolution: An Overview', in Benedict, ed., *Cities and Social Change in Early Modern France*, pp. 25, 28.

[14] The lower estimate is based on the evidence of church affiliation as indicated within those marriage contracts for the period 1605–9 joining two people of the same faith. The higher estimate derives from a comparison of the number of baptisms celebrated in the city's Catholic parishes and Reformed church for the years 1610–19.

[15] For the shifting demographic balance of the two faiths, and extensive comparative information about the size of Protestant communities in other cities, see above, chapter 2, pp. 61–3, 75–81. For the legislation concerning the composition of the city government, see Blanchard and Michel, 'De la place forte à la capitale provinciale', p. 190.

The third feature that commends Montpellier for the purposes of this study is the survival of good sources from which such comparisons can be made. Thousands of the marriage contracts that virtually every one of Montpellier's inhabitants, rich or poor, drew up when betrothed survive today in the city's archives. The quasi-universality of this practice can be inferred from the marriage records of the city's Reformed church, which for certain years list not only the dates on which the successive banns were read out for each couple, but also the date on which their marriage contract, if any, was signed. Almost without exception, each entry notes the existence of a marriage contract alongside the names of the couple intending to marry.[16] The records of some of the notaries whose names are found in these registers have subsequently been lost, with the result that the number of seventeenth-century marriage contracts preserved today in Montpellier's archives represents only about 60 per cent of the total number of marriages actually celebrated in the city at this time.[17] Furthermore, as will shortly be explained, certain peculiarities of local legal practice mean that a significant fraction of the surviving contracts do not convey as accurate a picture of the total assets with which the couples in question began their life together as do marriage contracts from other French cities. The most complete of Montpellier's marriage contracts none the less list the occupation of the prospective groom, his father and his bride's father, thereby allowing a look at changing patterns of occupational choice and the transmission of status across generations. Virtually all indicate the church in which the marriage was to be celebrated, thus revealing the religious affiliation of the future couple. And virtually all record a financial exchange between the contracting parties and their families, thus providing a rough indication of the prospective wealth of the couple-to-be. I have examined the archival resources of most of the larger French cities of the seventeenth century that contained a significant fraction of Protestants. For no other that I know of is it possible to obtain as widely representative and as richly revealing an insight into evolving patterns of wealth as is permitted by the marriage contracts from Montpellier.

---

16 For 1636 and 1637, banns were read for 93 people; reference is made to the existence of a marriage contract in all but one of these cases: A.C. de Montpellier, GG 367.

17 There is no reason to suspect that the lost notarial registers skew the representativeness of those that survive. The estimated survival rate of the registers is based on a comparison of the number of surviving marriage contracts for the years 1605, 1608 and 1665–69 that I was able to locate with the number of acts in the city's Catholic and Protestant marriage registers for these years. The estimate is only approximate, for the records of Montpellier's Reformed church do not list all marriages celebrated before the church, but rather all couples for whom banns were read. The years in question are the only ones for the three five-year sample periods used for this study (p. 129 below) for which full sets of parish registers exist for all of the city's different churches.

Marriage settlements, of course, may not be a fully reliable indicator of changing wealth trends, for historians have detected certain moments when elite groups in late medieval and early modern Europe invested a growing percentage of their wealth in procuring adequate matches for their offspring.[18] It is difficult to believe, however, that such 'dowry inflation' could by itself account for significant long-term changes in the size of marriage portions across the entire population of a variegated city, much of whose female population depended as much upon its own labour as upon the transmission of property from a previous generation to accumulate a dowry. For the eighteenth century in France, a period about which considerably more research has been undertaken utilizing both marriage contracts and other sources that shed light on individual wealth, it has been shown that marriage settlements and *post mortem* personal estates increased in Chartres in virtual unison over the course of the century.[19] No sources exist for seventeenth-century Montpellier that could be used to determine if the same held true there. Strictly speaking, therefore, the results presented in this chapter provide data about changes in family wealth only among newly formed couples. It would be surprising, however, if this were not roughly representative of broader wealth trends among the different components of the urban population.

For the purposes of this study, complete samples of all surviving contracts drawn up in the city and involving a prospective bridegroom residing in Montpellier have been selected for three five-year periods at 30-year intervals. The first sample covers the years 1605–9, the latter half of the decade of reconstruction and prosperity under Henri IV that followed the bitter civil wars of the late sixteenth century. The second covers 1635–39, another period of reconstruction following the renewed civil war and plague of the 1620s, but one which also coincided with the outbreak of war with Spain and which, to judge by the smaller number of marriages celebrated in this period and the particular scarcity of marriage contracts involving textile workers, appears to have been one of some economic difficulty. Finally, the third covers 1665–69, an era of renewed peace and prosperity during which the number of marriages celebrated rose to levels considerably higher than in either of the preceding five-year periods. Together, these three samples contain 1554 contracts. They permit one to form an idea of changes in the city's wealth and social structure across three generations from 1600 to the 1660s, to compare the Protestant and Catholic segments of the population, to see how their relative wealth and occupational contours changed over time,

---

[18] For the best-documented such case of which I am aware, see Lawrence Stone, *The Crisis of the Aristocracy, 1558–1641* (Oxford, 1965), pp. 641–2.

[19] Benoît Garnot, *Un déclin: Chartres au XVIIIe siècle* (Paris, 1991), p. 96.

and even, occasionally, to link members of the same family over several generations.[20]

In order properly to interpret the evidence provided by these 1554 marriage contracts, certain of their basic characteristics must first be understood. The overwhelming majority of Montpellier marriage contracts maintained a sharp distinction between the property of each of the two parties who intended to wed. Marriage involved a two-part exchange of property. First, 'since a dowry must be provided on the woman's part so that the expenses of marriage may be more easily borne' (to quote the conventional formula of the contracts), the family of the bride-to-be gave a combination of money and property to the future groom as a dowry, to be used by him during the duration of the marriage but to be returned to the woman or her family in the event that either he predeceased her or she died without children. Secondly, in order to help whichever party to the marriage might outlive the other to bear the burden of widowhood, each agreed to provide the other with a specified 'augmentation' of the dowry as a sort of insurance policy against being left bereft of a spouse. With only the rarest of exceptions, the augmentation provided by the man was exactly twice that provided by the woman. This may well be an indication of the relative contribution each party was assumed to make to the domestic economy.

Ninety-eight per cent of all contracts specify the size of the augmentation promised by each party, so virtually every contract provides some indication of the wealth of the couple-to-be. But many of the contracts, especially those drawn up by women whose parents were both dead, fail to indicate the precise size of the dowry, instead stating simply that the woman will provide 'all and each of her rights, names, shares and movable and immovable goods, present and future, wherever they might be situated'. In certain other localities where an augmentation of the dowry was a regular part of the marriage exchange, a fixed ratio obtained between the dowry and the augmentation. This, unfortunately, was not the case in Montpellier. The augmentations here clustered strongly around a few round

---

[20] The following notarial *liasses* were examined for the purposes of this study: A.D.H. 5 E 6011, 53035, 55034–9, 55074, 55092–6, 55122, 55126, 55128, 55136, 55139–43, 55172, 55206, 56036, 56070–71, 56106, 56158–62, 56181–2, 56191–2, 56194–5, 56204–7, 56219–22, 56225, 56255–9, 56307–10, 56327–8, 56344–5, 56351, 56372–6, 56406–10, 57025–34, 57037, 57071–5, 57104–6, 57134–8, 57171–5, 57202–6, 57216–18, 57245–9, 57266–7, 57270–71, 58008–10, 58031–5, 58039, 58067–72, 58408, 59012–16, 59029–31, 60011, 60015–20, 60057–63, 60086–7, 61008–12, 61018, 61031, 61040–44, 61112, 62031–2, 62043–5, 62051–2, 62078–82, 62131, 951611–13, 951636–8, 951645 and 951662–5. All marriage contracts within these registers were identified and examined, and those from the years in question involving a bridegroom resident in Montpellier retained for closer inspection. The sample contains 535 contracts from 1605–9, 420 from 1635–39 and 599 from 1665–69.

numbers – the sums of 30, 50, 60, 100 and 200 *livres* account for 66 per cent of all cases in my sample – and they are perhaps best interpreted as figures representing widely shared notions of the amount of money needed to help widows or widowers who had previously enjoyed a certain level of well-being to maintain their standard of living. The dowries, by contrast, varied far more from case to case. A few were smaller than the augmentation promised in return. Others exceeded the augmentation by a factor of ten. The majority were from two to four times as large as the augmentation. Some correlation can none the less be observed between the size of the two sums, and this permits the calculation of a rough estimate of the size of the dowry for those cases where its precise size is not specified, on the basis of the median ratio of dowries to augmentations in those cases where both are specified.[21] Because of the variations from case to case, these estimates must be recognized as nothing more than rough approximations, accurate when aggregated for large numbers of cases, but highly suspect for individual contracts.

In addition to frequently requiring the researcher to infer the approximate size of the dowry involved in a marriage from the amount of the augmentation, Montpellier's marriage contracts contain other, more predictable omissions that result from variations in the assiduity of individual notaries. Table 3.1 spells out just how complete the information is.

Bearing in mind the lacunae in the records, what can we learn from the marriage contracts? The first finding that they suggest, and one of the most interesting, is that the city as a whole enjoyed increased prosperity over the sixty-year period under discussion. This is worth highlighting, because so much of the literature on French economic and social history depicts the seventeenth century as a period of economic crisis or stagnation, a 'phase B' in the language of François Simiand made familiar to

---

21 The following procedure was used to calculate estimated dowries. It was observed that the ratio of dowry to augmentation tended to be higher for marriage contracts involving large dowries than for those involving smaller ones, with a 300-*livre* augmentation being the clearest watershed. Those marriage contracts indicating both dowry and augmentation were therefore used to calculate two ratios, one for contracts with augmentations greater than 300 *livres*, the other for contracts with augmentations at or below that threshold. The resulting ratios (3.6 : 1 and 3.33 : 1) were then used to generate a first estimation. In certain cases where the dowry is not specified in full, details are none the less provided about portions of it. In a few of these cases, the details indicate that the dowry must have been larger than the first estimate generated by extrapolating from the augmentations. For these cases, the evidence about dowry size provided directly by the contract has been taken to be the estimated dowry, despite its apparent incompleteness. Naturally, where the dowry is indicated in full, this information has been retained; for all other cases, the extrapolation from the augmentation has been used. Frederick Irvine employs similar, although not identical, procedures in his outstanding study 'Social Structure, Social Mobility and Social Change in Sixteenth-Century Montpellier: From Renaissance City-State to *Ancien-Régime* Capital' (Univ. of Toronto Ph.D. thesis, 1979), esp. pp. 248–9.

Table 3.1   Information contained in Montpellier marriage contracts

	% of all cases		
	1605–9	1635–39	1665–69
Dowry specified	42	26	38
Groom's occupation specified	88	89	88
Groom's place of birth specified	82	88	93
Groom's father's occupation given	35	44	57
Bride's place of birth specified	85	87	89
Bride's father's occupation given	46	49	59
Church of marriage known	95	99	99

Note and sources: For the sources of Tables 3.1–3.10, see n. 20. In a certain number of cases where the marriage contract fails to specify the church in which the wedding was to be solemnized, the religion of the parties to the marriage has been determined from the city's parish registers, which survive for both faiths for the greater part of the century.

historians of this period by Pierre Goubert.[22] From one period to the next, Montpellier's young people entered into marriage with increasing resources. The mean value of the augmentations specified in the contracts increased from 229 *livres* in the first period (n [number of marriages] = 525), to 283 in the second (n = 413), to 421 in the third (n = 595). In those smaller number of cases where the dowry was indicated, it rose from an average of 1250 *livres* (n = 222) in the first period, to 2258 in the second (n = 110), to 3008 in the third (n = 226). If the average dowry is calculated for all cases using the techniques for estimating missing dowries indicated above, these figures become, respectively, 840, 1152 and 1638 *livres*. In other words, the average sums of money that prospective marriage partners promised one another roughly doubled between 1605–9 and 1665–69.[23] This increase was in no way the result of inflation. Basic commodities remained stable in price across this period. The average price of a measure of wheat sold in nearby Béziers scarcely fluctuated at all between the three periods in question here.[24]

---

[22] François Simiand, *Recherches anciennes et nouvelles sur le mouvement général des prix du 16e au 19e siècle* (Paris, 1932); idem, *Les fluctuations économiques à longue période et la crise mondiale* (Paris, 1932); Pierre Goubert, 'The French Peasantry of the Seventeenth Century: A Regional Example', *Past and Present* 10 (Nov. 1956), 55–77; idem, *Beauvais et le Beauvaisis de 1600 à 1730: contribution à l'histoire sociale de la France du XVIIe siècle* (2 vols, Paris, 1960).

[23] Specifically, the increase was of 84 per cent in the average augmentation, 95 per cent in the average estimated dowry, and 140 per cent in the average dowry whose precise amount was specified in the contracts.

[24] The average price of a measure of grain in the market of Béziers for 1604–10 was 5.51

Furthermore, this growing prosperity appears to have been spread across all groups in the urban population – in sharp contrast to the preceding 60 years, when lawyers and robe officials increased their wealth far more dramatically than any other members of Montpellier's population. Between the two periods 1540–59 and 1600–19, as Frederick Irvine has shown, the average inflation-adjusted dowry received by lawyers and robe officials more than doubled, but the dowries of artisans and *laboureurs* increased by just 33 and 16 per cent respectively, while those received by merchants and bourgeois declined.[25] By contrast, as Table 3.2 reveals, the members of all major groups within the urban population were able by the sixth decade of the seventeenth century to promise dowries for their daughters or augmentations for their future brides that were between 66 and 109 per cent more generous than those provided by their counterparts 60 years earlier.[26] The increase was slightly greater among the high officials and nobles, but the prosperity of the period was shared remarkably evenly. Other recent studies have also provided evidence of a general enrichment of the population of two other cities of comparable character, Dijon and Bordeaux.[27] In light of that evidence and of the fact that marriage portions in Montpellier increased so consistently across the social hierarchy, it seems unlikely that the increase observed here is primarily due to an inflation of dowries. It offers instead further evidence that the larger cities of seventeenth-century France may have been more dynamic centres of economic growth and transformation than was previously thought.

A look at changes within the occupational makeup of the city provides still more evidence of this. Although the samples of marriage contracts are too small to permit fine-grained analysis of possible changes in the

---

livres tournois; for 1634–40, 5.34 *livres tournois;* and for 1664–70, 5.46 *livres tournois:* Emmanuel Le Roy Ladurie, *Les paysans de Languedoc* (2 vols, Paris, 1966), II, 821–2.

25 Irvine, 'Social Structure, Social Mobility and Social Change in Sixteenth-Century Montpellier', p. 117.

26 To compute an aggregate measure of the enrichment of each group, the index values of the augmentations and dowries have been averaged together, with due weight given according to the number of cases in each category. The results obtained are: agricultural or urban workers, 185; artisans, 166; merchants, 182; professionals, 189; nobles and high officials, 209.

27 James R. Farr, *Hands of Honor: Artisans and their World in Dijon, 1550–1650* (Ithaca, 1988), pp. 94–104; *idem*, 'Consumers, Commerce, and the Craftsmen of Dijon: The Changing Social and Economic Structure of a Provincial Capital, 1450–1750', in Benedict, ed., *Cities and Social Change in Early Modern France*, p. 158; Martin Dinges, *Stadtarmut in Bordeaux, 1525–1675: Alltag, Politik, Mentalitäten* (Bonn, 1988), pp. 63, 237. Dinges states that his data, drawn from probate inventories, suggest stagnation rather than growth in the real value of the personal property owned by members of the lower orders in Bordeaux, but it should be noted that he deflates the absolute values indicated in the documents on the basis of an index that overstates the degree of inflation between 1600 and 1675, computing change with reference to a single year (1602) of abnormally low grain prices.

Table 3.2   Mean augmentation and estimated dowry of selected occupational categories in Montpellier (n = number of marriages)

Category	1605–1609		1635–1639		1665–1669	
	Augm.	Dowry	Augm.	Dowry	Augm.	Dowry
Agricultural or urban workers	44	220	88	291	84	392
	n=106	n=50	n=102	n=42	n=99	n=86
Artisans	78	306	107	485	120	575
	n=228	n=96	n=173	n=88	n=247	n=140
Merchants	252	1573	498	1676	494	2460
	n=37	n=30	n=41	n=32	n=77	n=40
Professionals	645	2091	900	3508	1138	4366
	n=46	n=13	n=28	n=18	n=37	n=23
Nobles or high officials	1774	6080	3400	15 325	2884	16 629
	n=23	n=27	n=10	n=9	n=33	n=24

Note: monetary values provided are in *livres tournois*. The estimated dowries have been grouped according to the status of the bride's father. In practice, women accumulated their dowries from a variety of sources – inheritance from the paternal and maternal lines, contributions from other relatives and friends, and their own work – with the parental contribution diminishing in relative significance as one descended the social hierarchy. The parental contribution, understood as a combination of direct monetary provision and the provision of social capital, was none the less the largest element. Classifying the estimated dowries according to the status of the groom instead of that of the bride's father would not significantly alter the results obtained.

city's social structure, a rough classification utilizing the evidence about the grooms' occupations provided by the contracts suggests that the overall makeup of Montpellier's population changed little over these 60 years. (See Table 3.3.) Within this broadly static population, however, the number of people categorized as merchants of some sort expanded significantly, from 7.9 per cent of the young men married between 1605 and 1609 to 14.5 per cent of those married between 1665 and 1669. This attests a growing commercialization of the regional economy.

How did the two religious communities that lived alongside one another within this prospering city compare in wealth and occupational distribution? As already indicated, a great deal of scholarship over the past 25 years has been devoted to determining the sociological characteristics of those who embraced Protestantism in the years between 1555 and 1565 when the first permanent Reformed churches were established in the kingdom and thousands of people pledged their adherence. While the many local studies devoted to this question have revealed considerable variation from one location to another, most have reached the conclusion that the early Protestant movement drew very few

Table 3.3   The social composition of Montpellier's population,
1605–9 to 1665–69

Category	1605–9		1635–39		1665–69	
	No.	%	No.	%	No.	%
Nobles	4	0.9	3	0.8	12	2.3
Officiers	19	4.1	8	2.7	21	3.9
Bourgeois	6	1.3	6	1.6	9	1.7
Professionals	46	9.8	28	7.5	37	7.0
Merchants	37	7.9	41	11.1	77	14.5
Artisans	228	48.6	173	46.0	247	47.0
Agricultural or urban workers	108	23.0	102	7.5	104	19.6
Other	21	4.5	10	2.7	23	4.3
Total cases of known status	469		371		530	

of its adherents from the *vignerons*, *laboureurs* and other agricultural workers who might constitute as much as a quarter of the population of many French cities at this time, but that above this level of society the movement cut across all the major divisions of wealth and status within society. In many cities, the 'new religion' took somewhat stronger root among the legal and professional classes than among other groups; within the artisanate, the Protestants were often over-represented among the more skilled and literate crafts. These differences, however, are matters of minor statistical tendencies, not sharp social divisions. In one of the classic early studies of this type, Emmanuel Le Roy Ladurie found the following social breakdown among Montpellier's Protestants: nobles, 2.3 per cent; bourgeois, 4.2 per cent; 'intellectual professions', 15.4 per cent; merchants, 4.3 per cent; artisans, 69 per cent; agriculturalists, 4.8 per cent. The figures clearly reveal the near-absence of those involved in working the soil, the preponderance of artisans and the importance of the educated professionals. Le Roy Ladurie does not offer any information about the relative wealth of the Protestants and Catholics, and indeed few studies of the early years of the Reformed religion's establishment in France have provided hard data about the wealth of the new faith's adherents, although Natalie Davis has asserted that her evidence about Lyon indicates that 'the Calvinist movement ... drew from rich and poor ... in numbers roughly proportional to their distribution in the population at large', and David Rosenberg has provided crude statistical support for a roughly similar pattern using a small sample of inventories after death from Amiens.[28]

---

[28] Natalie Zemon Davis, 'Strikes and Salvation at Lyons', *A.R.* 56 (1965), 54, repr. in her *Society and Culture in Early Modern France* (Stanford, 1975), p. 7; David L. Rosenberg, 'Social Experience and Religious Choice: A Case Study. The Protestant Weavers and Woolcombers of Amiens in the Sixteenth Century' (Yale Univ. Ph.D. thesis, 1978), pp. 21–5.

Four-and-a-half decades later, as the reign of Henri IV neared its end, the social composition of the Protestant fraction of Montpellier's population had changed relatively little from that found in 1560 by Le Roy Ladurie. The occupational classification scheme that I have adopted for this study and that is reproduced in Table 3.4 differs from Le Roy Ladurie's in that it divides into separate categories the nobles, important royal officials, professionals and minor local officials whom Le Roy Ladurie grouped together as either 'nobles' or members of the 'intellectual professions'. (The minor officials have been placed in the 'other' category along with soldiers, innkeepers and a few others who do not fit easily into the major social categories of the era.) Keeping these differences in mind, the most important changes that seem to have taken place in the ranks of the Reformed between 1560 and 1605–9 were modest increases in the numbers of merchants and of agricultural labourers and day-labourers, and a decrease in the percentage of artisans. Since it is now possible to compare the Protestant portion of the population with a comparable sample of those remaining loyal to the Roman church, it can be seen that the Protestants occupied the clear majority of the leading positions within the royal courts and financial offices, the learned professions and trade.

Table 3.4   The social composition of the Protestant and Catholic fractions of Montpellier's population, 1605–9

Category	Protestants		Catholics	
	No.	%	No.	%
Nobles	1	0.4	2	1.1
Officiers	14	5.3	2	1.1
Bourgeois	5	1.9	1	0.5
Professionals	30	11.4	16	8.7
Merchants	25	9.5	10	5.5
Artisans	142	54.0	76	41.5
Agricultural or urban workers	29	11.0	73	39.9
Other	18	6.8	3	1.6
Total cases of known status	264		183	

A clear wealth gap also separated the two confessions by this period. Taken as a whole, Protestant grooms-to-be promised their future brides average augmentations 92 per cent higher than those promised by their Catholic counterparts. Protestant women entered into marriage pacts with estimated dowries 85 per cent larger. If the sums mentioned in the marriage contracts can be taken as a fair indication of the overall distribution of private wealth within the city, the Huguenot majority controlled 71 per cent of Montpellier's total private wealth, the Catholic minority 29 per cent. A similar pattern of Huguenot domination emerges from analysis of the 20 largest individual marriage contracts.[29] Fourteen involved couples who promised to marry before the Reformed church, and just three involved couples who intended to wed in the Catholic church. (Three contracts fail to specify the church in which the marriage was to be celebrated.) The greater average wealth displayed by the Protestant marriage contracts can be linked to two factors. First, the Huguenots were over-represented among the wealthier and more prestigious groups within the city. Secondly, as Table 3.5 shows, those Protestants in the higher ranks of society tended to be wealthier than their Catholic counterparts of similar occupational status. The same was not true for the agricultural segment of the population, however, where the Catholics were slightly wealthier on average than their Huguenot counterparts. Among the city's artisans, the Protestants maintained only a modest economic superiority.

The marriage contracts of the first period thus reveal a city in which the Huguenots were the more powerful group economically and socially as

Table 3.5 Mean augmentation and estimated dowry for members of each religion by selected occupational categories in Montpellier, 1605–9 (n = number of marriages)

Category	Protestants		Catholics	
	Augm.	Dowry	Augm.	Dowry
Nobles or *officiers*	1540	5035	1175	4614
	n=15	n=17	n=4	n=5
Professionals	731	2083	493	–
	n=29	n=12	n=16	n=0
Merchants	269	1786	189	720
	n=25	n=24	n=11	n=6
Artisans	80	316	76	275
	n=142	n=68	n=76	n=26
Agricultural or urban workers	40	206	44	239
	n=27	n=22	n=73	n=27

[29] The occupational status of the grooms in these contracts is as follows: eleven held offices in the most important royal tribunals in the city or in the upper reaches of the financial system; five were barristers with the doctorate in law; two were described simply as noblemen; one bore the title of 'medecin ordinaire du roy et son professeur stipendié en l'université'; and one, descended from a family of important merchants, was identified simply as a bourgeois of the city.

well as politically. And as a citadel of Protestant strength, the town attracted many well-to-do Huguenot immigrants. In this period, 57 per cent of all Protestant grooms and 45 per cent of all Protestant brides whose place of birth is given were born outside Montpellier, figures nearly identical to those for Catholics (grooms: 56 per cent immigrants; brides: 51 per cent). Furthermore, the average sums of money exchanged in the contracts involving Protestant men born outside the city were higher than in those involving natives. This stands in sharp contrast to the pattern among the Catholic fraction of the sample in this period, as well as to the pattern found among the members of either faith in the subsequent two periods.[30] This influx of relatively well-off immigrants reinforced the prominence of Montpellier's Huguenot community in this period. It accounts, however, for just a fraction of the wealth superiority of the Protestant component of the sample. Isolating those instances involving native-born residents of the city reveals that the native-born Huguenots were still 67 per cent wealthier than the native-born Catholics. This accounts for three-quarters of the total wealth differential between the two groups in the sample.

Over the course of the subsequent decades, the Protestants lost both their numerical and their political preponderance in the city. As this happened, the extent to which their average wealth per head outstripped that of the Catholics changed remarkably little. As Table 3.6 shows, the gulf between the average dowries and augmentations exchanged by Protestants and Catholics narrowed slightly between 1605–9 and 1635–39. This appears to have resulted above all from the conversion to Catholicism of a number of leading Huguenot citizens amid the political upheavals of the 1620s. Throughout the Midi, the ranks of the Roman church increased in this decade, thanks to the conversion of prominent former Protestants troubled by what they saw as the disloyal and excessively militant actions of their former co-religionists.[31] While the sources consulted for this study do not allow one to gauge the full extent of this trend in Montpellier, some indications can be obtained from those cases where the successive samples of marriage contracts yield documents concerning the same family. In 33 of these 36 cases, the children married in the same church as their parents, indicating fidelity to the church of origin. Two of

---

30 Mean estimated dowry: immigrants, 967 *livres*; natives, 857 *livres*. Mean augmentation: immigrants, 252 *livres*; natives, 231 *livres*. Within the Catholic fraction of the sample, the mean augmentation was 153 *livres* for natives and 121 *livres* for immigrants.

31 Elisabeth Labrousse, 'Conversion dans les deux sens', in *La conversion au XVIIe siècle: actes du XIIe Colloque de Marseille* (Marseilles, 1983), p. 164; Louis Desgraves, 'Un aspect des controverses entre catholiques et protestants: les récits de conversions (1598–1628)', ibid., pp. 98–101; Gregory Hanlon, *Confession and Community in Seventeenth-Century France: Protestant and Catholic Coexistence in Aquitaine* (Philadelphia, 1993), pp. 208, 234–5.

Table 3.6 Mean augmentation and estimated dowries for Protestants and Catholics in Montpellier, 1605–9 to 1665–69 (n = number of marriages)

	Protestant		Catholic		P.–C. index*
	Augm.	Dowry	Augm.	Dowry	
(1) 1605–9: total sample	261	944	136	510	189
	n=282		n=224		
Selected occupational categories					
Agricultural or urban workers	40	206	44	239	89
	n=27	n=22	n=73	n=27	
Artisans	80	316	76	275	108
	n=142	n=68	n=76	n=26	
Merchants	269	1786	189	720	191
	n=25	n=24	n=10	n=6	
Professionals	730	2083	493	–	148
	n=29	n=12	n=16	n=0	
Nobles or *officiers*	1540	5035	1175	4614	120
	n=15	n=17	n=4	n=5	
(2) 1635–39: total sample	381	1411	219	884	167
	n=153		n=263		
Selected occupational categories					
Agricultural or urban workers	67	221	81	308	74
	n=21	n=80	n=7	n=34	
Artisans	109	420	105	532	96
	n=71	n=37	n=102	n=51	
Merchants	527	1788	408	1428	127
	n=31	n=22	n=10	n=10	
Professionals	967	3849	867	2313	134
	n=12	n=14	n=15	n=4	
Nobles or *officiers*	1780	16 775	4250	13 875	36
	n=5	n=4	n=4	n=4	
(3) 1665–69: total sample	594	2227	348	1398	165
	n=171		n=427		
Selected occupational categories					
Agricultural or urban workers	88	466	84	378	114
	n=11	n=13	n=88	n=71	
Artisans	119	640	121	538	106
	n=77	n=50	n=170	n=90	
Merchants	639	2925	289	1892	198
	n=45	n=22	n=32	n=18	
Professionals	1614	3629	1026	4840	125
	n=7	n=9	n=30	n=14	
Nobles or *officiers*	3764	14 292	2682	18 031	114
	n=11	n=9	n=22	n=15	

Note: Monetary values provided are in *livres tournois*. The estimated dowries have been grouped according to the status of the bride's father.
*P.–C. index: ratio of average Protestant values to average Catholic values, expressed as an index. (Where the values are identical, the index is 100; where the average Protestant values are twice the Catholic, the index is 200; and so forth.)

the three cases where a conversion is evident from one generation to the next involved prominent families passing from Protestantism to Catholicism between the first and the fourth decade of the century. These cases alone are sufficient to account for the slight narrowing of the ratio between the sums of money exchanged in Protestant and Catholic marriage contracts in these two periods.[32] Over the years between 1635–39 and 1665–69, the ratio between the average sums of money exchanged by the members of the two religious groups then remained virtually constant. As the first decade of Louis XIV's personal reign drew to a close and the king began to multiply the legal disadvantages placed on the Protestants, the average Huguenot in Montpellier remained 65 per cent wealthier than the average Catholic.

The striking stability of the average relative sums exchanged at the time of marriage by the members of the two faiths suggests powerfully that neither encouraged markedly greater wealth accumulation than the other. But it must be recalled that in this age when high rates of both migration and mortality bred constant turnover in urban populations, the universe of families represented in the three samples utilized here was hardly stable. It appears that a disproportionate number of Huguenots either moved elsewhere or died as a result of the hardships of the 1620s.[33] Furthermore, a noticeable shift occurred in the catchment area from which the city drew its immigrants in the subsequent decades. A growing proportion of Montpellier's new residents arrived from the heavily Catholic uplands of the Massif Central, especially Rouergue.[34] This may have resulted from the expansion that began to characterize Nîmes's textile industries from 1640 onwards, making that nearby city an increasingly powerful magnet

---

32 In one of the two cases involving prominent families, both father and son were notaries (the father was also for a while the secretary of the *maison consulaire*); in the other, the father was an *avocat général* of the Cour des Aides and the son a *receveur général des finances*. The third case of conversion involves an artisan family that passed from Catholicism to Protestantism in the same period. If the sums involved in the marriage contracts of these three families are credited to their religious group of origin rather than to the church in which the sons were married between 1635 and 1639, the ratios of Protestant to Catholic augmentations and estimated dowries for 1635–39 become virtually identical to those for 1605–9.

33 This can be deduced from a simple calculation. Knowing the percentage of members of each faith within the population at each period sampled, one can then estimate the numbers of native-born members of each faith likely to appear in the subsequent sample on the basis of the persistence rates revealed by the samples as a whole. For each of the two later periods, a smaller percentage of native-born Protestants and a higher percentage of native-born Catholics turns up than the model predicts. The discrepancy is especially marked in the 1635–39 sample, after the troubled decade of the 1620s.

34 The distribution of the place of origin of the immigrants to the city (both men and women) whose birthplace is noted in the marriage contracts breaks down as follows (figures represent percentages of the total pool of immigrants for the period in question):

for migrants from the heavily Protestant Cévennes.[35] Whatever the cause, the consequence of this shift was that the large numbers of immigrants who filled the gaps left in Montpellier's population by the siege of 1622 and the plague of 1629 were preponderantly Catholic. (See Table 3.7.)

Table 3.7   Percentage of immigrants by sex and religion within Montpellier's marriage contracts, 1605–9 to 1665–69

	Protestants		Catholics	
	Men	Women	Men	Women
1605–9	57	45	56	41
1635–39	46	37	67	59
1665–69	40	27	57	46

In these periods, those Protestants who moved to the city, like their Catholic counterparts, were also less than half as wealthy as their co-religionists born in Montpellier; it seems that once the Protestants lost their political dominance in the city, the number and social prominence of the new Huguenot migrants also declined. With the Catholic segment of the population containing a higher percentage of poorer immigrants in the latter two samples, it would be expected that those members of the Roman church who were natives of the city actually improved their economic situation relative to their native-born Huguenot counterparts in these years. An analysis for these periods restricted to lifelong inhabitants of the city confirms this. (See Table 3.8.) Perhaps as a result of the upheavals of the 1620s and of the Protestants' loss of political control, the gap between the

Place of origin	1605–9 (%)	1635–39 (%)	1665–69 (%)
Other localities in the diocese of Montpellier	20	18	18
Diocese of Nîmes (Cévennes)	34	28	19
Diocese of Mende (Gévaudan)	8	10	9
Rouergue	5	8	14
Other regions of Bas-Languedoc	14	17	15
Haut-Languedoc and Aquitaine	7	7	9
Provence, Dauphiné and Comtat	5	3	5
Auvergne	2	2	4
Other	5	7	7

35 Line Teisseyre-Sallmann, 'Urban Economy and Industrial Development in the Early Modern Period: Nîmes in the Seventeenth and Eighteenth Centuries', in Herman Diederiks, Paul Hohenberg and Michael Wagenaar, eds, *Economic Policy in Europe since the Late Middle Ages: The Visible Hand and the Fortune of Cities* (Leicester, 1992), p. 45.

Table 3.8   Mean augmentation and estimated dowries provided by
Montpellier-born residents, 1635–39 to 1665–69

	Protestant		Catholic		P.–C. index*
	Augm.	Dowry	Augm.	Dowry	
1635–39	415	1616	368	1045	134
1665–69	564	2321	456	1567	136

Note: Monetary values provided are in *livres tournois*. Cases involving a change
in religion from one generation to the next have been classified according to the
familial region of origin.
*P.–C. index: ratio of average Protestant values to average Catholic values,
expressed as an index.

average sums exchanged by Catholics and Protestants was significantly
smaller among natives of the city by 1635–39 than it had been among
either natives of Montpellier or all those marrying in the city in 1605–9,
when the ratio of Protestant to Catholic contributions to the marriage
pact stood at 167 for the former group and 189 for the latter. Between
1635–39 and 1665–69, the disparity between the marriage contributions
of natives of each faith did not narrow further.

The shifting patterns of migration that made the Roman church the
majority faith, the growing Catholic domination of those levers of
power and wealth most closely linked to the crown and to royal
administration, and the conversion of some of the more prominent
Huguenots to the Roman church all combined to tilt the *cumulative*
economic weight of each group significantly in the Catholics' favour,
even if the per capita wealth gap narrowed only slightly. Each group
controlled precisely 50 per cent of the city's private wealth in 1635–39. By
1665–69, the Catholic share had grown to 60 per cent. The Catholics
were also now predominant among the city's wealthiest inhabitants,
accounting for 13 of the 21 marriages in which the largest sums of money
were exchanged.[36]

As the Protestant community shrank in numbers, its social composition
also changed. Table 3.9 shows the establishment by 1665–69 of Catholic
superiority within the royal tax-courts and other official positions linked

---

36 The occupational status of the grooms in these contracts is as follows: nine noblemen,
one of whom also held an office in the Cour des Comptes, Aides et Finance; six royal *officiers*
of *roturier* status; three doctors, two of whom were also professors in the medical faculty;
two doctors of law, one of them also a university professor; and one man of unknown
status. Seven of these men were married in the Reformed church. One marriage contract
does not indicate the church in which the marriage was to be celebrated.

Table 3.9 Occupational breakdown of grooms of known occupation in Montpellier, 1605–9 to 1665–69

Category	1605–09 Protestant No.	%	1605–09 Catholic No.	%	1635–39 Protestant No.	%	1635–39 Catholic No.	%	1665–69 Protestant No.	%	1665–69 Catholic No.	%
Nobles	1	0.4	2	1.1	1	0.6	2	1.1	4	2.5	6	1.6
Officiers	14	5.3	2	1.1	5	2.8	2	1.1	6	3.8	15	4.0
Lesser officials	14	5.3	2	1.1	1	0.6	1	0.6	1	0.6	5	1.3
Professionals	30	11.4	15	8.2	12	6.7	15	8.3	7	4.5	30	8.0
Merchants	25	8.9	10	5.5	31	17.2	10	5.6	45	28.6	32	8.6
Artisans	142	53.8	76	41.5	102	56.7	71	39.4	77	49.0	170	45.6
Agricultural or urban workers	29	10.3	73	39.9	21	11.7	80	44.4	13	8.3	91	24.4
Other	9	3.4	2	1.1	5	2.8	9	5.0	4	2.5	24	6.4
Total cases of known occupation	264		182		178		190		157		373	

to the crown.[37] The Catholics also took over more and more positions within the ranks of the learned professions. Meanwhile, the Protestants held their own far better amid the growing ranks of the city's merchants. As a result of these trends, the social composition of the Huguenot community looked quite different in the period immediately prior to the Revocation of the Edict of Nantes than it had in the earliest years of the movement's growth around 1560. Artisans still formed the largest single element within the Huguenot population, and there were still few *vignerons* and day-labourers, but where officeholders and members of the learned professions had bulked far larger than merchants within the upper ranks of the community in 1560 and 1605–9, those involved in commerce now far outstripped them in numbers. Meanwhile, at the very top of the social hierarchy, a somewhat larger group of élite Huguenots now pursued military careers or lived 'nobly'. As has already been suggested, these changes in the social composition of Montpellier's Protestant community appear to have been typical of those occurring in the larger urban congregations of seventeenth-century France.

This striking shift in the sociology of Montpellier's Huguenots might appear to substantiate the view that there was an association between Calvinist belief and commercial success, but the dominant tradition among historians of the French Protestant community has instead emphasized a second consideration: the legal disabilities increasingly placed on the members of the Reformed faith limiting their access to royal offices and to the learned professions. The evidence of Montpellier's marriage contracts offers some intriguing clues about the validity of each of these explanations.

If certain aspects of the Protestants' behaviour inclined them to business success, we would expect to find evidence that merchants and artisans of this faith increased their overall wealth or accumulated real property more quickly than their Catholic counterparts. Table 3.6 has already shown us, however, that while Protestant merchants and artisans were able to provide larger augmentations for their future brides and bigger dowries for their daughters than their Catholic counterparts at both the beginning and the end of the period studied, the sums they were able to furnish did not increase significantly more rapidly than did those provided by Catholic merchants and artisans. Nor was this result significantly influenced by the differences in the percentage of immigrants to the city found among each

---

37 This shift was aided by political pressure that the province's Catholic majority brought to bear on the crown to prevent the granting of key royal offices to Huguenots. In 1653 and again in 1666, the estates of Languedoc brought suit against the admission of Protestants to Montpellier's most important tribunal, the Cour des Comptes, Aides et Finances: A.T. van Deursen, *Professions et métiers interdits: un aspect de l'histoire de la Révocation de l'Edit de Nantes* (Groningen, 1960), p. 175.

group. In 1605–9, the average augmentation promised by Protestant artisans to their future brides was 6 per cent higher than that promised by Catholic artisans. For each of the following periods, an analysis restricted entirely to artisans who were natives of the city finds that the average augmentations promised by members of each confession were virtually identical.[38]

Furthermore, since the three samples of marriage contracts examined here are separated by roughly a generation, certain of the contracts involve individuals whose parents' marriage contract appears in the previous sample. These can then be compared to determine if the younger generation entered marriage with more or less money than their parents. The number of families which it proved possible to follow in this manner turned out to be smaller than had initially been hoped. As already indicated, only 36 links could be made between the marriage contracts of members of successive generations of the same family, involving 33 different families, fifteen of them loyally Protestant, fifteen of them loyally Catholic, and three experiencing a change of religion between the generations. Where the member of the younger generation in such cases was male, the augmentation that he was able to promise his bride-to-be was compared with that provided by his father. For daughters, the dowry that she and her parents promised was compared with that of her mother at the time of her marriage if the dowries of both generations were specified; if not, the two augmentations were compared as a rough substitute for the dowries. Such comparisons show that enrichment across the generations was the norm for members of both faiths. Twelve of the fifteen Protestant families were able to provide their younger generation with a larger dowry or augmentation than the older generation, while nine of the fifteen Catholic families were able to do so.[39] The most substantial increases over the generations were registered by two relatively humble Catholic families. Just as was the case with the entire universe of merchants and artisans, these two groups involving members of a stable universe of families registered virtually identical percentage increases in aggregate wealth – the aggregate Protestant contribution to the marriage pact augmenting from one generation to the next by 44 per cent, and the aggregate Catholic contribution by 45 per cent. It does not appear from this test that the Reformed of Montpellier accumulated wealth any more rapidly than

---

[38] For 1635–39, 103 *livres* for the Protestants and 104 *livres* for the Catholics; for 1665–69, 125 *livres* for both. The sample was too small to permit a reliable comparable analysis for the native-born merchants.

[39] In the cases of the families within which a change of religion occurred, the two passing from the Reformed church to the Catholic (both from relatively well-to-do families in legal offices) also showed an increase in wealth, while the one passing in the other direction (a relatively poor artisan family) showed a decrease.

their Catholic neighbours, nor did they suffer economically from their faith's loss of local political domination. The samples here are, however, extremely small.

The marriage contracts can also be used to trace patterns of occupational choice and social mobility across generations. Here, certain differences do emerge between the two faiths. First, the children of Protestant artisans appear to have been slightly more likely than their Catholic counterparts to achieve a measure of upward occupational mobility and to establish themselves as merchants, professionals, or officials by the time of their marriage. Combining the three periods, the marriage contracts offer us evidence about the occupation of 154 Protestants whose fathers were artisans. Of these, 23 (15 per cent) had established themselves in higher-status occupations, with sixteen of these, or 10 per cent of the total sample, becoming merchants. Another 143 sons of Catholic artisans can be similarly traced, of whom only eleven (8 per cent) moved into higher-status occupations, seven becoming merchants (5 per cent of all known sons). It should be recalled that the Protestant artisans were not a markedly wealthier group than their Catholic counterparts, so these slightly higher rates of upward mobility by artisans' sons may betray some genuine differences in occupational aspirations and strategies and in their successful implementation between the members of the two faiths.

If these slightly higher rates of movement from artisan to merchant ranks on the part of Montpellier's Protestants explain part of the tendency that we have observed for a growing percentage of the Huguenot community to devote itself to trade, much of this shift must also be attributed to a growing tendency for the Reformed to steer their children towards trade and away from the professions or the purchase of royal office. Table 3.10 assembles the evidence for all children of merchants, professionals and royal officers for those cases where the occupations of ten or more such children are known for a given faith during a given time period. As can be seen, over the course of these three generations Protestant families engaged in trade increasingly tended to encourage their children to follow artisan or commercial careers. A sharply declining percentage of sons entered royal officialdom or the learned professions. The sons of Catholic merchants, by contrast, were strongly drawn in the 1660s to become professionals or officials, more strongly even than their Protestant counterparts at the beginning of the century. Among the children of professional men, the differences between the two faiths were negligible in the 1660s, but once again this was not the case among the children of royal officials, for whom, unfortunately, evidence is particularly scanty. In the final sample period, young Huguenots from this rank in society succeeded their fathers in office or entered another royal office noticeably less often than their Catholic counterparts. Those of either faith who

Table 3.10 Occupational choices of children with fathers in selected occupational categories in Montpellier, by religion and time period

	Protestants						Catholics					
	1605–9		1635–39		1665–69		1605–9		1635–39		1665–69	
	No.	%	No.	%	No.	%	No.	%	No.	%	No.	%
(1) Occupational choices of children of merchants												
Merchants	6	26	19	61	14	88	–	–	–	–	8	32
Artisans or agriculturalists	5	22	5	16	2	13	–	–	–	–	3	12
Professionals	6	26	2	16	0	0	–	–	–	–	10	40
Officials	3	13	2	6	0	0	–	–	–	–	2	8
Other	3	13	3	10	0	0	–	–	–	–	2	5
Total	23		31		16				11		25	
(2) Occupational choices of children of professionals												
Merchants or artisans	4	24	–	–	6	40	–	–	1	9	10	42
Professionals	9	53	–	–	6	40	–	–	9	82	10	42
Officials	1	6	–	–	2	13	–	–	1	9	4	17
Other	3	18	–	–	1	7	–	–	0	0	0	0
Total	17				15				11		24	
(3) Occupational choices of children of officials												
Merchants or artisans	–	–	–	–	1	7	–	–	–	–	1	6
Officials	–	–	–	–	5	33	–	–	–	–	9	56
Military officers or living as nobles	–	–	–	–	9	60	–	–	–	–	1	6
Professionals	–	–	–	–	0	0	–	–	–	–	5	31
Total					15						16	

Note: A dash indicates that fewer than ten cases are available for the time period and religious group in question.

abandoned the robe rarely pursued a career in trade, however. This was simply too much of a comedown in status for families of this rank. Instead, most pursued a military career, chose to live 'nobly', or entered the professions. At the upper levels of urban society, the growing legal and political disadvantages imposed upon France's Huguenots clearly deflected patterns of social aspiration in significant ways.

The systematic comparisons undertaken here on the basis of a large sample of marriage contracts point towards conclusions similar to those advanced by Etienne François in his study of Augsburg.[40] Rather than suggesting that Calvinist doctrine or piety offered a distinctive, consistent stimulus to habits of thrift or industry, it would appear that the higher levels of wealth per head found throughout the seventeenth century among Montpellier's Huguenots – a superiority of fortune similar to that also observed for the Protestants of such religiously divided German cities as Augsburg, Colmar and Oppenheim – resulted from some combination of initial patterns of conversion to the faith and changes that may have occurred in the distribution of wealth between the rival confessions amid the upheavals of the wars of religion. Wealth per head was substantially higher among the Reformed than among the Catholics in 1605–9, less because the Reformed were substantially better off than their papist neighbours of comparable status than because they were over-represented within the higher-status and more lucrative occupations. A small number of conversions to Catholicism by high-status Protestants subsequently diminished this advantage slightly between 1605–9 and 1635–39, but otherwise the per capita discrepancy between the two faiths hardly changed at all, despite the fact that the Catholic sector of the population constituted a higher percentage of migrants to the city, who typically were less affluent than the native-born. Differences did mark patterns of intergenerational occupational mobility, and these produced clear transformations in the sociology of the Reformed community over the course of this period. Furthermore, as Montpellier's Catholic population grew, a greater share of private wealth came to be controlled by members of the Roman church. Nevertheless, examination of that fraction of the population that would appear to provide the best test of whether or not Calvinism bred distinctive attitudes that stimulated disciplined labour and economic success – Montpellier's native-born artisans – suggests no difference between Catholics and Calvinists in the rate at which they accumulated wealth over time. Similar conclusions emerge from the small sample of cases where it has been possible to follow the same family over several generations.

---

40 See p. 123 and notes 5 and 7 above.

The average sums that young people brought to marriages in Montpellier roughly doubled between the first and the seventh decades of the seventeenth century, but the general prosperity of the period was shared almost equally between Protestants and Catholics alike. In short, contingent historical circumstances, not habits of behaviour stimulated by the devotional culture of Protestantism, produced the pattern of greater wealth per head observable among Montpellier's Huguenots in the seventeenth century.

To be sure, the evidence examined here has not permitted a thorough examination of all the possible ways in which economic behaviour might have differed by confession in post-Reformation Europe. For example, Zschunke's finding that the Protestants of Oppenheim possessed more ample grain reserves than their Catholic neighbours, suggesting a greater tendency to plan for future contingencies, deserves further confirmation or contradiction.[41] Close comparative examination of inventories after death from religiously divided communities might still reveal possible differences in patterns of consumption, investment, or savings. Bankruptcy records or mercantile letters might reveal different entrepreneurial strategies or attitudes. The evidence of the marriage contracts examined here none the less leads unmistakably to the conclusion that the rising tide of prosperity in seventeenth-century Montpellier lifted Protestant and Catholic alike. In this instance, at least, confessional differences had implications for political identity that led the Huguenots to direct their occupational aspirations along different courses, but they did not cut so deeply as to produce significant differences in economic success between those in comparable occupations.

---

[41] See p. 123 and notes 5 and 6 above.

PART TWO
Religious Faith, Cultural Capital and Historical Consciousness

CHAPTER FOUR

Protestant and Catholic Book Ownership in Seventeenth-Century Metz

Compared with the voluminous literature on Anglo-American Puritanism, remarkably little is known about Huguenot religious culture. While the Puritan 'mind' has been dissected by a remarkable succession of scholars wielding analytic tools of all descriptions, the historiography of French Protestantism has been so dominated by the twin themes of persecution and resistance that the properly religious history of the movement has been all but neglected. Recently, Philippe Joutard's studies of the Camisards have explored the mental universe of the rural congregations of the Midi in the post-1685 period, while Walter Rex and Elisabeth Labrousse have written studies of Bayle that also reveal a great deal about the culture of Huguenot intellectuals more generally.[1] For the mass of the Protestant faithful in years between the Edict of Nantes and its Revocation, however, our best guide remains the pastor Paul de Félice's now century-old filiopietistic masterpiece, *Les Protestants d'autrefois*.[2] This work discusses the character of French Reformed services in considerable detail and depicts a community steeped in the Bible and the psalms, but that is the extent of its exploration of Huguenot religious culture.

The chief reasons for this relative neglect of Calvinist religious culture in the land of Calvin's birth undoubtedly lie with the preoccupations of those French Protestants who have written about their group's past and the marginal situation of this minority of less than a million people within the mainstream of French historiography. But it must also be admitted that this culture is not easy to penetrate. Unlike their Puritan brethren, France's Protestants kept few diaries of conscience or other personal records which provide direct access to their mental world. Indirect approaches to this world consequently become necessary. That is what this chapter seeks to offer, through an examination of the evidence about book ownership and reading patterns provided by several hundred inventories of personal possessions from the city of Metz.

---

1 Philippe Joutard and Henri Manen, *Une foi enracinée, La Pervenche* (Valence, 1971); Joutard, *Les Camisards* (Paris, 1976); *idem, La légende des Camisards: Une sensibilité au passé* (Paris, 1977); Elisabeth Labrousse, *Piere Bayle* (2 vols, The Hague, 1963–64); Walter Rex, *Essays on Pierre Bayle and Religious Controversy* (The Hague, 1965).

2 (3 vols, Paris, 1897–99).

An island of French control within the independent duchy of Lorraine, the erstwhile free imperial city of Metz contained one of seventeenth-century France's largest Protestant communities north of the Loire. It also possessed a local *coutume* which required or encouraged its inhabitants to have recourse to a notary in a wide range of situations to have inventories of their personal possessions drawn up. The surviving inventories are unusually precise in their notation of the books which people owned, and they consequently indicate a great deal about the texts which helped shape Huguenot culture and the characteristic intellectual preoccupations of the group. The question 'What books did the Huguenots own?' is a simple one, but answering it can provide a large first step toward a satisfactory reconstruction of the psychology and mentality of French Calvinism.

While the chief focus of this chapter will be on Metz's Huguenots, comparisons will also be made between Catholic and Protestant patterns of book ownership and devotional reading within the city in the hope of contributing to our understanding of the long-term consequences of the 'two Reformations'. A venerable tradition asserts that Protestantism was far more of a religion of the book than Catholicism. Among the parallels between the Protestant and Catholic Reformations noted by historians in the past decades, however, have been their common efforts to promote elementary education for catechitical purposes and to root out elements of popular culture deemed pagan or ungodly. Reforming Catholic prelates made the regular reading of edifying books by laymen an essential part of their strategy for spiritual renewal, just as the Protestant reformers did.[3] The emerging body of evidence provided by the growing number of studies of book ownership in different countries suggests that such efforts did not bear fruit in Catholic Europe to anything like the degree they did in Protestant lands. In Lutheran areas of Germany in the eighteenth century, the percentage of probate inventories revealing books was over twice that found in Catholic France.[4] But this could be attributed to the influence of Pietism as well as to the initial Reformation, and we shall see that the measure itself is not an entirely trustworthy guide to the actual circulation of books on both sides of the confessional divide. A study of a single religiously divided community can provide a clearer picture of the

---

[3] The 1693 synodal statutes of Châlons-sur-Marne ordered all believers 'd'avoir toujours dans leur maison, s'il y a quelu'un qui sache lire, quelque bon livre ... et d'en faire la lecture pour le moins les dimanches et les fetes dans leur famille, et souvent en particulier, avec attention et devotion'. The archbishop of Paris even ordered his *curés* to maintain *fiches* on all their parishioners and to note whether or not they read books of devotion within the family. Henri-Jean Martin, *Livre, pouvoirs et société à Paris au XVIIe siècle (1598–1701)* (Geneva, 1969), p. 953.

[4] Etienne François, 'Livre, confession et société urbaine en Allemagne au XVIIIe siècle: l'exemple de Spire', *R.H.M.C.* 29 (1982), 355.

relationship between the two Reformations and print culture than we possess so far.

The source and the setting

The inventory after death no longer requires extensive introduction as a source for cultural history. Ever since Lucien Febvre first demonstrated how much can be gleaned from these dry lists of personal possessions in his celebrated essay on Amiens,[5] they have become fundamental for historians seeking to add the dimension of social depth to cultural and intellectual history. Recent studies have used quantitative examinations of large numbers of library inventories to establish the popularity of different authors, to map the social contours of the book-owning public, and, in the remarkable essay of Jean-Luc Marais, to help suggest when 'popular literature' became truly popular.[6]

As such studies have multiplied, the silences and limitations of inventories have also emerged with increasing clarity.[7] First, those drawing up the documents often did not bother to specify all the objects they encountered as they made their way around a person's house. Worn-out or less valuable books were particularly likely to be consigned to this sort of oblivion; to take an example from Metz, the inventory of Louis Persod and his wife Susanne notes 'a folio bible printed in Geneva' evaluated at 24 *francs messins*, 'the history of the martyrs' worth 15 *francs*, six psalters together worth 20 *francs*, and 'twenty-five other books of various sizes and authors' whose total value was just 8 *francs*.[8] Since the range in value between a large but in no way exceptionally costly book such as the in-folio *Histoire des*

---

5 Febvre, 'A Amiens: de la Renaissance à la Contre-Réforme', *Annales d'histoire sociale* 3 (1941), 41–55, repr. in *Au coeur religieux du XVIe siècle* (Paris, 1957), pp. 274–90.

6 The fundamental reference points in a vast literature are Martin, *Livre, pouvoirs et société*; Albert Labarre, *Le livre dans la vie amiénoise du seizième siècle: l'enseignement des inventaires après décès (1503–1576)* (Paris–Louvain, 1971); Jean Quéniart, *Culture et société urbaines dans la France de l'Ouest au XVIIIe siècle* (Paris, 1978); Michel Marion, *Recherches sur les bibliothèques privées à Paris au milieu du XVIIIe siècle* (Paris, 1978); Jean-Luc Marais, 'Littérature et culture "populaires" aux XVIIe et XVIIIe siècles. Réponses et questions', *Annales de Bretagne et des pays de l'Ouest* 87 (1980), 65–105.

7 Excellent critical discussions can be found in Henri-Jean Martin, 'Culture écrite et culture orale, culture savante et culture populaire dans la France d'Ancien Régime', *Journal des Savants*, July–Dec. 1975, 225–6 and *passim*; and the pages by Roger Chartier in G. Duby, ed., *Histoire de la France urbaine* (5 vols, Paris, 1980–85) III, 274–82.

8 A.D.M., B 3363, inv. of Dec. 4, 1668. One *franc messin* was worth twelve-twentieths of a *livre messin* and approximately seven *sols*, four *deniers tournois*. Eustache Lenoble, *Traité de la monnoye de Metz* (Paris, 1675), provides a complete account of the 'bizareries' of Metz's unique system of money of account.

Evesques de Metz of Martin Meurisse and a cheap in-octavo collection of
Noëls could be as high as 125 : 1, many cheap books or pamphlets must
have gone entirely unrecorded.[9] Henri-Jean Martin's judgement that the
inventories reflect the cultural image that book-owners were trying to
convey rather than their true preoccupations and tastes[10] is perhaps a bit
excessive, for cheaper volumes that procured no status are occasionally
mentioned alongside the hefty legal treatises and abundant editions of the
classics that dominated most large libraries. Furthermore, clues as to the
identity of some of the books that remain unidentified or hidden in the
inventories of personal book collections are often provided by other
sources, notably the inventories of booksellers' stocks, which reveal the
sorts of cheap books available in large quantities. None the less, the source
unquestionably privileges weightier and more valuable tomes.

Beyond this, of course, by no means all books which an individual read
in the course of a lifetime ended up in what Roger Chartier has aptly
called 'that tomb', the inventory after death. Books were passed from
hand to hand and read aloud in groups, reaching more people than their
owner alone.[11] Many popular books may have died violent deaths from
decomposition; others were surely hidden from the *greffier* or notary, or
passed on as gifts before death. The percentages of people owning books
revealed by all the studies using inventories done so far are surely inferior
to the reality of the situation for reasons such as these. Can one believe
that only fifteen of 34 seventeenth-century Parisian *hommes de loi* owned
books, as one study using inventories suggests, or even only 62 per cent of
professional men in nine cities of western France at the end of the century?[12]
Conversely, mere possession of a book was no guarantee that the owner
had read it. The inventory of Jacques Couet du Vivier, an *avocat au
Parlement*, reveals a stunning collection of over 300 theological works,
including Socinus' *De Jesu Christo*. While one might be tempted to deduce
that he was a particularly theologically curious barrister and perhaps even
a secretly heretical one, that judgement changes when one learns that his
grandfather was a minister in Basel who wrote a number of treatises
including a volume against the Socininans.[13] Many of his theological works

---

9 A.D.M., B 3362, inv. of Jean Anthoine, *imprimeur juré du roi*.

10 Martin, 'Culture écrite et culture orale', p. 225.

11 Natalie Zemon Davis, 'Printing and the People', in *Society and Culture in Early Modern
France* (Stanford, 1975), pp. 212–14, and 'Beyond the Market: Books as Gifts in Sixteenth-
Century France', *Transactions of the Royal Historical Society*, 5th ser., 33 (1983), 69–88;
Duby, ed., *Histoire de la France urbaine*, III, 277.

12 Roland Mousnier, *Recherches sur la stratification sociale à Paris aux XVIIe et XVIIIe
siècles: l'échantillon de 1634, 1635, 1636* (Paris, 1976), p. 97; Quéniart, *Culture et sociétés
urbaines*, p. 267.

13 A.D.M., B 3355, inv. of 11 September 1652; Haag (2nd edn, Paris, 1877–88), III, cols
763–72; Emmanuel Michel, *Biographie du Parlement de Metz* (Metz, 1853), p. 108; Roger

must have been inherited, and indeed private libraries were often the product of several generations of book-buying. Even in cases where it seems relatively certain that a man's books were all ones he had acquired himself, it is obviously risky to assume too much about the contents of his mind from the mere fact of possession of a specific book. Anybody who has ever experienced temptation before a rack of books can recognize the variety of motives which can lie behind the purchase of a specific volume, and several recent studies have stressed the extent to which different readers will react differently to the same book.[14] All these critical considerations must be kept firmly in mind in evaluating the information gained from inventories. None is so damning as to undermine the clear value of the source as a guide to the circulation of books and to at least some of the mental baggage of the books' owners.

Certain peculiarities of Metz's local *coutume* must also be understood to assess properly the information presented here. As in many parts of France, local laws required that an inventory after death be drawn up in inheritance cases involving minor heirs, and it permitted adult heirs to have an inventory made in cases where they suspected their inheritance was so encumbered with debts that it might be to their advantage to renounce it. Beyond this, Metz's *coutume* allowed parties to a marriage an unusual degree of latitude in determining whether they would hold their goods separately or in common, and if they chose the latter course of action, in deciding which possessions they wanted to include among their common goods.[15] The possessions of a married couple might consequently be legally divided into as many as three categories: the wife's possessions, the husband's possessions, and goods held in common. This has two implications. First, marriage arrangements often generated notarized inventories, as the parties to the marriage sought to specify legally which goods would remain the personal property of each party and which would be jointly held. Second, any given inventory, whether drawn up at marriage or after a person's death, refers only to one of the different categories of goods and thus may include only a fraction of the total possessions of any household. Books were not immune from being divided among different categories of goods. The inventory after death of the personal possessions of Jean Baudoin, a *marchand tanneur* and elder of the Reformed church, lists two large Bibles printed in Geneva. An inventory of the goods he held

---

Mazauric, 'La vie courte et remplie d'un jeune Messin du XVIIe siècle: le Pasteur Jacques Couet du Vivier, aveugle de naissance', *B.S.H.P.F.* 104 (1958), 208–11.

[14] Davis, 'Printing and the People', p. 192 and *passim*; and especially Carlo Ginzburg, *The Cheese and the Worms: The Cosmos of a Sixteenth-Century Miller* (Harmondsworth, 1982), xx–xxii and *passim*.

[15] *Coutumes générales de la ville de Metz et Pays Messin* (Metz, 1730), pp. 145, 220, 260–62.

commonly with his wife, drawn up a day later, reveals the family copy of Crespin's *Book of Martyrs*.[16] The example warns us that, in the case of Metz's inventories, it is even more dangerous than normal to assume that any given library list is complete. One might also suspect that the percentage of inventories listing books would under-represent actual rates of book ownership even more than is the case in other studies from other regions. To minimize this tendency, only inventories after death of men, and of widows who held goods in common with their husbands, have been utilized in calculating statistics of book ownership, these sorts of inventories having been retained since they were least likely to omit the family books in cases where a household owned them. (Where other sorts of inventories mention books, these notations have been retained for the evidence they provide about the popularity of different authors and patterns of individual taste.) In fact, as we shall see, the percentages of book ownership thus calculated are in line with those revealed by other studies of French towns – at least so far as the Catholic population of Metz is concerned.

Still another consequence also follows from the fact that many *messin* inventories were drawn up simply to indicate which goods belonged to a certain legal category of possessions: only occasionally are valuations attached to the different goods. It is thus impossible to correlate patterns of different cultural objects with wealth, as has been done in other studies of book ownership.[17]

Set against these problematic characteristics stands the cardinal virtue of Metz's inventories, their remarkable precision in listing book titles. As is the case with such documents elsewhere, certain of the inventories frustratingly consign most or all of the books they mention to the limbo of anonymity. It has none the less been possible to identify or classify by subject matter 65 per cent of all books mentioned in the inventories. By contrast, Albert Labarre was able to identify only 22 per cent of the books mentioned in the inventories he examined from sixteenth-century Amiens, and Henri-Jean Martin just 38 per cent of the volumes in his one hundred *best* Parisian inventories from the period 1671–1700.[18]

---

16 A.D.M., B 3356, invs of 21 and 22 October 1655.

17 These studies show, as is hardly surprising, that book ownership increased with wealth among most groups in society. Quéniart, *Culture et société urbaine*, pp. 171–8; Marion, *Bibliothèques à Paris*, pp. 106–11.

18 Labarre, *Livre dans la vie amiénoise*, p. 154; Martin, *Livre, pouvoirs et société*, p. 927. By the eighteenth century, Parisian inventories are far more laconic yet, commonly listing books together in large groups by format and indicating the title of merely the first book in each group. Michel Marion could thus identify but 4 per cent of the books listed in 237 large libraries whose inventories he examined. *Bibliothèques à Paris*, pp. 118, 134.

Some 338 inventories from the years 1645–72 form the basis for this study.[19] The statistical sample used for calculating rates of book ownership among different groups in society is composed of 273 inventories. This initial sample was supplemented by 65 additional inventories which either fell outside the criteria for inclusion in the statistical sample but none the less mentioned books, or were deliberately sought out in an effort to fill out the picture of Protestant book ownership provided by the approximately one hundred Huguenot inventories turned up in the initial sample. As is typical of such studies, the sample is skewed toward the upper levels of society, the wealthier being more likely to have their possessions inventoried.[20] All levels of society from the First President of Metz's Parlement to simple *journaliers* are none the less represented, even if not in numbers proportionate to their importance within the population.

Since the inventories contain no explicit indications of religion, this had to be determined by comparing the names of those whose goods are listed with Metz's unusually complete set of Protestant registers of baptisms, marriages and burials, which run from 1561 to 1685.[21] The need to link two different sets of records introduces still another source of uncertainty into this study, for, aside from the ever-present possibility of human error in such an operation, not every member of a given community necessarily appears in its parish registers, especially in cities with their high rates of geographic mobility. After the two sets of records had been linked, nine cases remained such as that of Samuel de Saint-Aubin, whose Old Testament name and library, including the Bible, five psalters, and Lewis

---

[19] The overwhelming majority of inventories which I examined come from fifteen large *liasses* preserved among the records of the Baillage, A.D.M., B 3351–65. Other inventories are also scattered among the records of Metz's *amans*, or notaries. Time permitted me to examine just one such *liasse*: A.D.M., 3 E 3176. It might be noted here that the books have to be sought out within the different categories of goods that form the sections into which the inventories are divided. They usually appear among the 'meubles de bois'. Only on rare occasions is a special chapter of an inventory devoted to books. The article of Henri Tribout de Morembert, 'Bibliothèques messines du XVIIe siècle', *Annales de l'Est*, 5th ser., 33 (1971), 219–29, appears to be based exclusively on the inventories which list books separately. The author claims that few inventories reveal private libraries and bases his brief examination on just 23 cases from the years 1623–1702.

[20] The bias can be seen by comparing the occupations of the Protestants in the sample of inventories with the full 1684 census of the group, 'Extrait et estate général des habitants de la ville de Metz qui font profession de la religion Prétenduë Réfformée', *Annuaire de la Société d'Histoire et d'Archéologie de la Lorraine* 3 (1891), 345–75. Merchants, legal or medical personnel, *officiers*, and other titled members of the urban élite account for 47.4 per cent of the inventories in the sample, as opposed to just 28.8 per cent of the heads of household listed in the census.

[21] These are housed in the A.C., Metz, GG 236–53. I also used the index to the Protestant *état civil*, GG 259–59bis, and the genealogical *fichier Poirier*.

Bayly's very Protestant *La Pratique de Piété*, suggest strongly that he was Huguenot, but who could not be found in the Protestant registers. Even though such individuals were in all likelihood Huguenots, these cases have been classified 'Religion Uncertain' for the purposes of calculating statistics of book ownership, and all such statistics have been computed twice, once on the assumption that such people were Protestant and once on the assumption that they were Catholic. Simply to have assigned these cases to the Protestant column would have resulted in underestimating rates of Catholic book ownership, for there is no way of identifying those other Protestants without books in the sample of inventories whose true religion could not be identified using the *état civil*. As we shall see, the degree of uncertainty introduced by this procedure is only a minor one.

Having discussed the sources for this study, a word might also be in order about the city in question and the Protestant community within it. In the war-torn seventeenth century, Metz was a military citadel and administrative centre of critical importance, with a population of close to 20 000 in both the early decades of the century and around 1685, although a terrible plague in 1635–36 and the fighting brought to the region by the Thirty Years War cut into the population considerably in the middle years of the century.[22] The city was not a great manufacturing centre, and trade was primarily distributive, centring around military provisioning and supplying the local population with goods produced elsewhere.[23] The town was consequently dominated socially and economically by an old and wealthy bourgeoisie with extensive rural holdings, supplemented and increasingly supplanted by the military and legal personnel attached to the citadel and, from 1633 onward, the Parlement. These same circles, along with the clergy, also guaranteed the city such intellectual life as it possessed. Guez de Balzac passed a year in the city in the entourage of the military governor Epernon. Some remarkably distinguished clerics were attached to the local First Estate – not only the great Bossuet, but also Nicolas Coëffeteau, one of the leading controversialists and devotional writers of the first part of the century, and his successor as suffragan bishop, Martin Meurisse.[24] On the Protestant side, Paul Ferry was the great

---

22 Jean Rigualt, 'La population de Metz au XVIIe siècle: Quelques problèmes de démographie', *Annales de l'Est* 5th ser., 2 (1951), 307–9.

23 The best sources for the city's economy are the inventories themselves. See also Gaston Zeller, 'Marchands-Capitalistes de Metz et de Lorraine au XVIe siècle', in *Eventail de l'histoire vivante: Hommage à Lucien Febvre* (2 vols, Paris, 1953), II, 273–81; and Jean Rigault, 'La fortune d'un protestant messin du XVIIe siècle, Philippe de Vigneulles (vers 1560–1634)', *Annales de l'Est* 5th ser., 2 (1951), 79–88.

24 Roger Zuber, 'Metz et la Champagne, ou les frontières littéraires de la France au début du XVIIe siècle', in *Mélanges d'histoire littéraire (XVIe–XVIIe siècle) offerts à Raymond Lebègue* (Paris, 1969), pp. 175–83; M. Magendie, *La politesse mondaine et les théories de l'honnêteté en France au XVIIe siècle, de 1600 à 1660* (Paris, 1925), p. 424; Charles Urbain,

adornment of the Reformed church, and he was just one member of a small cenacle of learned pastors and professionals who met weekly to discuss matters historical and philological.[25] While not a university town or a major printing centre, Metz did support several printers and booksellers.[26]

Protestant ideas reached Metz early in the course of the Reformation, with Guillaume Farel preaching there in 1524. If the new faith soon won adherents, it was not able to gain legal recognition during the three subsequent decades during which Metz remained a free imperial city, but several years after the French asserted their 'protection' over the town a special grant of privilege provided toleration for the faith. Under this special regime of privilege, the new Reformed church quickly attained considerable proportions, and even though it suffered many of the vicissitudes experienced by other French congregations over the course of the Wars of Religion, it still possessed in 1635 over six thousand members, four pastors, and a special legal status that placed it outside the regime of the Edict of Nantes.[27] The church included people drawn from all sections of society, but as was typical of the larger urban Huguenot communities of the seventeenth century, its members tended to be over-represented within certain occupations, notably among the merchants, doctors and surgeons, and underrepresented among others, especially the world of officialdom and, somewhat unusually, the artisans. (See Table 4.1.) The Protestants may also have been more prosperous than their Catholic neighbours. One Catholic cleric, who noted the disproportionate number of Huguenots among the city's doctors and merchants, also complained that they were the richest merchants and goldsmiths, filled half the positions of authority within the town council and militia, and were avidly buying up all the *granges* in the nearby countryside.[28]

This substantial and solidly established community maintained an extensive network of elementary schools, closely supervised by the pastors

Nicolas Coëffeteau (Paris, 1893), *passim*; *Dictionnaire de Théologie Catholique* (Paris, 1910–51), X, s.v. 'Meurisse'.

25 Roger Mazauric, *Le pasteur Paul Ferry* (Metz, 1964), *passim*, esp. pp. 45–6.

26 Throughout the second half of the century, three to four printers appear to have been regularly active, and several other *libraires* also retailed books. Albert Ronsin, 'La communauté des imprimeurs libraires et relieurs de Metz (1656–1791)', *Annales de l'Est* 5th ser., 2 (1960), 203–26; C. Lanette-Claverie, 'La librairie française en 1700', *Revue Française d'Histoire du Livre* 3 (1972), 9; A.D.M., B 3352, inv. of 8 April 1647; B 3354, inv. of 21 February 1651; B 3358, inv. of 23 March 1658; B 3359, inv. of 21 July 1660.

27 Henri Tribout de Morembert, *La Reforme à Metz* (Nancy, 1969–71), provides an excellent history of Protestantism in Metz. On the size of the Huguenot community in 1635, see Rigault, 'Population', p. 309. The plague of 1635–36 reduced the community by over 20 per cent, and it never was able to replenish its ranks. On the eve of the Revocation, it numbered 4380 people.

28 A.D.M., D 11, 'Estat present de l'heresie dans la ville de Metz et pays messin'.

Table 4.1   Sociological distribution of Metz inventory sample by religion

Occupational category	Catholics	Protestants	Religion uncertain
Nobility	9 (5.2%)	4 (4.4%)	2 (22%)
Officiers	7 (4.0%)	4 (4.4%)	–
Clergy	5 (2.9%)	1 (1.1%)	–
Legal personnel	7 (4.0%)	7 (7.8%)	1 (11%)
Medical personnel	2 (1.1%)	8 (8.9%)	1 (11%)
Lesser officials	11 (6.3%)	3 (3.3%)	–
Merchants	15 (8.6%)	20 (22.2%)	2 (22%)
Artisans	60 (34.5%)	21 (23.3%)	2 (22%)
'Bourgeois'*	20 (11.5%)	11 (12.2%)	–
Soldiers	8 (4.6%)	–	–
Labourers and agricultural workers	11 (6.3%)	4 (4.4%)	–
Unknown	19 (10.9%)	7 (7.8%)	1 (11%)
Total	174	90	9

*The term 'bourgeois' is used somewhat differently in legal documents in Metz than is normal for records of the *ancien régime*. Many artisans, even quite humble ones, receive the appelation 'bourgeois', where typically this was reserved for rentiers or wealthy merchants elsewhere in France. The term is thus in many ways closer to the German 'Bürger' than 'bourgeois' in the usual *ancien régime* sense. Those classified as 'bourgeois' here are those for whom this term was the only socio-professional indication encountered in the documents and where a trade could not be safely deduced from the objects listed in the inventory.

and deacons. With attendance required of all children and this require-ment reinforced by a system of scholarships that provided the poor with tuition, books and even pens and ink, these schools created a population in which literacy was quite high. According to Jean-François Michel, of 1880 witnesses noted in the 1668 register of baptisms, marriages and burials, only 22 per cent were recorded as incapable of signing their name[29] – and this document includes acts concerning inhabitants of the surrounding countryside as well as the city itself. Such figures are not extraordinary for Protestant communities in this period; the signature rate for Reformed newlyweds in Rouen between 1668 and 1685 was 88

[29] Michel, 'Les écoles protestantes à Metz et en pays messin aux XVIe et XVIIe siècles', *Annales de l'Est* 5th ser., 21 (1969), 230, an excellent study.

per cent for men and 78 per cent for women.[30] But not all Huguenot communities could boast so well-established a network of schools – some fought a losing battle even to be able to maintain so much as one legally – and thus the findings here concerning rates of Protestant book ownership should not be generalized to all Huguenot communities.[31]

Small libraries and religious books

The first thing to strike one in examining Metz's inventories is how much more frequently books appear in Protestant hands. Sixty-nine to 72 per cent of all Protestant inventories note the presence of at least one book, while the comparable figure among the city's Catholics is just 21 to 25 per cent. These latter numbers are not out of line with the percentages found elsewhere in early modern France. Books are noted in 20 per cent of all Amiens inventories from the period 1503–76; in 25.7 per cent of inventories in Jean Queniart's nine cities of western France in 1697–98; and in 36.7 per cent of inventories in the same nine towns in 1757–58.[32] By contrast, the figures concerning Metz's Protestants can only be compared with percentages from other Protestant lands. Even here, they easily outstrip comparable figures from three Kentish towns in the 1630s (44–49 per cent), although they do not quite attain the levels found in three cities of eighteenth-century Germany, which vary from 77 to 89 per cent around mid-century.[33]

Part of the contrast between the two faiths in Metz must be attributed to the differences of wealth and social composition between them, but this only accounts for a small part of the explanation. As Table 4.2 shows, even within the same occupational classification Protestant inventories were far more likely to reveal books, so much more so that this can hardly be accounted for solely by differences in wealth.

---

[30] Jean-Pierre Bardet, *Rouen aux XVIIe et XVIIIe siècles. Les mutations d'un espace social* (Paris, 1983), p. 244. The comparble figures for the Catholic population were 69 and 44 per cent.

[31] The small and precariously established church of Amiens, composed overwhelmingly of cloth merchants and textile workers, provides a clear contrast. As yet incomplete research using inventories after death of seventeenth-century Protestant merchants and artisans is revealing a substantially lower percentage of households with books than in Metz, although a higher percentage than among their Catholic counterparts.

[32] Labarre, *Livre dans la vie amiénoise*, p. 105; Quéniart, *Culture et société urbaines*, p. 158.

[33] Peter Clark, 'The Ownership of Books in England, 1560–1640: The Example of Some Kentish Townsfolk', in Lawrence Stone, ed., *Schooling and Society: Studies in the History of Education* (Baltimore, 1976), p. 99; François, 'Livre, confession et société urbaine en Allemagne', p. 355.

Furthermore, Huguenots owning books also typically possessed more volumes than did their Catholic neighbours of similar status. (See Table 4.3).

Table 4.2   Rates of book ownership by occupational category in seventeenth-century Metz (statistical sample only)

Occupational category	Protestants		Catholics		Religion uncertain	
	Percentage of cases with books	Number of cases	Percentage of cases with books	Number of cases	Percentage of cases with books	Number of cases
Noblemen	75	4	22	9	100	2
Clerics	100	4	60	5		
Officiers	100	4	57	7		
Legal professions	86	7	29	7	100	1
Medical professions	88	8	50	2		
Lesser officials	100	3	18	11		
Merchants	85	20	33	15	100	2
Artisans	52	21	17	60	100	2
'Bourgeois'	73	11	5	20		
Soldiers	–	–	25	8		
Labourers and agric. workers	25	4	9	11		
Unknown	57	7	16	19	100	1

Table 4.3   Mean size of libraries among those owning books in seventeenth-century Metz (all inventories examined)

Occupational category	Protestants		Catholics	
	Mean number of books	Number of cases	Mean number of books	Number of cases
Nobles and *officiers*	22	13	37	9
Learned professions	124	17	37	7
Merchants, artisans, soldiers, lesser officials, labourers	6	53	2.5	20
'Bourgeois' and unknown	11.5	16	1	5

The confessional contrast is impressive, but before we leap to any conclusions about the relationship between religion and book ownership, let us look closely at the books found in the inventories. Particular attention should be given to the books in smaller libraries, since these libraries account for most of the observed statistical difference between Catholics and Protestants.

To begin with, the great majority of identified books in these small libraries were religious in character. This underscores the importance of religious considerations in leading those outside the ranks of the educated élites to acquire substantial books.

What religious books predominate? Looking at the Protestant books first, it comes as no surprise to discover that the Bible and the psalter were by far the most popular individual works. Bibles appear in 87 of 96 Calvinist inventories where one or more book is identified by title, and in 87 of 133 Protestant inventories overall.[34] Large folio editions predominate, but many smaller copies, often worn from heavy use, are also noted. Many families owned several, and Greek and Latin versions appear with considerable frequency in the hands of the better educated, testifying to the seriousness of their Bible study. Unlike in sixteenth-century Strasbourg, most of the Bibles were complete editions, not just New Testaments, with the Geneva Bible being by far the most frequently encountered version.[35] Psalters appear less frequently, being noted in 42 Protestant inventories, but it is impossible to know to what extent this is simply because they were less valuable than Bibles and hence less likely to be recorded. All Protestants were expected to have a copy of the psalter for use in services, and aside from being regularly sung at the temple, psalms formed a standard part of family services as well.[36] It is not uncommon to find six or seven copies in a single household, one for the use of each family member, and judging by the elaborate bindings lavished on the volumes, these were often highly treasured. In sum, the inventories provide ample confirmation of the place of the Bible and the psalter in Huguenot personal and family piety, although they also suggest that every Huguenot household may not have possessed them.

Considerably more surprising is the proliferation of other works of devotion, controversy and church history found in the hands of ordinary

---

34 This sample includes those cases classified as 'religion uncertain'.

35 Four Bibles are noted as being printed in Lyon, one Protestant owned a copy of the Louvain Bible, and one a Bible printed in La Rochelle. On the prevalence of New Testaments in Strasbourg, see Miriam Usher Chrisman, *Lay Culture, Learned Culture: Books and Social Change in Strasbourg, 1480–1599* (New Haven, 1982), p. 155.

36 The place of the psalms in Huguenot culture is discussed by de Félice, *Protestants d'autrefois* II, 63–7, 88; Félix Bovet, *Histoire du Psautier des Eglises Réformées* (Neuchâtel–Paris, 1872), pp. 111–35; Roger Zuber, 'Les psaumes dans l'histoire des Huguenots', *B.S.H.P.F.* 123 (1977), 350–61.

church members. The difference in rates of book ownership between Protestants and Catholics cannot be attributed primarily to the ownership of Bibles and psalters, for even when one eliminates all Protestant households where these are the only recorded books, the percentage of Huguenot households with books still stands at 59–62 per cent. Representative small libraries found in the hands of Protestants outside the ranks of the learned professions and the nobility are those of Abraham La Bausse, a *huilier*, with a Bible, a New Testament, the *Book of Martyrs*, two volumes of psalms and two volumes of prayers; or Philippe Moré, an innkeeper, with a Bible, Du Moulin's *Bouclier de la foi*, a volume of prayers and consolations by Daniel Toussaint, and four unidentified books; or the widow Marie Lindfoier, who owned two Bibles, the *Book of Martyrs*, 'l'abrégé de l'histoire en figures', d'Aubigné's *Histoire universelle*, *La Pratique de Piété* and 'several other small books in a large basket'.

Aside from the Bible and psalter, no individual titles appear with outstanding frequency in such small Protestant libraries, the most commonly encountered works being Crespin's martyrology (7 times), one of Calvin's commentaries (4), and Bayly's *Pratique de Piété* (3). Instead, it is the variety of titles which is impressive. In addition to the volumes just mentioned, religious books found in the hands of Protestant merchants, artisans and labourers with fewer than twenty books include such works of devotion as an unidentified 'livre de préparation à la cène', a 'tableau de la mort' and François de Combles's *Meditations consolatoires pour ceux à qui quelqu'un est mort*;[37] sermons by Calvin, Bullinger and Luther; several copies of Calvin's *Institutes*; such works of ecclesiastical history as Sleidan, Josephus's *Antiquité des Juifs* (owned by a *marchand pelletier* whose only other book was the Bible), and the *Histoire ecclésiastique des églises réformées au royaume de France*; and Drelincourt's *Abrégé des controverses*. Beyond simply encouraging psalm-singing and reading the Bible, Calvinism clearly also bred a personal religious culture that often included direct contact with the writings of important Reformed theologians and with major works of church history.

Since so little work has been done to date on Huguenot reading patterns, let us push this examination of the works which shaped Huguenot religious culture further by determining the popularity of different books and authors within all Protestant libraries, large and small. Table 4.4 identifies the most widely owned Protestant authors as revealed by the inventories, and this information has been supplemented by the evidence of a second, precisely contemporaneous source, the registers of the important Protestant

---

[37] De Combles was a pastor of the church of Metz.

Table 4.4   The most widely diffused Protestant authors and books in seventeenth-century Metz

Author	Most popular work(s)	Total number of volumes by author encountered in Protestant hands	Number of households with one or more works by author
Calvin	Bible commentaries (28 copies) *Institutes* (15) Sermons (9)	63	21
Du Moulin	*Bouclier de la foi* (10) *Nouveauté du Papisme* (7)	54	18
Du Plessis-Mornay		25	10
Drelincourt		19	10
Beza		17	5
Crespin	*Histoire des Martyrs* (15)	15	15
Bullinger		14	5
Paul Ferry	*Dernier Désespoir* (7)	13	10
Viret		12	4
Hall		11	2
Peter Martyr		9	2
Amyraut		8	6
Sleidan		7	6
Mestrezat		7	4
Bayly	*La Pratique de Piété* (6)	6	6
	Histoire ecclésiastique	6	6
Taffin		6	5
Daniel Toussaint	*Prières et consolations* (4)	6	5
Samuel Durand		6	3
Daillé		5	2
Cameron		5	2
Cappel		5	2
Napier	*Ouverture des tous les secrets de l'apocalypse* (4)	4	4
Thomson	*Chasse de la beste romaine* (4)	4	3
Luther		4	3
Zanchi		3	2
Zwingli		2	1
Bucer		2	2

bookseller of Grenoble, Jean Nicolas, which run from 1645 to 1668.[38] (See Table 4.5.) The two sources complement each other well, for the inventories reveal the composition of libraries that were often formed decades before the inventories were drawn up, while Nicolas's registers indicate those Protestant books which were selling best in precisely these middle years of the seventeenth century.

Table 4.5   Best-selling Protestant authors in the sales records of the Grenoble bookseller Jean Nicolas, 1645–68

Author	Most popular work(s)	Total volumes sold
Drelincourt	*Abrégé des controverses* (9 copies)	42*
Mestrezat		37**
Daillé		32***
Du Moulin		28
Amyraut		21
Hall	*De la tranquillité de l'esprit* (8)	18
Bayly	*Pratique de Piété* (13)	13
David Eustache		13
Calvin		1

*Excluding sales of his *Consolations de l'âme fidèle*, which Nicolas published himself and sold wholesale as well as retail.
**Primarily different editions of his sermons.
***Primarily his sermons and commentaries.

The man who stands out as the most widely owned religious author within the inventories is none other than John Calvin, at the top of Table 4.4 both in terms of the number of volumes of his works encountered in the inventories and in the number of different inventories which reveal at least one work by him. Abraham de La Cloche, one of Metz's pastors, owned 22 different works from his pen, more than any other author, while works by Calvin appear not only in the libraries of apothecaries, notaries and lawyers, but also those of a goldsmith, a master saddlemaker and a cobbler's widow. Overall, nearly one Protestant inventory in six notes a copy of Calvin.

This pre-eminence of the Genevan reformer may not appear terribly surprising, but it is none the less worth underlining, especially in light of

---

38 Henri-Jean Martin and M. Lecocq, *Livres et lecteurs à Grenoble: les registres du libraire Nicolas (1645–1668)* (2 vols, Geneva, 1977), II.

Brian Armstrong's finding that the defenders of neo-Calvinist orthodoxy among the French Reformed clergy in the early seventeenth century do not appear to have been well read in Calvin.[39] Calvin certainly did not sell well in the seventeenth century to judge by Nicolas's registers, and indeed his works were very infrequently reprinted in the period; after 22 French-language editions of the *Institutes* between 1541 and 1566, only one edition appeared over the course of the entire subsequent era up to 1685.[40] Most of the copies of Calvin revealed by Metz's inventories must thus have been copies passed down within the families that owned them from the sixteenth century, talismans of the family's attachment to the faith. As such, some copies may well have been more treasured than read. Yet it would be unwise to assume that this was always the case. Books were preserved and used longer in the early modern period than they are today,[41] and it is telling that two French editions of the *Institutes* were published in Bremen in the decades following the Revocation of the Edict of Nantes, indicating a continuing desire to consult the work by those Huguenot refugees who had been unable to take their copy with them into exile. Calvin still cast a long shadow over seventeenth-century French Calvinism.

One figure approaches Calvin in the frequency with which his works appear in the inventories: Pierre Du Moulin, the great champion of Reformed orthodoxy throughout the early decades of the seventeenth century. Du Moulin was a prolific writer whose works ranged from meditations and works of pastoral advice to abstract theology and works of controversy against Arminians, Amyraldians and Catholics alike. Quite significantly, amid this wide range of books, by far his most widely diffused works were the *Bouclier de la foi*, 'in which are decided all principal controversies between the Reformed churches and the roman church', which recurs ten times, and the *Nouveauté du Papisme*, an even more complete defence of the faith against Rome that ran to almost 1100 pages, which appears seven times, once in the possession of a *marchand tanneur*.[42] Already here one of the fundamental characteristics of Huguenot culture

[39] *Calvinism and the Amyraut Heresy: Protestant Scholasticism and Humanism in Seventeenth-Century France* (Madison, 1969), p. 188.

[40] Alfred Erichson, ed., *Bibliographia Calviniana* (Berlin, 1900), *passim*.

[41] One *messin* library, that of Louis Ferry, Paul Ferry's son, is inventoried in a fashion that includes the place and date of publication of all of the books. Only 30 per cent of Ferry's books were published during his lifetime (1626–66), and 11 per cent of them date from the 1560s or earlier. A.D.M., B 3362, inv. of 1 July 1667. François, 'Livre, confession et société urbaine en Allemagne', pp. 364–5, 371 provides even more striking evidence of the long life of books in this era.

[42] These were followed in popularity by the *Apologie pour la Sainte Cène* and his *Décades* of sermons, each of which appears five times.

emerges, the important place occupied by works justifying and defending the tenets of Calvinism against the champions of Rome. As Elisabeth Labrousse has written, 'The Huguenots were at once so small a minority and so constantly pressured to convert that every educated man among them was a capable controversialist'.[43] We shall have further occasion to confirm this judgement.

Among other important French Protestant writers of the seventeenth century, the turn-of-the-century 'Huguenot Pope' Philippe Du Plessis-Mornay appears next most frequently in the inventories, while the four dominant Protestant divines throughout the middle years of the century – Moise Amyraut, Jean Daillé, Charles Drelincourt and Jean Mestrezat – appear most frequently in Nicolas's registers, a contrast obviously explained by the different chronological focus of the two sources. Nicolas's registers also show that the frequency with which Paul Ferry's works appear in *messin* inventories bespeaks local rather than national influence. The relatively minor place that Amyraut occupies among these four divines is striking, for he was the most controversial and theologically important of the seventeenth-century Huguenot pastors. Unlike disputations against Catholicism, controversies within the Reformed church did not appeal widely to laymen. While Amyraut's *Traité de la prédestination*, the work which touched off the great quarrel over universal grace, appears twice in the inventories, none of the subsequent refutations and counter-blasts inspired by the controversy appears so much as once, and Du Moulin's attack on the Dutch Remonstrants, the *Anatome Arminianismi*, shows up only in the library of the pastor de La Cloche. The most frequently encountered work of Amyraut's in the inventories, by contrast, is his *Discours de l'estat des fidèles après la mort*, a discussion of the fate of both body and soul after death originally written to console his wife on the death of their child.[44] Works of controversy and apologetics once again bulk largest among the volumes by these Huguenot authors. Du Plessis-Mornay's most widely diffused works were *De l'Institution du saint sacrement de l'Eucharistie en l'Eglise ancienne* (5 copies), a defence of Reformed eucharistic theology; *De la verité de la religion chrestienne* (4 copies), an apology for Christianity against 'atheists, epicurians, pagans, jews, mahometans and other infidels'; and the anti-papal *Mystère d'iniquite* (4 copies). Ferry is similarly represented above all by his *Dernier désespoir de la tradition contre l'Escriture* (7 copies), a rebuttal of the Jesuit François

---

43 Quoted by Philippe Joutard, 'Les racines de la mémoire', *H-Histoire* 7 (1981), 13.

44 This work appears three times. It was also one of the three of his works of which Nicolas sold the most copies (4), along with the *Apologie pour ceux de la religion* and the *Considerations sur les droits par lesquels la nature a reiglé les mariages*, again works unrelated to Amyraut's controversial theological pronouncements.

Veron's *Brief et facile moyen ... de faire paraitre à tout ministre qu'il abuse et à tout religionnaire qu'il est abusé*; while Drelincourt's most frequently recurring books included his popular works of controversy, the *Abrégé des controverses, ou sommaire des erreurs de l'Eglise romaine avec leur refutation par des textes expres de la Bible de Louvain* (4 copies) and the *Dialogues familiers sur les principales objections des missionaires de ce temps* (3 copies), alongside his *Consolations de l'âme fidèle contre les frayeurs de la mort* (also 3 copies), a work which only appeared in 1651 and was destined to attain great popularity. Nicolas's registers also suggest a growing taste for sermons as the century progressed, a trend confirmed by publication figures which show such works attaining a considerable vogue between 1630 and 1660.[45]

The preoccupation of so much French Protestant writing with doctrine and its defence may well explain why English works of practical divinity and spiritual consolation proved so appealing when they were translated. 'Books written by Englishmen concerning the way to practise piety are running from hand to hand and enjoy a remarkable vogue', Amyraut wrote in 1660.[46] While he did not specify the works in question, the inventories and Nicolas's registers identify them for us. They are the various meditations and writings of Joseph Hall, the 'English Seneca', and Lewis Bayly's monumental handbook of meditations and prayers, *The Practice of Piety*. Hall's elegant and rather lengthy meditations, tinged with neo-Stoicism, appealed exclusively to men of education, while Bayly's more practical compendium, offering prayers for all occasions, seasons and times of the day, attracted some readers from farther down the social scale – an interesting reflection of the appeal of different spiritual styles to different groups.[47] Amyraut was in fact rather disturbed about the popularity of Bayly's work, which he saw as offering too mechanical a kind of piety, as if the author 'sought to teach a trade'.[48] Translations also introduced the Huguenots to British traditions of apocalyptic speculation, something that

---

[45] Martin, *Livre, pouvoirs et société*, fig. IX.

[46] Cited by Hartmut Kretzer, 'Die Calvinismus–Kapitalismus–These Max Webers vor dem Hintergrund Franzosischer Quellen des 17. Jahrhunderts', *Zeitschrift für Historische Forschung* 4 (1977), 425n.

[47] Those who appear in the inventories owning Bayly's work are two merchants, an apothecary, the *receveur de la ville*, a widow of uncertain status, and the pastor Abraham de La Cloche. Volumes by Hall appear only in the possession of de La Cloche and Jean Bancelin, a master goldsmith whose exceptional library is analysed in detail below, pp. 184–5. The identified purchasers of Hall's works in Nicholas's registers are all members of the high robe or *secrétaires* to the leading figures in the city – with the striking exception of 'Mgr. l'éveque et prince de Grenoble' (!). By contrast, a *maitre tailleur* and two merchants joined the eight lawyers and *officiers* who purchased *The Practice of Piety* from Nicolas – and clients from below the rank of lawyers and *officiers* appear very rarely in his registers.

[48] Kretzer, 'Calvinismus–Kapitalismus–These', p. 425.

was not much cultivated by the leading Huguenot divines throughout the period before the Revocation. Four copies appear of John Napier's landmark *Ouverture de tous les secrets de l'apocalypse*, which went through five editions in La Rochelle in a translation by George Thomson, himself the author of a tract which also appears in the inventories four times, *La Chasse de la beste romaine, ou est ... recerché et evidemment prouvé que le pape est l'Antichrist.*[49] In the absence of a native tradition, these works would have introduced curious Huguenots to the major themes and preoccupations of Protestant apocalyptics, thus providing a framework for interpreting events that would take on new relevance after 1685.

No other figure of the formative years of the Reformation approaches Calvin in the frequency with which his books appear in the inventories, but titles by certain other sixteenth-century theologians do recur with some regularity. The great names of the first generation of the Reformation such as Luther and Zwingli are striking for their scarcity, but Beza, Bullinger and Viret all appear in ten or more copies and four or more inventories. Their works cluster in a few large collections belonging to men of particular theological training or curiosity, but one or two books by each author found their way outside these restricted circles. Also noted in five inventories are works by Jean Taffin, the Walloon native and later court preacher to William of Orange who served as a pastor in Metz in the years just after the Reformed church was 'planted'.[50] Once again his popularity may represent local rather than national conditions, but his *Des Marques des enfans de Dieu* has also been found in a Protestant inventory in rural Lower Normandy, indicating the possibility of broader popularity.[51]

Aside from works of abstract theology, controversy and some devotional writing, volumes on church history also nourished the reflection of Metz's Protestants and shaped their outlook on the world. Foremost among these

---

[49] Paul Christianson, *Reformers and Babylon: English Apocalyptic Visions from the Reformation to the Eve of the Civil War* (Toronto, 1978), pp. 97–100; and Katherine R. Firth, *The Apocalyptic Tradition in Reformation Britain, 1530–1645* (Oxford, 1979), pp. 132–49, provide excellent discussions of Napier's work. I have been unable to discover anything about the mysterious Thomson other than his activity in La Rochelle, which is evident from Louis Desgraves, *Répertoire bibliographique des livres imprimés en France au XVIIe siècle* (Baden-Baden, 1978–), II, 134, 142, 147.

[50] On Taffin and his activity in Metz, Charles Rahlenbeck, 'Jean Taffin un réformateur belge du XVIe siècle', *Bulletin de la Commission pour l'Historie des Eglises Wallonnes* 2 (1887), 117–79; D. Nauta, 'De Kerk der Reformatie in Metz onder Leiding van Predikers uit de Nederlanden, 1559–1569', *Nederlands Archief voor Kerkgeschiedenis* 58 (1977–78), 49–84.

[51] Michel Reulos, ed., 'Les livres de Jean de Bouquetot, sieur du Breuil (1611)', *B.S.H.P.F.* 128 (1982), 366. It is also worth noting that Taffin's major works appeared after he left Metz.

was Jean Crespin's great compilation of accounts of those noble and 'abject', male and female, who won a martyr's crown. The *Histoire des Martyrs* was, along with Calvin's *Institutes*, the most frequently recurring single religious book after the Bible and the psalter, appearing in fifteen households, or nearly one Protestant inventory out of eight. Gilmont has shown that the later, folio, editions of this Protestant analogue to Catholic collections of the lives of the saints were particularly successful, far outselling the earlier small-format editions once they appeared.[52] The *Histoire des Martyrs* was an iconic centrepiece of family piety, made to be read aloud around the table. In addition to offering inspiring tales of commitment to the faith, the work cautioned against such doctrinal deviations or weaknesses as Nicodemism and Anabaptism and shaped the historical culture of its reading and auditing with historical sections on the early church, the progressive corruption of Rome, and the great events of the Reformation.[53] Other widely diffused historical works included, for the Reformation era, Sleidan (7 appearances) and the *Histoire ecclésiastique des églises réformées au royaume de France* (6 appearances), and for the time of Christ Josephus's history of the Jews (9 appearances), that staple of booksellers throughout this period.

From the Bible and the *Bouclier de la foi* to the *Institutes* and the *Histoire des Martyrs*, virtually all of the widely disseminated Protestant books mentioned so far were substantial tomes, precisely the sort of books most likely to be noted by title in such documents. What about those cheaper volumes such as the ones slumbering anonymously in Marie Lindfoier's large basket? Were there any popular genres of cheap Protestant literature which our survey has so far overlooked? Fortunately, three inventories of Protestant booksellers' shops from this period have survived. All of these *libraires* were quite modest tradesmen whose stocks of books were decidedly not such as to intimidate relatively unlettered customers.

---

[52] Jean-François Gilmont, *Jean Crespin, Un éditeur réformé du XVIe siècle* (Geneva, 1981), pp. 179–80.

[53] Scholars have long stressed the importance of Foxe's *Acts and Monuments* in shaping the consciousness of England's Protestants. Crespin's compilation seems to have played a comparable role for the French Huguenots and suggests the value of a close comparative study of the different martyrologies. Even the most cursory examination of Foxe and Crespin reveals several differences of significance. Foxe's work concentrates far more exclusively on national events, while Crespin conveys the image of a common cause uniting defenders of the Gospel in France, the Low Countries, the British Isles and even Spain and Poland. From this point of view, Foxe may have contributed more to the idea of England as the 'elect nation' than recent commentators on Foxe have suggested. The chronology of events recounted in Foxe is also set in a framework drawn far more clearly from the books of Apocalypse and Revelation than is the case with Crespin.

The shop of Pierre Chopine is the most fully inventoried of these Protestant bookshops.[54] Chopine offered two books for sale in particularly large quantities, one of them already familiar to us, the psalter (171 copies in different formats), but the other so far encountered only in a single notation, some 180 'preparations for the *cène* (Lord's Supper)'. This was a species of book at which a variety of Huguenot ministers tried their hand and which typically included an explanation of the sacrament, an exhortation to self-examination and good behaviour, and prayers and meditations to be said on communion day.[55] Chopine also stocked 50 small A.B.C.s, 36 'preparations for fast days', two dozen 'civilitez', or behaviour manuals for children, 16 Bibles, and approximately 50 other books whose titles are recorded in the inventory, all works of Protestant religiosity except a volume of Seneca, a history of the Valtelline, and seven copies of Pibrac's popular moralizing quatrains. Most of these works are again familiar from the inventories; Drelincourt (11 copies) and Du Moulin (7 works) are the authors who recur most often. Finally, some 67 'diverse books' are once again left unidentified, 19 of which are explicitly noted as being 'used'. The inventory highlights the broad availability of two sorts of books rarely mentioned in the inventories of private possession, schoolbooks and works of prayer and meditation in preparation for the Lord's Supper, but otherwise it corroborates nicely the impression of Protestant reading patterns gained from the individual inventories.[56] At the same time, the recurrence of a significant number of unidentified books drives home once again the fact that a certain number of works will always escape detection on the basis of inventories alone. This floating stock of cheap, often-used volumes can only be approached through efforts such as those of Robert Mandrou and Henri-Jean Martin to analyse the contours of the surviving copies of the *bibliothèque bleue* and the inventories of those printers specializing in this cheap *littérature de colportage*.[57]

---

[54] A.D.M., B 3354, inv. of 22 February 1651.

[55] *Le Voyage de Beth-el, avec les Preparations, Prieres et Meditations, pour participer dignement à la Sainte Cene* (Charenton, 1665) includes such tracts or meditations by Jean de Fauquembergues, Michel Le Faucheur, Samuel Durand, Pierre Du Moulin and Raymond Gaches, several of which have title pages of their own, suggesting they were also sold separately.

[56] The same can be said for the other inventories of Protestant libraries encountered. Daniel Tannoy (A.D.M., B 3358, inv. of 23 March 1658) sold primarily schoolbooks, writing materials and playing cards, but his shop also had a few Bibles and psalters, a copy of the *Coutumes de Metz*, and 22 'autres petits livres de diverses sortes'. The stock of Daniel Guepratte (A.D.M., B 3352, inv. of 8 April 1647) is less thoroughly inventoried yet, but he too had dozens of A.B.C.s and 'civilitez', a Geneva Bible, three 'praticques de piete', two 'boucliers de la foy' – and four 'jeux d'oye'.

[57] Mandrou, *De la culture populaire aux XVIIe et XVIIIe siècles: La Bibliothèque bleue de Troyes* (2nd edn, Paris, 1975), pp. 43–9; Martin, 'Culture écrite et culture orale', pp. 245–56.

By comparison with the Protestants, very few inventories of Catholic town-dwellers from below the level of the urban élite and the learned professions reveal books, and when books do appear it is common to find only one or two. Far less can consequently be said about the contents of Metz's small Catholic libraries.[58] But several points do stand out. As among the Protestants, these small libraries are predominantly composed of religious books, but the range of titles is far more restricted. Out of 26 books identified, 12 are volumes of the lives of the saints and ten are Bibles – also the two most widely diffused religious books in Paris in this era, although there Bibles were rarer in artisan hands.[59] Interestingly, no books of hours are noted in the inventories; even though this was the most frequently encountered sort of Catholic book in sixteenth century Amiens;[60] we shall see shortly that the absence of such books in the private inventories by no means signifies that they were not circulating in substantial numbers in the city. And only two devotional or historical works by Counter-Reformation authors appear in the small Catholic libraries: a copy of the works of Fray Luis de Granada and Meurisse's *Histoire des Evesques de Metz*, both of which appear in the possession of a widow of the *concierge des prisons* who also owned two portraits of Metz's governor, the cardinal de La Valette, suggesting someone with strong vertical ties to the élites. With a larger sample of small libraries belonging to Catholic artisans and merchants, a few more Counter-Reformation classics would undoubtedly have been encountered, as they were by Henri-Jean Martin in Paris.[61] None the less, his work shows clearly that the massive diffusion of the literature of the Counter-Reformation was only beginning to gather momentum around mid-century – and the rates of book ownership attained among Catholics even late in the century or in the next demonstrate that the dissemination of at least large books never approached the levels attained among France's Protestant population.

But 'large' is the word that needs to be stressed in the preceding sentence, for one of the attributes of the Counter-Reformation as it developed in France was that it was accompanied by the multiplication of small, cheap books aimed at a mass audience. Some of these works were targeted specifically at a certain group within society, as titles such as the *Boutique sacrée des saints et vertueux artisans* or *Le bon laboureur* indicate. Others were collections of Christmas carols (*Noëls*), small volumes of prayers, or

---

[58] There is, in any case, an extensive analysis of the most popular Catholic books in Martin, *Livre, pouvoirs et société*, pp. 99–189, 493–503, 775–805, 928–32.

[59] Ibid., pp. 494–500. The relative frequency of Bibles in Catholic hands in Metz may reflect a certain mimetism of Protestant practice. It may also simply result from a failure to identify some cases within the sample here as Protestants.

[60] Labarre, *Livre dans la vie amiénoise*, pp. 165–6.

[61] *Livre, pouvoirs et société*, pp. 516–17.

accounts of the virtues of a particular shrine that one presumes to have circulated primarily among the *menu peuple*, even if such an audience is not explicitly designated. Books of hours were also cheap popular books by this period; the large and often elaborately illustrated volumes of the waning Middle Ages had by now metamorphosed into crudely printed books of just a few sheets which combined in various proportions an almanac-like calendar, prayers for different occasions, and short biblical passages, occasionally illustrated by crude woodcuts. A hierarchical, paternalistic vision of society underpinned this proliferation of crude books. Certain of them were not even expected to be read directly by their stated audience. Instead, a preface invites those in high positions to buy the work and to read and explain it to those to whom it is addressed.[62]

Given the existence of this vast pool of cheap Catholic literature, booksellers' inventories modify our understanding of the circulation of books in Catholic hands far more than is the case with the Protestants. The inventory of Jean Anthoine, a Catholic printer–bookseller who settled in Metz in 1633 and successively obtained the positions of *imprimeur juré* to the Parlement, the bishop and the king, is particularly telling.[63] Anthoine is known as the publisher of Meurisse's *Histoire des Evesques* and Bossuet's *Réfutation du catéchisme de M. Paul Ferry*, but the 70 copies of the former and 45 of the latter still in his stock are dwarfed in number by 7900 A.B.C.s, 1200 'books of hours with twelve figures in fourteen sheets' and 750 'hours called *billot*'. His stock also included 1572 *Noëls*, 850 catechisms of different sorts, 650 'Prayers of the Missionary Fathers', and 450 copies of 'the mysteries of the rosary', all worth just a few *deniers* apiece. Here is an entire universe of Catholic religious books for sale in Metz which do not appear once in our inventories.

This hidden iceberg of cheap Catholic books obviously requires that the impression of Protestant–Catholic differences gained from the raw statistics of book ownership be nuanced. With a fuller understanding of the religious works circulating on both sides of the confessional divide, a more precise view of the relationship between religion and the world of print emerges. To begin with, the discrepancy between Catholic and Protestant rates of book ownership was less great than that statistics derived from the inventories would suggest, even if the high Protestant literacy rates, the very magnitude of the discrepancy revealed by the raw inventory statistics, and the fact that these statistics also underestimate actual Huguenot rates of book ownership all continue to suggest that the

---

[62] Ibid., pp. 123–69 and esp. 613–25 and 782–97; Albert Labarre, 'Heures', *Dictionnaire de Spiritualité* (Paris, 1937–), VII, part 1, cols 410–31.

[63] A.D.M., B 3362. On Anthoine, see the *Dictionnaire de biographie française* (Paris, 1933–), II, cols 1484–5.

dissemination of Catholic religious works did not attain the levels reached by Protestants. But far more telling than the simple rates of book ownership is the character of the books that circulated in large numbers within the ranks of each confession, and the kind of relationship between book and reader to which they lent themselves. The short Catholic books of hours, prayerbooks or *Noëls* could not support daily reading or foster the gradual mastery of a complex mass of information in the way in which a Bible did. Such books were in many ways ancillary pedagogic tools in a religion that remained centred upon ritual; they taught prayers or songs that might be used in devotions and helped to explain the officially sanctioned meaning of these practices, but they did not displace the experience of the ritual act as the central element in the devotion. The Protestant doctrines of *sola fide* and *sola scriptura* by contrast demanded that reading and absorbing the Bible become far more central to religious practice. Protestantism was indeed a religion of the book; Counter-Reformation Catholicism was a religion that used books. Furthermore, where the universe of Catholic devotional literature was highly stratified, the print culture of Protestantism was more unified and less patronizing in its assumptions about the intellectual capacities of ordinary readers. A shared biblical culture provided the bedrock, and works of abstract theology reached artisans as well as *avocats*, where only the better-trained clerics and a restricted élite of pious laymen read such works among the Catholics. In this respect, Abraham Louvanne, the *marchand tanneur* moved to acquire Du Moulin's 1100-page work of controversy, *La Nouveauté du Papisme*, while hardly typical of Huguenots of his station, is representative of a tendency fostered by Protestantism that finds no parallel within the church of Rome.

So far we have been examining exclusively religious titles, but the secular books in small libraries, while rare, are no less interesting. The greater familiarity with complex texts and the more extensive, regular reading which we have just seen associated with Protestantism could well have had significant implications for secular affairs as well as religious life. One hypothesis in particular suggests itself. Might this familiarity with books not have enabled the Huguenots to gain greater knowledge about the world around them and to learn of new craft or business techniques through the printed word?

Formulating such a hypothesis is easy, but verifying or falsifying it against the ambiguous evidence of the inventories is far more difficult. To judge by the books they owned, most of Metz's Huguenots did not frequently put their reading skills to practical use. Secular titles account for just 12 per cent of all identified books in Protestant inventories belonging to those outside the ranks of large book owners. Of 86 such inventories examined, works of a practical nature bulk large in just two: that of Jean Girard, a master surveyor, whose only books were seven works of mathematics and geometry, and Anne Moreau, the widow of a man who appears from his tools to have been a metalworker of some sort, with a 'book of mathematical figures' and three volumes of portraits alongside six prayer books.[64] An additional work on mathematics, two copies of the *Coutumes de Metz*, an 'essay on the marvels of nature' and three works of history appear in other Huguenot libraries. Yet this is a larger harvest of secular titles than one finds among 176 such Catholic inventories, where the only case which might be considered comparable to those of Girard and Moreau is that of Henry Ribon, a painter who owned 39 volumes of engravings that undoubtedly served him as models in his work, along with nine other unidentified books. Beyond this case, a 'wisdom of Solomon' and a copy of the *Coutumes* are the only secular titles appearing in Catholic hands. The comparison suggests a bit more access to legal and mathematical knowledge of potential practical value and a slightly broader range of curiosity expressed through reading among the Protestants. On the other hand, there is hardly extensive evidence of commercial or technical skills being mastered through reading.

Large libraries

The recent proliferation of studies on the possession and circulation of books during the *ancien régime* has made it clear that a bifurcated pattern of book ownership characterized urban society by the seventeenth century. Among all town-dwellers except for members of the learned professions, magistrates, and a fraction of the town-dwelling nobility, books show up in only a minority of inventories, libraries are generally small, and such books as appear are overwhelmingly religious in character. For many of these people, their chief contact with books would have come through the *littérature de colportage*, which catered primarily to an urban market in this period. The educated urban notables, by contrast, were the great consumers of substantial *livres de bibliothèque*. Libraries were the rule rather than the exception in their households. These libraries often contained several hundred volumes, including a broad range of historical and literary works as well as numerous books related to the owner's professional capacity.

We have just seen that Metz's Huguenot minority differed from this dominant pattern in that ownership of at least a few substantial books was the norm rather than the exception within the community. The differences between Protestants and Catholics among the city's educated élites were less marked. Educated Huguenots, like their Catholic

---

[64] A.D.M., B 3353, invs of 4 February and 26 March 1648.

counterparts, were steeped in the classical culture taught in the *collèges* and academies. Table 4.6, which sets forth the most common secular or non-Protestant authors in Metz's inventories (the table is composed overwhelmingly of books drawn from the large libraries of the élite[65]), looks very much like the similar tables compiled by Martin on the basis of Parisian inventories of this period.[66] If, for instance, the Protestant epic poet Du Bartas stands atop the category of modern poets in Table 4.6, his popularity cannot be ascribed to a particular affinity for his works among Metz's Huguenots; he was also the most frequently encountered poet in

Table 4.6   The most popular secular or non-Protestant authors and books in seventeenth-century Metz

Author	Total copies	Owned by Protestants
Cicero	34	29
Plutarch	28	20
Seneca	17	14
Aristotle	16	8
Ovid	14	12
Erasmus	12	12
Lipsius	12	12
Tacitus	12	12
Meurisse	12	5
Coutumes de Metz	11	7
Livy	11	9
Du Bartas	10	10
Montaigne	9	8
Bodin	9	9
Pliny	9	7
Quintilian	9	7
Josephus	9	9
Théophile de Viau	8	6
Caesar	8	6
Davity, *Les Etats, empires, royaumes et principautés du monde*	8	6
Du Vair	8	5

[65] The great proportion of these books owned by Protestants stems from (1) the important representation of Huguenots within the ranks of the learned professions; (2) the special effort made to seek out Huguenot libraries beyond those in the original sample; and (3) the fact that many of the largest Catholic libraries are poorly inventoried.

[66] Martin, *Livre, pouvoirs et société*, pp. 503–15.

the Parisian inventories. Similarly, the most popular secular authors in Paris in the years 1642–70 were (in descending order) Plutarch, Seneca, Aristotle, Tacitus, Livy, Pliny and Cicero, almost exactly the same authors who appear most often among Messin Protestants. (The Huguenots may have had more of a taste for Cicero and Ovid and less exposure to Aristotle than their Catholic counterparts.) Among the moderns, Erasmus, Montaigne and Bodin were once again extremely popular in Paris.[67] Finally, although Table 4.6 does not show it, such modish genres as novels, plays, works on *honnêteté* and treatises on the occult also appear regularly in Protestant hands, without it being possible, given the small size of our sample, to determine whether these were either more or less popular than among the Catholics. A common learned culture was shared by those on both sides of the confessional divide.

Two significant differences can, however, be seen. First, the libraries of Huguenot legists and medical personnel were less dominated by books directly related to their profession and contained a higher percentage of religious works than those of their Catholic counterparts. Since the sample of well-inventoried libraries of Catholic professionals in Metz is too small to offer a sound basis of comparison, the best statistical demonstration of this can be obtained by comparing the contents of eighteen libraries of Huguenot lawyers and medical men with Jean Quéniart's breakdown of the libraries of the 'bourgeoisie des talents' in his nine cities of western France at the end of the century. Quéniart found that 64 per cent of the books owned by legal and medical professionals were volumes relevant to their occupation, 5 per cent were devoted to religion, and 20 per cent were works of *belles-lettres*. The comparable figures among Metz's Protestants were 35 per cent professional books, 20 per cent works on religion, and 15 per cent *belles-lettres*.[68] The percentage of religious books among the Huguenots may be exaggerated because of the influence of one large and unusual library, that of Jacques Couet du Vivier, the *avocat* who inherited the books of his pastor grandfather. Eliminating this case from consideration, the figures become 41 per cent professional books, 12 per cent religious books, and 16 per cent *belles-lettres*, still substantially different from the Catholic figures. Again, the Huguenots' need to know and justify the elements of their faith manifests itself.

Second, while it cannot be confidently asserted that the Huguenots displayed a greater interest in history than their Catholic neighbours, the

---

67 The large number of copies of Lipsius appearing in Table 4.6 reflects the passion of one man, Josias Floris (we will meet him again later on), who owned nine of his works.

68 *Culture et société urbaines*, fig. 42. The three Catholic lawyers or medical men in Metz with substantial and well-inventoried libraries also possessed very few books on religion (5.6 per cent of identified titles).

volumes of history and current events that they possessed indicate a distinct interest in events related to the fate of international Protestantism.[69] Books on the history and institutions of England, the Low Countries and the Germanic lands were scarce in France in this era,[70] but among Metz's Protestants one encounters a number of histories of England, several volumes on Sweden or accounts of the progress of Swedish arms in Germany, four copies of Simler's *La république des Suisses*, and even the genealogy of the house of Nassau. Lest the popularity of Simler's survey of the history and institutions of the Swiss Confederation be taken as confirmation of the charge often levelled at the Protestants that they desired the establishment of a republic on the Swiss model, it should be noted that works such as Bodin's *Six livres de la république*, Le Bret's *De la souveraineté du roi*, and Barclay's *De Regno et regali potestate*, which enunciate strongly royalist views, appear with some regularity on the shelves of educated Huguenots, while no monarchomach tracts were encountered. The copies of Simler surely reflect the same identification with the Swiss confederation also revealed by the paintings of Geneva owned by two Huguenots.

Beyond the broad overall patterns of reading preference which they reveal, much of the interest of the large inventories lies in what they can tell us about different groups or specific individuals within the Protestant community. The well-inventoried library of the minister Abraham de La Cloche is a particularly valuable find, for no reconstruction of the cultural horizons of a Protestant community would be complete without some sense of the intellectual culture of its pastors, whose thrice-weekly sermons were of enormous potential influence in shaping the outlook of a Reformed churchgoer.

De La Cloche's library contained no less than 836 titles, a very impressive figure by the standards of the day, even if dwarfed by the 2596 volumes known to have been owned by Paul Ferry.[71] Not surprisingly, books on

---

[69] Elisabeth Labrousse has argued that the same pressures that drove Huguenots to immerse themselves in works of controversy also made them eager readers of works of history relevant to the disputed issues of the day. 'Tout huguenot cultivé était pour le moins un historien amateur'. (Cited in Joutard, 'Racines', p. 13.) Comparison of the libraries of Metz's Protestant professional men with Quéniart's 'bourgeoisie des talents' reveals that 9 per cent of the identified books among the former group were devoted to history and geography as opposed to perhaps 3 per cent among the latter. Quéniart, however, utilized a different classification scheme from that employed here, counting all works of 'antiquité' separately where I have included the ancient historians within the 'history' category. With works of 'antiquité' comprising nearly 30 per cent of all titles in Quéniart's sample, it is evident that this category may have included enough works of history to narrow the difference considerably.

[70] Martin, *Livre, pouvoirs et société*, pp. 202–3, 208, 511.

[71] A.D.M., B 3357, inv. of 13 April 1656; Mazauric, *Paul Ferry*, p. 124.

religion accounted for the lion's share, making up 458 of the 765 titles which could be identified. These reveal close study of the Bible, as would be expected from a minister who had to preach on a different scriptural passage each time it came his turn to mount the pulpit. De La Cloche owned eighteen different editions of the Bible in both the original languages and translations, several concordances and numerous commentaries by different theologians, not to mention Greek, Hebrew, Chaldean and Syriac grammars and dictionaries. The library also suggests extensive acquaintance with the Reformed theological tradition and recent Catholic–Protestant controversies in France. In addition to 22 works by Calvin and fifteen by Du Moulin, titles by all of the important recent French Reformed theologians appear, as do works by Bullinger, Vermigli, Musculus, Zanchi, Oecolampadius, Ursinus, Pareus, Gwalter, Alsted, Foxe, Hall, Whitaker and Perkins. Copies of the Augsburg confession and a 'liturgie angloise' suggest a certain curiosity about other traditions of Protestantism, but de La Cloche owned few theological works by Protestants outside the Reformed tradition; two books by Luther, two by Chemnitz (including his *Examinis Concilii Tridentini*, a work of obvious utility to a Huguenot pastor), and one by Bugenhagen represent the sum total. The Roman tradition was far better represented, and not only by statements of faith or defences of Catholic doctrine such as several Catholic catechisms, three controversial works by Bellarmine and Du Perron's treatise against the Protestant Tilenus, all of which the pastor undoubtedly owned the better to know the enemy. He also had such works as Jansenius's paraphrases and annotations of the psalms, Gabriel Biel's *De canone missae*, three devotional treatises by Luis de Granada, and sermons by Savonarola, Michel Menot and Saint Bonaventure that he may have read with appreciation.[72] Compared with these theologians, the church fathers were not heavily represented, although the complete works of Saint Augustine and volumes by Origen, Ambrose, Lactantius and Tertullian also were on the pastor's shelves. Copies of Napier, Foxe's commentary on the Apocalypse, and the *Chronicon Carionis* suggest an interest in apocalyptics.[73] If de La Cloche had read even the majority of these titles, his theological formation was impressive indeed.

While the majority of de La Cloche's books were devoted to religion, fully 40 per cent concerned secular subjects. Some 122 titles can be classified as works of *belles-lettres*, demonstrating a hearty interest in rhetoric, as

---

[72] Protestant doctrine taught, of course, that even amid the darkest days of the medieval church, sparks of true doctrine remained alive. Crespin saw Savonarola as a martyr for the Gospel, and both Saint Bonaventure and Grenada were much admired by Protestant devotional writers.

[73] This last work was a basic building block of the apocalyptic tradition. Firth, *Apocalyptic Tradition*, pp. 14–22.

might expected from a preacher, and a broad literary culture grounded in both the ancient authors and such moderns as Erasmus, Montaigne, Du Vair, Théophile de Viau, Ariosto and d'Aubigné. The Reformed church's hostility toward the theatre did not prevent de La Cloche from owning not only such classic, if debated, school texts as the comedies of Terence and Plautus, but also the plays of Garnier and even the *farceur* Bruscambille.[74] De La Cloche's reading in the literature of antiquity was backed by a certain acquaintance with the historians of the period as well, but most of his 86 works on history and geography concerned more recent periods and topics. These included the history of the Popes (John Bale's *Des vies des éveques et papes de Rome*, Platina and the illustrated *Antithèse des faits de Jesus Christ et du Pape*); French history, often from a Protestant perspective (d'Aubigné, Jean de La Serre's *Inventaire general de l'histoire de France*, the *Satire Ménipée*, an account of the siege of Montauban); foreign affairs, again with a clear Protestant slant (Simler's *République des Suisses*, *L'Histoire des guerres de Nassau*, *Le soldat suédois*, an *Apologie des Chrétiens exilés en Allemagne*, and a *Remontrance du roi d'Espagne sur l'Inquisition*); and travel accounts (Jean de Léry, Van Linschoten and Busbecq's Turkish letters).

Another 94 books were scattered among the fields of law, philosophy, mathematics, the sciences and medicine. Aristotle and his recent commentators dominated the works of philosophy, although de La Cloche owned one work by Ramus. His interest in mathematics was considerable, and he also had a few tomes on the mysteries of nature, including Bruno and Cardano as well as more prosaic treatises on fish and plants. His law books were overwhelmingly what might be called practical working volumes (i.e. law codes, commentaries); only a French version of James I's *Basilikon Doron* and a treatise by Charles Du Moulin concerning the limits of Papal authority in France touched on larger public issues or the nature and limits of political obligation. Some guidebooks of other sorts – *La maison rustique*, *Le chevalier françois*, *Le guide des chemins* and Castiglione's *Courtier* – rounded out the library. In sum, de La Cloche's secular books differed little from those that might be found in the library of a typical, non-clerical member of the educated Protestant *haute bourgeoisie*; no gulf separated the cultural universe of the Protestant clergyman from that of his élite parishioners, although this universe was of course quite different from that of ordinary members of the congregation.[75]

---

74 Martin remarks that Bruscambille's prologues were 'fort appréciées, des spectateurs, plus savantes peut-être qu'on ne l'imaginerait d'abord'. *Livre, pouvoirs et société*, p. 292.

75 Paul Ferry's biography suggests the same conclusion. As a student he wrote poetry and pastorals in the latest style of the day, and the small cenacle of his which mixed pastors and laymen has already been mentioned. Mazauric, *Paul Ferry*, pp. 24, 29–31, 45–6. The library

This same literary and historical culture built heavily around the classics left a particularly pronounced imprint on the libraries of the university-trained doctors and lawyers among Metz's Huguenots. The 695 volumes of the doctor Josias Floris, for instance, were classified by subject matter within the inventory itself and included 65 'poetae', 33 'humanisti', 42 'historici', 32 'oratores' and 57 'philosophi', an overwhelmingly Latin culture spiced by a few 'plaisants' such as Boccaccio, Rabelais and Noël Du Fail.[76] Floris also possessed 349 books on medicine, 33 scientific, astrological and hermetic works, and 30 titles on religion, most of them accounts of important Protestant–Catholic controversies.[77] Couet du Vivier's books reveal a similar immersion in Latin and neo-Latin literature, along with some volumes in French and even 43 works in German, primarily on current affairs or religious topics.[78]

Jean Quéniart has pointed out that whereas educated professionals derived much of their prestige and rhetorical power from their ability to master this culture of the classics, merchants and artisans were free to follow whatever intellectual interests they developed more spontaneously.[79] The remarkable library of the master goldsmith Jean Bancelin, containing no less than 271 books, reveals the interests of one substantial Huguenot tradesman.[80] Entirely in French, Bancelin's books included the works of a few ancient authors in translation – Plutarch, Tacitus, Pliny, Seneca, Plato and even Philo of Alexandria – but the dominant character of his library was resolutely modern. Two categories dominated: history (96 titles) and

---

of the Lyonnais pastor Jean de Brunes, who died young in 1604, also appears quite similar to de La Cloche's, both in general composition and in the important representation of non-theological works. Puyroche, 'La Bibliothèque d'un pasteur à la fin du XVIe siècle', *B.S.H.P.F.* 7 (1872), 327–37.

[76] A.D.M., B 3352, inv. of 2 July 1647.

[77] Aside from such classics of Protestant controversial theology as Du Moulin's *Bouclier de la foi* and Drelincourt's *Abrégé des controverses*, one notes several pieces from Du Moulin's extended debate with the Jesuit Coton, Du Plessis-Mornay's *Deux homélies sur les moyens de se resoudre sur les controverses de ce temps*, the 'Conference entre Gonteri jesuite et les ministres de Caen', and a 'lettre de Gontery Jesuite a Mr le Conte gouverneur de Sedan'. Floris also possessed the early Christian controversialist Arnobius's *Adversus gentes*, as well as works by Lactantius and Augustine. Other of his religious works of note: François de Sales's *Traité de l'amour de Dieu*; Luis de Granada's catechism; Jean Taffin the Younger's *L'Estat de l'Eglise*; Jean de L'Espine's *Traité de la reconnaissance et confession des pechés à Dieu*; a *Harangue consolatoire sur le deuil que les gens de bien ont eu pour le decez de Theodore de Beze*; and a treatise for deacons and elders on the proper administration of the eucharist.

[78] A.D.M., B 3355, inv. of 11 September 1652. Couet du Vivier was an 'interprète pour la langue germanique' and had accompanied the marquis de Feuquières on his diplomatic mission through the Empire in 1635.

[79] *Culture et société urbaines*, pp. 305–7.

[80] A.D.M., B 3355, inv. of 25 October 1653.

religion (86 titles). Bancelin had an enormous taste for the history of France, possessing two dozen general histories of the kingdom, not to mention eighteen volumes of the *Mercure français* and a half-dozen important memoirs of the period. More specific works such as Jean de Léry's *Histoire admirable du siège de Sancerre*, a *Histoire de la dernière guerre de Suède*, an account of the Interdict struggle between Pope Paul V and the Venetians, and a volume from the vigorous debate concerning the supposed Pope Joan, *La papesse Jeanne, ou dialogue entre un protestant et un papiste prouvant qu'une femme ... a été pape de Rome*, all testify at once to the breadth of his curiosity and his distinctively Protestant interests. Bancelin also treasured accounts of exploration and the history of other lands, owning volumes concerning Portugal, Spain, Flanders, England, Italy, the Holy Land, the Ottoman Empire, China, Africa and New France. Among 27 books on law and politics were Machiavelli's *Discourses*, Balzac's *Prince*, legal treatises on the salic law and the king of France's claim to Metz, and a *Receuil des édits de pacification*. A few works by Calvin, Viret and Taffin appear among his volumes on religion, but most of the volumes in this category were accounts of current controversies, sermons and the major works of seventeenth-century Protestant apologetics, seasoned by four volumes of Hall's spiritual writings and contemplations, Napier's *Ouverture*, and Bullinger's sermons on the Apocalypse. That other fascination of the period, witches, also attracted Bancelin's attention, as copies of Bodin's *Démonomanie* and the writings of the great Franche-Comtois witch-finder Henri Boguet indicate. Jean-Jacques's *Secrets et merveilles de nature*, the works of Girolamo Cardano, and three volumes by Francis Bacon show an interest in the natural as well as the supernatural world. Finally, the goldsmith owned several dozen works of *belles-lettres* and moral philosophy which bespeak a desire to obtain a broad culture and again show a preference for modern authors.[81] Touching virtually all of the great intellectual issues of the day, Bancelin's library suggests a range of knowledge and awareness that was decidedly exceptional for one of his status in this era.

The establishment in 1633 of a *parlement* in Metz brought a new set of prestigious official positions to the city, and apparently a corporate ethos that encouraged new patterns of social behaviour as well. A *mondain* character marks the libraries of the two Huguenot members of the court whose libraries were encountered, both of which date from the 1670s and thus stand on the far side of the 'mutation du siècle' highlighted by Martin.[82]

---

[81] Among the works in this category: Montaigne, Du Vair, Petrarch, Saint Amant, several volumes by Guez de Balzac, Barclay, d'Urfé's *Astrée*, *Le bouquet des plus belles fleurs de l'eloquence*, and Scipion Dupleix's introduction to moral philosophy.

[82] *Livre, pouvoirs et société*, Part 3, section 1.

Abraham Le Duchat, the scion of a noteworthy Protestant family who entered the court on its creation, seems to have strayed particularly far from the ways of earlier generations.[83] Eager to learn the arts of polite behaviour that led to preferment, Le Duchat owned several works on *honnêteté*, including Etienne de Réfuge's *Traité de la cour*, Bardin's *Lycée*, and the prince of Conti's *Devoirs des grands*. As was fitting for an *honnête homme*, he was also something of an amateur of art, at least if several volumes of engravings, including the works of Callot, are to be trusted.[84] His 31 works of *belles-lettres* included not only the classic ancient authors and such ubiquitous moderns as Du Bartas and Guez de Balzac, but also several plays, the *Sentiments de l'Académie Françoise sur la tragicomédie du Cid*, and a *Discours apologetique en faveur des femmes*, all of which give off a clear odour of the Parisian salons. Taxing works of abstract philosophy were decidedly not to Le Duchat's taste; his only works of philosophy (if the classification is even appropriate for certain of these works) were a Latin work on dialectics, Plato's *Republic*, Montaigne, Charron and La Mothe Le Vayer. History, on the other hand, he purchased avidly, especially recent history. His 91 works on this subject formed the largest section of his library other than the law, and they were even more resolutely centred around the recent history of France than were Bancelin's books on the subject. Volumes such as the *Journal de ce qui s'est passé aux assemblées du parlement à Paris en 1648–49* show a special concern for political events involving the courts.

Le Duchat's taste in religious books was highly idiosyncratic for a Huguenot – if not for a member of the *noblesse de robe* – since the author to appear most often among his 21 books on this subject was none other than the great Jansenist Antoine Arnauld. Although Arnauld was a vigorous anti-Protestant polemicist as well as a champion of Jansenism, this was not what impelled Le Duchat to acquire his works. The debate touched off by *La fréquente communion* particularly intrigued him; he owned that controversial discussion of the sacrament of penance, several refutations, and one of Arnauld's responses to his critics. Virtually all of Le Duchat's other books on religion also concerned the Jansenist issue or were anti-Jesuit polemics of a different stripe. The only Protestant classics in his library were Diodati's 1644 French translation of the Bible, the *Histoire ecclésiastique des églises réformées*, Du Plessis-Mornay's *De l'Institution ... du saint sacrement de l'Eucharistie*, and Thomson's *Chasse de la beste romaine*.[85] Few other large Protestant libraries are equally devoid of

---

[83] A.D.M., 3 E 3176, inv. of 29 May 1673; Michel, *Biographie du Parlement de Metz*, pp. 297–8. Le Duchat's library numbered 275 titles.

[84] He also owned a copy of *Les Tableaux de Philostrate*, the leading treatise on art of the time.

[85] He also owned the Catholic (but not Jansenist) Sénault's *L'homme criminel*.

works of Protestant devotion or controversy, yet Le Duchat's political savvy and diplomatic skill apparently made him a respected member of the temple, for the congregation chose him to represent its interests at court in 1656 during a dispute over the Protestants' right to hold services at nearby Courcelles.[86]

Since Metz housed a large garrison, a final category of inventories to appear with some frequency is that of Huguenot noblemen serving in the king's armies. Such men were hardly scholars, and each usually possessed only a few dozen books. Interestingly, a substantial proportion of these were on religion.[87] While the period witnessed the defection of many of the great Huguenot aristocrats, the lesser Protestant nobility demonstrated considerably more fidelity to the faith. The books on religion were usually blended with some standard works of history, a few volumes of practical use to a soldier such as medical books or treatises on horsemanship and military tactics, and occasional novels or *chroniques scandaleuses* to pass the idle hours. To take just one example, the 34 books owned by the captain Isaac de Saint Blaise included twelve works on religion, among them three Bibles, Crespin's *Histoire des Martyrs*, Marnix de Saint-Aldegonde's *Tableau des differens de la religion*, Du Moulin's *Apologie pour la Saincte Cene*, and Napier's *Ouverture des secrets de l'Apocalypse*.[88] Another dozen works were devoted to history, among them Josephus, Henri Estienne's *Traité préparatif à l'Apologie pour Hérodote*, Simler, the popular *Les Etats et empires du monde*, *Les amours de Henri IV* and a

---

[86] Tribout de Morembert, *Réforme à Metz*, II, 213. The other library of Huguenot *parlementaire*, that noted in the inventory of Anne de Villers, the wife of Jacques Herbin (A.D.M., B 3364, inv. of 12 October 1670), was less *mondain* and less political, and it suggests a deeper and more conventional Calvinist piety. The 25 religious works it contained were all by Protestant authors, excluding the three copies of the Bible and a psalter. No plays or novels appear, while Ronsard, Tasso, Nervèze, Alciati's *Emblems*, Aldus Manutius's *Elegantiae* and a wider range of philosophical works, primarily in Latin, reflect a literary culture still steeped in the traditions of the late sixteenth and early seventeenth century. Yet *honnêteté* was of concern here too. Both Bardin's *Lycée* and Faret's *Honnête homme* appear, while Sorel's *La Maison des jeux* offered the family parlour games and amusements fit for 'personnes de bonne condition, nourries dans la civilité de la galanterie'. Aside from de La Cloche's copy of the *Courtier* and an example of de Réfuge's *Traité de la cour* owned by an apothecary, the numerous volumes on *honnêteté* in these two libraries are the only copies of such works on manners to appear in the inventories examined, an interesting indication of the audience for such books.

[87] The proportion of works on religion in the libraries of Huguenot nobles of the sword ranged from one of three identified volumes in the seventeen-book library of Benjamin de Saint-Aubin (who also owned portraits of Metz's four pastors), to five books out of the nine in the possession of sieur Philippe Grandjambe: a Bible, a 'testament grec et latin', Calvin's *Institutes*, Drelincourt's *Abrégé des controverses* and Marnix's *Tableau des differens de la religion*.

[88] A.D.M., 3 E 3176, inv. of 12 November 1670.

Défense de M. Fouquet. Montaigne's *Essays*, Ovid's *Metamorphoses*, Mlle de Scudéry's *Cyrus* and *Le Courier dévalisé* (a novel) comprised the *belles-lettres* section, while *Les principes de l'art militaire*, *Le medecin charitable* (a self-help medical book), and a volume of maps testified to the captain's *métier*.

Conclusion

The variety of reading patterns and intellectual interests indicated by these last examples should warn us against any facile generalizations about 'the' Huguenot mind. As in any complex society, sub-communities of occupation and status existed that shaped the outlook of their members in numerous ways. As in any society whatsoever, differences existed from individual to individual in the depth of commitment to the religion they professed and in the style in which they interpreted and expressed that commitment. These variations must be kept in mind, but they do not preclude drawing a few conclusions about the character of Huguenot religious culture on the basis of the evidence presented here.

In a journal written for the edification of his children, the Poitou schoolmaster Jean Migault praised his wife in the following terms:

> She lived in the fear and love of God, and the study of his holy word comprised her fondest delectations, even from youth. She was equally well versed in the history of the martyrs, and she read avidly all works that were apt to fortify her against the fear of death. She also gave a large part of her time and attention to our psalms, and these were so deeply graven in her heart and memory that it was not uncommon, at night while she slept, to hear her sing fragments.[89]

While the example comes from the other side of France, the behaviour it describes appears to have been characteristic of the Huguenots, both in the way in which reading was seen as at once a mark and an aliment of piety, and in the choice of texts. The Bible, the psalms and (although less widespread) Crespin's *Book of Martyrs* were foundation stones of Huguenot religious culture.

Beyond merely confirming the centrality of these books, this study has also shown us that many other titles – Calvin's *Institutes* and Bible commentaries, Bayly's *Practice of Piety*, the great works of controversy written by the leading seventeenth-century theologians from Du Plessis-Mornay through Drelincourt, and finally the small, cheap books of preparation for communion – also circulated widely within the community. If the description of individual libraries indicates the variety of Huguenot

---

[89] *Journal de Jean Migault*, ed. P. de Bray (Paris–Geneva, 1854), p. 76.

reading patterns, certain preoccupations also recur within the libraries described, notably the interest in controversial theology and the concern to be informed about political events of possible consequence for the fate of international Protestantism.

Comparisons with other Protestant traditions illuminate the particular character of the stock of books encountered among Metz's Huguenots especially well. In Lutheran Germany, books of hymns, prayers and other devotional works encouraging the cultivation of an interior, often mystical, piety bulked far larger than was the case in Metz, while works of abstract theology, including Luther's own writings, were extremely rare.[90] That great staple of English religious literature, anatomies of the soul such as Arthur Dent's *The Plain Mans Path-Way to Heaven wherein every man may clearly see whether hee shall be saved or damned*, found few parallels in France. The popularity of British authors such as Bayly, Hall and Napier reminds us of the international character of Protestantism in this era; the world of religious ideas available to France's Huguenots was larger than that contained in the writings of Huguenot divines alone. Still, inward religious life seems to have been cultivated less intensely among French Protestants and to have been centred far more resolutely on the Bible than was the case within German Lutheranism. Those great questions that haunted so many raised within the English tradition – 'how can I know if I am among the elect?', 'what are the inward signs of saving grace?' – simply do not seem to have much preoccupied the Huguenots. As a religious minority under constant pressure from would-be *convertisseurs*, their great test lay in whether or not they remained faithful to their confession. The popular writings of their ministers were those that reinforced them in this struggle. Abstract theological issues took on particular importance in the French context of religious division, and the tenor of French Calvinism was consequently different from that of English Calvinism. If seventeenth-century Protestantism was international, the colouration of the movement in each country remained distinct.

The differences between Huguenot reading patterns and those of their Catholic neighbours were, of course, greater yet. The major findings on the issue of Catholic–Protestant differences have already been presented in detail. Suffice it to recall here that in light of the large numbers of small Catholic devotional works which we know to have been on sale in Metz but which were only considered worth recording if found by a notary in the hundreds in the stock of a bookseller, the extreme contrast in rates of book ownership between the two communities revealed by the inventories of private libraries is somewhat misleading. Yet even if, in its way too, the Catholic Reformation encouraged a growing role for the printed word,

---

90 François, 'Livre, confession et société urbaine en Allemagne', pp. 363–8.

there can be little doubt that Protestantism stimulated a book-centred devotional life considerably more effectively. In thinking about the relationship between the two Reformations and print culture simple figures on how many people owned books may be less revealing than the sorts of books owned and the kinds of relationships between book and reader to which these lent themselves.

CHAPTER FIVE

Toward the Comparative Study of the Popular Market for Art: The Ownership of Paintings in Seventeenth-Century Metz

Although art historians have long been interested in the nature of the art market and its influence upon the character of the art produced in different times and places, they have generally contented themselves with unsystematic and imprecise descriptions of the market and its organization. A hoary commonplace, for instance, asserts that a mass market existed for paintings in the seventeenth-century Dutch republic, and that this shaped many of the basic characteristics of Golden Age Dutch art. Until recently, however, statements about how widespread painting ownership actually was in seventeenth-century Holland rested on little more than the observations of a handful of foreign travellers. No attempt was made to quantify the scope of demand and to establish precisely how the structure of the market differed from that prevailing in neighbouring lands.[1]

In a similar fashion, while sociocultural historians, especially in France, have for some time regularly noted the sorts of paintings which inventories after death reveal to have hung in private homes, the visual culture of ordinary Europeans in the early modern period has been explored far less thoroughly than has book ownership and the world of print culture. Large French theses on a town or the members of a specific social group often include pages on the paintings owned by the people in question, but the analysis is typically cursory.[2] A few more detailed studies have been devoted exclusively to paintings in private hands, but these show little concern

---

[1] See, for instance, Arnold Hauser, *The Social History of Art* (2 vols, London, 1951), I, 461–73; K.H.D. Haley, *The Dutch in the Seventeenth Century* (London, 1972), pp. 130–32; J.L. Price, *Culture and Society in the Dutch Republic during the 17th Century* (New York, 1974), ch. 6, esp. p. 134; Madlyn Millner Kahr, *Dutch Painting in the Seventeenth Century* (New York, 1978), pp. 9–10.

[2] Maurice Garden, *Lyon et les lyonnais au XVIIIe siècle* (Paris, 1970), p. 471; Pierre Deyon, *Amiens capitale provinciale: étude sur la société urbaine au XVIIe siècle* (Paris–The Hague, 1967), pp. 284–6; Bartolomé Bennassar, *Valladolid au siècle d'or: une ville de Castille et sa campagne au XVIe siècle* (Paris–The Hague, 1967), pp. 507–9; Roland Mousnier, *Recherches sur la stratification sociale à Paris aux XVIIe et XVIIIe siècles: l'échantillon de 1634, 1635, 1636* (Paris, 1976), ch. 6; Philippe Rosset, 'Les conseillers au Châtelet de Paris à la fin du XVIIe siècle: étude d'histoire sociale', *Mémoires de la fédération des sociétés historiques et archéologiques de Paris et de l'Ile-de-France* 23–4 (1972–73), 187–9.

for establishing such basic statistical facts necessary for defining the size of the art market as the percentage of people owning paintings and the number of canvases per household.[3] They are meagre things in comparison with the distinguished examinations of *livre et société*.[4]

It is against this historiographic background that the recent work of the Yale economist John Michael Montias assumes its full importance. In his book, *Artists and Artisans in Delft*, and in several subsequent articles, Montias has explored in great detail the wealth, status and training of the members of Delft's painters' guild, the precise extent of painting ownership in the city, and some ways in which collectors' preferences varied according to status and religion.[5] Reviewers of *Artists and Artisans* have criticized the book for drawing only the narrowest conclusions from the prodigious quantities of archival material which it presents.[6] None the less, the unquestionable merit of Montias's work is that it moves the discussion of both the structure of the art market and the nature of collectors' preferences in early modern Europe to a new level of precision and empirical detail. As another reviewer has observed, the full implications of Montias's data will only emerge when comparable information about other countries and other time periods becomes available.[7]

The goal of this chapter is to provide such information on the ownership of paintings in a provincial city in seventeenth-century France and, in so doing, to suggest a few of the possible uses and implications of such

---

3 Georges Wildenstein, 'Le goût pour la peinture dans le cercle de la bourgeoisie parisienne autour de 1700', *Gazette des beaux-arts*, no. 1052 (1956), 113–94; Georges Wildenstein, *Le goût pour la peinture dans la bourgeoisie parisienne entre 1550 et 1610 d'après les inventaires après décès conservés au minutier central des Archives Nationales* (Paris, 1962); Jean Chatelus, 'Thèmes picturaux dana les appartements de marchands et artisans parisiens au XVIIIe siècle', *XVIII' siècle* 6 (1974), 309–24.

4 Henri-Jean Martin, *Livre, pouvoirs et société à Paris au XVIIe siècle, 1598–1701* (2 vols, Geneva, 1969); Jean Quéniart, *Culture et société urbaines dans la France de l'ouest au XVIIIe siècle* (Paris, 1978). Quéniart explains in his 'L'utilisation des inventaires en histoire socio-culturelle', in Bernard Vogler, ed., *Les actes notariés, source de l'histoire sociale XVIe–XIXe siècles: actes du Colloque de Strasbourg, mars 1978* (Strasbourg, 1979), p. 244, that in western France paintings are merely identified by their proportions, if at all, in probate inventories. For one important recent attempt to use visual materials to explore popular culture, see R.W. Scribner, *For the Sake of Simple Folk: Protestant Propaganda for the German Reformation* (Cambridge, 1981).

5 John Michael Montias, *Artists and Artisans in Delft: A Socio-Economic Study of the Seventeenth Century* (Princeton, 1982); John Michael Montias, 'Reflections on Historical Materialism, Economic Theory and the History of Art in the Context of Renaissance and 17th Century Painting', *Journal of Cultural Economics* 5 (1981) 19–38; John Michael Montias, 'Collectors' Preferences in 17th Century Delft: Evidence from Inventories'. I would like to thank J.M. Montias for sending me a copy of this unpublished paper.

6 Theodore K. Rabb, 'The Historian and the Art Historian Revisited', *Journal of Interdisciplinary History* 14 (1984), 648–50.

7 I.H. Montijn in *History* 68 (1983), 326.

information for both the social history of art and sociocultural history more broadly. The town of Metz might initially appear a peculiar choice for such an investigation. Although the duchy of Lorraine is justly celebrated for its distinguished school of painting in the seventeenth century, all the great Lorraine artists from Bellange to de La Tour worked in Nancy or Lunéville, in the shadow of the ducal court. So devoid of noteworthy painters was Metz that Guillaume Janneau's encyclopaedic *La peinture française au XVIIe siècle*, one of whose goals appears to be to mention every French painter known to art history, does not indicate so much as one artist active in this outpost of French control within Lorraine.[8] And not only was Metz a far cry from the Delft of Jan Vermeer, Pieter de Hooch and Carel Fabritius as a cradle of famous artists; it is not generally recognized just how common it was for ordinary French town-dwellers as well to own paintings at this time. Yet Metz's archives contain a series of unusually precise probate inventories, and these note the existence of paintings in the possession of the majority of people whose belongings were recorded. Furthermore, Metz was a religiously divided city with a large Protestant minority; its study consequently permits comparison of patterns of painting ownership between the members of the two different confessions which coexisted, if not always peacefully, within seventeenth-century France. As we shall see, exploration of the contents of Metz's inventories can establish the size of the private market for art in a provincial town of seventeenth-century France and permit comparisons with the Dutch situation; it can reveal certain patterns of Catholic and Protestant religiosity; and it can suggest certain insights about attitudes towards both the family and political authorities.

The sample on which this study is based is composed of 270 inventories from the years 1645–57 and 1667–72.[9] One hundred and four of these inventories belong to Protestants, who can be identified as such from the registers of baptisms, marriages and burials of the local Reformed church.[10] The sample contains people of all social levels from the First President of Metz's Parlement to a crippled old woman living off the charity of her neighbours, making comparisons between different social strata possible as well. As is typical of such studies, however, the sample is skewed towards the upper levels of society, since inventories were more frequently commissioned by families of high status.

Several deficiencies of the inventories must be noted. Only a small fraction of them attach valuations to the objects they list, making it

---

8 Guillaume Janneau, *La peinture française au XVIIe siècle* (Geneva, 1965).

9 A.D.M., B 3351–7, 3362–5. I utilized only those inventories concerning inhabitants of the city of Metz.

10 A.C. Metz, GG 236–53.

impossible to ascertain the precise wealth of most of the individuals in question, and thus to correlate painting ownership with wealth. Metz's inventories after death are also somewhat unusual in that they generally categorize objects according to the nature of the things in question (wooden furniture, clothing and the like), rather than according to the rooms in which they were found. They consequently make it impossible to offer any confident generalizations about the placement of different sorts of paintings in different locations around the house, although one or two inventories which do follow the layout of the house suggest that a logic often governed this. This is clearest in the case of Claude de Bretagne, marquis de Loisy, the First President of the Parlement. The central room of his house declared his political and corporate loyalties, displaying portraits of the king, the First President and his father, and 24 of the *conseillers* in the Parlement – as well as a portrait of St François de Sales and a genre scene depicting a fruitseller. 'La chambre de madame' was decorated more intimately with a Venus, several landscapes including one pastoral scene with shepherds and shepherdesses, and paintings of Joseph and 'Ste. Marie Egyptienne'. Meanwhile the marquis's son, himself also a president of the Parlement, had paintings of St John the Baptist, 'une charité nue', and the Maréchal de La Ferté, governor of the French-controlled parts of Lorraine during the Thirty Years War, in his bedroom.[11]

Metz may not have been known as an artistic centre, but the city contained a small group of painters none the less. Three appear on a 1637 census in which occupations are listed for eleven of the city's fourteen parishes – this at a time when Metz's total population stood at 15 023 in the wake of a killing plague.[12] Fortunately an inventory has survived for one of these artists, Henry Ribon, making it possible to gain an idea of how at least one of these painters organized his business.[13] Ribon is the classic example of the obscure painter. None of his works is known to have survived, and all that the standard French biographical dictionary of artists states about him is that he was born and died in Nancy, which may well be wrong.[14] Although Ribon unquestionably had certain links to court circles at Nancy – his first wife's uncle was a servant of the duke of Lorraine – his business at the time of his wife's death in 1648 was oriented entirely towards production for the urban market, both in Metz and elsewhere.

---

11 A.D.M., B 3364, inv. of 7 March 1670.

12 A.C. Metz, DD 13.

13 A.D.M., B 3353, inv. of 8 April 1648.

14 E. Bénézit, *Dictionnaire critique et documentaire des peintres, sculpteurs, dessinateurs et graveurs* (10 vols, Paris, 1976), VIII, 727. Bénézit's entry appears to follow Albert Jacquot, 'Essai de répertoire des artistes lorrains peintres, peintres verriers, faïenciers, émailleurs', *Réunion des sociétés des beaux-arts des départements* 23 (1899), 485–6. The 1637 Metz census lists 'Henry Ribon peintre' as being 'de la ville'.

His *boutique* contained 21 large oil paintings, which could have been either his own work or that of other artists, depicting such diverse subjects as the Crucifixion, the Virgin, a hunting scene, 'des mangeurs de fromage', Louis XIII and 'Madame la Mareschale de Schomberg'. Several unidentified works in tempera, some picture frames, and 39 volumes of portraits and engravings, which probably provided the models from which Ribon worked, were also scattered around the shop. No outstanding debts indicate any work which Ribon had done on commission.[15] By contrast, he told the notary that he had sent nine of his paintings to Paris and eight to Thionville to be sold by merchants in those cities. He was an artist who painted pictures for an anonymous urban market, rather than on commission.

That a substantial market existed for paintings such as those which Ribon produced is clear from the inventories. Among the possessions of Chrestienne Viviot, the widow of a tinsmith and a Catholic, we find paintings of the Crucifixion, the Descent from the Cross, and Louis XIII, as well as single-figure images of Christ, the Virgin and St Catherine. Abraham Baudouin, a Protestant *marchand tanneur*, owned Adam and Eve in the Garden of Eden, Christ Entering Jerusalem, the Resurrection of Lazarus, the Passsion, the Miracle of the Loaves and the Fishes, and a painted depiction of the Ten Commandments.[16] In all, paintings appear in 66 per cent of the inventories examined. Given the weighting of the sample towards the upper ranks of society, this means that paintings hung in approximately 58 per cent of all the city's households.[17] The mean number of paintings per household (those without paintings as well as those with them) was 5.5.

By contrast, roughly two-thirds of Delft's inhabitants owned canvases in this same period, and the average household there contained eleven, indicating an overall level of demand for easel paintings to be hung in private residences within the city just over twice that found in Metz.[18] To compare properly the market for ready-made paintings in France and the Netherlands it is necessary to recall that it was relatively common for artworks to hang in peasant households in the United Provinces by the mid-seventeenth century, something that was certainly not the case in

---

15 Cf. 'Inventaires du logis de Simon Vouet dans la Grande Galérie du Louvre, 1639 et 1640', ed. Gaston Brière, *Mémoires de la fédération des sociétés historiques et archéologiques de Paris et de l'Ile-de-France* 3 (1951), 117–72.

16 A.D.M., B 3356, invs of 16 March, 21, 22 October 1655.

17 This figure was computed by weighting the Protestant results against the 1684 'Extrait et estat général des habitants de la ville de Metz qui font profession de la religion Prétenduë Refformée', *Annuaire de la Société d'histoire et d'archéologie de la Lorraine* 3 (1891), 345–86, which includes a full occupational listing.

18 Montias, *Artists and Artisans in Delft*, p. 220.

France.[19] At the outside this represented a further doubling of the demand for paintings; Holland was 60 per cent rural in 1622, but it seems unlikely that peasants would have owned as many paintings per capita as town-dwellers.[20] A comparative perspective thus confirms that the market for art was unusually extensive in the Netherlands, but it also underscores the fact that the difference between France and the Netherlands in the size of the market for paintings to hang in non-aristocratic homes was a matter of degree rather than kind. It is inaccurate to assert, as Haley does, that outside the Netherlands paintings belonged exclusively to the crown, the nobility and the church.[21] At the same time the comparison of Metz and Delft confirms the frequently expressed observation that the situation of Dutch artists was a particularly difficult and competitive one. Where Metz had but a handful of painters among its 15 000 inhabitants (recall here that the 1637 census omits occupational listings in three parishes), Delft, with a population of 28 to 30 000 inhabitants around the same time, housed 58 master painters – and, of course, the church did not offer them the additional source of commissions that it did French artists.[22] That many Dutch artists should have failed, or taken up other occupations, is hardly surprising in light of these figures, and one can see how the highly competitive situation of painters in a town such as Delft would have served as a forcing-house for talent and innovation.

The unsystematic character of earlier studies of painting ownership in French towns makes it hard to determine exactly how much the French urban market expanded over time, but some evidence can help place the figures from Metz in better perspective. On the basis of information gathered by Georges Wildenstein, it can be calculated that paintings appear in 46 per cent of Parisian inventories from the years 1556–65 and 54 per cent from the period 1600–10.[23] The 66 per cent figure from Metz thus indicates the continuation of a steady, but hardly revolutionary, expansion of the market during the late sixteenth and first half of the seventeenth centuries. While Wildenstein's exploration of Parisian inventories unfortunately fails to indicate how many paintings are listed in each document, it does suggest that a broadening of the range of paintings in private hands also occurred during this period. In late sixteenth-century

---

19 Jan de Vries, 'Peasant Demand Patterns and Economic Development: Friesland, 1550–1750', in William N. Parker and Eric L. Jones, eds, *European Peasants and their Markets: Essays in Agrarian Economic History* (Princeton, 1975), p. 222.

20 Jan de Vries, *The Dutch Rural Economy in the Golden Age, 1500–1700* (New Haven, 1974), p. 86.

21 Haley, *Dutch in the Seventeenth Century*, p. 130.

22 Montias, *Artists and Artisans in Delft*, pp. 136, 220.

23 Figures calculated from Wildenstein, *Goût pour la peinture dans la bourgeoisie parisienne entre 1550 et 1610*.

Paris privately owned paintings were overwhelmingly religious in character, with portraits forming the only other genre of importance. By the mid-seventeenth century in Metz such other kinds of works as genre scenes, historical paintings, and landscapes formed 32 per cent of the total. After this expansion of the market between 1550 and 1650 the percentage of town-dwellers acquiring easel paintings appears to have levelled off, but the number of works owned per household may have continued to increase, largely as a result of the continued multiplication of non-religious paintings. Canvases appear in 'over two-thirds' of all inventories in later eighteenth-century Lyon, with the average number of paintings *and listed engravings* per household standing at 8.2. The percentage of religious paintings among different groups in society was markedly lower than in Metz.[24] These figures are partial and must be interpreted with caution. None the less, they suggest overall growth in the demand for paintings on the part of French town-dwellers between the sixteenth and eighteenth centuries. Further exploration could enable us to understand the exact course and extent of this expansion, the comparative importance of aristocratic and ecclesiastical demand, and thus the precise significance of the urban market for what is unquestionably the central theme of a social history of French art in this period, namely the rise of French painters from a peripheral to a central position within the world of European art.

What sort of paintings did Metz's inhabitants own? Most of the paintings listed in the inventories were in all likelihood works such as those produced by Ribon, for they fall within a restricted range of subjects which appear to have been reproduced with regularity. Only a few were so closely tied to the specific interests or attributes of their owners as to suggest that they must have been specially commissioned. Where the medium is specified, it is usually oil or tempera.[25] Most works for which a valuation is provided are appraised at just a few *livres messins* each, about the same as a small piece of wooden furniture and more than most books, although not as much as a folio Bible in good condition. A few more valuable works also appear; one painting of Troy burning owned by the *parlementaire* Louis Maguis was assessed at 60 *livres*. Tellingly, however, no works are attributed to a specific artist, and the descriptions of the paintings are brief and include no observation about their style. Unlike in the Netherlands, a speculative art market in which the authorship of a painting was important for its value and in which even relatively modest public officials could identify the styles of specific masters had not yet

---

24 Garden, *Lyon et les lyonnais*, p. 471.

25 A few works are described as 'tableaux en taille douce'. These have been eliminated from consideration in all calculations, as they probably represent only the tip of the iceberg of engravings. Many cheap woodcuts and etchings were surely of too little value to be recorded in the inventories.

developed in Metz in the mid-seventeenth century. Only in the eighteenth century, especially after 1750, do attributions begin to appear with frequency in French inventories.[26]

Much of the interest of the paintings listed in the inventories lies in what they can tell us about the religious culture of those who owned them. Surprisingly little difference appears between Metz's Protestants and Catholics when one compares the *number* of paintings owned by the members of each religion. Even though Reformed Protestantism rejected any use of images which bordered too closely on idolatry and although the rise of the French Calvinist movement was accompanied by vigorous outbursts of iconoclasm, paintings hung in almost precisely the same number of Huguenot households in mid-seventeenth-century Metz as in Catholic ones. (The exact figures are 65 and 66 per cent.) The median number of paintings owned in both cases is also the same. Metz's Protestants tended to be of slightly higher status than the city's Catholics, and when the two communities are broken down along occupational categories, small differences emerge which suggest a slightly greater propensity to acquire paintings among Catholics than among Protestants of similar status. (See Table 5.1.) Catholics of similar status also tended to own slightly more paintings, and nine of the ten largest collections belonged to members of the Roman church, with the result that the mean number of pictures owned by Catholic painting-owners was 8.9, as opposed to

Table 5.1   Painting ownership of selected occupational categories by religion in seventeenth-century Metz

	Protestants			Catholics		
	No. of cases	% of inventories noting paintings	Mean no. of paintings	No. of cases	% of inventories noting paintings	Mean no. of paintings
Nobles and *officiers*	10	80	8.0	16	100	20.5
Learned professions	18	82	9.3	13	77	9.3
Merchants and lesser officials	26	77	6.9	26	88	8.2
Artisans, 'bourgeois', labourers and unknown	50	52	4.4	111	55	6.0

26 On attributions and comments on style in Delft inventories, see Montias, *Artists and Artisans in Delft,* pp. 230–38. On the appearance of attributions in eighteenth-century France, see Wildenstein, 'Goût pour la peinture dans la bourgeoisie parisienne, autour de 1700', pp. 135–6, 138; Garden, *Lyon et les lyonnais,* p. 471.

6.5 for the Huguenots. But these differences were small. If the case of Metz is at all typical, Calvinism may have brought about the collapse of large-scale ecclesiastical commissions in those lands in which it became the dominant religion, but it cut into the private market for works of art far less than one might imagine.

Strong contrasts emerge, however, when one examines the kinds of paintings owned by the members of each confession. Religious paintings were far rarer in Protestant than in Catholic households. As Table 5.2 shows, they account for 61 per cent of all works owned by members of

Table 5.2   Types of paintings owned by religion in seventeenth-century Metz

	Protestants	Catholics	Total
Religious	66 (27)	357 (61)	423 (51)
Portraits	32 (13)	112 (19)	144 (17)
Historical/mythological	35 (14)	24 (4)	59 (7)
Genre	40 (16)	45 (8)	85 (10)
Encyclopaedic	49 (20)	13 (2)	62 (7)
Landscape	19 (8)	28 (5)	47 (6)
Still life	3 (1)	9 (2)	12 (1)

Note: Figures in parentheses denote percentages.

the Roman church and just 27 per cent of the canvases in Reformed hands. The Huguenots also appear to have had a slight reticence about acquiring portraits. In compensation, they purchased many more genre paintings, historical and mythological works, and the sorts of encyclopaedic series such as the Four Seasons, the Five Senses, and the Twelve Months of the Year that were quite popular in the early seventeenth century and had to be classified as a separate category of paintings, since artists variously represented these either as landscape or genre scenes, or as allegorical personifications. Comparison of the Protestant figures with those from Delft reveals that the percentage of religious paintings among Metz's Huguenots was very close to that among Delft's population as a whole (24 per cent). The Dutch, however, owned considerably fewer historical/mythological works (7 per cent) and genre scenes (5 per cent) and were far more partial instead to those classically Dutch genres, landscapes (33 per cent) and still lifes (14 per cent).[27]

---

[27] Calculated from Montias, *Artists and Artisans in Delft*, Table 8.3, combining figures for the period 1640–69.

The contrast between Protestant and Catholic taste is even more striking when one examines the specific subjects of the religious paintings owned by members of the two faiths. (See Table 5.3.) Religious paintings were, of course, far more than decorative objects in this period; they were valued for what they represented. Many devotional writers of the later Middle Ages recommended the use of images as aids to meditation and prayer, and the same prescriptions were reiterated and spread even more widely by confraternity statutes in the early modern period. Thus the White Penitents of Toulouse were required to pray each evening with a fellow brother of the association 'in a suitable place in the house where they will keep a votive image of Our Lord or of the Blessed Virgin Mary, and there, on bended knee, they will make an examination of conscience and, beating themselves, they will humbly ask pardon of God for their sins'.[28] The four most popular religious subjects in Catholic households in Metz – the Virgin, paintings of saints, the Crucifixion and Deposition, and the Magdalen – were all topics which lent themselves to such devotional uses. The Crucifixion and the Virgin were precisely the sorts of subjects recommended by the Penitents, while the Magdalen became an important symbol of penance in the Catholic art of the seventeenth century, and the votive character of saints' images is obvious. Among the saints, St Francis was the most frequently encountered figure (13 appearances), a reflection of the considerable influence exercised by the Franciscans in seventeenth-century Lorraine.[29] He was followed in turn by St Catherine (12 appearances) – and by Joseph (6 appearances), whose cult was strongly stimulated by the Counter-Reformation. This order of ranking is very different from that found in later sixteenth-century Paris, where St John and St Jerome were the most frequently honoured.[30]

While Metz's Catholics favoured images of devotion and veneration, the city's Huguenots shunned these with remarkable uniformity. Whereas 90 paintings of the Virgin (with or without Child) appear in Catholic

---

28 Sixten Ringbom, *Icon to Narrative: The Rise of the Dramatic Close-Up in Fifteenth-Century Devotional Painting* (Acta Acad. Aboensis, Human., ser. A, XXXI, no. 2, Åbo, 1965), ch. 1; Marguerite Pecquet, 'La Compagnie des Pénitents Blancs de Toulouse', *Annales du Midi* 84 (1972), 218. See also *Les papiers des dévots de Lyon: recueil de textes sur la Compagnie secrète du Saint-Sacrement, ses statuts, ses annales, la liste de ses membres, 1630–1731*, ed. Georges Guigue (Lyon, 1922), p. 49: 'Each *confrère* will keep in a visible place in his house an effigy of the Holy Sacrament in the form of an image or painting, so that his children and domestics may revere it.' I would like to thank Philip T. Hoffman for calling these papers to my attention.

29 See here René Taveneaux, 'Jacques Callot, témoin de la Réforme catholique', *Le pays lorrain* 49 (1968), 99–116.

30 Wildenstein, *Goût pour la peinture dans la bourgeoisie parisienne entre 1550 et 1610*, p. 25. One presumes that the St Catherine in question in Metz was St Catherine of Alexandria, although the inventories do not provide any more precise identification.

Table 5.3 The most popular painting subjects in seventeenth-century
Metz

	Number owned by		
	Catholics	Protestants	Total
Religious			
Virgin Mary	60	2	62
Virgin and Child	22	1	23
Virgin with Saints	8	–	8
Annunciation	12	1	13
Saints	77	2	79
Mary Magdalen	24	1	25
Nativity	12	7	19
Holy Family	4	1	5
Christ	15	3	18
Christ and Saints	2	1	3
Life of Christ	15	3	18
Last Supper	4	2	6
Passion scenes	4	1	5
Crucifixion	39	–	39
Descent from the Cross	12	1	13
Entombment and Resurrection	5	–	5
Other New Testament scenes	16	15	31
Susannah	2	5	7
Judith	3	1	4
Other Old Testament scenes	15	18	33
Miscellaneous	6	1	7
Portraits			
Family members	18	4	22
Royalty	14	6	20
Other noteworthy figures	44	11	55
Unidentified people	23	11	34
Dogs	13	–	13
Historical/mythological			
Roman emperors	15	11	26
Venus	3	–	3
Other	6	24	30
Genre			
A courtesan	6	12	18
Shepherds	7	–	3
Other	32	28	60
Encyclopaedic			
The Four Seasons	10	14	24
The Twelve Months	–	22	22
The Five Senses	3	7	10
The Four Elements	–	5	5
Other	–	1	1
Landscape			
'Un paysage'	27	14	41
City of Geneva	–	2	2
Other	1	3	4
Still life	9	3	12

hands, along with another 12 paintings of the Annunciation, just 4 canvases of these topics appear in Protestant households. A similar contrast emerges when one examines paintings of the saints, the Crucifixion and the Magdalen. The contrasting patterns of painting ownership revealed by Table 5.3 show the strength of Huguenot antipathy towards the veneration of images and the cult of the saints, reinforced by the confessional polarization which occurred during the century following the rise of Protestantism in France and which turned images such as the Crucifix into bitterly contested symbols, ardently embraced by Catholicism and therefore just as bitterly detested by the Huguenots.

'Nevertheless', Calvin had written, 'I am not so scrupulous as to consider that one should tolerate no images at all.'[31] Paintings of sacred histories were permissible, and indeed most of the religious paintings owned by the Protestants were illustrations of different biblical episodes – in effect, visual complements to their intense biblical culture. These show clearly the Huguenot identification with the world of the Old Testament; 37 per cent of the Protestant-owned religious paintings were devoted to Old Testament subjects, as opposed to just 6 per cent of the Catholic-owned religious paintings. The rare characteristically Catholic images which do turn up in Protestant inventories usually suggest no serious inclination towards Catholic patterns of religiosity. The exception is the apothecary Pierre Piot, who owned paintings of the Virgin, Mary Magdalen and St Sebastian along with six other works on religious subjects. More typical is the case of Moyse Richard, whose painting of the Madonna and Child is explicitly described as old; Richard also owned six other canvases recounting episodes from the Old and New Testaments – and a view of Geneva.[32] The overall impression gained from the pattern of painting ownership among Metz's Huguenots is of a community remarkably united in its rejection of things papistical.

The sorts of paintings found in private hands in Metz varied not only according to religion, but also to status. As Table 5.4 shows, not only did noblemen, high royal officials and garrison officers own the largest number of paintings; they also owned the smallest percentage of religious paintings and were by far the greatest acquirers of portraits. While the percentage of religious works increases regularly as one descends the social scale, this is primarily because the members of the lower orders bought fewer paintings overall. The members of the aristocracy and the learned professions owned more religious paintings per capita than did their humbler neighbours; they simply surrounded these with a greater profusion

---

31 John Calvin, *Institution de la religion chrestienne*, ed. Jean-Daniel Benoit (5 vols, Paris, 1957–63), I, 135n.

32 A.D.M., B 3357, inv. of 7 December 1657; B 3352, inv. of 15 December 1646.

Table 5.4 Types of paintings owned by members of selected occupational groups in seventeenth-century Metz

Category	Religious	Portraits	Historical/ mythological	Genre	Encyclopaedic	Landscape	Still life
Nobles, *officiers* and military officers (34 cases)	106 (38)	88 (32)	25 (9)	28 (10)	1 (0)	20 (7)	10 (4)
Learned professions (31 cases)	45 (48)	13 (14)	3 (3)	14 (15)	10 (11)	9 (10)	–
Merchants (38 cases)	52 (54)	4 (4)	15 (16)	16 (17)	5 (5)	3 (3)	1 (1)
Artisans (87 cases)	90 (76)	5 (4)	13 (11)	3 (3)	1 (1)	7 (6)	–

Note: Figures in parentheses denote percentages.

of other canvases. The strong classical culture of the educated members of the learned professions did not translate into a great penchant for large-scale history paintings recounting episodes from classical mythology or history. Historical and mythological paintings were owned in larger numbers by merchants and members of the aristocracy, although the frequency of such works among the former group is exaggerated by one case of a merchant who owned a set of twelve paintings of 'les douze empereurs romains'. Genre scenes, by contrast, appealed to all groups, but seem to have been particularly favoured by merchants and members of the learned professions. Landscapes appealed to all strata and still lifes, a new and a rare genre, were especially favoured by the aristocracy.

Portraits form a particularly revealing group of pictures. Specially commissioned portraits regularly expressed loyalty to individuals or corporate bodies, or reflected the interests and status of their owners. The 24 portraits of members of the Parlement of Metz displayed in the *hôtel* of the court's First President, Claude de Bretagne, are one example of this. More striking yet, the *grande gallerie* of Jean de Ligniville, comte de Bey, contained 'un chasseur assis son chien près de luy', paintings of two stags, and ten portraits of hunting dogs, each with the dog's name beneath it. De Ligniville, the reader will hardly be surprised to learn, was the *Grand Veneur* of the duke of Lorraine and the author of a treatise on hounds and the hunt. His *hôtel* also contained a portrait of the count of Vaudémont, a member of the ruling house of Lorraine.[33]

Alongside such specially commissioned portraits were numerous paintings of important public figures produced to satisfy a broader demand. Paintings of the king were the most common of these, appearing in seventeen households, or roughly one in sixteen. In the great majority of cases where the inventory indicates the identity of the king displayed, this was Louis XIII or the young Louis XIV. These portraits were thus generally expressions of loyalty to the reigning monarch, not of attachment to a popular king of the past, admiration for whom could also imply ambivalence towards the man currently seated on the throne. Royal portraits appear in Catholic and Protestant households with roughly equal frequency, and they were owned by people in all social strata. They were, however, most common in the households of officials or military men directly in the royal service. Only one artisan and one merchant in the sample owned such portraits.

One of the consequences of the virtually complete rejection of political history on the part of French historians of the past few generations is that virtually nothing is known even about those points where politics might

---

33 A.D.M., B 3364, inv. of 7 March 1670; B 3354, inv. of 18 October 1650; François-Georges Pariset, *Georges de La Tour* (Paris, 1948), p. 351.

intersect with the concerns of a historiography which seeks to reconstruct the total historical experience of ordinary people of the past – as, for instance, the question of how strongly ordinary Frenchmen of the *ancien régime* were aware of political events at the centre, felt loyalty towards their king, and participated in a national political culture. We know it was customary during the numerous popular rebellions of the seventeenth century for the *insurgés* to appeal to an idealized figure of the king, but otherwise the history of popular attachment – or indifference – to the crown has hardly begun to be written. For this reason the proper context into which to place the frequency with which royal portraits appear in private homes in Metz is unavailable. It is obvious that such portraits brought a distant monarch closer to his subjects and betoken a degree of attachment to the figure of the king. At the same time, some comparative information suggests that the frequency of such portraits in Metz was anything but exceptional. In eighteenth-century Paris, royal portraits hung in the house of nearly one merchant or artisan in ten, a rather ambiguous contrast that could be attributed either to a growing sense of attachment to the crown over the intervening period or to Parisians' particularly close proximity to the person of the king. In seventeenth-century Delft about one family in four owned a portrait of a member of the House of Orange. In the republican United Provinces, attachment to national heroes was apparently considerably stronger than in monarchical France.[34]

Portraits of other noteworthy political figures, such as Richelieu, Anne of Austria, the First President de Bretagne, and above all Metz's successive governors, also recur with some frequency, but these are far more exclusively confined to the houses of military officers or royal officials, among whom they may indicate clientage ties to the figures in question. Since such positions were held predominantly by Catholics, these portraits turn up overwhelmingly in Catholic hands. Huguenot loyalties were meanwhile occasionally expressed by portraits of important Protestant figures. Paintings of Metz's four pastors, of the early Huguenot poet Clément Marot, and of the great ministers Pierre Du Moulin and Theodore Beza all appear in Calvinist hands. So too do two views of Geneva, one of which represents the city besieged by the duke of Savoy.

By contrast with the portraits of important public personages, family portraits were still relatively rare, especially in comparison with the massive diffusion they would experience from the end of the century onwards (an interesting reflection of the sentimentalization of the family group made famous by Philippe Ariès – as well, perhaps, as a weakening of religious

---

34 Chatelus, 'Thèmes picturaux dans les appartements de marchands et artisans parisiens', p. 315; Montias, 'Collectors' preferences in 17th Century Delft', Tables 1, 2.

strictures against vanity).[35] Family portraits appear in eleven *messin* households, all belonging to members of the aristocracy or the urban élite, whereas in eighteenth-century Paris these are found by the hundreds among the city's merchants and artisans.[36] Most of the portraits in Metz depict either the deceased or members of his or her immediate nuclear family. A few aristocrats, however, displayed portraits of their father or other members of a preceding generation, while the 'tableau representant la généalogie des Le Duchat' found among the possessions of Adam Le Duchat, a *bourgeois*, shows that a concern for lineage could extend to the *haute bourgeoisie* as well.

To recapitulate, paintings may not have hung in the houses of ordinary town-dwellers in seventeenth-century France in as great a profusion as they did in the Low Countries, but works of art were, none the less, widely disseminated objects whose investigation, where probate records note their subject-matter with some care, clearly has a great deal to teach not only historians of art and of religion, but students of the family and of political authority as well. The evidence presented here from Metz confirms that the popular market for art was particularly large and particularly competitive in Holland; it also indicates the contours of the market in France and suggests a certain expansion between the later sixteenth century and the middle of the seventeenth. The members of Metz's sizeable Huguenot minority were almost as likely as their Catholic neighbours to own paintings, but the sorts of paintings owned by the adherents of each faith revealed the radical dichotomy in religious sensibilities between the two groups in this era of confessional polarization. The paintings Metz's inhabitants owned also reveal a good deal about their attachment to the monarchy and to powerful political patrons and show that town-dwellers below the level of the urban aristocracy were still reticent about displaying portraits of themselves and had not yet begun to honour and to sentimentalize the family group in the way they would increasingly come to do from the end of the century onwards.

This study has been based on a relatively small sample of inventories from one town during a restricted period of time. More ambitious enquiries along similar lines could define still more precisely the evolving contours of the popular market for art during the *ancien régime*. Such studies could be used to reveal changes over time in religious sensibilities, particularly in the attachment to different Catholic saints and devotional practices. They ought, as this chapter has already tried to suggest, to be an essential element of a still much needed investigation of popular attitudes towards

---

[35] Philippe Ariès, *Centuries of Childhood* (New York, 1962).

[36] Chatelus, 'Thèmes picturaux dans les appartements de marchands et artisans parisiens', pp. 315–16.

political authority and the person of the king. Along slightly different, but related, lines, statistical exploration of the extent of royal, aristocratic and ecclesiastical patronage, as well as further examination of the pattern of artistic production revealed by the probate inventories of painters both famous and anonymous, could illuminate the precise importance of different forms of economic relationships within the art world and help us to understand just how large the crown, church and aristocracy bulked within this world. Since Philippe Ariès, historians of the family have been aware of the value of iconographic evidence for their subject, yet the rise and transformations of the family portrait have never been properly charted. In short, a great deal more work calls to be done. The statistical investigation of paintings which the researcher cannot even see will never become the dominant mode of art-historical research. None the less it offers one valuable means towards the creation of a truly historical art history, free from the distortions introduced by selective survival and judgements of quality, and capable of integration into a democratic history of culture. It also promises to enable us to situate the production of art more precisely in its socioeconomic context than previous, more impressionistic, methods have generally allowed. An important field of research beckons historians and art historians alike.

CHAPTER SIX

Two Calvinisms

What is the hold of a religion on those who hold it? One of the classic explorations of this problem is Max Weber's in *The Protestant Ethic and the Spirit of Capitalism*. As he stressed at the outset of his discussion of the 'religious foundations of worldly asceticism', Weber was not concerned with the formal ethical teachings of the different Christian churches and their possible influence on the development of capitalism, but with the 'psychological sanctions which, originating in religious belief and the practice of religion, gave a direction to practical conduct and held the individual to it'.[1] Here the Calvinist doctrine of predestination was central, because once it was expressed openly the question was bound to arise for individual believers: how can I know if I am among the elect or not? 'For Calvin himself this was not a problem. He felt himself to be a chosen agent of the lord, and was certain of his own salvation', Weber wrote. But for later followers, beginning with his successor at Geneva, Theodore Beza, such confidence was impossible, and the answer which many Calvinist divines began to offer those anxious about their election was: look to your works. An upright life in the service of God became the best proof that one was indeed elected. Thus the tensions engendered by predestination created in believers a constant pressure to live a godly life. An inner-worldly asceticism and a systematization of ethical conduct resulted. One particular mark of this systematization of ethical behaviour which Weber noted was the practice of diary-keeping as a way of monitoring one's behaviour and one's progress in grace. In 30 pages on Calvinism, the essay sketched out a brilliant picture of the psychological tensions implicit in a certain system of theology gradually unfolding themselves over time and coming to shape the behaviour of those raised within that system in profound and unexpected ways.[2]

While the Weber thesis has generated a massive literature of exegesis and debate, the debate, as many commentators have observed, has largely been a dialogue of the deaf. Historians have been Weber's most frequent critics, but they have focused most of their fire on positions which the master never held, thereby leaving sociologists free to retain their faith in what remains a canonical text of their discipline.[3] Two questions have

---

[1] Max Weber, *The Protestant Ethic and the Spirit of Capitalism*, trans. Talcott Parsons (New York, 1958), p. 97.

[2] Ibid., pp. 98–128, esp. pp. 110, 124.

[3] It would be impossible to list all the studies relating to the Weber thesis. Good reviews of the literature, with extensive bibliographies, are Philippe Besnard, *Protestantisme et*

particularly attracted the attention of historians of religion of the early modern period. First, a substantial literature has grown up on church teachings on business ethics, especially the question of usury, with the central issue being whether or not Calvinist writings were more favourable to capitalist practices than those of other faiths – in other words, focusing on precisely the sort of formal ethical teachings that Weber explicitly declared he was not concerned with.[4] Second, certain commentators on Calvin have sought to defend him against the charge of being capitalism's spiritual godfather by demonstrating the quite substantial distance between his social, economic and theological teachings and the Calvinism depicted by Weber – a cogent defence of Calvin, but not a very damaging critique of Weber, who was clear about the distinction between Calvin and later Calvinism.[5] My intention here is not to go over this well-trodden ground once more. It is to explore the religious culture of Calvinism in two different countries, France and England, taking Weber's account of the psychology of the religion as my point of departure. Put differently, this chapter attempts to assess and refine Weber's depiction of the faith in the period of its mature development in the light of both work done in religious history since Weber's time and some original research in the diaries, spiritual autobiographies and popular religious literature of the period.

One caveat and a preliminary point of method first: I should make it clear from the outset that I am speaking here only of the culture of the godly, of that fraction of the population which took the models proposed by preachers and devotional writers seriously and sought to shape its behaviour accordingly. How large this fraction of the population was and

---

capitalisme (Paris, 1970) and Gordon Marshall, *In Search of the Spirit of Capitalism: An Essay on Max Weber's Protestant Ethic Thesis* (New York, 1982).

[4] R.H. Tawney, *Religion and the Rise of Capitalism* (New York, 1926); B. Groethuysen, *Origines de l'esprit bourgeois en France, I L'Eglise et la Bourgeoisie* (Paris, 1927); H.M. Robertson, *Aspects of the Rise of Economic Individualism* (Cambridge, 1933); J. Brodrick, S.J., *The Economic Morals of the Jesuits: An Answer to Dr. H.M. Robertson* (London, 1934); Benjamin Nelson, *The Idea of Usury: From Tribal Brotherhood to Universal Otherhood* (Princeton, 1945); John T. Noonan, Jr, *The Scholastic Analysis of Usury* (Cambridge, Mass., 1957); Ernst Beins, 'Die Wirtschaftsethik der Calvinistischen Kirche der Niederlande, 1565–1650', *Nederlandsch Archief voor Kerkgeschiedenis* 24 (1931), 81–156; C.H. and K. George, *The Protestant Mind of the English Reformation 1570–1640* (Princeton, 1961); Jean Lejeune, 'Religion, morale et capitalisme dans la société liégeoise du XVII siècle', *Revue Belge de Philologie et d'Histoire* 22 (1943), 109–54; Rene Taveneaux, 'L'usure en Lorraine au temps de la Réforme catholique: Les controverses sur le prêt à l'intérêt', *Annales de l'Est* 5th ser., 26 (1974), 187–216; *idem, Jansenisme et prêt à intérêt* (Paris, 1977); Hartmut Kretzer, 'Die Calvinismus–Kapitalismus–These Max Webers vor dem Hintergrund Französischer Quellen des 17. Jahrhunderts', *Zeitschrift für Historische Forschung* 5 (1978) 415–27.

[5] André Biéler, *La pensée économique et sociale de Jean Calvin* (Geneva, 1959).

who composed it are not my concerns here, although it might be observed that there was surely a difference between England, where the godly viewed themselves as a minority of the population and set themselves clearly apart from their fellows in matters such as their ordinary forms of recreation,[6] and the *petit troupeau* of French Huguenots, a well-structured minority community whose devotional culture, as we shall see, made less insistent demands on its members.

The rich historical literature on Anglo-American Puritanism and on English church history more broadly has only occasionally been inspired by an explicit Weberianism. A devout Weberian could none the less find a good deal to confirm his faith in this literature, something which is perhaps not too surprising since Weber relied heavily on English sources. First of all, such scholars as Basil Hall, R.T. Kendall and Lynn Tipson have underscored the shift that occurred with regard to the question of predestination as Calvin's thought became systematized as Calvinism.[7] Calvin, most scholars now agree, was not a man whose thought should be associated above all with one doctrine, predestination. He certainly enunciated more clearly than the other Reformers the 'awesome decree' that some men were destined for salvation and others for damnation, but this was by no means the central organizing principle of his thought, and he was careful to treat of predestination only after he had discussed at length justification by faith and the nature of saving faith.

The men who gave predestination a new prominence in Calvinist thought were the theology professors of the next generation, notably Theodore Beza and Girolamo Zanchi. Where Calvin was the creator of a theology which he sought to render as true to the Bible as possible, the tasks facing these men were to defend this theology against the spokesmen of rival creeds and to expound it clearly and systematically to subsequent generations of students. In their effort to present theology as effectively as possible, these men often drew on the tools of scholastic logic for help. They also naturally began their expositions at the beginning, with God, his nature, and his will, and once they were on this topic they moved quickly to discuss that central aspect of the divine will in so far as humans are concerned, the double decree of election and reprobation. Predestination consequently took on a new prominence and organizational centrality.

---

6 Patrick Collinson, *The Religion of Protestants: The Church in English Society, 1559–1625* (Oxford, 1982), pp. 189–241, esp. pp. 191, 230.

7 Basil Hall, 'Calvin against the Calvinists', in G.E. Duffield, ed., *John Calvin* (Abingdon, 1966), pp. 19–37; Lynn B. Tipson, Jr, 'The Development of a Puritan Understanding of Conversion' (Yale University Ph.D. diss., 1972); R.T. Kendall, *Calvin and English Calvinism to 1649* (Oxford, 1979).

Such theologians of the second generation as Beza and Zanchi also explicitly taught supralapsarianism, an issue on which Calvin was ambiguous. This is also a matter with implications for the question of assurance about salvation, for a basic corollary of supralapsarianism was the view that the efficacy of Christ's atonement extends only to the elect. Christ cannot be said to have died for all men. Calvin had always encouraged those in doubt about their faith to look to Christ's promises, even if he had also indicated that good works were proofs of the indwelling of the Holy Spirit that could 'undergird and strengthen faith'. 'If Pighius asks how I know I am elect, I answer that Christ is more than a thousand testimonies for me.'[8] Supralapsarianism discourages looking to Christ and encourages introspection. Beza drew the logical conclusion: 'When Satan putteth us in doubt of our election, we may not search first the resolution in the eternal counsel of God, whose majesty we cannot comprehend, but on the contrary we must begin at the sanctification which we feel in ourselves.'[9]

By the second generation, then, two important shifts can be traced in the writings of certain continental Calvinists. Predestination had come to be placed front and centre, and the need to look to one's own sanctification when in doubt about salvation had been adduced. But it should also be stressed that on the continent the theologians I have mentioned so far were just some among many Reformed theologians, many of whom spoke with different voices on these issues. The importance of Beza and Zanchi for English Calvinism lies in the fact that these authors exercised a growing influence in England over the course of the Elizabethan period and were to be two central theological influences on the Cambridge theologian William Perkins.[10] Perkins in turn was the most frequently reprinted English author of the period 1590–1620 and the fountainhead of subsequent Puritan theological writing. He teaches both supralapsarianism and strict predestination quite emphatically, and even lays his doctrine out in diagram form as an 'ocular catechism to them which cannot read' in the introduction of his major doctrinal work, the *Golden Chain*.

---

8 Quoted in Kendall, *Calvin and English Calvinism*, p. 28.

9 Quoted in Tipson, 'Puritan Understanding of Conversion', p. 119.

10 C.M. Dent, *Protestant Reformers in Elizabethan Oxford* (Oxford, 1983), pp. 74–102, traces well the growing influence of Beza and Zanchi in English theological circles. Perkins not only cites both of these authors frequently; he excerpted from Beza's works 'an Excellent Treatise of Comforting such, as are troubled about their Predestination' and published this as an appendix to his *Golden Chain*, while he attached 'A Briefe discourse taken out of the writings of Her. *Zanchius* Wherein the foresaid case of Conscience is disputed and resolved' to his *A Case of Conscience, the greatest that ever was: How a man may know whether he be the Child of God or no* (London, 1592).

Perkins was not simply important as England's first systematic Reformed theologian to attain international stature. In Fuller's endlessly quoted phrase about him, he 'brought the schools into the pulpit, and, unshelling their controversies out of their hard school-terms, made thereof plain and wholesome meat for his people'. Personally linked to that early group of Puritan preachers and spiritual writers whom William Haller has labelled 'physicians of the soul' (Richard Greenham, Arthur Hildersham, Richard Rogers, John Dod and Henry Smith), Perkins was the first of these men to publish his works and attain considerable success as a practical theologian.[11]

Here we have to introduce some considerations which Weber did not mention. A striking characteristic of all these early Puritan writers is that they not only had mutual interconnections to each other and to Cambridge, but were also pastors of rural parishes. As such, these men had to face the problem of bringing the Protestant message of justification by faith alone, increasingly set within a theology that stressed the division of the world into the elect and the reprobate, to an audience whose grasp of doctrinal abstractions was often shaky at best. Furthermore, they had to do so in the context of a church about whose liturgical practices they had serious reservations, which lacked in their eyes the proper means of godly discipline, and within which ministers licensed to preach were a small, although growing, minority. The consequence of this situation was to lead the zealous preachers and spiritual writers to emphasize the prophetic element in their calling – ministers had to be the agents of salvation for men from many miles around – and to develop techniques for teaching and reinforcing proper moral behaviour that would encourage godliness in the absence of a proper formal scheme of discipline.[12]

---

11 On Perkins, see especially, *The Works of that Famous and Worthie Minister of Christ, in the Universitie of Cambridge, M. W. Perkins* (Cambridge, 1605); Ian Breward, ed., *The Work of William Perkins* (Appleford, 1970); H.C. Porter, *Reformation and Reaction in Tudor Cambridge* (Cambridge, 1958), pp. 288–313; Tipson, 'Puritan Understanding of Conversion', ch. 4; Kendall, *Calvin and English Calvinism*, pp. 51–76. On the wider context, see William Haller, *The Rise of Puritanism* (New York, 1938), pp. 10–82; Porter, *Tudor Cambridge* pp. 215–73. Perry Miller emphasizes the importance of Perkins for the later Puritan tradition in 'The Marrow of Puritan Divinity' in *Errand into the Wilderness* (Cambridge, Mass., 1956), p. 57.

12 'The theological achievement of the Puritans, from William Perkins onwards, can be roughly interpreted as the adaptation and domestication of Calvinism to fit the condition of voluntary Christians whose independence of the ordered, disciplined life of the church Calvin would have found strange and disturbing.' Patrick Collinson, 'Towards a Broader Understanding of the Early Dissenting Tradition', in *Godly People: Essays in English Protestantism and Puritanism* (London, 1983), p. 539. See also David Zaret, *The Heavenly Contract: Ideology and Organization in Pre-Revolutionary Puritanism* (Chicago, 1985), *passim*, esp. chs 4, 5.

The pastoral strategy which these godly ministers adopted in the face of this situation involved three parts. Patrick Collinson has characterized the attitude dominant among England's rural parishioners as a 'rustic pelagianism', a point of view which the author illustrates with the figure Atheos from George Gifford's *Countrie Divinitie*: 'I mean well: I hurte no man; nor I thinke no man anye hurt: I love God above all: and put my whole trust in him: What woulde you have more?' Another example is Asunetus, 'An Ignorant Man' of Arthur Dent's *The Plain Man's Path-Way to Heaven*.

> If a man say his Lords praier, his Ten Commandments, and his Beliefe, and keeps them, and say nobody any harme, and doe as he would be done to, have good faith to God-ward, and be a man of Gods beliefe, no doubt he shall be saved, without all this running to Sermons and pratling of the scripture.[13]

First, to combat what they saw as this misplaced confidence in the view that a man could be saved if he simply tried to do good and left the rest up to God, the godly ministers directed their attention to bringing their auditors to salvation by preaching first the Law and then the Gospel. The members of their audience initially had to be convinced of 'their wretched state by nature' by having all the implications of the Ten Commandments expounded to them so that they might see the impossibility of living up to such standards. Then, once they were sufficiently cast down into despair over their wretchedness, the Gospel's promises of salvation could be announced.

Once believers were led to recognize that salvation could only come from faith alone, it was then necessary for the godly minister to assist them in recognizing the presence of that saving faith within. 'Give no rest to yourselves, till you can prove that you be in the estate of salvation', Richard Rogers told his readers, and this phrase could well be taken as the watchword of Puritan pastoral writings.[14] In order to help troubled souls prove this to themselves, the Puritan spiritual writers explored the mysteries of the conversion process and provided lists of marks of election, or 'glasses of godliness', against which people could measure themselves in order to answer that fundamental question which they were now invited

---

[13] Collinson, *The Religion of Protestants*, p. 202 and, more broadly, pp. 201–4; Dent, *The Plain Mans Path-Way to Heaven* (London, 1607), p. 25. Thomas Boston, *A General Account of My Life* (London, 1908), pp. 73, 112, provides a nice account of the continuance of this state of affairs in one rural Scottish parish at the close of the seventeenth century.

[14] Quoted in Tipson, 'Puritan Understanding of Conversion', p. 292. Similar sentiments in Perkins, 'A Treatise Tending unto a Declaration Whether a Man be in the Estate of Damnation or Salvation', in Breward, ed., *Work of Perkins*, p. 361; William Bradshaw, *A Preparation to the Receiving of the Sacrament*, quoted in Edmund S. Morgan, *Visible Saints: The History of a Puritan Idea* (New York, 1963), p. 76.

to consider: am I a child of God or no? The detailed exploration of the process of growth in assurance and the use of such 'glasses of godliness' are the elements in Puritan devotional literature that seem most novel with the generation of Perkins, Greenham and the other Elizabethans, although antecedants can be found in the writings of the earlier English reformers William Tyndale and John Bradford, both of whom were sources for Perkins.[15]

Finally, once believers were brought to some assurance of salvation, it was necessary to provide guidance as to how they should order their subsequent behaviour. To this end Puritan writers multiplied volumes of cases of conscience, tracts on 'domesticall duties', and such vast compendia of prayers, meditations, and directions for all events in life as Lewis Bayly's *The Practice of Piety, Directing the Christian how to walk that he may please God*. Until volumes such as this have received the close study they deserve, the precise origin of all the various meditations and rules for living which their works contain cannot be known clearly. Those scholars who have written about Puritan meditation and devotion have, however, all pointed to its debt to Catholic devotional literature and practice.[16] Richard Rogers explicitly states at the beginning of his *Seven Treatises*, one of the first guides to daily walking, that he wrote the book to refute the taunts of Catholic authors such as Parsons 'that we have nothing set out for the certaine and daily direction of a Christian, when yet they have published (they say) many treatises of the argument'.[17] In replying to the challenge of these works, the Puritan authors in fact adopted certain of their elements. For instance, the counsel that every evening one should review and examine one's behaviour during that day – a clear example of the systematization of ethical conduct taught by these books – descends from St Bernard and is recommended by Loyola and François de Sales as well. The guidelines for the daily behaviour of a pious Christian found in

---

15 Bradford, *Writings* I, 43–65; 'A Dialogue of the State of a Christian Man Gathered Here and There Out of the Sweet and Savoury Writings of Master Tyndale and Master Bradford', in Breward, ed., *Work of Perkins*, pp. 362–8. Donald Dean Smeeton, *Lollard Themes in the Reformation Theology of William Tyndale* (Kirksville, Mo., 1986), p. 140, observes that Tyndale's concern for and treatment of the issue of assurance is one of the most original aspects of his thought, unanticipated by either Luther or the Lollards.

16 Louis L. Martz, *The Poetry of Meditation: A Study in English Religious Literature of the Seventeenth Century* (New Haven, 1954), esp. pp. 108–75; Charles E. Hambrick-Stowe, *The Practice of Piety: Puritan Devotional Disciplines in Seventeenth-Century New England* (Chapel Hill, 1982), pp. 25–39; Frank Livingstone Huntly, *Bishop Joseph Hall 1574–1656: A Biographical and Critical Study* (Cambridge, 1979), 75–81; Elisabeth Bourcier, *Les journaux privés en Angleterre de 1600 à 1660* (Paris, 1976), pp. 353–4.

17 Rogers, *Seven Treatises containing such direction as is gathered out of the Holie Scriptures, leading and guiding to true happines, both in this life, and in the life to come* (London, 1603), unpaginated preface.

Bayly's *Practice of Piety* and the multi-authored collection *A Garden of Spirituall Flowers* could have been drawn almost directly from one of the first Catholic devotional manuals translated into English, Gaspar Loarte's *The Exercise of a Christian Life.*[18]

The themes and genres pioneered by the early 'physicians of the soul' were then reiterated and amplified in the vast outpouring of popular devotional books which streamed off English presses throughout the seventeenth century. The most frequently reprinted book of the period 1603–40, for instance, was Bayly's *Practice of Piety*. After a catechism, the next biggest seller was Dent's *Plain Man's Path-Way to Heaven*, whose subtitle, significantly, is 'Wherein every man may clearly see, whether he shall be saved or damned'. This is an exposition of many of the basic points of Protestantism set in dialogue form. It includes lists of 'notes and tokens of a regenerate mind' and applies the Law–Gospel means of presenting religion in a long and compelling stretch of dialogue in which Asunetus is brought to see the depth of his sinfulness and then to feel 'som perswasion, that the promises doe belong unto me, my sins are forgiven, and that I am one of them that shall be saved'.[19] The habit of providing lists of the marks of election became so entrenched over the course of the century that writers in the emerging Anglican tradition regularly supplied them as well as did Puritans.[20]

And what were the signs of election that these books set forth? Here, the extensive scholarship on the Puritan 'morphology of conversion' requires that Weber's understanding be given certain nuances, although not rejected altogether. The many authors who addressed this question provided a bewildering array of probable marks of election. Early in the *Plain Mans Path-Way*, for instance, the reader is informed that these are the eight signs of salvation:

> A love to the children of God
> A delight in his word
> Often and fervent prayer
> Zeale of Gods glory
> Deniall of our selves
> Patient bearing of the crosse, with profit, and comfort
> Faithfulness in our calling
> Honest, just, and conscionable dealing in all our actions among men.

---

[18] *A Garden of Spirituall Flowers* (London, 1625); *The Exercise of a Christian Life Written in Italian by the Reverend Father Gaspar Loarte D. of Divinitie, of the Societie of Jesus. And new translated into Englishe by I.S.* (n.p., [1579]; reprint edn, Menston, 1970).

[19] Dent, *Plain Mans Path-Way*, 393. On the popularity of Bayly and Dent, see H.S. Bennett, *English Books and Readers 1603 to 1640* (Cambridge, 1970), pp. 213–14; Geraint H. Jenkins, *Literature, Religion and Society in Wales, 1660–1730* (Cardiff, 1978), p. 114.

[20] J. Sears McGee, *The Godly Man in Stuart England: Anglicans, Puritans, and the Two Tables, 1620–1670* (New Haven, 1976), pp. 65–7.

Later on Dent mentions:

> reverence of God's name
> keeping of Sabbath
> truth
> industrie
> sobrietie
> compassion
> humility
> chastity
> contentation.

At this point, one character in his dialogue asks if some of these marks cannot be found in the reprobate as well. Yes, his godly interlocutor admits, and he offers eight further signs set forth by Saint Peter himself:

> faith
> virtue
> knowledge
> temperance
> patience
> godliness
> brotherly kindness
> love.

Doesn't the same objection apply to this list, Theologus is again asked? Yes, he admits again. Here are the most sound evidences of salvation of all:

> assured faith in the promises of God
> sincerity of heart
> the spirit of adoption
> sound regeneration and sanctification
> inward peace
> groundedness in the truth
> continuance to the end.[21]

If this was supposed to provide reassurance, one can see how that was not necessarily always the result.

As Dent's lists show, good works bulked large among the signs of salvation. But the precise degree of emphasis devoted to them varied from author to author. Indeed, debate about this issue was one of the central dialogues within the world of English theology throughout the century. Some writers, notably John Downame, stressed so much that the proper method of gaining assurance was to begin with sanctification and work backward to election that certain passages in their writings came perilously close to sounding like a doctrine of justification by works. 'We are therefore sanctified that we may be saved, and also assured of our salvation',

---

21 Dent, *Plain Mans Path-Way*, pp. 30, 232–4.

Downame wrote in his *Christian Warfare*, while in urging charity in *The Pleas of the Poore* he could assert, 'by these works of mercy we are furthered notably in the way to salvation'.[22] For those writers denounced as Antinomians, on the other hand, sanctification had no place at all in the business of assurance. If one can define a modal position within this dialogue, it would be that the inward experience of grace working upon the heart was central to assurance, and yet this alone was likely to be insufficient in what was normally a long, drawn-out quest. Perkins tells his readers that there is always a single moment when a person is first converted from a state of corruption to a state of regeneration, but his pastoral experience taught him that for most people this was not an overpowering and instantly recognizable experience. To explain the usual workings of faith in an individual, he introduced a distinction between 'weak faith', the first faint stirrings in a person when he becomes persuaded that his sins are pardonable, even if he does not have full confidence that they are in fact truly pardoned, and the 'strength or ripeness of faith', which only comes gradually and after periods of doubt.[23] This distinction enabled the pastor, if he found only the slightest trace of faith in a member of his congregation, to apply the soothing balm of predestination. Given that the elect were predestined to persevere, even this tiny bit of faith, the 'graine of musterd seed' that was the title of one of Perkins' works, was enough for a person to know that he was among the elect. It was its applicability to contexts such as this that led Puritan authors constantly to insist that predestination was a 'comfortable' doctrine, not one which bred anxiety about salvation. Unfortunately, the comfort Perkins offered with one hand he took away with the other, for he followed Calvin in believing in the possibility of temporary faith.[24] Both observation and biblical example taught that it was possible to display all the outward marks of godly behaviour that the elect did, even to experience almost the same inward feeling that they did, and then to fall away from faith. How could an individual recognize the difference between weak faith and temporary faith? The difference, it had to be admitted, was almost impossible to discern at once. Unless the first fruits of grace increased in time, however, they were clearly counterfeit. Full assurance thus only came

---

[22] Quoted in Dewey D. Wallace, Jr, *Puritans and Predestination: Grace in English Protestant Theology: 1525–1695* (Chapel Hill, 1982), p. 51; A.L. Beier, 'The social problems of an Elizabethan country town: Warwick, 1580–90', in Peter Clark, ed., *Country Towns in Pre-industrial England* (New York, 1981), p. 72.

[23] Breward, ed., *Work of Perkins*, p. 230. Tipson, 'Puritan Understanding of Conversion', pp. 244–6, provides the best exposition of this question and Perkins's understanding of conversion more generally.

[24] Breward, ed., *Work of Perkins*, pp. 359–61; Kendall, *Calvin and English Calvinism*, pp. 67–74.

'in some continuance of time, after that for a long time he hath kept a good conscience before God, and before men, and hath had divers experiences of God's love and favor towards him in Christ'.[25]

Such an understanding of faith obviously stretched the process of conversion out over a long period of time, and it is what made the Puritan's life an extended pilgrimage toward both ever greater assurance and sanctification. During this pilgrimage, the feeling of faith would ebb and flow. Because of this, strenuous effort was required and often rekindled along the way, since periods of doubt and despair would recur. That effort could be moral effort, Perkins's 'keeping a good conscience before God'. It could also be devotional effort, as prayer, reading of Scripture and partaking in communion were all seen as means of fortifying one's faith. All might stimulate further inward testimonies of God's grace, and Puritan devotional writings offered instruction in cultivating these. The implications of the Puritan understanding of conversion as it was developed in the wake of Perkins are perhaps most sensitively set out by Charles Hambrick-Stowe:

> Faithful New Englanders were men and women spiritually driven toward the goal of union with Christ. This inner drive was an essential force in their devotional practice. The nature of conversion was in part responsible for the sustained power of the yearning of union. Even when conversion was a decisive personal event, it left many questions unanswered and opened new doors of spirituality. The questions centered around the search for assurance that God was indeed imparting grace. Although much has been written about the anxiety that accompanied the Puritan's inner quest for assurance, it is significant that the quest led to an ever-deepening relationship with the God of salvation. Diaries indicate that a spiraling effect commonly marked Puritan experience. The intensity of each crisis contributed to an ever greater intensity of assurance. Ongoing anxiety served a beneficial purpose and was one way that Puritans felt God leading them on to the ultimate end of their pilgrimage.[26]

The concern of the English devotional tradition with both personal self-control in the absence of institutional means to enforce discipline and the intense self-scrutiny to discern and reinforce the signs of election also helps to explain why the Puritans were such regular diary-keepers. Diaries could provide a tool for monitoring one's own behaviour while at the same time offering a record of God's particular providences to his children and a

---

25 Breward, ed., *Work of Perkins*, p. 404; Tipson, 'Puritan Understanding of Conversion', p. 246.

26 Hambrick-Stowe, *Practice of Piety*, p. 89. On the Puritan doctrine of conversion more generally, see also Morgan, *Visible Saints*, pp. 65–75; Miller, *The New England Mind*, esp. ch. 10; William K.B. Stoever, *'A Faire and Easie Way to Heaven': Covenant Theology and Antinomianism in Early Massachusetts* (Middletown, Conn., 1978).

memento of personal spiritual experiences that could be re-read in those periods when the feeling of faith ebbed and doubt began to raise its ugly head. The first evidence of spiritual diary-keeping in England comes in a 1574 account of the life of John Bradford:

> he used to make unto himself an ephemeris or a journal, in which he used to write all such notable things as either he did see or hear each day that passed. But whatsoever he did see, he did so pen it that a man might see in that book the signs of his smitten heart. For if he did see or hear any good in any man, by that sight he found and noted the want thereof in himself, and added a short prayer, craving mercy and grace to amend. If he did hear or see any plague or misery, he noted it as a thing procured by his own sins, and still added *Domine miserere me*, 'Lord have mercy upon me.' He used in the same book to note such evil thoughts as did rise in him ... And thus he made to himself and of himself a book of daily practices of repentance.[27]

The first surviving diaries of this sort originate precisely in the Cambridge circle of the 1580s and 1590s. Perkins urged their maintenance in the conclusion of his *Graine of Musterd-Seede*. By the middle of the seventeenth century, this prescription had been taken up by other spiritual writers and such diaries are numerous.[28]

Better than any other documents, these journals and autobiographies testify to the particular set of experiences that characterized the inner life of English Puritanism and demonstrate that the devotional writings of the godly ministers provided a template which moulded the experience of those who read them. Periods of profound depression in which the conviction of one's sinfulness and certain damnation was so intense as to breed thoughts of suicide; the searching of conscience for the faint signs of grace; the subsequent roller-coaster ride of assurance and renewed doubt; an intense life of 'closet devotions' combined with close surveillance of one's personal behaviour – all of these appear repeatedly in these documents. Often, it is clear, anxieties about not possessing saving grace arose not out of any abstract contemplation of the 'awesome decrees' of predestination, but when individuals were convinced by a book they read or a sermon they heard that simply living the sort of upright life they had felt themselves to be living up until that moment was insufficient for salvation, or when their spiritual experiences did not conform to the morphology of conversion set forth in their works.[29] In other words, the

---

27 Bradford, *Writings*, I, 35.

28 Breward, ed., *Work of Perkins*, pp. 406, 408; Owen C. Watkins, *The Puritan Experience: Studies in Spiritual Autobiography*, esp. pp. 18–24; Bourcier, *Les journaux privés en Angleterre*, pp. 69, 323–60; Hambrick-Stowe, *Practice of Piety*, pp. 186–93.

29 See, e.g., Richard Baxter, *Autobiography*, ed. N.H. Keeble (London, 1974), p. 10; Morgan, *Visible Saints*, p. 71.

traditions of preaching to conversion and seeking to spell out the precise stages of a true conversion themselves heightened lay concern with the issue of assurance.

During the years in which the contours of Puritan spirituality were taking shape in Elizabethan England, France's Huguenots were involved in a life-and-death struggle for the survival of their faith. The Wars of Religion were hardly hospitable to the establishment of settled patterns of devotion, so these are best approached from the vantage point of the seventeenth century, after the promulgation of the Edict of Nantes instituted an 87-year period of unbroken toleration and relative calm. Even in this period, for reasons which will soon become apparent, the sources are far less revealing than they are for Puritan culture. Nevertheless, the picture that appears to emerge from them is of a religious culture whose patterns and stress points were different from those of Anglo-American Puritanism in a number of important ways.

A sense of the differences between the two Calvinisms emerges first of all from the books which circulated most widely in Huguenot hands in the seventeenth century. Aside from the inevitable Bibles and psalm books, occasionally leavened with Crespin's *Histoire des martyrs*, two categories stand out for the frequency with which they appear in private libraries: the writings of Calvin himself, and works of controversy written by seventeenth-century French theologians, works which seek to demonstrate the truths of the Reformed religion and the errors of papistry such as Pierre Du Moulin's *Bouclier de la foi* and *La Nouveauté du papisme* or Charles Drelincourt's *Abrégé des controverses, ou sommaire des erreurs de l'Eglise romaine avec leur refutation par des textes expres de la Bible de Louvain*. Printed sermons also enjoyed a growing vogue as the century progressed. By contrast, the works of practical divinity and personal spirituality which so dominated the book market in seventeenth-century England occupied a far smaller place.[30]

In Huguenot sermons or those devotional writings which did find their way into print, many of the chords which sound so clearly in the English sources are also muted or non-existent. I have found no traces of Huguenot preachers first trying to convince the members of their audience of the extent of their sinfulness under the Law, then preaching the Gospel. The division of the world into the reprobate and the elect is not broadcast as openly and as insistently by Huguenot writers as it is by the English; nor

---

[30] Louis Desgraves, *Répertoire bibliographique des livres imprimés en France au XVIIe siècle* (Baden-Baden, 1978), esp. vol. 1, Saumur, vol. 2, La Rochelle, vol. 6, Montauban, Niort, vol. 9, Montpellier, Nîmes; above, Chapter 4, pp. 166–74.

is there the same emphasis that each individual must make his or her own election sure. With relatively few exceptions, most notably Amyraut's 4560-page *Morale chrétienne*, which was clearly not intended for a broad popular audience, the French Protestants also did not write many treatises on such matters as the proper conduct of family life, business affairs, or other aspects of applied morality; nor did they author extended devotional manuals.

English books in translation could and did fill certain of these gaps, but the pattern of English translations and the reception these books received is also revealing. Two English devotional writers attained considerable popularity in France: Joseph Hall, the author of numerous guides to the art of meditation and works of spiritual consolation whose writings contain a strong neo-Stoic element that fitted well with the emerging classical culture of the *grand siècle*; and Lewis Bayly, whose *Practice of Piety* went through at least twenty French editions.[31] With its sabbatarianism, its practical moral guidelines for everyday behaviour, and its promotion of a regime of self-discipline reinforced by nightly meditations on the sins of the preceding day, this book displays many characteristic preoccupations of Puritan devotion. Its diffusion could thus have introduced or reinforced these practices among a significant fraction of the Huguenot population. Yet the book received a cool welcome from the Huguenot pastorate. Amyraut saw it as threatening a return to works righteousness. Instead of being subject to rules, he wrote, 'piety should be supremely voluntary and practised with full alacrity of courage and even gaiety'. 'It is an enemy of that peace and joy ... to feel scruples and remorse that importune one's conscience.'[32]

Does this mean that the issue of whether of not they possessed saving faith never arose for Huguenots? Certainly not. Four times a year, before the celebration of holy communion (in which virtually all church members above the age of twelve appear to have participated each time it was celebrated[33]), church members were exhorted to prepare themselves for the ceremony by examining their behaviour of the past three months,

---

31 Above, Chapter 4, pp. 171–2; Georges Ascoli, *La Grande Bretagne devant l'opinion française au XVIIe siècle* (2 vols, Paris, 1930) II, 312. On Hall, see Huntley, *Bishop Joseph Hall*; idem, *Joseph Hall and Protestant Meditation in Seventeenth-Century England* (Binghamton, 1981). The latter work, p. 44, argues that Hall's neo-Stoicism has been overemphasized, but it is unmistakable in the work of his that attained the greatest popularity in France, *De la tranquillité de l'esprit* (Paris, 1648). There is no good study of Bayly and his book, even though *The Practice of Piety* was *the* great international best-seller of seventeenth-century Calvinism, being translated into Dutch, German, Italian, Hungarian, Czech, Welsh and the 'Massachusetts Indian language' as well as French.

32 Kretzer, 'Die Calvinismus–Kapitalismus–These Max Webers', pp. 425, 427.

33 A.C. Montpellier, GG 369–70 (these church registers record the number of participants at each quarterly *cène*); Janine Garrisson-Estèbe, *Protestants du Midi, 1559–1598* (Toulouse, 1980), p. 243.

repenting for their sins, and ensuring that they had a genuine faith in Christ without which to participate in the sacrament was to pollute it. The words of the liturgy, also reiterated in hymns that became popular, intoned:

> Let each person examine himself
> If he believes Jesus his Savior
> If he fears God, serves and loves him
> And all his brothers with a true heart.
>
> If he knows and feels his misery
> And weeps bitterly because of it
> If his repentance is sincere
> And he wants to live in holiness.[34]

This exhortation was reiterated and amplified in certain Huguenot manuals of preparation for communion, a genre of small devotional works that attained widespread circulation.[35] In such a situation, it seems inconceivable that the issue of assurance would not have arisen for some believers. Certain tracts and sermons, especially from the late sixteenth and early seventeenth century, indicate that it did.

Probably the earliest important treatise which dealt with this issue and which obtained considerable diffusion in France was Des *marques des enfans de Dieu* by the Walloon minister Jean Taffin, who served for a while as pastor of Metz. Although written primarily to encourage the faithful of the Low Countries to persevere in the faith despite the afflictions of the times, the tract, which went through seven known French editions following its initial publication in Haarlem in 1584, also recognizes that 'nothing troubles tender consciences more grieviously than doubts and fears of not being the child of God'.[36] Several chapters are devoted to allaying these fears. Two marks distinguished the children of God according to Taffin: the exterior mark, which is membership in the true church; and the interior mark, which comprises both 'the witness of the Holy Spirit in our hearts' and good works done in the fear and service of God.[37] In providing this exterior mark, Taffin thus used the question of assurance to fortify attachment to the Reformed church, even while he makes church

---

34 Charles Bost, 'Poésies populaires huguenotes du Vivarais (du XVIe siècle à la fin de la révolte camisarde)', *B.S.H.P.F.* 89 (1940), 209.

35 Samuel Durand, 'Espreuve du fidelle, pour se preparer a la Sainte Cene', and Raymond Gaches, 'Preparation a la Sainte Cene', in *Le Voyage de Beth-el, avec les Preparations, Prieres et Meditations, pour participer dignement à la Sainte Cene* (Paris-Charenton, 1665 and numerous subsequent editions); Jean Claude, *L'Examen de soy-mesme pour se bien preparer à la communion* (Paris–Charenton, 1682).

36 Taffin, *Des marques des enfans de Dieu, et des consolations en leurs afflictions* (Saumur, 1606), pp. 33–4.

37 Ibid., p. 21.

membership something that can itself provide a source of reassurance to the troubled believer. In counselling those who do not find the above marks precise enough to satisfy their anxiety about election, he echoes Calvin's advice. Instead of looking to themselves, they should look to the Scriptures. Trust those passages which announce salvation through Christ, he urges. If you were banished from a city and a good prince then issued a general pardon, he asks in an analogy that must have seemed particularly pertinent to his readers in both France and the Low Countries at the time he was writing, wouldn't you believe that you were included in the amnesty? 'Have recourse to Him, and believe in Him, and you are assured that he will be equally generous in mercy to you.'[38]

Another exploration of the question of assurance arises in the Languedoc minister Daniel Pérol's *Discours familier touchant la certitude de salut que les fideles doivent avoir*. This is not a work of pastoral advice but a turgid piece of controversy dedicated to proving, against Rome, that believers can attain certitude about their salvation. The first part recognizes that 'fearful consciences' are occasionally troubled by the issue of predestination. Against such fears it simply opposes the promises of God. Not only is no appeal made to good works as marks of election; the author criticizes the Catholic theologian Medina for making works a sign of faith. With this issue duly disposed of, Pérol is free to turn the full weight of his argumention against the errors of Rome.[39]

The writings which return the most insistently to the question of assurance are the sermons of the most prominent Huguenot minister of the first part of the seventeenth century, Pierre Du Moulin.[40] Du Moulin, significantly, studied at Cambridge between 1589 and 1592, and his discussion of the issue of assurance is very much akin to that of the English writers. Unlike Taffin or Pérol, he did not appeal to God's promises of salvation, but advised his listeners to look to their own experience and behaviour. 'Do you wish to know if God is with you, then see if you are with him, sound yourself to see if you love him, if you fear him, and if you are touched to the heart with the zeal of his service.'[41] Good works are

---

[38] Ibid., p. 38.

[39] D.P. [Daniel Pérol], *Discours familier touchant la certitude de salut que les fideles doivent avoir* (Montpellier, 1611), *passim*, esp. pp. 36–7. A copy of this rare work survives in the B.P.F. in Paris. Another one was discovered among a cache of Huguenot books brought to light in 1948. Jean Cadier, 'Livres huguenots retrouvés à Montpellier en 1948', *B.S.H.P.F.* 97 (1950), 165–9.

[40] Extended treatment of the issue of assurance of election may be found in Du Moulin's *Cinquieme Décade de Sermons* (Geneva, 1645), sermons II and III; and *Sixieme Décade de Sermons* (Geneva, 1647), sermons V and VII.

[41] Pierre Du Moulin, *Cinquieme Décade de Sermons*, p. 35. A good biography of Du Moulin is provided by Lucien Rimbault, *Pierre Du Moulin 1568–1658: Un pasteur classique à l'age classique* (Paris, 1966).

signs of election for him, and his sermons urge his auditors to pursue the process of sanctification without respite. Regeneration, he warns, is not like writing a book; it cannot be put down and then resumed at the same point later.[42] Time is not to be wasted in idleness, for 'we will have to render account to God for our days and our hours, and for the advancement in piety that we achieved during them'.[43] In passages such as these, Du Moulin comes closer than any other Huguenot writer to the themes dear to Puritanism.

If a degree of concern with the issue of assurance of salvation thus began to develop within French Protestantism from Taffin through Du Moulin, such concern receded in the subsequent generations. Alexandre Vinet, the historian of seventeenth-century Huguenot preaching, observes that the themes of election and certitude of salvation largely disappear from French sermons after Du Moulin.[44] I have encountered just one exception to this assertion, the sermons of Jean Claude, the pastor of Nîmes and Montauban called to Paris in 1666. His sermons and devotional treatises insist that genuine saving faith is difficult to distinguish from temporary faith and prod believers to look closely at their own situation, providing a series of characteristics whereby they can distinguish each form of faith from the other.[45] It would appear that Claude was familiar with depictions of the morphology of conversion found in the writings of the English practical divines, but it cannot be said that this morphology was ever spelled out in any detail by the French themselves.

The Huguenots thus ultimately did not develop as strong a preoccupation in their religious literature with personal assurance and the means whereby this might be attained as did the English. In consequence, Huguenot culture lacked the powerful impulse toward self-scrutiny found across the Channel, just as it lacked as extensive a literature urging methodical self-discipline. This in turn helps to explain why the Huguenots also appear to have lacked a tradition of spiritual journal-keeping.

Certain Huguenots kept journals, of course, just as did other people of the time.[46] Virtually all, however, are accounts of business and personal

---

42 Du Moulin, *Sixieme Décade de Sermons*, p. 142.

43 Quoted in Peter Bayley, *French Pulpit Oratory 1598–1650: A Study in Themes and Styles, with a Descriptive Catalogue of Printed Texts* (Cambridge, 1980), p. 132.

44 Alexandre Vinet, *Histoire de la prédication parmi les Réformés de France au dix-septième siècle* (Paris, 1860), pp. 83–4. My reading of selected sermons generally confirms Vinet's judgement.

45 Jean Claude, *Sermon sur ces paroles de l'epistre de Saint Paul aux Ephesiens Chap. 4 vers 30 'Ne contristez point le S. Esprit de Dieu, par lequel vous avez été séellez pour le jour de la Redemtion'* (Paris–Charenton, 1666); *L'Examen de soy-mesme*.

46 A search for Huguenot journals and autobiographies has revealed the following documents, which serve as the basis for the assertions which follow: Bibliothèque Municipale de Rouen, MS M 281, 'Livre de raison de Jacques Papavoine'; Algemeen Rijksarchief (The

affairs or noteworthy events, with very little to distinguish them from the journals kept by their Catholic neighbours. More uniquely Huguenot, and not just because of their subject matter, are the numerous accounts of the Revocation of the Edict of Nantes and of its attendant sufferings, written from exile. To a greater or lesser extent, these are all moral tales emphasizing for subsequent generations the importance of fidelity to the church of one's ancestors. The anguish felt by those induced by bribery or considerations of personal safety to abjure, God's admirable providences in delivering his children from bondage, and heroic examples of suffering and of daring escape are all variously underscored. In the preface to his autobiography, Jacques Cabrit tells his children that the era of the Revocation should be one they keep constantly before their memory as a 'powerful cause for humility, detachment from the things of the world, and the most hearty gratitude toward our divine liberator'.[47] The memory of past persecutions is a central theme in Huguenot culture, but it is obviously a very different motive for diary-keeping than that impelling Puritan diarists.

One journal brings the reader closer to the lived religious experience of a French Protestant than any other. This is the diary of the eminent classical scholar and minister's son, Isaac Casaubon. As time is a precious commodity, Casaubon declares at the outset of his journal, he has decided to keep a record so that he can observe his use of the time which remains to him in this world. 'I praise you, God, for the time which remain to me

---

Hague), Eerst Afdeling, Familie-archief Collot d'Escury, no. 390, Daniel Collot d'Escury, 'Livre de ma généalogie et des evennemens les plus remarquables qui me sont arrivez dans ma vie'; Jacques Fontaine, *Mémoires d'une famille huguenote, victime de la Révocation de l'Edit de Nantes* (Toulouse, 1887); 'Extrait du journal manuscrit ou diaire autographe du ministre Jaques Merlin, pasteur de La Rochelle', in J. Gaberel, *Histoire de l'Eglise de Genève* (Geneva, 1855), 2, 153–207; 'Diaire de Jacques Merlin, ou "Receuil des choses [les] plus mémorables qui se sont passées en ceste ville" [de La Rochelle] de 1589 à 1620', ed. Charles Dangibeaud, in *Archives Historiques de la Saintonge et de l'Aunis*, 5 (1878), 63–380; Jean Rou, *Mémoires inédits et opuscules*, ed. Francis Waddington (Paris, 1857); Pierre Du Moulin, 'Autobiographie', *B.S.H.P.F.* 7 (1858), 170–82, 333–44, 465–77; 'Journal inédit d'un fidèle de l'ancienne Eglise Réformée de Metz', *B.S.H.P.F.* 11 (1862), 163–79, 281–99; Jacques Cabrit, 'Autobiographie', *B.S.H.P.F.* 39 (1890), 530–45, 587–98, 635–45; 'Mémoires de la famille de Chaufepié', eds J.-H. Dompierre de Chaufepié and N. Weiss, *B.S.H.P.F.* 52 (1903), 231–54; 'Pierre de Vernéjoul, procureur au Parlement de Guienne et son journal inédit', eds D. Benoit and P. de Felice, *B.S.H.P.F.* 53 (1904), 401–37; Isaac Dumont de Bostaquet, *Mémoires*, ed. Michel Richard (Paris, 1968); Isaac Casaubon, *Ephemerides* (Oxford, 1851); Jean Migault, *Journal*, ed. P. de Bray (Paris–Geneva, 1854); Jean Olry, *La persécution de l'église de Metz*, ed. O. Cuvier (Paris, 1860); 'Pierre Lézan, secrétaire du consistoire de St-Hippolyte 1663–1700: Extraits de ses mémoires in Clément Ribard, *Notes d'histoire cévenole* (Cazillac, 1898), pp. 54–61.

47 Cabrit, 'Autobiographie', p. 533. See also the memoirs of Rou, Olry, Fontaine, Migault and Collot d'Escury.

in this life, and I shall do all I can to know you, to adore you without measure, to promote your glory and help knowledge, and to procure my salvation and that of all who are mine.'[48] True to the stated purpose of the diary, the daily entries note Casaubon's daily round of activities. His morning prayers, the progress of his studies, and whether or not he was able to spend each morning and afternoon working or was interrupted by illness, family concerns, or (most exasperating of all) his friends, 'or better yet enemies', who were constantly dropping by to talk with him are all duly noted. The recorded events are strictly external ones; the author does not sound the character of his faith and note whether his devotions were warm or cold, nor does he spell out his sins and inattentions to duty. His faith is not problematic to him. On the contrary, he explicitly states his certainty that, although unworthy, he is one of those predestined to salvation through Christ's merits.[49] What shines through above all else in the diary are the same sentiments that are so powerful in Calvin's own writings, namely a sense of God's absolute sovereignty and of man's duty to serve and honour him in all his actions. The most insistent refrain in his prayers is the petition that God grant him the health and the power to be useful in his service – although whatever God wills for him he declares he is ready to accept. It is this which makes him so concerned about using his time well.

Both the socio-historical context in which French Protestantism found itself and its specific theological traditions can help us to understand why the anxieties revolving around predestination do not seem to have come to the fore within French Calvinism and why the character of Huguenot religiosity differed as it did from Puritan devotion. First, French Calvinism was a minority religion. At no point in the seventeenth century did members of the French Reformed church comprise more than 6 per cent of the entire French population.[50] Where a committed Elizabethan clergyman faced a congregation composed of virtually the entire local population, many of them ill versed in Protestant doctrine, a French Reformed pastor was presented with a congregation of people who had voluntarily embraced the faith or were descendants of people who had voluntarily embraced the faith, who had remained loyal through the terrible years of the Wars of Religion, and who were still being constantly solicited to convert to Catholicism. In such a context, the chief concern of pastoral activity was naturally not to awaken individuals to conversion, but to seek to rebut the adversaries of the faith and maintain the community of the faithful.

---

[48] Casaubon, *Ephemerides*, p. 1.
[49] Ibid., p. 79.
[50] Above, Chapter 2, pp. 92–3; Jacques Dupâquier, *La population française aux XVIIe et XVIIIe siècles* (Paris, 1979), pp. 11, 34.

(Preaching to those outside the ranks of the church was forbidden by law.) Even for those ministers who believed in strict supralapsarian predestination, the central division which they observed in the world around them was that between Huguenots and Papists, not between the reprobate and the elect. Meanwhile, for the members of this small band of Protestants in a vast Catholic sea, the words 'pauci Electi' must have had a considerably less terrifying ring. Good Calvinists knew that the church visible and the church invisible were not the same, and preachers occasionally warned that there were hypocrites among the flock, but the temptation was none the less strong to assume that those who remained faithful to the church and did not behave in a manifestly dissolute fashion had saving faith. Preaching at Charenton on a communion day on the text, 'He who has the Son has life; he who has not the Son of God has not life' (1 John 5: 12), Jean Daillé told his flock that he did not wish to dampen the joy of the occasion by setting forth the horrors of damnation that awaited those who did not have the Son. 'In any case, I would like to think that such an effort would be needless.'[51]

Theological developments also caused the doctrine of predestination to assume diminishing importance in seventeenth-century France. The high Calvinist orthodoxy of Beza and Perkins that was enshrined in the canons of the synod of Dort never fully triumphed in France. Although the decisions of Dort were accepted by the French Reformed church at the urging of Pierre Du Moulin in 1620, a rival position was being defined in precisely these years by the theologians of the Academy of Saumur, notably John Cameron and Moyse Amyraut. These men consciously opposed Beza and appealed to Calvin instead. They rejected supralapsarianism, argued that predestination had to be confined to being discussed as a corollary of justification and not in the context of the divine will, and developed the idea of 'hypothetical universal grace', which stressed that God offered grace to all men, even if they did not all have the grace to receive it. In effect, they reversed the steps that had been taken in the passage from Calvin to Calvinism. Amyraut also propounded a concept of faith in which intellectual assent to the truths of the Bible was emphasized and inward experience downplayed.[52] All the most frequently reprinted Huguenot preachers of the subsequent generation were men who allied themselves with Amyraut in the disputes which developed over his teaching.[53] It is

---

[51] Jean Daillé, *Mélange de sermons* (Amsterdam, 1658), part II, p. 123.

[52] Brian G. Armstrong, *Calvinism and the Amyraut Heresy: Protestant Scholasticism and Humanism in Seventeenth-Century France* (Madison, 1969), esp. chs 4, 6.

[53] François Laplanche, *Orthodoxie et prédication: L'oeuvre d'Amyraut et la querelle de la grace universelle* (Paris, 1965), pp. 308–9, identifies the leading allies and disciples of Amyraut. Among them were Jean Mestrezat, Jean Daillé and Michel Le Faucheur. The sermons of these men were respectively the first, second and fourth most frequently reprinted volumes

hardly surprising, then, that the Huguenot sermons of the time offer no hints of the division of the world into elect and reprobate and are not much concerned with the issue of assurance of election.

In conclusion, as Elisabeth Labrousse has already observed in two brilliant paragraphs which anticipate many of this chapter's major conclusions, the Huguenots did not live their faith in the same way as the English Puritans.[54] The central drama of a Huguenot's life was not the progress from conviction of sin through conversion to the gradual movement toward full assurance. It was the demonstration of genuine conviction by remaining firm to the true faith in the face of pressure to abjure. The conversion of a family member to Catholicism was experienced by Huguenot households as a major family tragedy, and confidence about salvation was intimately tied up with fidelity to the church.[55] It is this context which explains why works of controversy and abstract theology bulked so large in Huguenot libraries, for it was necessary to be well versed in the elements of the faith and the arguments that undergirded them in order to be able to resist the *convertisseurs*. It is this context which explains why so intellectualist a conception of faith as Amyraut's should be developed in France.

In sum, the experience of French Calvinism appears to have been significantly different from that of English. The hold which Calvinism exercised upon its adherents was not simply a matter of the psychological tensions implicit within a system of theology gradually unfolding themselves over time. It was a consequence as well of the socio-historical situation in which different Calvinisms found themselves, the pastoral strategies developed in response to these situations, and specific theological traditions.

---

of sermons of the period 1600–50. (Du Moulin ranked third in number of editions; Amyraut tied Le Faucheur for fourth.) Statistics calculated from Bayley, *French Pulpit Oratory*, Descriptive catalogue of printed texts.

54 Elisabeth Labrousse, *Pierre Bayle*, II *Heterodoxie et rigorisme* (The Hague, 1964), pp. 296–7.

55 Katherine L.M. Faust, 'A Beleaguered Society: Protestant Families in La Rochelle, 1628–1685' (Northwestern University Ph.D. diss., 1980), pp. 339–40; Charles Bost, 'La Piété protestante au XVIIe siècle', *Revue Chrétienne* 60 (1913), 855–6.

CHAPTER SEVEN

Print and the Experience of Ritual: Huguenot Books of Preparation for the Lord's Supper

Amid the ever-widening stream of devotional books which flowed off Europe's presses in the centuries following Gutenberg and Martin Luther, one clearly identifiable genre, which emerged in the Catholic, Lutheran and Reformed worlds alike, was that of books on how to prepare for and participate in holy communion. These small treatises reveal how the leading devotional writers of each tradition understood the experience of communion and tried to shape believers' participation in it. In so far as the guidelines proposed by these works were internalized by the faithful, they also indicate what participation in the eucharist might have been like for ordinary believers. While a comparative study of these works could surely shed a great deal of light on the range of meanings attached to communion across the religious map of Europe, this brief essay must confine itself to examining the treatises of preparation for communion of just one early modern confession, the French Reformed church, a group for which these books have the added interest of being one of the relatively few forms of small, widely diffused devotional works produced in the centuries following the Reformation. Such an examination, it is hoped, will contribute to our still underdeveloped understanding of Huguenot religious culture. More broadly, it may also illuminate some of the ways in which books were used in this era to complement ritual, and thus to shape and give it meaning.

The history and diffusion of Huguenot communion books

The roots of the communion manual can be traced back to several kinds of late medieval devotional works: books of hours, which often included instructions on 'how one should think during the Mass'; confession books, which told believers how to prepare themselves for that sacrament; and prayer books, which frequently included prayers to be said during the celebration of communion.[1] Such early writings of the Reformers as

---

1 Paul Saenger, 'Prier de bouche et prier de coeur. Les livres d'heures du manuscrit à l'imprimé', in Roger Chartier et al., *Les usages de l'imprimé (XVe–XIXe siècle)* (Paris, 1987), p. 210; Johannes Geffken, *Bilderkatechismus des fünfzehnten Jahrhunderts* (Leipzig, 1855);

Luther's 1524 *Sermon von Beichte und Sakrament* and Calvin's 1540 *Petit Traicté de la Sainte-Cène* also helped shape this genre in Protestant lands, although these works differ from the later books of preparation for communion in that much of their energy is devoted to defending a specific theological interpretation of the sacrament, rather than simply attempting to explain to believers how they should partake of the sacrament within a theological system which is taken for granted. Perhaps the first book which one can identify as a typical communion manual of the sort that would become common from the later sixteenth century onward was the Lutheran Christophorus Lasius's *Beichtbüchlein* of 1557. In the subsequent years, such books proliferated in Lutheran Germany, across Catholic Europe, where they appear to have been a particular speciality of the Jesuits, and within those countries which drew inspiration from the Reformed tradition.[2]

The first known French Protestant treatise of preparation for communion appeared just a few years after the establishment of permanent Reformed congregations, with the 1563 publication of the Saintongeais minister Yves Rouspeau's *Traitté de la preparation à la saincte Cène de nostre seul sauveur et rédempteur Jesus-Christ*, reprinted twice in the following two years.[3] The subsequent publishing history of Huguenot communion manuals is difficult to trace in full, for these works were small, cheap volumes (editions survive in formats as small as in-32o, with individual treatises typically including no more than 50 to 100 pages), and it is clear that many editions have been entirely lost. What is certain is that many of the most celebrated Huguenot ministers of this era wrote prayers or meditations concerning communion, often as part of larger devotional works or prayer books.[4]

Steven Ozment, *The Reformation in the Cities: The Appeal of Protestantism to Sixteenth-Century Germany and Switzerland* (New Haven, 1975), pp. 16–17, 23–7; Hermann Beck, *Das religiöse Volkslitteratur der evangelischen Kirche Deutschlands in einem Abriss ihrer Geschichte* (Gotha, 1891), p. 11; René Bornert, *La réforme protestante du culte à Strasbourg au XVIe siècle (1523–1598)* (Leiden, 1981), pp. 25–6.

2 Brief surveys of this genre in Lutheran Germany may be found in Beck, *Religiöse Volkslitteratur* and *Theologische Realenzyklopädie* (Berlin, 1976–), s.v. 'Gebetbücher'. The Jesuit contribution may be discerned from Carlos Sommervogel, *Bibliothèque de la Compagnie de Jésus* (11 vols, Brussels–Paris, 1890–1932). A good survey of these works in England is offered by E. Brooks Holifield, *The Covenant Sealed: The Development of Puritan Sacramental Theology in Old and New England, 1570–1720* (New Haven, 1974). Important Dutch Reformed communion books include Willem Teelinck, *Het geestelijck cieraet van Christi bruyloftskinderen*; Willem Saldenus, *Het geestelijk Avondmaal, vertoont in zijn vertroostende en heyligmakende kracht*; and the collective *'t Recht gebruyck van des Heren Heylige Avondtmaal*, all frequently reprinted.

3 Eugénie Droz, *L'imprimerie à La Rochelle, 1 Barthélémy Berton 1563–1573* (Geneva, 1960), pp. 23–4, 54.

4 This is evident from the prefatory dedication of Charles Drelincourt, *Prieres et Meditations pour se preparer à la Communion* (Saumur, 1668), fol. Aiii, as well as from the number of different works of preparation for communion which would be compiled in later anthologies.

At least three of these were published as books in their own right: Charles Drelincourt's *Prières et Méditations pour se préparer à la Communion*, which went through a minimum of four editions between 1621 and 1668; Raymond Gaches's *Préparation à la sainte cène*, of which only the fourth edition of 1661 survives; and Pierre Du Moulin's *Meditation pour se preparer à la Sainte Cene*, published in Saint-Maixent in 1665.[5] A 1643 *Receuil de plusieurs préparations et prières pour la sainte Cène par plusieurs auteurs* also brought together texts by Du Moulin, Daniel Toussaint, Jean Mestrezat and Michel Le Faucheur.[6]

Because these books were of such little value that officials seldom thought them worth recording in inventories of private possessions, the precise extent of their diffusion is harder still to reconstruct. Evidence about the activity of Protestant booksellers from the mid-seventeenth century shows that works of preparation for communion had come to play a noteworthy role in their affairs by the 1650s. Inventories from around mid-century of the goods of three small Huguenot booksellers in Metz reveal stocks dominated by multiple copies of a few books which obviously formed the staple of their trade. Schoolbooks, psalters and an unidentified 'preparation a la saine' were by far the most abundant of these works.[7] The account books of Jean Nicolas, the important Huguenot printer–bookseller of Grenoble, show that he sold seventeen copies of an unnamed work of preparation for communion between 1650 and 1661. Here we know the identity of the purchasers; all were members of the city's social élites, the sort of clientele to which Nicolas generally catered, but several bought multiple copies, which suggests they may have distributed them to family members or servants.[8] Perhaps the most striking evidence of the diffusion

---

5 These and all subsequent figures regarding the number of known editions of a book of preparations for communion are based upon an examination of the published library catalogues of the B.N. and B.L.; the American National Union Catalogue; Haag; Alexandre Cioranescu, *Bibliographie de la littérature française du dix-septième siècle* (Paris, 1965–66); Louis Desgraves, *Répertoire bibliographique des livres imprimés en France au XVIIe siècle* (Baden-Baden, 1978–); and a possibly incomplete search of the card catalogues of the B.P.F., the Koninklijke Bibliotheek in The Hague, and the university libraries of Amsterdam and Utrecht. It is possible that the edition of Du Moulin's *Meditation* published in Saint-Maixent in 1665 and listed in Desgraves, VI, 217, should not be considered a separately published work but merely part of a copy of *Le Voyage de Beth-el* completed by the same printer, François Mathé, in the subsequent year.

6 This work is listed in Haag, s.v. 'Drelincourt'.

7 A.D.M., B 3352, inv. of 8 April 1647; B 3354, inv. of 22 February 1651; B 3358, inv. of 23 March 1658. All the 'preparations a la saine' appear among the goods of a single bookseller, Pierre Chopine, but the number of such volumes in his possession alone made them almost as numerous as the total number of the psalters found in all three of the inventories combined. The A.B.C.s were more numerous yet.

8 Henri-Jean Martin and M. Lecocq, *Livres et lecteurs à Grenoble. Les registres du libraire Nicolas (1645–1668)* (Geneva, 1977), II, 740.

which devotional works intended for use in conjunction with the celebration of communion had achieved by the second half of the seventeenth century comes from the decisions of the provincial synod of Basse-Guyenne, which observed in 1661 that 'in the greater part of churches several people, both men and women, hold to reading certain books of prayers during the celebration of the Lord's Supper'. The synod condemned this practice, enjoining the faithful to 'attach themselves religiously to the hearing of the word of God and the singing of psalms without seeking elsewhere in temple the consolation and joy that they will find abundantly in these practices'.[9] Clearly, the spread of prayer books and works of preparation for communion had reached widely enough to begin transforming the character of the *cène* along more individualistic lines, even before the appearance of the work destined to become by far the most popular Huguenot manual of preparation for communion, *Le Voyage de Beth-el, avec les Preparations, Prieres et Meditations, pour participer dignement à la Sainte Cene.*

Le Voyage de Beth-el was first published in 1665 by the Parisian printer Etienne Lucas for sale at Charenton. The title of this work derived from a new vade-mecum written by the Dieppe minister Jean de Focquembergues, *Le Voyage de Beth-el, ou sont representez les devoirs de l'Ame Fidele en allant au Temple, et en retournant.* The Lucas edition also contained prayers and meditations concerning communion by Du Moulin, Gaches, Le Faucheur and Samuel Durand – both Du Moulin's and Gaches's were preceded by title pages of their own, suggesting that they could also be sold independently – as well as the psalms sung on communion day. Within the twenty years that elapsed between its initial publication and the Revocation of the Edict of Nantes, at least seventeen further editions of *Le Voyage de Beth-el* issued from presses in Paris, Rouen, Caen, Saumur, Niort, Saint-Maixent, Bergerac and Montauban. Further French-language editions of this work appeared after the Revocation in no less than seven cities outside France for the use of Huguenot refugee communities. Virtually all of the copies whose full contents I have been able to ascertain were, like the 1665 edition, collections of works by various authors, although the precise authors represented varied from edition to edition. As Table 7.1 shows, the prayers and meditations of Le Faucheur and Durand gave way in the eighteenth century to those of Drelincourt and the early eighteenth-century Genevan minister Benedict Pictet. Some pre-Revocation editions also contained morning and evening prayers, the former including passages asking blessings for 'the sacred person of the King' and the other members of the royal family. A post-Revocation edition with the same prayers, upon reaching the passage in

---

9   A.N., TT 248 (12), article 5.

Table 7.1 The contents of some editions of *Le Voyage de Beth-el*

	Paris 1665	Saumur 1668	Paris 1670	Paris 1674	Saumur 1677	Rouen 1681	Amsterdam 1686	London 1737	The Hague 1759	Utrecht 1766
Jean de Focquembergues *Le Voyage de Beth-el*	×	×	×	×	×	×	×	×	×	×
Michel Le Faucheur Prayers	×			×	×	×	×			
Samuel Durand 'Espreuve du fidelle pour se preparer à la Sainte Cene'	×		×	×	×	×				
Pierre Du Moulin *Meditation pour se preparer à la Sainte Cene*, Prayers	×		×	×	×	×	×	×	×	×
Raymond Gaches *Préparation à la sainte cene*, Prayers	×		×	×	×	×	×	×	×	×
Jean Mestrezat Prayers					×					
Benedict Pictet 'Preparation à la Communion'								×	×	×
Charles Drelincourt Prayers & Meditations								×	×	×

the morning prayer concerning political superiors, simply asks 'protect this state'.[10]

The great popularity obtained by *Le Voyage de Beth-el* did not prevent still further Huguenot pastors from trying their hands at writing communion manuals. The year 1682 witnessed the appearance of two additional ones: Jean Claude's *L'Examen de soy-mesme pour se bien preparer à la communion*, and Pierre Allix's *Preparation à la Sainte Cene*. The first of these threatened for a while to attain a level of popularity comparable to *Le Voyage de Beth-el*; printers in Paris, Niort, Montauban, The Hague and London saw fit to print no less than seven French and one English editions between 1682 and 1684. The book's success was as short-lived as it was spectacular, however, for only one further French-language and one English edition are known after 1684. Allix's tract went through three French editions and was also translated into English.

The character of the works

Since the manuals of preparation for communion were essentially glosses upon the ritual itself, some understanding of how the sacrament was celebrated within the French Reformed church is necessary before one can understand the manuals themselves. Although the church never specifically prescribed a standard eucharistic liturgy, the form of services instituted by Calvin in Geneva predominated overwhelmingly in the first centuries of the church's life.[11] Communion was celebrated quarterly – at Christmas, Easter, Pentecost and in September – with the sparse evidence available suggesting that, unlike in many other Protestant churches during the later sixteenth and seventeenth century, the overwhelming majority of church members deemed mature enough to participate in the ceremony in fact did so.[12] The ceremony began with the reading of verses 23 through 29 of Chapter 11 of Paul's first epistle to the Corinthians:

10 Cf. the edition of Paris–Charenton, 1673, published by Louis Vendosme, and that of Amsterdam, 1686, published by Pierre Mortier (both at B.P.F.).

11 The account of French Reformed liturgical practices which follows depends primarily upon Yngve Brilioth, *Eucharistic Faith and Practice: Evangelical and Catholic* (London, 1930), ch. 5, esp. p. 179; Emile Doumergue, *Essai sur l'histoire du culte réformé principalement au XVIe et XIXe siècle* (Paris, 1890), part 2, ch. 1; John Calvin, *Opera quae supersunt omnia*, ed. G. Baum, E. Cunitz and R. Reuss (59 vols, Brunswick–Berlin, 1863–1900), VI, cols 192–202; 'La Maniere de Celebrer la Sainte Cene', in *Le Voyage de Beth-el* (Paris–Charenton, 1665), pp. 81ff; John Lough, *France Observed in the Seventeenth Century by British Travellers* (Stockfield, 1985), p. 245.

12 Janine Garrisson-Estèbe, *Protestants du Midi, 1559–1598* (Toulouse, 1980), p. 243; A.C. Montpellier, GG 369–70.

> For I have received of the Lord that which also I delivered unto you,
> That the Lord Jesus the same night in which he was betrayed took
> bread: And when he had given thanks, he brake it, and said, Take,
> eat: this is my body, which is broken for you: This do in rememberance
> of me. After the same manner he also took the cup, when he had
> sucked, saying, This cup is the new testament in my blood: this do ye,
> as oft as ye drink it, in rememberance of me. For as often as ye eat this
> bread, and drink this cup, ye do shew the Lord's death till he come.
> Wherefore whosoever shall eat this bread, and drink this cup of the
> Lord, unworthily, shall be guilty of the body and blood of the Lord.
> But let a man examine himself, and so let him eat of that bread, and
> drink of that cup. For he that eateth and drinketh unworthily, eateth
> and drinketh damnation to himself, not discerning the Lord's body.

In keeping with the text's warning against unworthy participation, the
minister then excommunicated all

> idolators, blasphemers, mockers of God, heretics and those who form
> sects apart to rupture the unity of the church, perjurers, those who
> rebel against their fathers, their mothers, and their superiors, seditious
> souls, mutineers, troublemakers, adulterers, fornicators, thieves,
> ravishers of other men's property, avaricious souls, drunkards, gluttons
> and all those leading scandalous and dissolute lives.

He next exhorted all church members to examine themselves for evidence
of true penitence for their faults, faith in God's mercy, and a desire to
renounce all enmity and hatred and to live in concord with their fellows.
At this point, he sought to reassure those who might be excessively hard
on themselves and felt themselves unworthy to take part in the ritual.
Those who could find evidence in their heart of the sentiments just
mentioned were worthy to communicate, even if they might also have a
consciousness of their own sinfulness. 'For we do not come to proclaim
that we are perfect or just in ourselves; on the contrary, in seeking life in
Jesus Christ we confess that we are dead in ourselves.'

Exhortation followed to see in communion the signs of Christ's mercy
to his people and a token that the result of his passion was the imputation
of righteousness to them, while warning against seeing Christ as corporally
present in the elements of the ceremony. 'Let us raise our minds and hearts
on high, where Jesus Christ resides in the glory of his Father ... And let us
not amuse ourselves in seeking him in these earthly and corruptible elements
that we see with our eyes and touch with our hands, as if he were contained
in the bread and in the wine.' Following this, the members of the
congregation lined up to receive the bread and wine, with the minister(s)
partaking first, then the other church officers, the men of the congregation,
and finally the women, all proceeding in groups as large as could be
accommodated at the table set up before the pulpit. As each group sat at
the table to receive communion, the remainder of the congregation was
supposed to sing psalms or listen to scriptural readings concerning the

passion, although, as we have already seen, the habit of reading from prayer books threatened with time to weaken these common activities at the expense of personal prayer and meditation.

In building his eucharistic liturgy around Paul's letter to the Corinthians, Calvin created an order of service characterized by considerable tension between the appeal for all believers to take part in the ceremony as a public testimonial of their faith and the warning against polluting it by unworthy participation. Many of the Huguenot communion manuals would be structured around this tension. The evidence of true faith that the liturgy exhorted believers to search themselves for – penitence for their faults, faith in God's mercy, and the desire to live in peace and charity with their neighbours – also established three benchmarks around which the manuals of preparation for communion organized many of their meditations. Different manuals, in fact, could be distinguished according to the amount of emphasis they put on each of these elements. The clearest distinctions of all between the various manuals, however, arise from the different rhetorical strategies adopted by their authors. Three can be discerned, which I shall loosely call the didactic, the meditative and the prophetic/penitential.

As befits a work written for a newly established church, the first French Protestant treatise of preparation for communion, Rouspeau's *Traitté de la preparation à la saincte Cène de nostre seul sauveur et rédempteur Jesus-Christ*, was strongly didactic in character, setting forth to believers just how they should come to the sacrament in order not to profane it. This task was necessary, Rouspeau declared in the work's prologue, since the just-completed First Civil War and its attendant cortège of plague and famine demonstrated God's anger at the widespread profanation of the sacrament, not only among those still mired in Romish error, but also among those who professed to believe the true word of God and yet came to the communion table 'some ... as ignorant asses, other as swine leading a dissolute and slanderous life'.[13]

The first part of the tract details the self-examination that would-be communicants must undertake before the ceremony. First, they must verify that they have faith, defined as 'a certain and infallible assurance ... that God is a merciful father unto us in the name of his son Jesus Christ our Lord'. Second, they must truly repent for their 'wicked life passed, using a true and severe examining of our selves', the points of which Rouspeau does not specify. Third, they must give thanks to the Lord in their heart as well as in their words, recognizing that it is from God that faith comes.

---

13 I have consulted Rouspeau's treatise in the English edition of Lucas Harrison, *A Treatise of the preparation to the holy Supper of our onely Saveour and Redeemer, Jesus Christe* (London, n.d. [1577?]), unpaginated.

Finally, they must show the effects of this thankfulness by keeping God's commandments. In these sections, Rouspeau places a good deal of stress on communion as a ritual which expresses and furthers love within the community. Before the ritual, church members must reconcile themselves with any fellow member with whom they have quarrelled. Having done this, they may then be bound together into a community, as 'bread is made of many grains and wine of many clusters of grapes', a simile which Rouspeau borrows from Calvin.

The final sections of the treatise then explore a series of ancillary issues surrounding participation in the sacrament. Rouspeau was clearly concerned that communion might become an occasion for recrimination between church members. He stresses that communicants should stick to examining their own lives and not pry into those of others. In this world, the good will always be mixed with the bad, so believers should not be offended if some of their neighbours whom they might feel were unqualified to participate in communion none the less did so. He then addresses those who abstain from communion, adducing their unworthiness. Those who do so, he argues, spurn Christ's command to take and eat with him, not recognizing that one purpose of the sacrament is precisely to strengthen the faith and quicken the virtue of believers still burdened by sin. On the other hand, there are those who should indeed abstain from communion. The last part of the book spells 43 categories of people who should be barred from the Lord's Table, including atheists, magicians, idolaters, whoremongers, usurers, incontinent buggerers and drunkards.

Another treatise in the didactic mode was the *Préparation à la sainte cène* of Raymond Gaches (*c.* 1615–1668). Longer than Rouspeau's *Traitté de la preparation* and less an exposition of the rules governing admission to communion than an exposition of the meaning of the sacrament, this work none the less bears numerous similarities to Rouspeau's treatise. The conviction that too many believers approach the sacrament with excessive nonchalance; the listing of true repentance, true faith, and true charity as the *sine qua non* of participation; and the emphasis on the sacrament's role in uniting the congregation in charity, illustrated by the analogy of the congregation to the bread formed out of many grains and the wine of many grapes, all recur here. The minister of Castrais called to Paris in 1654 did feel compelled to explain at somewhat greater length just what defines true faith. This is not necessarily a strong faith, he explains, but a sincere faith that Christ truly loves us, and it is manifested in good works. 'The most certain mark for knowing the sincerity of our faith is the one that Saint James teaches us in the second chapter of his Epistle. "Show me," he says, "faith by thy works"'.[14] Gaches also was

---

[14] Raymond Gaches, *Le Voyage de Beth-el* (Paris–Charenton, 1674), p. 237.

one of the first authors of these treatises to encourage his readers to supplement the public celebration of communion with family devotions, urging them to read aloud the Biblical passages concerning the passion upon their return home from the temple.[15]

Still another essentially didactic treatise, Pierre Allix's *Preparation à la Sainte Cene*, offers a strikingly historicized explication of the meaning of the sacrament. 'No man', claims Allix, 'can, with any benefit, receive this Sacrament unless his Spirit be filled with the same thoughts, which Our Saviour did thereby suggest to his apostles.'[16] The first part of his work consequently focuses upon the biblical account of the Last Supper, setting this in its context of Jewish Passover services in order to indicate the ways in which it at once drew upon and departed from the ritual which had preceded it. Following this account of the origins of communion, the treatise then spells out the doctrinal truths conveyed by the ceremony, the comforts it brings believers, and the duties it imposes upon them.

While these didactic treatises spelled out the rules for the proper participation in the sacrament and offered information about the ritual intended to enable believers to participate in it in full understanding of what they were doing, the manuals in what I have labelled the meditative mode were either composed exclusively of prayers and meditations set in the first person or alternated such first-person meditations with detailed instructions about how to behave at every stage before and during communion. The manner in which this was done made these works, at least potentially, nothing less than blueprints of just how believers were supposed to behave and what they were supposed to feel as they prepared for and took communion. Particularly critical here was the extensive use of the first person, by which the authors of these treatises literally put words into the mouths of those readers who repeated the prayers they offered. 'O Lord!' exclaims one, 'I feel you approaching me in your mercy! My soul shivers with joy.'[17] Through exclamations such as this, these communion books conveyed to readers not simply the sentiments but even the sensations deemed appropriate during communion.

Two particularly important works of this sort were Drelincourt's *Prières et Méditations pour se préparer à la Communion* and Du Moulin's *Meditation pour se preparer à la Sainte Cene*. 'My Lord and My God!' begins the former. 'You welcome me by your mercy to the solemn feast of your only Son, my Saviour Jesus Christ; but when I meditate what you are, and what I am, how rich and excellent are the goods that you prepare for

15 'Ce que l'on doit lire estant de retour à la maison' in ibid., p. 275.

16 Allix, *A Preparation for the Lord's Supper* (London, 1688), preface.

17 Charles Drelincourt, 'Priere et Méditation pour le fidèle qui se présente à la Communion', in *Le Voyage de Beth-el* (Utrecht, 1766), p. 91.

me, and how little disposed I am to receive them, my soul is in anguish, and I tremble at the approach of your glorious Majesty.'[18] Du Moulin's work likewise opens with a confession that the first-person meditator – and the reader, of course, is invited to become that person – feels unworthy of the honour of dining at the Lord's table and frightened by the invitation. Both works then proceed to a detailed confession of specific sins, with Du Moulin focusing with particular acuity on inward thoughts and dispositions. His meditator declares that even his best actions are filled with imperfections and that his mind wanders during prayer. 'In giving alms I feel that wicked flesh that tells me, you could well need this, and these poor people are unworthy, and there are others richer than you who can help them.'[19] But Christ calls sinners, not the just, both works recognize. Can his command to take and eat be disobeyed, especially when one has some evidence that God has pardoned one, has given one a serious hatred for one's sins, and has planted his love in one's bosom – all elements of the spirit of adoption which God grants his children? Having found those, 'Behold how I who trembled and dared not approach, whose conscience was troubled by the vastness of my sins, now I approach with confidence, and having my soul altered by your grace, I hasten ardently to my Saviour Jesus, who holds out his hand to me.'[20] Further prayers and meditations testify to the blissful feeling that Christ is drawing near as the meditator/author/reader comes to communion, request the grace necessary to continue to walk in the path of the Lord following the ritual, and petition that it thereby engender the spirit of sanctification and adoption which is the mark that one is a child of God. These meditations thus move readers from a recognition of unworthiness to the affirmation that they none the less possesses faith, through eager participation in communion, and finally to the post-communion interpretation of the event as a reason to desire all the more strongly to advance in virtue.

Where Du Moulin and Drelincourt present the experience of communion as the passage from hesitation to renewed commitment, Focquembergues's *Voyage de Beth-el* turns the physical voyage which the Protestants of many cities had to make to temples which the law required be located outside the city which they served into a metaphor for the spiritual detachment from the things of the world which true Christians were supposed to cultivate. This work is a travel guide for the journey to the temple, 'by which we leave the world of our country and our kin ... to enter into a

---

18 Drelincourt, 'Priere & Meditation pour le fidele qui se prépare à la Communion', in *Le Voyage de Beth-el* (Utrecht, 1766), p. 63.

19 Pierre Du Moulin, 'Meditation pour se preparer à la Sainte Cene', in *Le Voyage de Beth-el*, (Paris–Charenton, 1674), p. 161.

20 Ibid., p. 170.

little Canaan, a Holy Land dedicated to the Lord Jesus'.[21] The work has much of the practical advice typical of travellers' guides. Before leaving, a short meditation is in order, expressing one's desire to see and serve God and asking for the grace to be present in the Lord's house in heart and spirit as well as in body. It is then advisable to walk gravely and modestly to the temple, avoiding all gossip and discussion of worldly affairs along the way if one should be travelling with others. 'If insults are thrown your way, take care not to react,' he adds – a reminder of the hostility which the sight of the Huguenots going in groups to church not infrequently aroused.[22] Further prayers and meditations are offered to be said during the voyage to the temple and on approaching and entering it.

Focquembergues then specifies in particular detail proper behaviour inside the temple. After kneeling and offering a prayer, one should listen devoutly to the reading of the Gospel and join in the singing of the psalms. These are not simply to be repeated coldly from memory, but sung with spirit and understanding. A brief meditation is offered which can be said between each psalm: 'O Eternal One I have celebrated you with the saints here on Earth that one day, O God raised up in Heaven, I may, together with the fortunate Souls, render you glory, honour and praise for the centuries.'[23] Once the pastor has arrived, the members of the congregation should focus their full attention upon him, neither sleeping nor talking during his sermon. 'Do not come [to the temple] to reproach (*reprendre*), but to learn (*apprendre*),' he urges – a bit of advice which hardly seems surprising coming from a minister.[24] As communion is administered, particular reverence is in order. The meditation suggested for the moment of taking communion expresses the hope that God will make this a true 'communion with his life-giving blood', a 'a seal of the justice that comes by faith, an assurance that all of my sins are forgiven me'.[25] A prayer of thanksgiving to be said after communion follows, asserting that one has indeed experienced such sentiments:

> I have savoured the foretastes of your eternal beatitude. I have received the pledges of blessed immortality and the glorious Resurrection, and the helpful and ineffable impress of the Seal of the Living God ... Grant me that I find all my joy and pleasure in savouring and tasting with rapture how benign you are ... Grant that I thoroughly renounce Sin and the World and all the urgings of the flesh.[26]

---

21 Ibid., pp. 4–5.

22 Ibid., p. 13. One of the most common times for seventeenth-century incidents of religious violence to occur was indeed when the Huguenots were either going to or returning from church.

23 Ibid., p. 23.

24 Ibid., p. 25.

25 Ibid., pp. 30–31.

26 Ibid., pp. 34–6.

For their last acts before leaving the temple, Focquembergues urges his readers to offer a second prayer of thanksgiving, stating that they have felt the truth of the assertion, blessed are those who hear the word of God and keep it, then to offer alms to the poor. As they return home, they should discuss all they have just heard. But even if Focquembergues urges his readers to take the pastor's words to heart and to discuss them on the way home, he does not encourage their uncritical acceptance. Once home, he advises believers, they should imitate the Bereans, who searched Scripture to see whether what they heard was so. (This attempt to encourage a certain lay independence of mind is parallelled in Jean Claude's *L'Examen de soy-mesme pour bien se preparer à la Communion*, where believers are urged not to make frequent use of a director of conscience lest they lose the habit of thinking for themselves and become slaves to other men.[27]) *Le Voyage de Beth-el* closes with a final prayer for the moment of return home, requesting the grace to avoid falling prey to the temptations of the world even though one is returning to one's ordinary place of residence: 'May I live in the world as if I were beyond it ... May my conversation be that of a citizen of Heaven (*Bourgeois de Cieus*).'[28] Not that this means an entire renunciation of wealth. The ideal state for a Bourgeois of heaven is an *aurea mediocritas*: 'Give me neither poverty nor riches. Nourish me with the bread of the quotidian, lest that in excess I renounce you ... or in poverty I falter. ... Bless my labour. Arrange the work of my hands and allow me to prosper in my calling.'[29]

The final category of Huguenot communion treatises elaborated in detail upon the liturgy's call for personal self-examination, in so doing turning them into instruments of self-scrutiny and personal improvement comparable to Catholic or Lutheran manuals of confession and communion. The 'Espreuve du fidelle pour se preparer à la Sainte Cene' of the Parisian pastor Samuel Durand (c. 1574–1626) warned that Christ's demand that believers examine themselves before communion was an obligation of the utmost seriousness. In an extended legal metaphor – is the reliance on this sort of metaphor, not commercial ones as in so many English devotional tracts, a telling commentary on the nature of French society? – Durand urged his readers to examine all the documents in the sack of their case (all the pieces in a French legal case were kept together in a sack) to be sure that they could find evidence of their repentance for all their transgressions, of their possession of Christ's letters of pardon, and of their obedience to the 'ordinance by which God constrains [them] tightly to devote [their] life to his glory and to the edification of his

---

27 Ibid., p. 44; Claude, *Examen de soy-mesme* (Paris–Charenton, 1682), p. 136.

28 Focquembergues, *Voyage de Beth-el* (Paris–Charenton, 1674), p. 47.

29 Ibid., p. 49.

Church'.[30] He then adopts the tone of an aggressive prosecuting attorney, peppering the reader with questions derived from each of the ten commandments in an eleven-page-long paragraph, of which, understandably, only a representative passage can be cited:

> God forbids fornication. But alas! Have you ever been free from disordered lust? Has your eye never wandered? How many times have words that encouraged dissolution escaped from your lips? How many times have you corrupted your good behaviour in wicked company? And see if your clothes do not still display worldly vanity. God forbids theft: but is your heart free from avarice, the root of all evils? Have your agreements and your dealings always been without injustice? ...[31]

The first part of a true preparation for communion, this tract continues, is to feel sorrow for these sins. 'Do you have downcast eyes and a downcast heart like the publican? Do you dissolve in tears like the poor sinning woman?'[32] Once believers have admitted their sinfulness, they can then pass to the next step, which is to recognize that they also are raised up at times by their faith. Finally, they must also desire to serve God. Durand, like Gaches, sees good works as the best evidence that a believer possesses saving faith. 'There O Christian, there is the touchstone: There, there you will see how serious is your repentance and how true your faith.'[33] The 'Espreuve' ends with a warning that only those who have resolved to keep God's commandments, who will devote their lives to furthering his glory, and who are eager to profess publicly the true religion despite all worldly considerations should come to communion. Several prayers follow which, once again, place in the mouth of those who said these prayers statements that they have felt God's mercy and are fortified in their faith.

Durand's 'Espreuve' was included in most seventeenth-century editions of *Le Voyage de Beth-el*, but it was replaced in eighteenth-century editions by a summons to an even more systematic process of self-examination, the 'Preparation à la communion' of the Genevan pastor Benedict Pictet (1655–1724). In Pictet's view, preparation for communion must extend over a number of days, with several hours being set aside each day for meditation upon one's sins. For the entire week before communion day, one should avoid reading anything that might turn one's thoughts away from God, i.e. anything other than the Bible, words of moral philosophy, sermons, or accounts of the lives and deaths of worthy men. To aid would-be communicants in their process of self-examination, Pictet provides 35 numbered questions for them to ask themselves, e.g.:

---

30 Ibid., p. 102.
31 Ibid., p. 108.
32 Ibid., p. 116.
33 Ibid., p. 124.

1. If it is not true that we like living beings more than God? ...
6. That we perform pious duties more out of custom than devotion ...
16. If it is not true that we have done some harm to our neighbours
    by bearing false witness of slander? ...
31. If we have not given too much time to our pleasures.[34]

That these take the form of a list seems particularly telling, for in such a format they could become not simply a means for convincing believers of their own sinfulness, but questions which could be meditated upon at length, one by one, and thereby serve as a basis for systematically reviewing one's recent behaviour As believers measured their behaviour against these questions, Pictet urged, they should pay particular attention to identifying certain categories of sins which could then become the target of a future campaign for eradication: those they have committed most often; those they have committed unknowingly; those committed despite an effort not to commit them; and those committed after a resolution to amend one's ways. 'One must not content oneself with meditating just once about these matters; they must be thought about until we have drawn tears.'[35] Only after such a self-examination, and only after making amends for any failings against or violation of the rules of honest dealing, should one come to communion. Interestingly, after several prayers and thanksgivings which once again express gratitude for God's mercy and for the peace and joy brought by the sacrament, Pictet then feels compelled to add a word of consolation for those who do not feel such sentiments. They should not worry, he explains: God often refrains from granting these joyful sensations as a way of testing believers' faith. Pictet also offers advice on how believers should spend the hours of the communion day which remain to them after the end of services. The entire communion day must be given over to God, he warns. Only activities such as reading the Bible or another devotional work, meditating upon God's mercies and one's transgressions, or righting quarrels with neighbours are acceptable.

Jean Claude's lengthy *L'Examen de soy-mesme pour bien se preparer à la Communion* also offers lists which can be used for systematic self-examination, but these, interestingly, are organized around the attributes that distinguish believers with true faith from those who lack it. It might have been expected that a eucharistic liturgy that placed as much emphasis as the Genevan and French one did on the dangers of participating in communion without true faith would have stirred later commentators to elaborate at length on just what constituted saving faith and how believers could be sure they had it. As we have seen, however, most Huguenot treatises of preparation for communion were content simply to reiterate

---

[34] *Le Voyage de Beth-el* (Utrecht, 1766), pp. 30–33.
[35] Ibid., p. 36.

the classic Calvinist definition of saving faith as a certain knowledge of God's mercy towards oneself, occasionally supplementing this with the observation that faith is not sure unless displayed in works. Claude went well beyond this. The list of characteristics which his tract sets forth as distinguishing the truly regenerate from the *mondain* is daunting indeed. The former, for instance, possess all of the virtues, even if only weakly, while the latter never attain 'complete justice'. The former never do a good deed or turn away from a sinful one without feeling an ardent desire to become still better.[36] A particularly critical distinction between those whose faith was true and those whose faith was not was their behaviour in the face of affliction. At such times, true believers glory in their tribulations, are moved to repent for their sins, and, if the tribulations are for religion's sake, hold firmly to the true faith and profess it proudly, even while avoiding all violence or sedition in its defence. The falsely regenerate lose confidence in God's grace.[37] In the course of this extensive description of the characteristics of the truly faithful, Claude also raises an alarming possibility which Calvin had already spoken of his writings, but which was not much discussed within Huguenot devotional literature more broadly, namely that the faith of certain believers might be only temporary faith, a faith which looked to all appearances very much like genuine saving faith but was fated to be only passing. Doubts about one's faith, Claude tells his reader, are common to 'the true faithful' and 'those called *temporels*, that is to say who only have a temporary faith'.[38] The difference is that these doubts are accompanied by anguish for the former and joy for the latter. The considerable popularity attained by Claude's treatise in the years just before the Revocation may well have derived from this extensive preoccupation with the characteristics of saving faith. As calamities rained down upon the Huguenots in these years, these must have provoked many to ask themselves if they might not be polluting communion by participating in it without true faith, and consequently to look for guidance as to what constituted such faith. Claude's treatise clearly spoke to such anxieties, even as it also attempted to use them to stimulate steadfastness to the church and the non-resistance to the crown that most Huguenot clergymen agreed was the proper response to the intensification of persecution.

After devoting more than half of his treatise to outlining the characteristics of genuine faith, Claude then enjoined those who believed they could discern such faith within themselves to proceed to a more detailed review of their recent behaviour and their sins great and small.

---

36 Claude, *Examen*, pp. 38–40, 45, 47.
37 Ibid., pp. 69–80.
38 Ibid., p. 51.

This review should stimulate them to advance in the process of sanctification. His treatise closes with an appeal to his readers to intensify their devotional life by meditating frequently on the mysteries of the faith. Some think that it is enough to know the chief elements of Christianity and to read a chapter or two of the Bible each day, he asserts. Such people miss out on an infinity of beautiful things.[39]

The Huguenot manuals of preparation for the Lord's Supper thus provided a great variety of both observations about and interpretations of communion. We still know too little about theological developments within the seventeenth-century francophone Reformed world, and about the precise place within that world of the authors whose works have been examined here, to know if the differences between these treatises can be fruitfully related to the outlook of each author. In concluding, however, we might ask if it is possible to discern any unifying characteristics or clear evolutionary trends within this corpus.

It is tempting to seek to isolate what was distinctive about the Huguenot communion manuals by contrasting them with similar treatises from other traditions. Comparing them with the Jesuit Emond Auger's 1571 *Maniere d'ouir la messe, avec devotion et fruict spirituel*, for instance, highlights Calvinism's particularly thorough disenchantment of the world; where Auger, like the Calvinist works, depicts attendance at the eucharist as a source of consolation, as a stimulus to more upright behaviour in the future, and as a generator of concord and charity among Christians, he also stresses its utility as a shield against 'evil spirits' and as protection against sickness or calamity.[40] Comparison with the Puritan William Bradshaw's 1609 *A Direction for the weaker sort of Christians, shewing in what manner they ought to fit and prepare themselves to the worthy receiving of the Sacrament of the body and blood of Christ* calls attention to the fact that English Calvinist devotional writing gave considerably more, and more precocious, attention to the detailed analysis of the characteristics of true faith than did Huguenot; Bradshaw offers a series of means whereby his readers can test their faith.[41] But the temptation to engage in such comparisons is probably one which should be resisted until surveys like this one of the full range of communion manuals which circulated within each country and confessional tradition have been carried

---

[39] Ibid., p. 120.

[40] [Auger], *La maniere d'ouir la messe, avec devotion et fruict spirituel* (Paris, 1571), unpaginated.

[41] William Bradshaw, *A Direction for the weaker sort of Christians, shewing in what matter they ought to fit and prepare themselves to the worthy receiving of the Sacrament of the body and blood of Christ* (London, 1609), pp. 71–105.

out, for one lesson of this study is surely how varied were the treatises which circulated at the same time within a single devotional tradition, and consequently how misleading it could be to take any single treatise as typical of Huguenot communion manuals in general.

As we have seen, the Huguenot manuals of preparation for communion fall into three identifiable sub-genres: didactic works, which sought to prepare believers for the sacrament by instructing them about its history and meaning; calls to self-examination, which sought to intensify the introspection demanded by the Pauline phrase given pride of place in the liturgy, 'let each examine himself'; and collections of prayers and meditations, which sought to guide believers' thoughts and feelings from the onset of the period of preparation for the ritual through its completion. Some evolutionary trends are discernible. The didactic treatises moved with time from being a simple exposition of the guidelines governing participation in communion to richer reflections upon the sacrament's meaning and history. It seems possible to detect within the calls to self-examination an escalating rigorousness and degree of systematization. It could also be noted that the short-lived success of Jean Claude's *Examen de soy-mesme* appears revealing of the era in which it was published. But what finally seems most noteworthy about this corpus of devotional works is not the time-bound character of certain treatises or the evolutionary trends discernible within certain of its sub-genres. Instead, it is the endurance over decades and even centuries of the most important of these treatises and the continued coexistence of all of the sub-genres. Indeed, by far the most frequently and enduringly reprinted work of all encountered in this study was an anthology which encompassed between its covers the full range of different glosses on the sacrament. The reader of *Le Voyage de Beth-el* would at once have been instructed in the meaning of the Lord's Supper, stimulated to moral introspection and amendment, and offered models for experiencing the ritual which made it at once a passage from repentance and doubt to renewed faith and commitment and a metaphor for the detachment from the things of the world that the good Christian was supposed to cultivate.

Was this in fact how the book was read? Until sources are discovered which give voice to the experience and understanding of communion by large numbers of ordinary believers, we will not be able to know with certainty how fully the models proposed by the different works examined here were internalized by those who read them.[42] As the studies of Roger Chartier have suggested, however, examination of the authorial and editorial strategies embedded in the texts themselves can also serve to

---

42 None of the copies of these books I have examined contained marginalia which provide significant clues as to how they were used.

illuminate the nature of the dialogue between books and their readers in this period.[43] Here, these works call our attention to the complex and even contradictory consequences of the rise of the book for European religious life. The greatly increased dissemination of religious texts in the centuries following Gutenberg and Luther multiplied the stimuli for the construction of personal religious worlds – including decidedly heterodox ones, as the celebrated example of Menocchio clearly shows. The dissemination of books also encouraged forms of religious life built around silent reading, thereby encouraging the construction or enrichment of interior worlds of devotional life, to some degree at the expense of the public world of vocal prayer and shared ritual; the spreading Huguenot practice of reading devotional manuals during communion that was denounced by the provincial synod of Basse-Guyenne of 1661 is an excellent example of this. But while the spread of the book thus stimulated the creation of pluriform personal religious worlds, tendencies in this direction were also counteracted at the very same time by the diffusion of other books disseminating the understanding of religious practices and doctrines deemed orthodox, proposing models of proper behaviour to adopt during religious worship, and even, as in the case of those communion manuals written in what I have called the meditative mode, quite literally putting words into the mouths of the faithful and suggesting to them what they were to feel at certain moments in worship. In this way, books could also be a powerful force for the standardization of religious experience. It would clearly be mistaken to assume that these books of preparation for communion exercised such influence on every person who possessed one. But given what several recent outstanding studies have shown us about the 'intensive reading' of this period and the eager, thorough internalization of books and their messages which this could breed,[44] it would be equally unwise to dismiss these works too lightly as a source for understanding the experience of communion of one religious group in early modern Europe.

---

[43] Roger Chartier, *The Cultural Uses of Print in Early Modern France* (Princeton, 1987), especially chs 5, 7, 8.

[44] Robert Darnton, 'Readers Respond to Rousseau: The Fabrication of Romantic Sensitivity', in *The Great Cat Massacre and Other Episodes in French Cultural History* (New York, 1984), pp. 215–56; Paul S. Seaver, *Wallington's World: A Puritan Artisan in Seventeenth-Century London* (Stanford, 1985).

CHAPTER EIGHT

The Owl of Minerva at Dusk: Philippe Le Noir de Crevain, a Pastor–Historian under Louis XIV

In November 1656, Philippe Le Noir, sieur de Crevain, pastor of the Reformed church of Blain, was nearing the midpoint of a life that had already brought him considerable pain and disappointment.[1] His wife had died in childbirth six months ago. He had just written her verse epitaph, 'Les Larmes Chrétiennes' ('Christian Tears'). The flock to which he ministered amounted to just a few hundred souls scattered among the market towns and manor houses of south-eastern Brittany, not far from Nantes. Finally, the 32-year-old pastor had always loved to write. As a student at the Academy of Saumur, he had composed a copious summary of the theology lessons he had attended and a précis of universal history. Since becoming a pastor he had written, in addition to his wife's epitaph, a treatise on civil and ecclesiastical rhetoric, a catechism of the disputed points of Protestant–Catholic controversy, a treatise on arithmetic using counters, an epic poem of the life of Jesus based on the four gospels, and a rhyming version of the Reformed liturgy. He had even begun a revision of that cornerstone of French Reformed religious life, the metrical psalter of Marot and Beza. But he had just been advised against completing this project, probably by ministerial colleagues.[2] He may also have become convinced that participating in the little circle of poets that gathered around the duchess of Rohan at Blain, and even aiding members of this circle in writing love poems, was not a seemly activity for a minister.[3] In any event, even though his gospel epic, *L'Emmanuel*, would be published the following

---

[1] This chapter is based primarily on three documents written by Le Noir de Crevain: 'Reflexions ou Remarques sur la lecture de quelques uns de mes livres', B.P.F., MS 388; H.G.; H.E.B. Unless otherwise noted, all information is drawn from these sources. Brief biographical accounts of Le Noir de Crevain and his milieu may be found in Haag, VI, 552–4; B. Vaurigaud, *Essai sur l'histoire des Eglises réformées de Bretagne 1535–1808* (Paris, 1870), II, 254–8; Jean-Yves Carluer, 'Les Protestants bretons XVIe–XXe siècles' (thèse de doctorat, Université de Rennes II, 1991), II, 457; *idem*, *Protestants et Bretons* (Carrières sous Poissy, 1993), 101–6. I would like to thank Jean-Luc Tulot for bringing his publication of Le Noir's genealogical history of his family to my attention.

[2] He would later write that he had been advised against completing it at the 1659 national synod of Loudun (H.G., p. 1381), although the acts of this synod published by John Quick, *Synodicon in Gallia reformata* (London, 1692) contain no reference to Le Noir or his project.

[3] This is suggested by Carluer, *Protestants et Bretons*, p. 101.

year by the Parisian printer René Rousseau and win enough esteem to merit at least eleven further printings over the following century,[4] he now professed to be convinced of his shortcomings as a writer. 'When I reflect upon my own works, I am not so blinded by self-love that I cannot see their weakness. Writing much is for great men; all others just waste paper, that often is more valuable than their time. I have thus resolved to abandon composition despite the diversion it brings me.'[5]

Needing to find another pastime, Le Noir de Crevain decided that it would be both amusing and useful to combine his two greatest pleasures, reading and writing, by recording his observations about the most important books that passed through his hands. Although, as we shall subsequently learn, he did not entirely abandon other forms of composition, he kept his resolution to note his reflections on what he read for virtually all of the remaining 35 years of his life. From 1656 to 1690 he filled 1023 large pages with his handwritten notes. The two volumes of his 'Reflections or Remarks about the reading of some of my books or those lent me' have been preserved among the manuscript holdings of the Bibliothèque de la Société de l'Histoire du Protestantisme Français in Paris. They offer a remarkable window into the life and mind of a member of that still little-known social group, the Huguenot pastorate of the seventeenth century.[6]

Le Noir de Crevain began his notebook with a self-portrait and set of pious meditations. 'God who placed me on earth', he declared, 'gave me four kinds of occupations: the first concerns the present life; the second that to come; the third the exercise of my vocation; and the last my honest recreations.' The first, he said, was the least of his concerns, 'even if after the death of my dear wife whom God took away from my embrace six months ago, I am necessarily obliged to think about the conduct of my household and the sustenance of my children'. 'I just acquit myself of this task as if in passing, without worrying myself or losing sight of the torch of God's providence, for He will dispose of my affairs as it is meet, and thus do I put all my cares on Him, knowing that he takes care of that

---

4 I have found references to the following editions of *Emmanuel*: Charenton, 1657; Paris, 1658; Charenton, 1664 '4e édition'; Niort, 1666; Leeuwarden, 1671; Amsterdam, 1672; Rouen, 1673; Saumur, 1678; Amsterdam, 1729; Amsterdam, 1758; and, in Italian translation, Erlangen, 1716. Le Noir himself indicates that the work was also published in Dieppe and four times in Saumur. H.G., p. 1380.

5 B.P.F., MS 388, I, 3.

6 The social history of the French Protestant pastorate is still all but unwritten, with the most useful overview remaining Paul de Félice, *Les Protestants d'autrefois* (2nd edn, Paris, 1897–99), vol. 3. Biographies have been written of some of the most notable pastors of the period, most importantly Lucien Rimbault, *Pierre du Moulin, 1568–1658. Un pasteur classique à l'âge classique* (Paris, 1966); Roger Mazauric, *Le pasteur Paul Ferry* (Metz, 1964), and Elisabeth Labrousse, *Pierre Bayle. I Du Pays de Foix à la cité d'Erasme* (The Hague, 1963).

which concerns me.' His faith, and an openly stated concern to seek a
neo-Stoic tranquillity of mind, evidently brought him a measure of
equanimity. So too, in all likelihood, did the absence of serious material
wants afforded him by his descent from a family enriched and ennobled
in the preceding century in the service of the high Protestant nobility.[7]

'The matter of the salvation of my soul and the future life, my sole
consolation, should be what occupies me the most,' Le Noir continued.

> My creator and saviour leaves me on earth so that, in acquiring an
> ever greater knowledge of his divinity, his great works, and his truth,
> I am led to a repentance that is followed by a faith in his divine
> promises, and is accompanied by works of charity and piety that
> seal my adoption in my conscience, and serve as a pledge of the
> sovereign good that heaven reserves for me. But I must confess that I
> do not give myself over to these things as seriously or as frequently as
> I should, and that ordinarily I prefer what is accessory to what is
> foremost. This does not prevent me from knowing my duty and
> attempting to do it, and for that reason I write on this paper and
> refresh in my memory this divine precept of my redeemer, Seek first
> the realm of God and his justice and all others things will be given
> you as well. Lord, do in me what you command, then command what
> you will.
>
> The third of my occupations consists of the exercise of my calling
> both in visiting the afflicted and in preaching the gospel that God
> placed in my charge, which requires the reading, reflection, and writing
> essential for so onerous and so glorious a job. In this I employ myself
> with zeal, care, and pleasure, in keeping with such small talents as
> God has given me. The corruption of this century, the small size of
> my church, the weakness of my constitution, and the little success
> with which I work are incapable of discouraging me. On the contrary,
> they serve as prods to me, and make me redouble my efforts in my
> powerful passion to render myself acceptable to the divine master I
> serve, if I cannot render myself agreeable to men.
>
> There remain my honest diversions. Games of any sort have no
> place in them, for I do not find that they are in accordance with a life
> above reproach, nor do they contribute to the repose of the mind that
> I try to obtain for myself. Social gatherings are not my element; I am
> not fit for them, for I lack the talents necessary for conversation; that
> is why I only participate in them to the degree required by civility and
> to visit the families of my church as is my duty. Travel also occupies
> me as little as possible for it is the enemy of my health, and the station
> in which Jesus Christ placed me does not require it. As for the pleasures
> of the flesh, God gave me the grace to feel these so little and to regard
> them with such disdain that, instead of occupying myself in pursuing
> and tasting them, I build my glory and my joy in depriving myself of
> them.[8]

---

7 B.P.F., MS 388, I, 1.
8 Ibid., I, 1–2.

In view of his calling and his predilections, writing down his reflections on the books he read was thus a perfect solution. Humanist pedagogues had long advised their students to keep two kinds of notebooks as they read, commonplace books in which they arranged particularly telling observations or quotations according to topic or subject-matter, and *adversaria* or running notes and observations about the books they read. Certain leading scholars even published their *adversaria*.[9] Although there is no direct evidence that Le Noir de Crevain had ever read any of these published collections of notes or works advising their compilation, he was in all likelihood inspired by this tradition. In any event, he articulated a series of reasons why such a pastime would be particularly fruitful for him. Not only did it agree with his profession and his humour; it would prevent him from being idle, increase his profit from his reading, and permit him to advance in the study of true virtue 'by consulting at all moments the great minds (*bons esprits*) and taking down in writing their advice'. Furthermore, his memory was weak, but he could compensate for this by re-reading his notes in the future in order to 'retrace in my mind the general picture of an author who has passed through my hands'.[10]

The need to supplement a weak memory may have seemed particularly urgent to Le Noir de Crevain, since his deficiencies in this domain had led him as a teenager to question his aptitude for a calling that had been placed on him as much by his earthly father as by his heavenly one. Like many seventeenth-century pastors, he was not the first in his family to enter the ministry; his father and uncle were both also pastors. His father, Guy Le Noir, sieur de Crevain and pastor of La Roche-Bernard, died when he was just seven. Philippe was sent to board with several pastors of the region to learn the rudiments of Latin and the humanities, then went off at fourteen to the Academy of Saumur to complete his humanities. At sixteen, he was already reading with pleasure (but little comprehension) one of the many works of the era that placed historical questions at the centre of Protestant–Catholic disputation, Edme Aubertin's *L'Eucharistie de l'ancienne Eglise*. But he struggled with Latin and Greek, to the point where his uncle pulled him out of school before allowing him to move to the next stage in his education and brought him to live with him. Neither he nor a second uncle had much success in sparking Philippe to learn through private tutoring. Philippe grew discouraged by his evident lack of aptitude for ancient languages and began to think he was better suited for a literary career or a post in an aristocratic household. Ultimately, as he

---

9 Jean-Marc Chatelain, 'Les receuils d'*adversaria* aux XVIe et XVIIe siècles: des pratiques de la lecture savante au style de l'érudition', in Frédéric Barbier et al., eds, *Le livre et l'historien* (Geneva, 1997), 169–86.

10 B.P.F., MS 388, I, 4.

later recalled the sequence of events, he grew reconciled to a pastoral career through his relatives' constant reminder that such a career had been his late father's wish for him. He returned to Saumur after a hiatus of four years and studied with two of the greatest figures of seventeenth-century Reformed thought: the learned Hebraist and champion of the application of historical–critical methods to the Old Testament, Louis Cappel, 'my master in Hebrew and rabbinics with whom I was very close'; and the controversial exponent of the doctrine of hypothetical universal grace, Moyse Amyraut, whom he found 'inaccessible' but possessing *'hautes lumières* in theology and an admirable fluidity, precision, and presence of mind'.[11] At 26 he finally earned his degree in theology.

His family connections then helped him obtain his pastorate. Soon after leaving Saumur, he visited his infirm 70-year-old uncle André Le Noir, sieur de Beauchamp, and sought to persuade him to turn the church of Blain over to him. His uncle initially resisted, considering the resignation of his post to be a 'humiliating degradation'. In this society without a regular system of retirement after a given age, the resignation of an office was often regarded as the 'ruin' or 'fall' of the person who relinquished the post.[12] But when a faction within the church began to scheme to have another candidate named instead, he reconsidered and resigned his position in Philippe's favour, with the approval of the duchess of Rohan, who exercised seigneurial jurisdiction over Blain. Like so many other positions within old regime society, Huguenot pastorates could evidently be passed on within a family under the right circumstances, albeit at some cost in family tension.[13]

Le Noir de Crevain had been Blain's minister for five years when he began to record his reflections on his reading. 'Wherever they have been preserved, the notebooks of *adversaria* of an educated man constitute an inestimable source for his thought,' Jean-Marc Chatelain has noted.[14] This is certainly true of Le Noir de Crevain's. They also shed considerable light on the circulation and accessibility of books in a provincial milieu. Blain may have been far from Paris, but the Rohan connection created a link

---

11 H.G., pp. 1376–9; B.P.F. MS 388, I, 69, 79. Both Amyraut and Cappel are discussed at length in François Laplanche's masterpiece, *L'Ecriture, le sacré et l'histoire. Erudits et politiques protestants devant la Bible en France au XVIIe siècle* (Amsterdam, 1986). See also Laplanche, *Orthodoxie et prédication. L'oeuvre d'Amyraut et la querelle de la grâce universelle* (Paris, 1965); and Brian Armstrong, *Calvinism and the Amyraut Heresy: Protestantism Scholasticism and Humanism in Seventeenth-Century France* (Madison, 1969).

12 Jonathan Dewald, 'Deadly Parents: Family and Aristocratic Culture in Early Modern France', in Barbara Diefendorf and Carla Hesse, eds, *Culture and Identity in Early Modern Europe (1500–1800): Essays in Honor of Natalie Zemon Davis* (Ann Arbor, 1993) pp. 230–31.

13 H.G., pp. 1376–9.

14 Chatelain, 'Receuils d'*adversaria*', p. 173.

with the world of the capital and the court. Furthermore those with literary or intellectual aspirations around the small town lent books to one another; seven of the 66 books on which Le Noir de Crevain took notes were recorded as borrowed. This reclusive pastor was thus able to learn of the issues being discussed in the Parisian salons, albeit with a time lag. In 1662, a neighbour lent him three volumes of Descartes's works published between 1637 and 1651. Although he only began to read them 'in order to please', he soon found himself fascinated by natural philosophy and subsequently followed the scientific discussions of the day with considerable interest. To be sure, he could not procure every book he sought. In writing about Gassendi's ideas in 1682, he had to make do with Bernier's 1675 *Abrégé de la philosophie de Gassendi*, since 'the major volumes of Gassendi have not come this far'. He also never managed to obtain the blockbuster treatise on Hebrew punctuation by his teacher Cappel, whose challenge to the antiquity of the Masoretic text of the Old Testament so troubled Reformed orthodoxy that the work could only be published under Catholic auspices. Additionally, the need to depend upon the generosity of others could limit his access to a given book, as when the duchess of Rohan only allowed him to keep her copy of the English liturgy for a single day.[15] Like everyone at the time, he read old books as well as new. Overall, the median age of the books that he read at the time he read them may be computed to have been approximately fifteen years. But this diminished with time. For the first decade during which he recorded his reflections on his readings, his reading matter often consisted of histories of events that had occurred decades previously and of treatises on theology or moral philosophy written around 1600. With the passage of time, he increasingly turned to more recent works of controversial theology or natural philosophy in what appears to have been a conscious effort to keep abreast of the issues of the day.

Le Noir de Crevain was an engaged reader. His literary interests made him a keen judge of writing, and he often penned remarks about the style of the books he read. His philosophical training at the academy had also given him a strong formation in logic, and he frequently recorded the steps of an author's demonstration and proposed objections to particular arguments. He lingered over certain books and dashed through others. The 730 in-folio pages of Cappel's *Critica Sacra*, on which he took nine pages of notes, absorbed him for nearly four months in 1660. By contrast, he devoted just nine days and four pages of notes to Philippe Du Plessis-Mornay's nearly as lengthy, but dated, account of the papacy and its usurpation of power over the centuries, *Le Mystère d'iniquité*. Over the years, the number of books about which he wrote notes diminished, but

---

15 B.P.F., MS 388, I, 108; II, 517; I, 107.

the length of his notes increased. Over 120 pages of his second notebook were given over to Samuel Bochart's *Hierozoicon*, a description of all animals mentioned in the Bible. Here, as with his notes on many books, he was particularly concerned to record factual information that he found interesting, making his notebooks a treasure trove of miscellaneous historical, ethnographic and natural philosophical details. His notes on theological and controversial writings spelled out their arguments, assessed their sources and their strengths, and again recorded many details relevant to the disputed issues of the time. Here, it appears as if he were amassing an armoury of arguments and anecdotes that he could wheel out and use in his own sermons. Late in his life, he expressed the hope that his notebooks would also prove useful to his son, likewise a pastor.[16]

In all, Le Noir de Crevain provided commentary on or took notes from 66 books. (These are listed in the Appendix.) As a rapid breakdown of these books by subject-matter suggests, his greatest interest lay in two domains: theology, especially the works of controversy that were so germane in the context of perpetual intellectual conflict that marked the relations between the Catholic and Reformed churches in France in this period; and history, both ecclesiastical and civil. A classification of the books annotated in his notebooks yields 20 works of theology, 18 works of secular history and geography, 12 works of ecclesistical history, and 4 books that might be best classified as biblical studies. He also retained an interest in literature and moral philosophy (4 works) and grew increasingly interested with time in natural philosophy (8 works). It must be added immediately that this classification is necessarily very imprecise, since much religious controversy in this period revolved around historical details concerning the early church, rendering it hard to differentiate between church history and theology. And what is the proper category for the *Hierozoicon*: natural history, or biblical studies?

The theologians he read were above all the leading French Reformed authors of his century, such as Amyraut, Du Moulin, Bochart, Le Faucheur and Claude. His favourite was undoubtedly Jean Daillé: he read eight of his works and gushed about his combination of eloquence and historical erudition, calling him 'an almost incomparable theologian and historian'.[17] Daillé was another Saumur alumnus, Amyraut's greatest defender in the disputes that agitated the French church about his theology, and an expert on the church fathers and their use in religious controversy. Two sixteenth-century works by Reformed theologians also seemed valuable enough to him to merit notes: the *Commonplaces* of Peter Martyr Vermigli, an 'excellent author to whom the Reformed church owes much'; and the

---

[16] H.G., p. 1381.
[17] B.P.F., MS 388, I, 215.

Zurich theologian Rudolf Hospinian's account of the development of holidays among the Jews and pagans, with its abundant documentation about its subject and, more broadly, the pagan character of many Catholic holidays.[18]

The overwhelming tilt of his reading towards the questions of church history and theology that occupied Protestant–Catholic controversy reveals how much the outlook of the seventeenth-century Huguenot ministry was shaped by the need to defend the faith against the constant assault of would-be *convertisseurs*. Everything that served this cause was grist to his mill. He was particularly quick to note examples of Catholic credulity or attachment to 'empty' rituals. He copied faithfully the case reported by Daillé of a woman advised by a Jesuit that she could obtain the conversion of her uncle by saying 16 000 Ave Marias in eleven days. He lauded the second part of Du Moulin's *Anatomie de la Messe* for 'report[ing] historically a great quantity of factual matters that it is good to learn in order to see clearly how ridiculous and superstitious the Roman cult is in many ways'.[19]

While Le Noir de Crevain was deeply attached to the Protestant cause and prone to believe the worst of its Catholic adversaries, he was at the same time widely curious. His most surprising choice of books in matters religious was undoubtedly the Koran, which he read in the translation of André Du Ryer, first published in 1647. He carefully copied Du Ryer's prefatory exposition of the chief points of Islam and searched the Koran to verify whether or not the text offered a basis for each doctrine. He also noted the points at which it departed from the Bible. His overall judgement was that the work contained many excellent things drawn from natural reason, the Law and the Gospel, especially its moral precepts and its depiction of God and his attributes. The work was none the less 'spoiled' by its numerous confusions, its 'mix of false doctrines, pernicious maxims, fabulous histories, and false miracles' contrary to the Bible, and, most importantly, the immense 'injustice' of its denial of Christ's divinity.[20]

Le Noir de Crevain's reading about historical subjects likewise started from a firmly Protestant point of view but ranged widely. He took abundant notes on Crespin's *Book of Martyrs*, Agrippa d'Aubigné's universal history and Theodore Beza's life of Calvin. After recording Crespin's estimate that the Saint Bartholomew's Massacre cost 30 000 Huguenots their lives (most specialists today would say 10 000 or less), he added in the margin 'or 100 thousand'.[21] He followed the fate of the

---

18 Ibid., I, 104.
19 Ibid., I, 249, 207.
20 Ibid., I, 190–97.
21 Ibid., I, 69.

Protestant cause in nearby lands through Heinsius's account of the siege of 's-Hertogenbosch, a genealogical history of the house of Orange–Nassau, and an account of Guy Fawkes's ill-fated gunpowder plot. The *Mercure François* offered him information about recent events in French history from the perspective of the monarchy's official historiographers. He also displayed a wide-ranging curiosity about distant lands, reading histories or travel narratives concerning Portugal, Greenland, the West Indies, the American continent, Muscovy and Persia. The ancient world likewise fascinated him, as it did so many of his learned contemporaries. He read Herodotus, Thucydides, Josephus and Eusebius; laboriously compiled a 41-page description of Rome surveying the history and location of all of its ancient gates, baths and other monuments; and reconstructed and sketched the topography of Jerusalem and the plan of the temple after Josephus. He was also interested in the art of historiography. The edition of Thucydides that he read contained Lucian's observations on how to write history properly. He summarized these in the form of 23 rules.

While history and theology remained the two chief poles of his reading throughout his life, his interests evolved with the times. His encounter with Descartes was a turning point. 'Almost everywhere,' he initially recorded, 'I cannot understand a thing because of the novelty and strangeness of his opinions, which he generally bases on mathematical demonstrations that are beyond my grasp.' This did not prevent him from carefully recopying the chain of deductions and the proof of God that Descartes offers in the *Discourse on Method*, before noting with a combination of disappointment and indignation: 'That is the only proof he uses to demonstrate that there is a God, and in my opinion the reasoning is very weak, falling well short of the expectations I had of a transcendent mind who boasts of having discovered so many beautiful insights (*tant de belles lumieres*).' Descartes's *Meditations* bothered him even more. Philosophers who offer weak arguments in favour of the existence of God ran a great risk of encouraging atheism, he wrote presciently; the only thing more distressing was that other philosophers who claimed to be Christians refuted their proofs.[22] Le Noir de Crevain also dared to express doubts about elements of Descartes's natural philosophy. He could not believe, for instance, that blood circulated through the body several hundred times a day as Descartes maintained, and expressed scepticism

---

22 Ibid., I, 108, 109, 115. Le Noir de Crevain's prescience emerges clearly from Alan Charles Kors, *Atheism in France 1650–1729. Volume I: The Orthodox Sources of Disbelief* (Princeton, 1990), which demonstrates that something that may fairly be labelled atheism was first espoused by a Catholic cleric who does not appear to have known any of the most advanced heterodox authors of the preceding century but had read with care the fratricidal debates that set Cartesians against anti-Cartesians over the proof of God.

that it circulated at all except when one was bled or cut.[23] Despite his
reservations and professions of incompetence, he filled fully fifteen pages
with notes on Descartes and subsequently read other works of natural
philosophy, including Willem Blaeu's treatise on how to use globes to
understand the superiority of the Copernican cosmology to the Ptolemaic,
Theophraste Renaudot's *Conferences* of the Bureau d'Adresse, Sir Kenelm
Digby's widely reprinted treatise on sympathetic healing, and a study of
the tides. Just as he compiled his own description of Rome from several
sources, he also drew up an exposition of the world systems advocated by
a variety of ancient and modern authors, and even dared to propose a
system of his own.

Like many other educated Frenchmen of his generation, Le Noir de
Crevain remained loyal to many aspects of the Aristotelianism he had
imbibed at school, could not accept the Copernican world-view in its
entirety, and sought instead to blend the new astronomical discoveries of
the century with features of the traditional Ptolemaic vision of the cosmos.
When he read Blaeu's treatise in 1663, he found it impossible to follow its
demonstration of the superiority of the Copernican system without owning
a globe of the sort that Blaeu described, so he simply copied down the
essential features of Copernicus's cosmology, adding with exasperation
'Let he who can understand this.' He then noted several reasons why
Copernicus's theory seemed implausible of the sort that were quite
frequently advanced in the first part of the century but that had come to
be rejected by 1650 by most better-informed French professors of natural
philosophy, such as that the earth could not possibly revolve around the
sun at the speed Copernicus suggested, for if it did people would find
themselves pinned against the globe unable to move, like mites against a
speeding cannonball.[24] He mistrusted yet more thoroughly Digby's
'sympathetic powder', which promised to heal wounds by being applied
not to the wound but to an object that had been in contact with it, such as
a piece of clothing or even the weapon that had inflicted it. After listing
numerous reasons why this could not possibly work, he concluded, 'there
is every appearance that this art contains something diabolical' and vowed
that he would not recommend it until he was better informed about
successful cures it had achieved.[25] The scientific work that most pleased
him was *Le flux et reflux de la mer* by the Bordeaux lawyer César d'Arcons.
He expressed astonishment that he had never heard anybody talking about

---

23 B.P.F., MS 388, I, 109.

24 Ibid., I, 155–6. On the history of these arguments and the broader story of the reception
of Copernicus in seventeenth-century France, see L.W.B. Brockliss, *French Higher Education
in the Seventeenth and Eighteenth Centuries: A Cultural History* (Oxford, 1987), pp. 341ff,
esp. p. 341.

25 B.P.F., MS 388, I, 352.

this book, even though it had appeared sixteen years before he first read it in 1671. While Copernicus, Sacrobosco, Tycho and Descartes had seemed to him to retail improbabilities and chimeras, he felt on reading d'Arcons as if the clouds had parted and the truth stood clearly revealed. The chief argument of d'Arcons, who rejected Copernicanism, was that the tides resulted from the tilting of the earth from north to south and then from south to north every six hours. The one flaw in this work in Le Noir de Crevain's eyes was that its author failed to explain this movement's final cause – that Aristotelian category – which was to give witness to the grandeur and wisdom of God.[26]

The pastor's own system of the universe, revised several times, ultimately incorporated elements from d'Arcons and Copernicus into still another of the systems of the universe that obtained wide circulation during this century of proliferating astronomical models, the so-called Capellan system.[27] This identified Mercury and Venus as satellites of the sun, but kept the earth at the centre of the universe, with the sun, the other planets, and the fixed stars revolving around it. In Le Noir de Crevain's updated version, the earth spun on its axis every 24 hours as Copernicus said, and tilted from north to south and back as d'Arcons asserted. Around it revolved (1) the moon; (2) the sun and its satellites Mercury and Venus; (3) Mars; (4) Jupiter with its four moons; (5) Saturn with its five satellites; and (6) the stars. While Le Noir's common-sense objections to the Copernican system were already dated when he first wrote them down, his attachment to the Capellan model of the universe did not mark him as particularly *retardataire* in the French context, for most of the kingdom's schoolteachers of natural philosophy hesitated to embrace the full Copernican system before the eighteenth century, and one declared in 1699 that Capella's model was accepted by the 'greatest part of the moderns'.[28] Le Noir de Crevain stressed in any event that he did not feel himself strongly wedded to the details of his cosmology, and that he was convinced that reflecting on such matters had value even if he made errors. Better scientific minds could undoubtedly propose numerous objections to his schema, he noted.

> It suffices that I have cheered my mind with the discovery of a system for my own personal use, without harming anyone and without becoming excessively subtle. It is no small matter that I may regard my system as easier than any other and devoid of a thousand complications, and that within it I can easily see shining the power, order, wisdom and goodness of our great God.[29]

---

26 Ibid., II, 39–54.

27 Named after the fifth-century encyclopaedist Martianus Capella, credited with first mentioning it.

28 Brockliss, *French Higher Education*, pp. 341ff; Christine Jones Schofield, *Tychonic and Semi-Tychonic World Systems* (New York, 1981), pp. 172–9, esp. p. 179.

29 B.P.F., MS 388, II, 528.

While Le Noir de Crevain read and took notes in the quiet of his study, the situation of France's Reformed churches deteriorated. Although his 'Remarks' give no indication of this, we know from other sources that shortly after Louis XIV instituted his policy of enforcing the Edict of Nantes according to the strictest letter of the law, Le Noir de Crevain was chosen by the provincial synod of Brittany to gather all available documentation about the history of the Reformed churches of the province, in order to demonstrate to the king's commissioners that the churches met the legal and historical criteria that governed their right to assemble. His antipathy to travelling notwithstanding, he was sent to court to plead the case of the province's churches. The enterprise was unsuccessful. Among the temples whose demolition was ordered by the royal commissioners was that of Blain. The church henceforward had to assemble in the chateaux of noblemen in the region.[30]

Notwithstanding his 1656 vow to abandon composition, Le Noir de Crevain continued to write throughout the latter half of his life. Various sources testify that he kept a 'journal ... of all his domestic affairs' and drew up a set of a thousand biblical emblems, explicated with French verses and classical citations, both now lost.[31] A sonnet eulogizing a Saumur professor has survived.[32] But his chief interests were historical. Between 1677 and 1684, as both his own family situation and that of France's Reformed churches grew ever more precarious, he wrote a résumé of ecclesiastical history organized in chronological tables, now also lost, and two works that have survived: a brief 'Genealogical History of Philippe Le Noir Pastor of the Reformed Church of Blain composed by himself', and a far more ambitious ecclesiastical history of Brittany's Reformed churches from the Reformation to the time of his writing, of which he was able to complete only the first half.

Le Noir de Crevain first began to think about writing the history of Brittany's Reformed churches after gathering the extant documentation about them to defend their rights of assembly to Louis XIV's commissioners.[33] This plan was what inspired him to read the great Greek historians in 1665 and to make his notes on how to write history. But he did not begin actively writing for nearly two more decades, when a series of even graver threats to his church, his faith and his family's safety finally prompted him to pass from idea to action. In 1681, Louis XIV's escalating persecution of the Huguenots reached its first paroxysm in the neighbouring province of Poitou, when the intendant Marillac unleashed the initial

---

30 Benoist, IV, 7–8; H.E.B., pp. xxx–xxxi; H.G., p. 1382; Vaurigaud, *Essai*, II, 306ff, and especially III, pièce justificative 2.

31 Vaurigaud, *Essai*, III, xlv; H.G., p. 1381; B.P.F. MS 388, II, 21.

32 Vaurigaud, *Essai*, II, 257.

33 *H.E.B.*, p. 3.

dragonnades against the Protestants of that province. Fearing that the use of troops to extort conversions might spread into Brittany, Le Noir de Crevain decided late in that year to send his two younger children away to safety in Holland. In 1682, a member of Blain's church was tried and convicted for calling the Catholic church 'the devil's religion' and other 'contemptuous and hot-headed phrases'. The year after that, the minister's own son-in-law was indicted for a similar offence. The young man decided to spare himself further legal troubles by converting, but his disloyalty to the faith prompted his wife to leave him and join her siblings in Holland, where six months later she gave birth to their child. This so embittered her husband that he initiated a law suit against his father-in-law. A failed reconciliation and further legal troubles finally convinced Le Noir de Crevain that he had to follow his children and flee for Holland. It was in the midst of these difficulties that his historical muse took wing. His 'Remarks' contain the following entry:

> Nota: In the years 1682, 1683, 1684 I did not make any extracts from my reading, because I was completing the 21 tables of my ecclesiastical history and drew from them two clean copies correcting, augmenting, and retouching the original. Beyond that in these three years I had to digest bitterness beyond belief, such as the absence of my children sent to Holland, family persecution by my son-in-law, and public persecution by the law courts against both me and my church: also the concern of seeing to the establishment and sustenance of my family in Holland. This does not count the composition of the history of the Reformation in Brittany, that I carried down to my father and uncle's reception in the holy ministry, from 1560 to 1611, the draft of which, without a copy but fairly clean, remained behind in Ponthus, borrowed by the marquis of La Mure at the end of 1684.[34]

In these same years, he also recopied and corrected his genealogical history that he had first written in 1677 at his children's request.[35]

Although it is a minor work destined strictly for family consumption, Le Noir de Crevain's genealogical history sheds fascinating light on the personal and family dimensions of Huguenot identity and historical consciousness in this period, as well as on the emotional tenor of his household. The pastor was troubled enough by the very act of drawing up a family history to begin with a set of reflections on the value of genealogies. They could be dangerous instruments of pride, he noted, but the Bible abounds in genealogical information; hence they could not be entirely bad. On the contrary, they could serve virtue by providing positive examples that might inspire subsequent generations within a family.[36]

---

34 B.P.F., MS 388, II, 527; Carluer, *Protestants et Bretons*, p. 106.
35 H.G., p. 1308.
36 Ibid., pp. 1308–9.

The virtue that Le Noir evidently wanted above all to inspire in his children was that of fidelity to the true religion. The work may be seen as one part genealogical history of a branch of God's chosen people, explicitly analogous to the Bible, and one part chronicle of fidelity to the cause in the manner of Crespin's *Book of Martyrs*. The lineage of each branch of the family, both Le Noir's and his wife's, is traced back to the first members of the family to embrace the Reformed faith. The biographical details provided about the earliest converts consist primarily of tales of exemplary fidelity to the cause and narrow escapes from massacres and persecutions, tales that presumably had become part of the family's oral tradition. Le Noir de Crevain even staked a claim to descent from an early martyr for the faith, a source of considerable pride within Huguenot pastoral families, on the rather shaky ground that one of his maternal ancestors was disinterred after death and dragged naked through the streets of Rennes: 'although unable to feel anything he suffered humiliation in Christ's name'.[37] The fidelity to the cause of virtually all later members of the family is likewise stressed, and his children are explicitly exhorted to remain equally faithful. Le Noir even gave voice with breathtaking assurance to the confidence in his own election that many Huguenots may have felt as a result of their status as a small and faithful minority: 'My dear children, since we are children of God you and I, we are the elect offspring and the family of he whose lineage is called that of heaven and earth. We shall be servants of God and coinheritors of Jesus Christ. Amen.'[38]

Despite his fear of the danger of pride, Le Noir de Crevain clearly also took satisfaction in the family's worldly renown and shared the interest in lineage that was so much a part of seventeenth-century élite culture. The Le Noirs were a 'good and ancient family of Orléans', he told his children. He duly noted the positions and titles of those family members who held royal offices or fiefs. He also recorded the value of various family members' dowries or estates, perhaps in the event that the children might have a future claim to the inheritance of that branch of the family. On passing through Orléans on the way back from court in 1665, he had made inquiries about distant cousins who might still be living there. He had also received inquiries from a Catholic relative of his wife's, a counsellor in the presidial court of Angers, who had contacted him in quest of information about his side of the family.[39] Interest in kinship ties within this milieu evidently transcended the confessional boundary.

---

[37] Ibid., p. 1367. Other claims of descent from more genuine martyrs may be found in Pierre II Du Moulin, 'La Vie de Pierre Du Moulin', printed in Rimbault, *Pierre Du Moulin*, p. 196; Charles Drelincourt, dedicatory epistle to *Neuf dialogues contre les missionaires sur le service des Eglises réformées*, reprinted in *La France Protestante* (2nd edn, Paris, 1876–87), V, 486–7.

[38] H.G., p. 1309.

[39] Ibid., pp. 1310, 1375, 1435, 1426.

The 'Genealogical History' also offers a small portrait gallery of those family members Le Noir de Crevain had known personally. The pastors in the family are memorialized for a variety of gifts: his father for his skill at visiting and consoling the sick, his uncle and predecessor in Blain for his eloquence in the pulpit and his wisdom in political and ecclesiastical affairs, which merited him several selections as the province's representative to national synods or Huguenot political assemblies. His maternal grandmother, with whom he had lived between the ages of four and seven, had been 'sweet and reasonable as she was perfectly instructed in religion'. Her husband was an excellent tennis player. The family also had its black sheep. His cousin Henry, also a pastor's son, failed to apply himself to his studies, 'being debauched and a libertine', and ended up dying a soldier's death in the regiment of the duke of La Trémouille.

Finally, Le Noir de Crevain used the genealogical history to give expression to certain feelings about his wife and children that display the complex and even contradictory attitudes toward the ties of the nuclear family prevalent in the upper strata of seventeenth-century France.[40] 'I did not have much inclination to marry and surely would have remained celibate if my mother had been alive and willing to come live with me,' he told his children, expressing again the lack – or denial – of interest in sexuality that he also stated in his preface to his reading notes. His marriage, he protested, was only prompted by his need to have somebody to look after his household and his inability to find a situation in Blain in which he could live as a boarder. His gaze settled on one of his parishioners, Anne Henriet, despite her modest dowry of 5000 *livres* and the fact that certain of her relatives, largely military men, looked askance at the marriage. She was short and squat, but in other ways a paragon of seventeenth-century womanhood:

> [She was] most agreeable, of a charming humour, incapable of the slightest outburst of anger, and knew how to maintain her station [*tenir son rang*]. She spoke beautifully as if she had spent her entire life at court and it seemed as if she was born for conversation with the great, so polite and civil she was. In all of her conduct a character of noble virtue reigned that made her esteemed and cherished by all. She had as facile and clever a mind and as enlightened a judgement as I have ever seen.

These virtues rendered her precious to her self-styled 'tender and good husband'. Although their marriage lasted for just four years before she died giving birth to their third child, he asserted that he became so attached

---

[40] A particularly sensitive examination of these attitudes that has informed much of this and the following paragraph is Jonathan Dewald, *Aristocratic Experience and the Origins of Modern Culture: France, 1570–1715* (Berkeley, 1993), ch. 3.

to her in this time that his grief on her death was 'unequalled' and convinced him that he could never marry again. Admiration for and attachment to a beloved spouse evidently warred within his breast against a mistrust of sexuality and marriage.[41]

Her death left him with the burden of raising their three children. His sister agreed to take in and bring up their eldest daughter for about twelve years 'at no charge', an act of considerable generosity in an age when the cost of caring for relatives was often an object of family negotiation, the outcome of which was specified by written contract. Le Noir de Crevain kept his only son with him and personally supervised his education for eighteen years before sending him off to Saumur and Leiden to become a pastor. He also kept the younger daughter with him, except for a few brief stays with aunts who could offer her elements of a girl's education that he could not. (Unfortunately he does not specify what these were or how he himself educated her.) Ultimately, he was not averse to telling all his children that this younger daughter became his favourite, even though his attitude toward her had initially been complicated by the fact that her mother had died during her birth, and even though he recognized that a father should treat all his children equally. 'Even though my grief was without equal, I looked upon the innocent murderer of my beloved wife and her worthy mother with compassion and tenderness, and I felt my affection for the dead one reawakening and perpetuating itself in the living child.' The long time that they lived together and the fact that she was as sweet as her mother cemented his predilection for her.[42] Yet Le Noir de Crevain professed himself deeply bound to all his children. When he finally felt compelled to arrange for their flight to Holland and was separated from them for several years, the pain and grief were, he asserted, even worse than after his wife's death.[43]

While Le Noir de Crevain's genealogical history reveals the familial component of later seventeenth-century Huguenot historical consciousness, his *Ecclesiastical History of Brittany from the Reformation to the Edict of Nantes* describes the regional history of the cause with a level of care and detail matched by few, if any, works of the period. It has been well known to historians of early modern Brittany since it was first published in 1851 by Benjamin Vaurigaud on the basis of a slightly incomplete eighteenth-century copy of the manuscript that the author had left behind in the possession of the marquis of La Mure. It deserves to be more widely known among all historians of sixteenth- and seventeenth-century France,

---

[41] H.G., pp. 1322.

[42] Dewald notes that love for children was often presented as being conditional and tied to their particular merits in aristocratic writings from this period.

[43] H.G., p. 1380.

both for what it can contribute to our understanding of the French
Reformation and for what it reveals about Huguenot historical writing in
the second half of the seventeenth century.

What first strikes the reader of the *Ecclesiastical History of Brittany* is
its density and precision of information, its careful use and systematic
identification of primary sources, and its sparseness of moralizing
commentary about the events reported. Le Noir de Crevain had at his
disposition many documents that are now lost, including sixteenth-
century baptismal registers for six churches (today the registers of just
one survive from this period), a memoir covering the period 1561–1604
written by the first pastor of La Roche-Bernard, and an account of the
first years of the church of Nantes that the author inherited from his
maternal ancestors. He not only drew from these sources numerous vivid
anecdotes, he also read them attentively to establish just where, when and
under whose direction the province's various churches met. On one
occasion, he even had recourse to simple quantitative techniques to
indicate the size of one of the churches, noting that the baptismal
register of the church of Nantes recorded nearly 400 baptisms from 1560
to 1572.[44] Virtually every paragraph contains within the text an
indication of the sources used. (He did not use footnotes.) Begrudg-
ingly, the eighteenth-century Benedictine Charles Taillandier admitted
that Le Noir de Crevain 'is a man of good faith, who narrates without
passion and sets forth the facts as he finds them in the memoirs that he
follows'.[45]

In light of what we have already learned about Le Noir de Crevain's
formation and reading, these features of his work should come as no
surprise. From Eusebius onward, ecclesiastical history was a branch of
history in which the direct citation of original documents occupied
particular prominence. Among Lucian's precepts that Le Noir de Crevain
had copied were that historians should always write without partiality,
and that they should indicate the sources for their assertions. Many of the
other works of history Le Noir de Crevain had read had offered him
instruction in the practical application of the techniques of historical
criticism, as his teacher Cappel had already done when he was a student
at Saumur. The task of defending the rights of assembly of Brittany's
churches had not only required him to assemble the extant documentation
about these churches, but to comb through it to determine when the various
churches of the province were functioning, and to present his findings to
hostile judges in a manner that was at once as probative and as inoffensive
to Catholic sensibilities as possible.

---

[44] H.E.B., p. 73.
[45] Cited by Vaurigaud, ibid., p. xxxii.

This is not to say that the work does not betray Le Noir de Crevain's concerns and values. It is clear that he was particularly anxious to preserve for posterity the works and deeds of the exceptional souls who braved great dangers to found the first Reformed churches. After expressing regret about the absence of information about the first pastors of Nantes, he added, 'If I had been able to find out all these details, I would have reported them with great care; ... such is the veneration we should have for the memory of those first founders of our most ancient churches, who did so much and suffered so much to procure the truth and freedom for us.'[46] His great concern to track the fate of each individual church also suggests a desire to keep alive for posterity, in the face of the threat of the definitive suppression of the province's churches, the knowledge that once upon a time 27 congregations gathered at precise dates and places within Brittany.

Writing at a furious pace that allowed him to draft 334 printed pages-worth of text in less than three months, Le Noir de Crevain organized his abundant information according to some simple chronological patterns. He divided the full history of the province's churches that he initially intended to write into four ages. The first covered the infancy of the churches, or the era of their birth and establishment, running from 1558 to 1561. The second examined the youth of the churches, or 'the time of troubles', running from 1562 to 1598. The third, never written, proposed to explore the virility of the churches, or the era during which the Edict of Nantes was faithfully observed, running from 1598 to 1660. The last, also unwritten, proposed to treat the old age of the churches, or 'the time of decadence and final decline, under the weight of the declarations that harmed the Edict of Nantes and gradually undermined it to topple it', from 1660 to 1683. Although he wrote the work before the final Revocation of the Edict of Nantes, he had no doubt about the destination toward which royal policy was headed. He organized his account of the second age, 'the time of troubles', in part around the classic narrative of the successive civil wars, but also in part, with greater originality, around the successive legal proscriptions and 'great re-establishments' of the church. From 1568 to 1570, 1572 to 1576, and 1585 to 1593/8, royal edicts outlawed the public exercise of the Reformed faith throughout the kingdom, and virtually all of Brittany's churches had to cease assembling. A significant part of the story he tells is that of the efforts of the province's ministers to rebuild their decimated con-gregations after each of these periods. The history of these successive 're-establishments' has been largely neglected by subsequent historians of the Reformed churches.

---

46 Ibid., p. 67.

Although above all a gold mine for the local historian of Breton Protestantism, the *Ecclesiastical History of Brittany* also records certain details that are significant for the history of France's Reformed churches as a whole. Brittany emerges from this work as one of those regions where the first institutions of the Reformed churches differed from those that ultimately came to be established throughout the kingdom. The first standing organism created to oversee the affairs of the religion in the province was not a synod of ministers and elders such as was established elsewhere, but a council composed of four noblemen that was created in May 1560 by an assembly of 'several gentlemen and other people with offices in the church'. The four members of this council were to be renewed every six months by a synod-like assembly of delegates from every one of the province's churches. 'Soon thereafter, in polishing the government of the church on the basis of the national synods and the common discipline, provincial synods were substituted for these perpetual councils of four gentlemen delegated by assemblies.'[47] The work also makes it clear that a strong sense of solidarity subsequently developed among the province's ministers. The pastor of La Roche-Bernard whose memoir Le Noir de Crevain so frequently cited called the collectivity of ministers 'our college' and followed as carefully as possible the fate of each one when they were scattered by the League. A separate Breton church, with its own consistory and its own celebration of the Lord's Supper, was established during this era in La Rochelle, a magnet for refugees from the province.[48]

The distinctive features of Le Noir de Crevain's *Ecclesiastical History of Brittany* emerge most clearly when it is compared with the sole ecclesiastical history of an individual French Reformed church or province to come down to us from the preceding century, Nicolas Pithou's *Histoire ecclésiastique de la ville de Troyes*, written in 1594. Le Noir de Crevain lets slip his scorn for the Roman church at the beginning of his *Ecclesiastical History of Brittany*, where he attributes Protestantism's slowness to develop in the province to the stupidity of its inhabitants and their extreme superstitiousness.[49] But the extent of his partisanship is modest in comparison with Pithou, whose history drips with disdain for Catholic practices, expressed in the mocking tones of the anti-Roman satires of the sixteenth century. Pithou's work also occasionally assumes prophetic overtones that are absent in Le Noir de Crevain, as when, narrating the slow re-establishment of Troyes's church in 1576 and 1577, it denounces the cowardice of those members who were not prepared to sacrifice their worldly ease for the cause of the faith. At other moments providential

---

47 Ibid., pp. 37–8.
48 Ibid., pp. 270, 1438.
49 Ibid., p. 5.

notes appear and God's judgements are clearly displayed, as when one of the chief figures in Troyes's local Saint Bartholomew's Massacre is said to have died in 1579, crying out horribly as a mini-tempest swirled around his deathbed.[50] The disappearance from Le Noir de Crevain's work of the providential, prophetic and vehemently moralizing tones that are so pronounced in Pithou's history all testify to the important changes that had taken place in Huguenot historical writing over the course of the intervening century. The royal edicts that forbade expressions of disrespect to the Catholic church, the recognition amid the numerous Catholic–Protestant controversies of the era that the sober recital of facts was often the most effective rhetoric in historical debates, the growing prestige of classical rhetorical models, and an increased reliance on the tools of historical criticism had all chastened Huguenot historiography.[51]

The flight to Holland that obliged Le Noir de Crevain to leave his *Ecclesiastical History of Brittany* incomplete took place in March and April 1685. He recuperated from his voyage for three months in The Hague, then took up a new post as pastor of the French church in Hoorn. There, in 1687, he began once again to record his observations on his reading in the notebooks that he had carried with him. The first two books on which he wrote notes concerned that problem then being hotly debated within Huguenot refugee circles and that has so often been of intense interest to persecuted groups of Christians: the interpretation of the apocalyptic books of the Bible. He pronounced himself particularly convinced by Pierre Jurieu's deciphering of the mysteries of Revelation, according to which an end to the persecution was imminent and would soon be followed by the destruction of the papal Antichrist. 'Nothing better [than Jurieu's book] can possibly be done until God brings us a time and doctors of greater vision through the very accomplishment of his prophecies, both with the final fall of Babylon and the happy reign of a thousand years.'[52] Le Noir de Crevain's new apocalypticism also found its way into his final revision

---

[50] B.N., Paris, MS Dupuy 698, fols 16ff, 421v, 444v, 450. The first part of this important work has now been edited and published by Pierre-Eugène Le Roy: Nicolas Pithou de Champgobert, *Chronique de Troyes et de la Champagne durant les guerres de religion (1524–1594)* (Reims, 1998). Mark Greengrass, 'Nicolas Pithou: Experience, Conscience and History in the French Civil Wars', in A. Fletcher and P. Roberts, eds, *Religion, Culture and Society in Early Modern Britain* (Cambridge, 1994), pp. 1–28, offers a sensitive reading.

[51] In the following generation, respect for historical veracity would assume still more force as a moral imperative for two other Saumur alumni, Pierre Bayle and Isaac de Beausobre. Bertram E. Schwarzbach, 'Politics and Ethics in the Huguenot Diaspora: Isaac de Beausobre in Berlin', in John Cristian Laursen, ed., *New Essays on the Political Thought of the Huguenots of the Refuge* (Leiden, 1995), p. 118, makes this point well about Beausobre.

[52] B.P.F., MS 388, II, 567.

of his world-system, which he completed in 1687. He ended this by expressing doubt that the true system of the world would ever be revealed in his dark century; only God could reveal it, and he would probably wait until the next century, 'when in penetrating us with his light he will make himself known to us and will give us perfect understanding of his works'.[53] Like Isaac Newton, that other, more brilliant student of natural philosophy who was at that very moment working out in Cambridge the system of planetary motion that would soon be hailed as revealing God's light to the world, this devotee of historico-critical approaches to the Bible was also susceptible to the appeal of apocalyptic prognostication.

But with his final exercises in annotation, Le Noir de Crevain returned to his old interests, controversial theology and ecclesiastical history. The penultimate book to appear in his 'Remarks' is Friedrich Spanheim's survey of the various forms of error that have challenged the truths of Reformed Christianity over the centuries and the key points that refute each one. The last book, aptly enough, is the same author's *Introduction to Ecclesiastical History*, whose erudite corrections of Baronius's classic work furnished the pastor with many supplementary details that he regretted he could not insert into his own tables of ecclesiastical history. Le Noir de Crevain finished copying information from this book at the end of October 1690. A year later he was dead.

One of the fascinations of biographies of relatively obscure men is that they serve to illuminate aspects of their subject's time and milieu while reminding one at the same time of the stubborn uniqueness of each individual life. The reader who has come this far may well wonder to what extent Le Noir de Crevain was representative of his time and milieu. Only a relatively small minority of pastors could join him in boasting a title of nobility, but most did come from families of some local notability and intermarried and associated with the best families of the region, especially in the northern half of the kingdom.[54] Not all found their retreat in their study and earned a reputation for erudition; the variety of skills of the pastors in Le Noir's immediate family has shown us that. Still, when an unknown royal agent drew up a rapid sketch of the 80 ministers of the synod of Haut-Languedoc and Haute-Guyenne with an evident eye to determining which ones might be likely candidates for conversion, the

---

53 Ibid., II, 528 ter.

54 De Félice, *Protestants d'autrefois*, I, 209–18, and, for further illustrations of this encountered in the course of research into other questions, A.D. Drôme, 1 Mi 490 R 23, baptism of 25 October 1671; A.D. Tarn, E 5198 ter, baptism of 30 May 1625; A.D. Loir-et-Cher, I 9, marriage of 28 February 1677.

attribute he most commonly commented on was their degree of learning, and his judgements were overwhelmingly positive: 41 of the pastors were said to be 'scavant', while 22 were praised for their 'esprit', 20 for their preaching, and just 4 for their skills as 'consistoriens' or 'hommes de conduite pour l'eglise'.[55] Many of the features of Le Noir de Crevain's intellectual interests and outlook were what we might expect from a Saumur graduate of his generation. Others, such as the interest in religious controversy, were more broadly typical of the French Reformed pastorate as a whole. Still others, such as his response to Cartesianism and Copernicanism, were shared by many of his university-educated contemporaries regardless of their confessional affiliation. Nor was Le Noir de Crevain the only Huguenot whose historical muse was awakened by the events leading up to and following the Revocation. By far the largest subset of surviving Huguenot personal documents is that of escape narratives and family memoirs written for the benefit of future generations in the wake of 1685, and the event also inspired such histories as Elie Benoist's *Histoire de l'Edit de Nantes* and Jean Olry's *La persécution de l'église de Metz*.[56]

Yet to see in Le Noir's life and writings nothing more than an illustration of his milieu and generation would be to miss his distinctive voice and to diminish the interest of his biography and his writings. None of his contemporaries wrote a work quite like the *Ecclesiastical History of Brittany*. Few wrote family histories as detailed as his. Understanding what led him to write these as he did casts a fascinating light on the interplay of personal memory, oral tradition, written records, ancient rhetorical models, and the tools of historical criticism in the construction of one man's multi-layered relationship to both the past and the future. It also helps us to understand why his *Ecclesiastical History* not only furnishes an abundance of raw material that later generations of historians can

---

55 'Notes sur les Ministres de la province de Haute-Guyenne et du Haut-Languedoc', published in Robert Garrisson, *Essai sur l'histoire du Protestantisme dans la Généralité de Montauban sous l'intendance de N.-J. Foucault 1674–1684* (Musée du Désert en Cévennes, 1935), pp. 247–60. The emphasis on learning within the Huguenot pastorate is also highlighted by Elisabeth Labrousse, *Un foi, une loi, un roi? La révocation de l'édit de Nantes* (Geneva, 1985), pp. 51–2.

56 Benoist; Jean Olry, *La persécution de l'église de Metz*, ed. O. Cuvier (Paris, 1860; orig. edn Hanau, 1690); Philippe Le Gendre, *Histoire de la persecution faite à l'Eglise de Rouen sur la fin du dernier siècle*, ed. Emile Lesens (Rouen, 1874). On the escape narratives and memoirs sparked by the Revocation, see Carolyn Lougee Chappell, ' "The Pains I Took to Save My/His Family": Escape Accounts by a Huguenot Mother and Daughter after the Revocation of the Edict of Nantes', *French Historical Studies* 22 (1999), 1–64, esp. 2n; Philip Benedict, 'Some Uses of Autobiographical Documents in the Reformed Tradition', forthcoming in Kaspar von Greyerz, ed., *Von der dargestellten Person zum erinnerten Ich. Europäische Selbstzeugnisse als historische Quellen*.

weave into patterns of their own design, but has the capacity to reach across the generations and enter into dialogue with modern historians, suggesting to them patterns to that history that they might not have seen. Above all else, to follow his life story and to encounter his distinctive voice is to find oneself briefly transported into another time and another sensibility, at once distant yet tragically familiar.

Appendix: works read by Le Noir de Crevain

Listed here are the works read by Le Noir de Crevain as listed in the 'Catalogue des Auteurs' that he placed at the beginning of each volume of his 'Remarks', together with full bibliographic citations of the works in question in so far as I have been able to identify them. Details provided within Le Noir de Crevain's notes often facilitate this identification. The precise edition used is rarely noted; where no indications are available, I have listed here the earliest edition of each title in question to appear in the catalogue of the Bibliothèque Nationale.

'La vie de Calvin par Beze'. [*Calvini vita a Theodoro Beza Genevensis Ecclesiae Ministro accurate descripta*, accompanying *Ioannis Calvini Epistolae*. Geneva, 1575.]

'La Geographie sainte de Bochart'. [Samuel Bochart. *Geographiae sacrae pars prior, Phaleg, seu de Dispersione gentium et terrarum divisione facta in aedificatione turris Babel. Pars altera, Chanaan, seu de Coloniis et sermone Phoenicum.* Caen, 1646.]

'Les VI Sermons de la grace, par M. Amyraud'. [Moyse Amyraut. *Six sermons de la nature, étendue, nécessité dispensative et efficace de l'Evangile.* Saumur, 1636.]

'Les Characteres des passions, par la Chambre'. [Marin Cureau de La Chambre. *Les Charactères des passions.* Paris, 1640. Le Noir de Crevain also later read vols 2–4, published in 1659–60.]

'La Sagesse de Charon'. [Pierre Charron. *De la sagesse.* Bordeaux, 1601.]

'Discours sur la creche & sur la croix, par Spanheim fils'. [Ezechiel Spanheim. *Discours sur la crèche de Nostre Seigneur. Discours sur la croix de Nostre Seigneur.* Geneva, 1655.]

'Histoire de Portugal, par Osorius et Lopez'. [Jeronymo Osorio da Fonseca and Fernão Lopes de Castanheda. *Histoire de Portugal contenant les entreprises, navigations et gestes mémorables des Portugallois ... depuis l'an 1496 jusques à l'an 1578.* Geneva, 1581.]

'Mystere d'Iniquité, ou histoire des Papes; du Plessix'. [Philippe Du Plessis-Mornay. *Le Mystère d'iniquité, c'est-à-dire l'Histoire de la Papauté ... où sont aussi défendus les droicts des empereurs, rois et princes chrestiens contre les assertions des cardinaux Bellarmin et Baronius.* Saumur, 1611.]

'Histoire des Martyrs par J. Crespin'. [Jean Crespin. *Histoire des martyrs persécutez et mis à mort pour la vérité de l'Evangile, depuis le temps des apostres jusques à l'an 1597.* N.p., 1597.]

'Critique Saincte, de Louys Cappel'. [Louis Cappel. *Critica Sacra, sive de variis quae in sacris Veteris Testamenti libris occurrunt lectionibus libri sex*. Paris, 1650.]

'Le Siege de Boleduc, par Heinsius'. [Daniel Heinsius. *Histoire du siège de Bol Doc et de ce qui s'est passé ès Pais Bas Unis l'an 1629*. Leiden, 1631.]

'L'Eucharistie de l'anciene Eglise, par Aubertin'. [Edme Aubertin. *L'Eucharistie de l'ancienne Eglise*. Geneva, 1633.]

'Traitté de la Cene contre du Perron, par le faucheur'. Michel Le Faucheur. *Traitté de la Cène du Seigneur ... avec la Réfutation des instances et oppositions du Cardinal du Perron*. Geneva, 1635.]

'La Mythologie de Noel le Compte'. [Natale Conti. *Mythologie, c'est-à-dire Explication des fables, contenant les généalogies des dieux, les cérémonies de leurs sacrifices, leur gestes, adventures, amours et presque tous les préceptes de la philosophie naturelle et morale*. Lyon, 1604.]

'Les Lauriers de Nassau, par un flamen'. [Jan Janszoon Orlers. *La Généalogie des illustres comtes de Nassau novellement imprimée avec la description de toutes les victoires lesquelles Dieu a octroyées aux nobles, hauts et puissants seigneurs Messeigneurs les Estats des Provinces unies du Pais bas sous la conduite et gouvernement de Son Excellence le prince Maurice de Nassau*. Leiden, 1615.]

'Le Mercure francois, par Jean Richer'. [*Le Mercure François*, vols 1, 2, 5. Paris, 1617–48.]

'Histoire des Antilles, sans nom d'Auteur'. [Charles de Rochefort. *Histoire naturelle et morale des iles Antilles de l'Amerique*. Rotterdam, 1658.]

'Relation de Groenland, sans nom d'Auteur'. [Isaac de La Peyrère. *Relation de Groenland*. Paris, 1647.]

'Diverses Poesies de Breboeuf'. [Georges de Brébeuf. *Poësies diverses*. Paris, 1658.]

'Lieux Communs de Pierre Martyr'. [Pietro Martire Vermigli. *Loci communes ex variis ipsius aucthoris et libris in unum volumen collecti*. London, 1576.]

'Oeuvres de des Cartes'. [René Descartes. *Discours de la methode ... Plus la Dioptrique. Les Meteores. Et la Geometrie*. Leiden, 1637. *Meditationes de prima philosophia*. Amsterdam, 1642. *Les principes de la philosophie*. Paris, 1651.]

'Origine des festes, par Hospinian de Zuric'. [Rudolf Hospinian. *De Origine, progressu, ceremoniis et ritibus festorum dierum Judaeorum, Graecorum, Romanorum et Turcarum libri tres*. Zurich, 1592.]

'Usage des Globes, par Blaeu flaman'. [Willem Blaeu. *L'Institution astronomique de l'usage des globes et sphères célestes et terrestres, comprise en deux parties, l'une suivant l'hypothèse de Ptolémée ... l'autre selon l'intention de Copernicus.* Amsterdam, 1642.]

'Estats & Empires de davity'. [Pierre Davity. *Les Estats, empires et principautez du monde, representez par la description des pays, moeurs des habitans, richesses des provinces, les forces, le gouvernement, la religion et les princes qui ont gouverné chacun estat.* Paris, 1619.]

'Conferences du Bureau d'adresse, par Renodot'. [Théophraste Renaudot. *Recueil général des questions traictées ès conférences du Bureau d'adresse.* 4 vols. Paris, 1655–56.]

'Alcoran de Mahomet, traduit par du Rier'. [*L'Alcoran de Mahomet. Translaté d'arabe en françois. Par le sieur Du Ryer.* Paris, 1647.]

'Foucade d'Angleterre'. [I have not been able to identify this work. Le Noir de Crevain's notes indicate that it is an account in Latin of the Gunpowder Plot written by a well-informed Englishman.]

'Histoire d'Aubigné'. [Agrippa d'Aubigné. *L'Histoire universelle.* 3 vols. Maillé, 1616.]

'Anatomie de la Messe, par du Moulin'. [Pierre Du Moulin. *Anatomie de la messe, où est montré par l'Escriture Saincte ... que la messe est contraire à la parole de Dieu et esloignée du chemin de salut.* Geneva, 1636.]

'Replique au Pere Adam et a Cottibi par daillé'. [Jean Daillé. *Réplique aux deux livres de MM. Adam et Cottiby.* Geneva, 1662.]

'herodote, traduit par du Ryer'. [Herodotus. *Les histoires, mises en francois par P. Du Ryer.* Paris, 1645.]

'Thucydide de la traduction d'Ablancourt'. [Thucydides. *L'Histoire de Thucydide ... continuée par Xenophon, de la traduction de Nicolas Perrot, sieur d'Ablancourt.* Paris, 1662.]

'Object du Culte religieux, par Daillé'. [Jean Daillé. *Adversus Latinorum de cultus religiosi objecto traditionem disputatio.* Geneva, 1664.]

'Confession auriculaire par M. Daillé et des Images'. [Jean Daillé. *De sacramentali sive auriculari Latinorum confessione disputatio.* Geneva, 1661. Jean Daillé. *De imaginibus.* Leiden, 1642.]

'Art des Emblemes, par Menestrier'. [Claude-François Ménestrier S.J. *L'Art des emblèmes, où s'enseigne la morale par les figures de la fable, de l'histoire et de la nature.* Lyon, 1662.]

'Description de Rome, de plusieurs auteurs'. [A topographical description of Rome compiled from various sources, among which Le Noir de Crevain cites: Giovanni Bartolommeo Marliani. *Urbis Romae topographia.* Rome, 1544. Alessandro Donati. *Roma vetus ac recens.* Rome, 1639. Nicolas de Bralion. *Les curiositez de l'une et de l'autre Rome, ou Traité des plus augustes temples ... de Rome chrestienne et des plus nobles monuments ... de Rome payenne.* 2 vols. Paris, 1655–59. Henri de Rohan. *Voyage du duc de Rohan, fait en l'an 1600 en Italie, Allemaigne, Pays-bas uni, Angleterre et Escosse.* Amsterdam, 1646.]

'Paradoxe de Mathieu Cottiere'. [Matthieu Cottière. *Paradoxe, que l'Eglise romaine, en ce qu'elle a de différent des Eglises dites réformées, n'est ancienne que de quatre cents ans environ, et qu'en plusieurs chefs elle est beaucoup plus récente.* Geneva, 1636.]

'Poudre de sympathie du chevalier digby'. [Kenelm Digby. *Discours fait en une célèbre assemblée, par le chevalier Digby ... touchant les guérisons des playes par la poudre de sympathie, où sa composition est enseigné, et plusieurs autres merveilles de nature sont développés.* Paris, 1656.]

'des Peines & satisfactions, et purgatoire, Daillé'. [Jean Daillé. *De poenis et satisfactionibus humanis libri VII.* Amsterdam, 1649.]

'histoire d'Eusebe, traduite par Henry Valois'. [Eusebius. *Historiae ecclesiasticae.* Paris, 1669.]

'faux denys Areopagite et Ignace. Daillé'. [Jean Daillé. *De scriptis quae sub Dionysii Areopagitae et Ignatii Antiocheni nominibus circumferuntur.* Geneva, 1666.]

'Perpetuité de la foi du Sr Arnaud, respondu par Mr Claude'. [Jean Claude. *Réponse aux deux traitez intitulez 'la Perpétuité de la foy de l'Eglise catholique touchant l'Eucharistie'.* Paris, 1665.]

'L'Office du sacrement, repondu par Mr de Larroque'. [Mathieu de Larroque. *Réponse à un livre intitulé: 'L'Office du S. Sacrement, ou Tradition de l'Eglise touchant l'Eucharistie'.* Paris, 1665.]

'Du Jeusne et du Caresme, par Mr. Daillé, en latin'. [Jean Daillé. *De jejuniis et quadragesima liber.* Deventer, 1654.]

'Ville & temple de Jerusalem, description tirée de Josephe'. [Josephus. *Histoire des Juifs ... traduite sur l'original grec revu sur divers manuscrits, par M. Arnauld d'Andilly.* Paris, 1668.]

'Hierozoïcon, des Animaux de l'Ecriture, par Sr Bochart'. [Samuel Bochart. *Hierozoicon, sive Bipertitum opus de animalibus Sacrae Scripturae.* London, 1663.]

'Flux & Reflux de la mer, par Cesar d'Arcons'. [César d'Arcons. *Le Secret du flux et reflux de la mer et des longitudes*. Rouen, 1655.]

'Voyages d'Olearius et de Mandeslo, en Moscovie, Perse, Indes'. [Adam Olearius. *Relation du voyage de Moscovie, Tartarie et de Perse, augmentée en cette nouvelle édition ... d'une seconde partie contenant le voyage de Jean Albert de Mandeslo aux Indes Orientales*. Paris, 1659.]

'Deffense de la Reformation, par Mr Claude, et Mr Pajon'. [Jean Claude. *La Défense de la Réformation contre le livre intitule: 'Préjugez légitimes contre les calvinistes'*. Rouen, 1673. Claude Pajon. *Examen du livre qui a pour titre: Préjugés légitimes contre les calvinistes*. Orléans, 1673.]

'De la Confirmation & Extreme Onction, par Jean Daillé'. [Jean Daillé. *De Duobus Latinorum ex unctione sacramentis confirmatione et extrema ut vocant unctione disputatio*. Geneva, 1659.]

'Histoire de l'Amerique par herrera'. [Antonio de Herrera y Tordesillas. *Histoire générale des voyages et conquestes des Castillans dans les isles et terre firme des Indes occidentales*. 3 vols. Paris, 1659–71.]

'Remarques sur l'Ecriture de Jean d'Espagne'. [Jean d'Espagne. *Oeuvres*. 3 vols. Geneva, 1671. Le Noir de Crevain's notes show that he read all of the works in this collection of short treatises on various religious questions by the minister of the French church of London; *Remarques sur l'Ecriture* is the first treatise in the compilation.]

'Culte des Latins, au bapt. & Euchar. oeuvre posthume de Mr Daillé'. [Jean Daillé. *De Cultibus religiosis Latinorum libri novem*. Geneva, 1671.]

'Theatre du Monde, de Boussingaut'. [Adam Boussingault, *Le Nouveau Théatre du monde, ou l'Abrégé des estats et empires de l'univers*. Paris, 1668.]

'Les Systemes du monde, au nombre de six'. [A précis of various cosmologies based upon a variety of sources, of which Le Noir de Crevains identifies: Claude Gadroys. *Le Système du monde selon les trois hypothèses, où, conformément aux loix de la méchanique, l'on explique dans la supposition du mouvement de la terre: les apparences des astres, la fabrique du monde, la formation des planètes, la lumière, la pesanteur, etc*. Paris, 1675. Claude Mallemans de Messanges. *Nouveau système du monde*. Paris, 1678. Francois Bernier. *Abrégé de la philosophie de M. de Gassendi*. Paris, 1675.]

'Eclaircissements sur l'Apocalypse. par m. Filipot'. [Jacques Philipot. *Défense des Eclaircissements sur l'Apocalypse de S. Jean, au sujet de l'effusion des phioles, contre l'Apologie pour l'accomplissement des prophéties*. Amsterdam, 1687.]

'Accomplissement des Propheties. mr Jurieu: 2e edition'. [Pierre Jurieu. *L'accomplissement des prophéties ou la prochaine delivrance de l'Eglise, Ouvrage dans lequel il est prouvé, que le Papisme est l'empire antichrétien: que cet Empire n'est pas éloigné de sa ruine; que cette ruine doit commencer dans peu de temps; que la persecution presente doit finir dans trois ans et demi. Apres quoy commencera la destruction de l'Antechrist, laquelle se continuera dans le reste de ce siècle, et s'achevra dans la commencement du siècle prochain: Et enfin le regne de Jesus Christ viendra sur le terre.* Rotterdam, 1686.]

'Indice des controverses controversiarum elenchus in 16o de Monsr Spanheim'. [Friedrich Spanheim. *Controversiarum de religione cum dissidentibus hodie Christianis, prolixis et cum judaeis, elenchus historico-theologus.* Amsterdam, 1694.]

'Introduction a l'histoire Ecclesiastique. Spanhem'. [Friedrich Spanheim. *Introductio ad chronologiam et historiam sacram, ac praecipue christianam, ad tempora proxima Reformationi, cum necessariis castigionibus Caesar. Baronii.* 2 vols. Leiden, 1683–88.]

PART THREE

Coexistence and Confessionalization

Un roi, une loi, deux fois: Parameters for the History of Catholic–Reformed Coexistence in France, 1555–1685

At first glance, France's history in the sixteenth and seventeenth centuries seems to present a series of paradoxes for the historian of tolerance and intolerance. In 1562, the country became one of the first powerful monarchies of the Reformation era to grant freedom of worship to more than one Christian confession, yet over the following decade this pioneer in religious toleration witnessed the era's bloodiest and most horrifying episodes of popular religious intolerance, culminating in the Saint Bartholomew's Massacre. Over the subsequent decades, France moved more successfully toward establishing peaceful coexistence between Catholics and Protestants. Then, despite this success, Louis XIV earned himself an enduring place in the annals of intolerance by revoking the Edict of Nantes. This essay will suggest that the apparent paradoxes of this situation disappear when certain of the potential oversimplifications and pitfalls contained within that somewhat Whiggish construct, the 'history of toleration', are recognized, and when the effort is made to write a history of Catholic–Reformed coexistence in France adequate to the complexity of the phenomena. The essay will also try to outline the basic elements of such a history – not always an easy task, since many aspects of the subject remain poorly understood.

The 'history of toleration'

Toleration is a quality that most members of modern liberal societies prize – until they have to put up with something truly intolerable. Where they then draw the line is infinitely varied. Some in America today would draw it at the open expression of racist attitudes, others at government support for statues of Christ submerged in urine, still others at smoking at the next table. In other words, the history of tolerance and intolerance is an extremely amorphous subject, for the question immediately arises: tolerance of what? Tolerance is not a polymorphously perverse attribute, capable of extension in any direction, possessed by certain individuals or societies and lacked by others. Instead, the toleration or prohibition of specific forms of thought or behaviour is intimately bound up with prevailing ideas about both the particular matter at stake and the larger nature of the political community, with practical considerations of power, and with the extent and character of the personal contacts between those who might do the persecuting and those who might be persecuted. There can be no unified history of toleration, except perhaps a history of the idea itself and of the migrations of arguments for toleration from the contexts in which they originally developed to other ones deemed analogous. A history of the social practices normally denoted by the concept involves multiple, if sometimes interconnected, histories of the tolerance or intolerance of specific groups or forms of behaviour.

When applied to the context of Reformation Europe, the history of toleration is usually understood to mean the history of religious toleration, the matrix out of which the modern idea of tolerance in fact grew. Even circumscribed in this manner, the topic remains multifaceted. Much of the best scholarship on this topic has focused upon the history of ideas concerning the appropriateness of tolerating two or more religions within the same polity. This has revealed that contemporaries often made important distinctions between different aspects of what is today often lumped together as religious freedom or toleration – most importantly between freedom of worship (the right to hold religious ceremonies and assemblies), freedom of religious speech (the right to proclaim what one chooses about religion), and freedom of conscience (the right to hold whatever ideas about religion one chooses in the intimacy of one's own mind). At the same time, ideas about each of these freedoms were intimately bound up with views about a variety of other connected issues, ranging from questions of political theory concerning the origins, duties and needs of the state, through questions of biblical exegesis concerning church–state relations in ancient Israel and the extent to which these offered binding examples for Christian practice, to historical questions about whether or not certain contemporary religious groups had shown themselves to be too seditious to be safely tolerated.

At the same time, as John Dunn has aptly observed, 'toleration may often be claimed by human groups and individuals as a matter of right – of intrinsic entitlement. But it is only ever conceded by incumbent political authorities as a matter of practical political judgement'.[1] Thus, while there

---

[1] John Dunn, 'The Claim to Freedom of Conscience: Freedom of Speech, Freedom of Thought, Freedom of Worship?', in Ole Peter Grell, Jonathan I. Israel and Nicholas Tyacke, eds, *From Persecution to Toleration: The Glorious Revolution and Religion in England* (Oxford, 1991), 172. Malcolm C. Smith, 'Early French Advocates of Religious Freedom', *The Sixteenth Century Journal* 25 (1994), 50, makes a very similar observation.

is a complex history of ideas about religious toleration that laps over into broad reaches of the history of political thought, of theology and of historiography, power relations between the different religious groups in any given society are equally or more important for making sense of the history of the legislation granting or revoking rights of religious toleration. An adequate history of the practice of toleration must furthermore survey not only the relevant legislation on the matter, but also how faithfully it was observed, for history provides numerous examples of societies that formally legislated against certain kinds of religious assemblies or practices, but none the less allowed them to continue. Finally, tragic contemporary examples have shown how swiftly peaceful coexistence can break down and give way to violence between religious or ethnic groups living within the same polity, even where these have lived in peace with one another for a generation or more. Isolating the preconditions for either stable or unstable situations of religious tolerance requires investigating the pattern of everyday relations between the members of the different religious groups, the cultural practices and historical memories that shaped their visions of themselves and of 'the other', and the political decisions that impelled leaders either to play upon or to seek to abate these cultural and historical differences and the grievances that so often accompany them. The history of the tolerance or intolerance of any specific religious group thus comes to encompass vast areas of the intellectual, political, social and cultural history of the time. When the variety of different groups or practices whose toleration could be explored is factored in, the subject becomes immense indeed.

To keep the scope of this essay within manageable proportions, the focus here will be entirely upon the largest religious minority to emerge in early modern France and the one whose existence within the realm posed the most disruptive and enduring questions of public order: the Reformed Protestants.[2] Between 1555, when the first churches were established in France along the lines urged by Calvin and the ministers he sent out from Geneva, and 1562, when the first of the Wars of Religion broke out, Reformed churches proliferated across France with extraordinary rapidity. A thousand or more Reformed churches may have been founded in those years. Many emerged from clandestinity to meet in public, often seizing Catholic churches for their own use. Some attracted the majority of the population of the community in which they were located. In one or two such towns, such as Castres, the ideas of the 'new religion' were so

---

[2] Other histories of toleration could be written about the Lutherans, the Anabaptists, the Jews, those Catholic movements that with time came to be defined as heterodox such as the Jansenists, the treatment of 'atheists' and 'libertines', and the problems raised by the criminalization of blasphemy and sodomy.

thoroughly dominant by late 1561 that the city magistrates had carried through the equivalent of a civic Reformation. Although the exact strength of the movement in this period may never be known, its adepts probably numbered at least a million and a half people by the time its growth had run its course. Over the next three centuries, its ranks would be thinned at several moments by the blows that would befall it, but until the end of the nineteenth century, the questions of what claims the Reformed could make upon the political nation, what rights the faith was to be accorded, and how its members interacted with their Catholic neighbours were the most pressing issues that religious, racial, or ethnic divisions posed for France.

The sudden emergence of so large a religious minority is the basic historical fact from which any history of Catholic–Reformed relations in France must start. How thoroughly did the transformation of the religious situation alter prevailing views about the wisdom of tolerating two faiths within the kingdom? How did the law grapple with the existence of a large religious minority and with the challenge to public order created by the sudden emergence of deeply antagonistic understandings of Christianity? How deep were the social fissures that opened up between the two faiths, and to what extent did the existence of these religious divisions trouble the social order? These are the fundamental historical questions posed by this transformation. The exploration of these questions for the period from 1555 to 1685 offers three sets of parameters for understanding the apparent mixture of tolerance and intolerance that marked the history of Catholic–Reformed coexistence over these years.

Ideas about freedom of conscience and worship

It is useful to begin with the *Begriffsgeschichte* of the phrases 'toleration' and 'freedom of conscience'. As the detailed semantic analysis of William H. Huseman has shown, nobody in sixteenth-century France conceived of the former as a good thing. The verb 'tolérer' was most often employed around 1560 by the partisans of a hard line against heresy to denote a distressing course of action that they opposed. Roughly synonymous with 'souffrir' or 'endurer', the word denoted the unpleasant experience of being subjected to some evil.[3] The first edition of the dictionary of the Académie Française, published in 1694, put only a slightly more positive spin on the word, defining 'tolérance' as 'condescension or indulgence for what one cannot prevent', as in the phrase 'it is not a right, but a tolerance'. Only in the eighteenth century did the word take on the range of positive

---

[3] Huseman, 'The Expression of the Idea of Toleration in French During the Sixteenth Century', *Sixteenth Century Journal* 15 (1984), 293–310.

connotations most famously expressed in the classic entry on the subject in the *Encyclopédie*, where tolerance is presented as the humane recognition of our species' incapacity for arriving at moral or intellectual certitude, and of the consequent unfairness of punishing anybody for their beliefs.[4]

As for the expression 'freedom of conscience', Joseph Lecler has shown that its initial appearance in the Reformation era, in the writings of Luther, Melanchthon and, with slightly different phraseology, Calvin, denoted something quite different from the modern concept. The phrase initially referred not to the freedom that individuals might enjoy from having their deepest religious convictions subject to government constraint and punishment, but to the conscience's liberation through faith from the fear and doubt that were its fate for those still mired in the errors of Catholicism. It was in France between 1559 and 1561 that authors first began to speak of 'liberté de conscience' in the sense in which the phrase is understood today. Typically, such liberty was simply proposed as a remedy for the problems facing the country rather than as a positive good in itself, but the phrase entered into the law codes in the Edict of Amboise of 1563 and was linked in the writings of certain authors with opposition to the forcing of consciences, depicted as a form of oppression. The phrase thus had more positive semantic associations. But many contemporaries resisted this. Theodore Beza called 'liberté aux consciences' 'a thoroughly diabolical dogma'.[5]

Just as the semantic associations of 'tolerance' were largely negative, so the strongest traditions that French political culture inherited from its medieval past were profoundly antithetical to the acceptance of religious division within the kingdom. The precocious development of French national identity in the later Middle Ages had highlighted the kingdom's special fervour for the defence of the church as one of the most evident marks of its status as God's chosen nation. The country was believed to

---

4 *Encyclopédie, ou Dictionnaire raisonné des arts et sciences* (3rd edn, Geneva, 1777), XXXIII, 590. The changing attitudes toward toleration in the eighteenth century can be nicely traced through successive editions of the *Dictionnaire* of the Académie Française. The second edition of 1718 defines the word as 'sufferance or indulgence for what one cannot prevent, *or believes should not be prevented*' (emphasis mine). This edition also adds that the word is at times applied to 'the prudent policy sometimes followed by rulers of allowing the exercise of another religion from that established by the laws of the state'. The 1765 edition includes for the first time entries for the adjective 'tolerante' and the noun 'tolerantisme', the latter being 'the system of those who believe the state should tolerate all sorts of religions'. See further Jean Delumeau, 'La difficile émergence de la tolérance', in Roger Zuber and Laurent Theis, eds, *La Révocation de l'édit de Nantes et le protestantisme français en 1685* (Paris, 1986), 359–64; Elisabeth Labrousse, *'Une foi, une loi, un roi?' La révocation de l'édit de Nantes* (Geneva, 1985), p. 95.

5 Joseph Lecler, 'Liberté de conscience. Origines et sens divers de l'expression', *Recherches de Science Religieuse* 54 (1966), 370–406.

have entered into a special covenant with the divinity at the time of Clovis that subsequently linked its continued existence to its enduring fidelity to the faith. 'I am famed for always having been Catholic, never having nourished heresy, and never will,' spoke the figure of France in Georges Chastellain's fifteenth-century mystery play, *Le Concile de Basle*.[6] From 1215 onward, the coronation oath sworn by all new monarchs included a pledge to be diligent in expelling from their lands all heretics designated by the church.[7] Theological and legal circles were meanwhile dominated by the views of Saint Augustine, incorporated into both canon law and scholastic thought, that justified the civil punishment of heresy by Christian rulers on the grounds that this (1) protected society against pestilential doctrines that threatened to lead others astray; (2) advanced the glory of God by demonstrating abhorrence for doctrines contrary to his honour; and (3) contributed to the potential redemption of the heretics themselves by providing the sort of sanction that was often necessary to induce people to abandon erroneous views.[8]

Although these traditions would powerfully shape the response to heresy in the sixteenth century, European culture was sufficiently varied at the end of the Middle Ages to provide intellectual resources to defend as well as oppose the extension of rights of worship to more than one Christian church. Political theories presenting secular government as a purely human construction whose highest priority was maintaining civil order had been articulated by scholastic theorists. Erasmus combined an emphasis on the virtues of peace with scepticism about the possibility of arriving at certain knowledge – a set of attitudes that led him to suggest, when the German evangelicals began organizing their own forms of worship, that allowing non-seditious sects to worship as they chose was a lesser evil than trying to suppress them and provoking war.[9] At least one French author of the early sixteenth century followed Erasmus in articulating certain of the premises that would subsequently undergird defences of freedom of conscience. Pierre Du Chastel, a scholar who briefly lodged with Erasmus in Basel and subsequently became Francis I's royal librarian, Grand Almoner, and the bishop of Tulle, Mâcon and Orléans, declared in 1547 that nobody should be executed for heresy, 'since no mortal man, whoever

---

6 Colette Beaune, *Naissance de la nation France* (Paris, 1985), pp. 207–16, esp. p. 213.

7 Richard A. Jackson, *Vive le Roi! A History of the French Coronation from Charles V to Charles X* (Chapel Hill, 1984), p. 58.

8 On the development of the ideas justifying the punishment of heresy within the medieval church, see Ernest W. Nelson, 'The Theory of Persecution', in *Persecution and Liberty: Essays in Honor of George Lincoln Burr* (New York, 1921), pp. 3–20, and Edward Peters, *Inquisition* (Berkeley, 1989), pp. 11–67.

9 Joseph Lecler, *Histoire de la tolérance au siècle de la Réforme* (2 vols, Paris, 1955), I, 134–8.

he may be, can through any human argument or reasoning judge with certainty what is true'.[10]

Du Chastel, however, was an isolated voice. Active debate about whether or not magistrates should punish heresy or permit more than one manner of worship really only began in France as the Reformed churches proliferated in the later 1550s. Then pamphlets, political and legal assemblies, and handwritten memoranda took up with urgency the issue of how to repair the widening religious schism. One current of opinion advocated a policy of concord that sought to obtain the agreement of all parties to a moderate reform of the Gallican church that would be acceptable both to Rome and to those who had left the communion of the church, and would thereby bring about the reunion of both parties. Certain of the 'moyenneurs' who championed this course advanced as one argument in its favour the impropriety or unworkability of any 'forcement de conscience', although they were often far more reluctant to envisage granting freedom of worship, which they saw as threatening to social unity and stability.[11] Others were willing to defend granting the Reformed freedom of worship, especially once the failure of the Colloquy of Poissy dampened hope that a reunion of the churches might be possible. Those who argued in favour of this position, most notably the Chancellor Michel de L'Hôpital, a friend of Du Chastel's, did so overwhelmingly on pragmatic grounds: the Reformed had simply grown too numerous and too strong to be denied rights of worship without irreparable harm to the kingdom, while the example of both the Roman Empire under those Christian emperors who had allowed the Arians churches of their own and contemporary Switzerland (far more than Germany the great illustration of successful religious coexistence at this time) demonstrated that polities could house several Christian churches and still thrive. More principled arguments also appear briefly in a few of these tracts: specifically that forcing people to act contrary to the promptings of their conscience was an illegitimate form of violence, and that the political order did not depend on Christianity, since excommunicates remained citizens.[12]

Against this view, hard-line Catholics defended the traditions of Catholic France, reiterated the Augustinian arguments for punishing heresy, and recalled the king's coronation oath. One even maintained in a Sorbonne debate that the Pope could excommunicate a king who favoured heretics and release his subjects from their obligations of obedience to him. The

---

10 Smith, 'Early French Advocates', p. 34.

11 Mario Turchetti, *Concordia o tolleranza? François Bauduin (1520–1573) e i 'moyenneurs'* (Geneva, 1984); Smith, 'Early French Advocates', pp. 38–40.

12 *Mémoires de Condé* (London, 1740), II, 732–42, 892–929; Lecler, *Histoire de la tolérance*, II, 36–62, 68–72; Smith, 'Early French Advocates', pp. 37–8, 40–48.

hard-line Catholics also charged that Calvinism was seditious by nature, a charge soon buttressed with references to the Huguenot efforts to advance their cause by force from the conspiracy of Amboise onward. By the later 1560s, certain Catholic polemicists had developed an account of the country's recent past that was little more than an extended chronicle of Huguenot efforts to destroy the country's churches and exterminate its royal family.[13] Catherine de Medici – a foreigner to the kingdom's political traditions – had been receiving reports from the provinces throughout 1560 and 1561 illustrating the difficulties of maintaining order between members of the rival faiths. When, eager for the support of the heavily Protestant Bourbon family, she accepted the arguments of the partisans of toleration and, with the Edict of Saint-Germain of January 1562, granted the Reformed freedom of worship 'until such time as God by his grace reunites [our subjects] in one sheepfold', the majority of the kingdom's Parlements protested vigorously. The descent into civil war was swift. The bulk of the political nation, it appears, was unwilling as yet to accept such a policy.[14]

For their part, the kingdom's Protestants were also divided over the desirability of religious tolerance, with the most powerful voices again being hostile to it. Calvin and Beza, of course, were both strongly committed from the 1553 execution of Michael Servetus onward to the view that civil magistrates were obliged to use the power of the sword to defend the true faith against heretics. A 1561 synod of the churches of Guyenne and Haut-Languedoc similarly declared the suppression of heresy to be a magistrate's duty, while the majority of the petitions and appeals that the Reformed addressed to the crown between 1559 and 1561 sought to persuade the rulers not to allow two kinds of churches in the kingdom, but to embrace the one true church, and to stamp out popish idolatry as a most Christian king should.[15] Some within the new Reformed churches dissented. The influential Pierre Viret opposed state punishment of heresy and was more willing than either Calvin or Beza to extend toleration to sectarians and

---

13 Barbara B. Diefendorf, 'Simon Vigor: A Radical Preacher in Sixteenth-Century Paris', *The Sixteenth Century Journal* 18 (1987), 399–410; *idem, Under the Cross: Catholics and Huguenots in Sixteenth-Century Paris* (Oxford, 1991), pp. 50–61; Philip Benedict, 'Of Marmites and Martyrs: Images and Polemics in the Wars of Religion', *The French Renaissance in Prints from the Bibliothèque Nationale de France* (exhibition catalogue, Los Angeles, 1994), pp. 111–14, 121.

14 A. Lublinskaja, ed., *Documents pour servir à l'histoire des guerres civiles en France* (Moscow, 1962), docs 1–13; André Stegmann, ed., *Edits des guerres de religion* (Paris, 1979), p. 10; Lucien Romier, *Catholiques et huguenots à la cour de Charles IX* (Paris, 1924), p. 303ff; Diefendorf, *Under the Cross*, p. 62.

15 Robert M. Kingdon, *Geneva and the Coming of the Wars of Religion in France, 1555–1563* (Geneva, 1956), p. 87; *Mémoires de Condé*, I, 341–96, 409–80, II, 481–530, 546–60, 578–84, 644–59, 743–5, 807–11, esp. 647.

to believe that people of different religions could live peacefully together. An early member of the church of Beaugency, Jean Bonneau, was called before the consistory for maintaining that it was wrong for the magistrates to punish heretics. Significantly, however, Bonneau was made to retract his views.[16] The Beza–Calvin position was the dominant one.

Active discussion of issues of freedom of conscience and worship continued throughout the subsequent century and a third. No comprehensive effort has yet been made to survey the entire discussion, but its contours appear to have been modified in three ways.

First, Catholic opinion about the practical wisdom of tolerating two faiths oscillated significantly as the Wars of Religion advanced. In the later 1570s, after more than a decade of bloodshed had taken a vast toll of lives without resulting in the elimination of heresy, certain of those who initially favoured defending unity of religion by force swung around to accept the most powerful prudential argument against this, namely that its human and political costs were simply too great to bear. At the Estates-General of 1576, a number of leading Catholic noblemen who had previously been ardent persecutors of the Huguenots were willing to advocate peace and toleration of Reformed worship 'until by means of a council, another meeting of the estates, or any other means ... God can bless us with only one religion'. A bare majority of the Third Estate voted in favour of renewed war and repeal of the generous conditions granted the Protestants under the Peace of Beaulieu, despite vigorous royal lobbying in this direction.[17] The pendulum swung in the other direction after the duke of Alençon's death raised the spectre of a Protestant succession. No precedents existed of Protestant monarchs who had not sought to bring the religious establishment of their kingdoms into line with their own personal beliefs. Many Catholics consequently feared that their faith would be subjected to the sort of persecution then being meted out to their co-religionists in England unless Protestantism was quickly eradicated and Navarre's accession to the throne blocked. When the bishop of Le Mans

---

16 Robert Dean Linder, *The Political Ideas of Pierre Viret* (Geneva, 1964), ch. 8; Yves Gueneau, 'Protestants du Centre 1598–1685 (Ancienne province synodale d'Orléanais-Berry). Approches d'une minorité' (thèse de 3e cycle, Université François Rabelais de Tours, 1982), pp. 33–4. See also *Opera Calvini*, eds G. Baum, E. Cunitz and E. Reuss (59 vols, Brunswick–Berlin, 1863–1900), XV, 435–46.

17 Lecler, *Histoire de la tolérance*, II, chs 4–5. For the details on the Estates-General of 1576: Mark Greengrass, 'A Day in the Life of the Third Estate: Blois, 26th December 1576', in Adrianna E. Bakos, ed., *Politics, Ideology and the Law in Early Modern Europe: Essays in Honor of J.H.M. Salmon* (Rochester, 1994), pp. 73–90; Mack Holt, *The French Wars of Religion, 1562–1629* (Cambridge, 1995), pp. 108–9. Montaigne's views similarly evolved over the early decades of the Wars of Religion towards the acceptance of two faiths within the kingdom. Malcolm C. Smith, *Montaigne and Religious Freedom: The Dawn of Pluralism* (Geneva, 1991).

tried to argue at the Estates-General of 1588 that good example, teaching and prayers were the only proper weapons for combating heresy, he was shouted down and censured. Opinion shifted once more after Henry IV converted in 1593, reducing the threat of a Protestant king. The especially intense devastation of the wars of the League, combined with the fact that the Protestants again survived a period of proscription and emerged with their power intact, further reinforced the view that there was no practical alternative to toleration. By the early seventeenth century, even the Assemblies of the kingdom's Catholic clergy professed their willingness to tolerate Reformed worship until such time as it might be possible to reunite the country once again in the true faith. The arguments of those Catholic historians and political writers of the early seventeenth century who defended allowing Reformed worship rarely recognized a generalized right to freedom of conscience or worship, however. Both Jacques-Auguste de Thou and Jean Silhon, for instance, asserted that rulers could legitimately strive to maintain unity of religion. Once a heresy had grown strong, though, it was wisest to leave it in peace.[18]

Second, a number of Reformed thinkers came with time to articulate stronger and more generally applicable arguments for freedom of conscience and worship. In the tracts and memoranda written by Philippe Du Plessis-Mornay between 1576 through 1597, this influential Huguenot statesman began to defend rights of worship for Catholic and Reformed alike, even embracing certain of Castellio's ideas on freedom of conscience after spending time in the circles around William of Orange in the Low Countries.[19] In the generations following the Edict of Nantes, the broadest current within Huguenot opinion sought to solidify the rights of worship that the Edict granted the Reformed with the narrow legal argument that the decree was perpetual and irrevocable by virtue of its frequent confirmation and more akin to a treaty between the king and his subjects than an ordinary law. Since kings were obliged to respect the treaties they entered into, they could not annul it. But a few thinkers built upon the

18 Bernard Dompnier, *Le venin de l'hérésie. Image du protestantisme et combat catholique au XVIIe siècle* (Paris, 1985), pp. 116–18; Lecler, *Histoire de la tolérance*, II, 108; François Laplanche, *L'Ecriture, le sacré, et l'histoire. Erudits et politiques protestants devant la Bible en France au XVIIe siècle* (Amsterdam, 1986), p. 392; Etienne Thuau, *Raison d'état et pensée politique à l'époque de Richelieu* (Paris, 1966), pp. 207, 274–5. As this last work makes clear, a few Catholic authors advocated freedom of conscience or worship as a broader value, on the grounds that only God controlled people's consciences.

19 Du Plessis-Mornay's various writings on this subject may be found in his *Mémoires et Correspondances* (Paris, 1824). Lecler, *Histoire de la tolérance*, II, 90–91, 181–4; and Marie-Madeleine Fragonard, 'La liberté de conscience chez Du Plessis-Mornay (1576–1598)', in Hans R. Guggisberg, Frank Lestringant and Jean-Claude Margolin, eds, *La liberté de conscience (XVIe–XVIIe siècles): Actes du Colloque de Mulhouse et Bâle (1989)* (Geneva, 1991), pp. 135–52, provide important secondary treatments.

historicization of Old Testament precedents by the humanists and theologians of the Academy of Saumur and the new emphasis on natural-law arguments that Grotius and his successors deployed to meet the sceptical challenge of the late sixteenth century, in order to articulate general arguments for freedom of conscience. Moyse Amyraut's vast *Morale chrestienne* (1652–60) argued that God was the author of the laws of nature and good government as well as of religion. In affairs of state, the laws of nature and good government took priority, and dictated that constraint was of no value in matters of conscience, since only persuasion and good example could convince people of religious truth. The examples of ancient Israelite rulers who had destroyed idols were irrelevant to Christian practice, since all of the events of the Old Testament were purely figurative except for the proclamation of the Ten Commandments.[20] At the end of the century, Pierre Bayle defended freedom of conscience for all, even atheists, with a battery of arguments that turned the classic religious justifications for persecution inside out. Thus he observed that while those who punished heretics claimed to be defending God's honour against those who affronted it, the majority of those guilty of heresy in fact acted from a sincere effort to honour God as they understood this was supposed to be done. In such a situation, the persecutors were themselves guilty of offending God by arrogating to themselves his function of judging each individual's faith. Bayle also drew upon natural law to argue that the functions of secular government were purely temporal, and he had no difficulty imagining a town in which the members of ten religions lived together in 'the same concord ... as in a city where various kinds of artisans support one another' – so long as all embraced 'the tolerance I support' and did not try to harm the others through persecution.[21] Under pressure to defend the constantly challenged rights of worship granted their minority faith, a number of Huguenot theorists thus contributed significantly to the development of the far richer and more powerful set of arguments for toleration that had emerged within the European republic of letters by the end of the seventeenth century.[22]

---

20 For the development of Amyraut's views on toleration, see Laplanche, *L'Ecriture, le sacré, et l'histoire*, pp. 387–9, 484–9. More generally, this magisterial work demonstrates the importance of the new exegetical methods of the school of Saumur. Richard Tuck, 'The "modern" theory of natural law', in Anthony Pagden, ed., *The Languages of Political Theory in Early-Modern Europe* (Cambridge, 1987), pp. 99–119; and *idem, Philosophy and Government 1572–1651* (Cambridge, 1993) are no less important in demonstrating the nature and advance of natural-law thinking in the seventeenth century.

21 Elisabeth Labrousse, *Pierre Bayle* (The Hague, 1964), II, 497–591.

22 A development remarked upon by Bayle himself in his *Supplément* to his *Commentaire philosophique sur ces paroles de J.C. contrains-les d'entrer*. Labrousse, *Bayle*, p. 542n. Delumeau's contrary assertion that 'tout avait été dit dès le XVIe siècle' is unconvincing. Delumeau, 'Difficile émergence de la tolérance', p. 374.

Third, another argument was added to the arsenal of toleration's defenders with the advance of modes of thinking that emphasized the needs of the state and its financial and military well-being. At the moment of the Revocation of the Edict of Nantes, the most forthright argument against the measure by a Catholic figure of influence came from the military engineer and army officer Sebastien le Prestre de Vauban, who stressed the costs to the state of driving abroad a group with the military and commercial skills of the Huguenots.[23]

The overall universe of discourse thus grew more favourable to arguments for freedom of conscience or worship by the end of the seventeenth century. Still, the great majority of political and legal theorists remained opposed to the principle of either freedom of conscience or worship at this time. The professors at the kingdom's law schools continued to teach that obdurate heresy was quite properly a capital offence. The Paris faculty of theology censured an English Benedictine who declared in a book published in France in 1627: 'the prince is required by God's law to maintain each person in his kingdom in whatever religion he professes without molesting them for their consciences'.[24] The majority of the Reformed were scarcely better disposed to generalized freedom of conscience or worship. In 1690, a synod of the then-Huguenot-dominated Walloon churches in the Netherlands censured the propositions that reason and piety require the toleration of all heresies, that the magistrate has no right to use his power to abolish idolatry or stop the progress of heresy, and that all people may not just believe but also teach what they wish.[25] The Revocation was no anachronistic throwback to a bygone era of intolerance. Instead, it was the act of a monarchy that had grown considerably in strength since the sixteenth century, could imagine that the eradication of heresy was within its grasp with few of the costs that had been associated with pursuing the goal a century earlier, and was pleased to carry out a policy that the great majority of the Catholic majority continued to consider fitting for a most Christian king.

The law and its observance

Government policy thus evolved within a field of discourse dominated by the idea that the king ought to repress false belief, but which at the same

23 Geoffrey Adams, *The Huguenots and French Opinion 1685–1787: The Enlightenment Debate on Toleration* (Waterloo, Ontario, 1991), pp. 19–30.

24 L.W.B. Brockliss, *French Higher Education in the Seventeenth and Eighteenth Centuries: A Cultural History* (Oxford, 1987), pp. 323–4.

25 Frank Puaux, *Les précurseurs français de la tolérance au XVIIe siècle* (Paris, 1881), p. 122.

time contained space for the conviction that political necessity might occasionally impel the toleration of two or more forms of worship. The law itself followed a complicated course. From 1562 to 1598, legal measures granted, revoked and modified permission for Reformed worship in rapid succession, with the measures granting permission attempting at the same time to define terms on which the two confessions could peacably coexist. During the period from 1598 to 1685, the fixed star of the Edict of Nantes lent considerably greater stability to the broad parameters of the law, but details continued to be modified. At every point from 1562 to 1685, a gap existed between the letter of the law and its implementation.

It is more difficult than might be imagined to establish just what the law decreed in the matter of religious toleration from 1560 to 1598. Eight different edicts, all but the first of them edicts of pacification bringing a civil war to a close, accorded the Reformed more or less generous freedom of worship. The evolution of their provisions betrays an effort to define terms acceptable to both sides. The Edict of January 1562 allowed the Protestants to assemble wherever they chose outside the walls of the kingdom's cities; the following four edicts restricted Protestant worship to a limited number of localities; the more generous 1576 Peace of Beaulieu restored complete freedom of worship for the Reformed except in the vicinity of Paris or the royal court, but this provoked the formation of the first nationwide Catholic League; and the subsequent edicts of pacification, including the Edict of Nantes, again limited the Reformed to a specified set of localities. Four other royal decrees formally revoked all Reformed freedom of worship – in 1568, 1572, 1577 and 1585. The measure of 1585, occasioned by the spectre of a Protestant succession to the throne and the formation of the second Catholic League, was particularly severe. It suspended freedom of conscience as well as of worship for the Reformed, made the practice of Catholicism obligatory for all Frenchmen within six months, and gave all ministers a month to leave the country. From 1585 to 1591, and longer in those parts of the country controlled by the League, Reformed belief was once more punishable as heresy.

What must be stressed is that royal ordinances provided only a general framework for the law in early modern France. Decisions of special royal commissions and arrêts of the country's *parlements* could modify the law to fit local conditions. For instance, a commission sent in the autumn of 1561 to pacify the Agenais, one of the corners of southern France most troubled by clashes between Huguenots who sought to take over Catholic houses of worship and Catholics determined to stop their assemblies, allowed the Protestants of this area a measure of toleration in October 1561, several months before the Edict of January granted them rights of worship throughout the kingdom. This measure ordered the principal church in localities with two or more churches that the Huguenots had seized to be restored to its Catholic clerics, who were not to be disturbed in their services. The Protestants were given tacit permission to retain one or more church for their own use. In localities with only one church, the rival parties were commanded to work out an agreement to share it.[26] Conversely, although kingdom-wide proscriptions of Protestant worship came only in 1568, 1572, 1577 and 1585, the decisions of local authorities led to its prohibition in many regions upon the outbreak of other civil wars as well. During the First Civil War of 1562–63, the Parlement of Normandy, which had fled Huguenot-controlled Rouen and reassembled in Louviers, decreed that Protestant worship would be outlawed in all cities that returned to obedience to the king over the course of the conflict. In Tours in the same period, those Huguenots who were not massacred when the city was retaken by the royal and Catholic forces were required to make a confession of faith before representatives of the archbishop and to leave town if the views they expressed were deemed contrary to the Catholic religion.[27]

In practice, the chronology of the civil wars and the local balance of power determined when the Reformed were actually able to assemble for worship in any given community. The rare surviving Protestant baptismal registers from this era provide the best evidence about when different churches were able to meet. The pattern varied from locality to locality. In such Protestant strongholds as La Rochelle, Montauban, Nîmes and the Cévennes, the Reformed assembled for worship throughout the period in sovereign disregard of the legislation that intermittently prohibited this. In cities that remained under effective royal control for most of the period, Reformed services were recurrently, although not absolutely consistently, interrupted by each civil war except the brief, localized Seventh Civil War of 1580. In localities where the military balance swung back and forth between the two faiths, the royal legislation was respected at certain moments but defied at others. During Henry IV's long battle against the Catholic League, Reformed worship resumed in many predominantly Catholic but none the less royalist towns (e.g. Caen, Gien, Vitré) even before the Edict of Mantes of July 1591 formally annulled the 1585 prohibition of the faith.[28] In at least a few places and times, we know from

---

26 Estienne de la Boëtie, *Memoire sur la pacification des troubles*, ed. Malcolm Smith (Geneva, 1983), pp. 9 and 100–106; Smith, *Montaigne and Religious Freedom*, p. 56.

27 A.D. Seine-Maritime, B, Parlement, Arrêts, Arrêt of 26 August 1562; David Nicholls, 'Protestants, Catholics and Magistrates in Tours, 1562–1572: The Making of a Catholic City during the Religious Wars', *French History* 8 (1994), 17.

28 I have now traced the pattern of Protestant worship in greater detail in 'Les vicissitudes des églises réformées de France jusqu'en 1598', *B.S.H.P.F.* 144 (1998), 53–72, also separately published as Michel Grandjean and Bernard Roussel, eds, *Coexister dans l'intolérance. L'édit de Nantes (1598)* (Geneva, 1998).

other sources, Protestant congregations met secretly for worship even when outlawed, as for instance in Paris after 1563, or in heavily Protestant Dieppe during the First, Second, Fifth and Sixth Civil Wars.[29] A number of French cities thus housed the equivalent of the Dutch 'churches under the cross' at certain moments in the religious wars. Such assemblies were decidedly dangerous, for individuals were executed for heresy or for participating in prohibited worship at several moments during the Religious Wars when such gatherings were outlawed. Executions for one or the other offence took place in Paris in 1562, 1569 and 1588–89.[30]

For their part, the Protestants did not hesitate to forbid Catholic worship in those localities that they dominated politically and numerically during the initial years of the Wars of Religion. Castres and Montpellier were two towns where a combination of anti-clerical violence and civic legislation forced Catholic worship to cease in the autumn and winter of 1561–62, even before the outbreak of the First Civil War. In both, the toleration granted the Reformed throughout the kingdom by the Edict of January did not beget similar toleration for Catholics in response. Roman worship did not resume in either town until the Peace of Amboise in 1563. When the Huguenots secured control of Orléans and Rouen at the outset of the First Civil War, Catholic services were initially allowed to continue there, but within less than a month they were forced to cease: in Orléans by decree of the city fathers following the massacre of Protestants in Sens; in Rouen following a local wave of iconoclasm, the seizure of arms from the city's Catholics, and the flight of the Parlement and much of the clergy. In Lyon, toleration of Catholic worship did not even last a few weeks, but was forbidden as soon as the Protestants took control of the city. In Montpellier, the Huguenot authorities went further yet in October 1562, making attendance at the *prêche* mandatory.[31] After the First Civil War, however, the initial Protestant impulse to uproot the abominations of the mass was tempered by the recognition that respecting the terms of successive edicts of pacification was beneficial for the cause as a whole. In La Rochelle, the great Huguenot stronghold from 1568 until 1628, Catholic

---

29 Diefendorf, *Beneath the Cross*, p. 123; Guillaume and Jean Daval, *Histoire de la Reformation à Dieppe*, ed. Émile Lesens (Rouen, 1878) I, 35, 41–2, 94, 120, 123.

30 William Monter, 'Les exécutés pour hérésie par arrêt du Parlement de Paris (1523– 1560)', *B.S.H.P.F.* 142 (1996), 209–10.

31 Jean Faurin, 'Journal sur les guerres de Castres', in M. de la Pijardière, ed., *Pièces fugitives pour servir à l'histoire de France* XV (Montpellier, 1878), 13; Charles d'Aigrefeuille, *Histoire de la ville de Montpellier* (Montpellier, 1877; repr. Marseille, 1976), I, 438; Philip Benedict, *Rouen during the Wars of Religion* (Cambridge, 1981), pp. 97–8; Bernard de Lacombe, *Les débuts des guerres de religion (Orléans 1559–1564): Catherine de Médicis entre Guise et Condé* (Paris, 1899), pp. 170–96, 328; Richard Gascon, *Grand commerce et vie urbaine au XVIe siècle: Lyon et ses marchands* (Paris, 1971), pp. 482, 492.

worship was permitted in each period of peace between those dates, although outlawed during each period of civil war.[32]

Some localities tried to follow an independent course of establishing a stable regime of religious coexistence even amid the periods of open civil war. The inhabitants of two communities in Dauphiné, Nyons and Saint-Laurent-des-Arbres, took formal vows in the 1560s to 'live in peace, friendship, and confederation' with one another despite 'the diversity of religion that is among them', and to defend their communities against attack by the troops of either religious party. A decade later, the duke of Montmorency-Damville sought to promote the toleration of both faiths over a broader area as the leader of the 'Protestants et Catholiques unis' in Languedoc. Such efforts succeeded intermittently in Montpellier, where both faiths worshipped side by side between 1574 and 1577 and again after 1582, although a regime of Protestant exclusivity prevailed between 1577 and 1582. They likewise succeeded in the little town of Saillans in Dauphiné, where the commissioners sent to oversee the implementation of the Edict of Nantes in 1599 found that both churches had exercised their religion 'for a long time ... in pure liberty'. Elsewhere, however, they broke down, as in Nyons, which by 1576 was a Huguenot *place de sûreté* where Catholic worship was forbidden in times of war.[33] Overall, the successful establishment of such regimes was probably rare. More often, the problem was enforcing the restoration of toleration decreed by the successive edicts of pacification. Particularly in the first decade of the civil wars, each new edict met with official foot-dragging and violent popular opposition in many cities, Catholic and Protestant alike. It often took the dispatch of special royal commissioners and a period of months or even years before those of the minority faith who had fled town dared to return home. Indeed, Michel Antoine has recently argued persuasively that the frequent use of royal commissioners to implement these edicts was an important step in the early development of the institution of the *intendant*.[34]

---

32 Etienne Trocmé, 'L'Eglise réformée de la Rochelle jusqu'en 1628', *B.S.H.P.F.* 99 (1952), 138. Catholic worship likewise ceased during the period of the League in the Protestant bastions of Die, Montélimar, Loriol, Livron and Nyons in Dauphiné. Elisabeth Rabut, *Le roi, l'église et le temple. L'Exécution de l'Edit de Nantes en Dauphiné* (Grenoble [?], 1987), pp. 73, 89, 100, 108, 168.

33 Marc Venard, *Réforme protestante, Réforme catholique dans la province d'Avignon au XVIe siècle* (Paris, 1993), p. 935; Stegmann, *Edits des guerres de religion*, p. 117; Rabut, *Le roi, l'église et le temple*, pp. 78, 168; Gérard Cholvy et al., *Histoire de Montpellier* (Toulouse, 1984), p. 152; A.C. Montpellier, GG 3–4 (demonstrating the resumption of Catholic worship after 1582).

34 Michel Antoine, 'Genèse de l'institution des intendants', *Journal des Savants* (1982), 293–6. For examples of local resistance to the resumption of toleration, see Claude Haton, *Mémoires*, ed. Felix Bourquelot (Paris, 1857), pp. 532–4, 604; Gascon, *Grand commerce*, pp. 523–7; Benedict, *Rouen*, pp. 114–15, 120–21; Nicholls, 'Protestants, Catholics and Magistrates in Tours', 17–21; Lacombe, *Débuts des guerres de religion*, p. 328.

A far more stable and enduring regime of coexistence followed Henry IV's triumph over the Catholic League. The Bourbon accession brought into the kingdom the little principality of Béarn, where Reformed Protestantism had been established as the religion of state and Catholicism outlawed under Jeanne d'Albret. Henry IV's Edict of Fontainebleau of 1599 allowed the limited reestablishment of Catholicism as a *quid pro quo* for the privileges granted France's Protestants under the Edict of Nantes, but local resistance initially stalled the implementation of this edict. The effective restoration of Catholic worship only came after Louis XIII led a small army into Béarn in 1620.[35] During the renewed civil wars of the 1620s, the rights of the Protestants to gather for worship remained undisturbed in both principle and general practice, although following the troubles these rights were revoked in certain localities to punish the inhabitants of the 'R.P.R.' (religion prétendue réformée) for their participation in the rebellion.[36] Catholic worship fared less well in many cities that took up the standard of revolt in these years, as the exaltation of a militant and triumphalist Protestantism gripped the population for a final time. In Montpellier, many of the scenes of the early 1560s were replayed: the churches were systematically purged of their idols; Catholics were driven to the *prêche* with sticks jocularly baptized 'the consistory's dusting rods'; and the mass ceased, as it also did in La Rochelle.[37] With the exception of these incidents, however, the general principle that both faiths had the legal right to gather for worship was not challenged until the Revocation. Instead, contestation over rights of worship by the militants on both sides shifted to arguments and legal battles over whether or not the Reformed had the right to assemble in specific localities under the complicated terms of the Edict of Nantes.

Establishing the legal parameters for the peaceful coexistence of two religious faiths in France involved more than simply decreeing that each one had the right to assemble for worship. From the start, every edict that granted the Reformed freedom of worship also contained provisions designed to mitigate the possibility of violence between the members of each faith and to specify the rights and obligations of the Reformed

---

35 Pierre Tucoo-Chala and Christian Desplat, *La Principauté de Béarn* (Pau, 1980), pp. 277–87, 311–14; above, Chapter 2, p. 88.

36 The national synod of 1637 listed 38 localities where churches had been closed since the civil wars of the 1620s. Jean Aymon, *Tous les Synodes Nationales des Eglises Reformées de France* (The Hague, 1710), II, 597. For evidence demonstrating the temporary closure of other churches: Benedict, *The Huguenot Population of France, 1600–1685: The Demographic Fate and Customs of a Religious Minority*, (Philadelphia, 1991), pp. 132–4.

37 André Delort, *Mémoires inédits sur la ville de Montpellier au XVIIe siècle (1621–1693)* (Montpellier, 1876–78, repr. Marseille, 1980), pp. 7–9; D'Aigrefeuille, *Histoire de la ville de Montpellier*, II, 48; Trocmé, 'Eglise de la Rochelle', p. 138.

minority. The number of such provisions tended to increase with each successive edict, as new sources of resentment and potential conflict were constantly revealed.[38]

To minimize friction, each edict from 1562 onward specified that butchers' shops were to remain closed on all *jours maigres* and that the Protestants were to respect Catholic feast days. The burial of deceased Protestants soon proved to be a particularly nettlesome issue, as the interment of heretics in hallowed ground proved so offensive to Catholic sensibilities that incidents recurred in which Huguenot corpses were dis-interred or dragged to the local refuse heap. From 1570 onward, successive edicts obliged the Protestants to obtain their own burial grounds, forbade Catholic attempts to interfere with their doing so, and sought to spell out procedures whereby Huguenot corpses might be taken to these burial grounds without creating 'scandal' or 'tumult'. Beginning with the 1570 Peace of Saint-Germain, each edict also guaranteed the Protestants access to educational and caritative institutions and to royal and municipal offices, creating an equality of civil rights that contrasts markedly with the situation of the dissenters in post-1688 England. That Peace of Saint-Germain was also the first to grant the Protestants control over a certain number of fortified towns as places of refuge in the event of further civil wars.

The Saint Bartholomew's Massacre of 1572, in the wake of which thousands of panicked Protestants abjured their faith and thousands of others fled abroad, opened new wounds. As the crown sought to close these, it decreed that past abjurations were not binding on those who chose to resume their prior faith and that the children of French subjects born abroad were French *regnicoles* if they chose to return to the country. Catholics were forbidden to continue holding processions to commemorate the events of Saint Bartholomew's Eve, and reparations were even granted the widows and children of the massacre victims in the form of six-year tax exemptions. Once again, these royal decrees of nationwide scope must be recognized as providing only the broad framework for the coexistence of the two faiths. Additional measures might be decreed locally. One particularly important tactic to which royal governors began to have recourse from early on in the Wars of Religion was that of dividing the seats in certain city councils between members of the two faiths in numbers roughly proportional to their strength within the community, creating a French equivalent to the regimes of parity of certain German free imperial cities.[39]

---

[38] The paragraphs that follow are based above all on the edicts collected in Stegmann, *Edits des guerres de religion*.

[39] The city councils of Lyon, Montpellier and Orléans were all divided in this fashion following the Peace of Amboise.

From 1598 to 1685, a string of edicts, *arrêts*, and declarations emanating from the *conseil du roi* and the *parlements* modified details of the civil situation of the Reformed in ways that became considerably more restrictive once Louis XIV began to rule on his own. Henry IV attempted a deliberate balancing act, alternately gratifying one party and then the other when faced with petitions alleging violations of the terms of the religious peace or requesting modifications of these terms. With the increasing influence of the *dévot* party at court and the death or disgrace of many of Henry IV's old councillors, royal policy grew more hostile to the Reformed by the later 1610s. Louis XIII and Richelieu sought particularly to erode Protestant political power, as illustrated by the 1629 repeal of the military concessions granted the Huguenots by the secret articles of the Edict of Nantes and by numerous decisions tilting the balance in *consulats mi-partis* in favour of the Catholics. An edict of 1634 prohibited Protestant ministers from preaching in the 'annex' churches attached to certain congregations, while three years later members of the faith were forbidden from gathering in their temples for prayer meetings or other acts of worship without a minister present. After the death of Louis XIII and Richelieu, the loyalty that the Protestants showed to the crown during the Fronde and the need to rally as much support as possible for the war against Spain led Mazarin to demonstrate more generosity toward the Huguenots on occasion – especially in 1654–55, when Cromwell, whose support he sought, made a diplomatic issue of their situation. In these years, the Protestants regained lost rights of worship or representation in city government in a number of localities. With the onset of Louis XIV's personal rule in 1661, however, the aggressively pro-Catholic policy that would culminate in the Revocation of the Edict of Nantes began in earnest. Teams of royal commissioners were dispatched to the provinces in 1662 to verify the titles of each local church and to close down those found to be in violation of the strict terms of the Edict of Nantes. Measures limited the size of the parties that could accompany Reformed funeral convoys, banned the singing of psalms in the street, and required members of the faith to respect the Catholic *temps clos* for marriages of Lent and Advent. Old guarantees of impartial justice were eliminated by first cutting back the jurisdiction of the bi-partisan Chambres de l'Edit and then, between 1669 and 1679, dissolving them. Still other measures removed the equal access to civil employment that the Reformed had previously enjoyed by imposing quotas on them in many guilds and professions and excluding them entirely from some. Particularly bitterly resented were the measures that restricted parental authority over their children by decreeing that all children of a Catholic father and Protestant mother must be raised as Catholics, and that parents must respect the wishes of children as young as seven who expressed a desire to convert to the Roman church. In 1680, Catholic conversion to Protestantism was entirely forbidden, as was intermarriage with a member of the faith.[40]

The events that greased the final slide to the Revocation have often been narrated, and need only be quickly recapitulated. The growing piety of the king; the discovery and ruthless exploitation by several iron-fisted administrators of the capacities of royal dragoons billeted in Huguenot houses to generate conversions; exaggerated reports of the numbers of conversions thus obtained and of the virtual extinction of the Protestant cause; and finally the pressures on the king to restore his lustre as a defender of the faith after his inaction in face of the Turkish siege of Vienna and his conflict with the Pope over the issue of the *Régale* – all these contributed their part. As recent historians have stressed, however, a deeper logic was also at work. The enduring hostility to religious pluralism on the part of the successive Bourbon kings, the Catholic church and so much of the political nation created a larger ideological context that encouraged the Revocation. If so many Protestants were now returning to the true faith and the crown's strength had increased to the point where it could no longer be argued that the revocation of tolerance for the Huguenots would produce an unacceptable level of internal warfare, what was the point of retaining a regime of toleration that had always been viewed as a necessary evil, especially when there was important symbolic capital to be obtained by doing away with it?[41] Strikingly, the Edict of Fontainebleau that replaced the Edict of Nantes made an awkward bow toward the principle of freedom of conscience by declaring that the members of the R.P.R. would not be troubled for their beliefs until such time as God illuminated them as to the true religion, so long as they did not gather for public worship or group prayers. But this was rendered meaningless by the highly organized military operation that had anticipated the Revocation and pressured the Reformed into abjuring the faith *en masse*. Furthermore, unlike the imperial legislation

---

40 Daniel Ligou, *Le Protestantisme en France de 1598 à 1715* (Paris, 1968), chs 3–5; Dompnier, *Venin de l'hérésie*, ch. 9; G. Bonet-Maury, *La liberté de conscience en France depuis l'Edit de Nantes jusqu'à la séparation (1598–1905)* (Paris, 1909), pp. 26–30; Janine Garrisson, *L'Edit de Nantes et sa révocation. Histoire d'une intolérance* (Paris, 1985); Ruth Kleinman, 'Changing Interpretations of the Edict of Nantes: The Administrative Aspect, 1643–1661', *French Historical Studies* 10 (1978), 541–71; *Edits déclarations et arrests concernans la réligion p. réformée 1662–1751* (Paris, 1885); Paul Gachon, *Quelques préliminaires de la Révocation de l'Edit de Nantes en Languedoc (1661–1685)* (Toulouse, 1899); A.T. van Deursen, *Professions et métiers interdits. Un aspect de l'histoire de la Révocation de l'Edit de Nantes* (Groningen, 1960).

41 Ernest Lavisse, *Histoire de France*, vol. 7, Part 2, (Paris, 1906), 39–80; Jean Orcibal, *Louis XIV et les Protestants* (Paris, 1951); Garrisson, *Edit de Nantes et sa révocation*, pp. 9–27, 184–262; Labrousse, *'Une foi, une loi, un roi?'*, pp. 25–6, 167–95; Pierre Chaunu, 'La décision royale (?): un système de la Révocation', in Zuber and Theis, eds, *Révocation de l'Edit de Nantes*, pp. 13–28.

on such matters, the Edict of Fontainebleau forbade Huguenot emigration. Their legal identity now redefined as 'Nouveaux Catholiques', the erstwhile members of the 'so-called Reformed religion' thus found themselves legally obliged to participate in Catholic communion, if they did not wish to take the risks of illegal flight.

The history of how the law was modified to adjust to the presence of France's Reformed minority can thus be envisaged as a movement in two parts. Over the course of the Wars of Religion, the crown groped along a twisting path to define a set of terms to govern the toleration of two faiths that were neither so generous as to provoke massive Catholic resistance, nor so restrictive as to prompt the same from the Reformed. In the formula that finally proved successful, Catholicism's position as the established faith of the kingdom was reaffirmed by a variety of measures that required the Protestants to respect Catholic practices and that restricted Reformed worship to a defined set of localities. At the same time, the Protestants were accorded impressive guarantees of equal civil rights and special arrangements to ensure their security and their access to impartial justice. All of the edicts of pacification, however, included wording to the effect that their provisions were only a temporary necessity until such time as the entire kingdom might be reunited in the true faith, always the fondest hope of royal policy. Once a stable regime of toleration was established, successive rulers whittled away at the various rights and privileges granted the Reformed, until at last they were entirely revoked.

How effectively enforced were the laws that defined the civil rights of the Reformed and the character of their obligations toward Catholic customs or rituals? A set of remonstrances that the Reformed presented to Henry IV in 1596 and published in the following year detailed more than 50 recent violations of the provisions of the Peace of Bergerac, which then governed affairs in those areas that recognized the prince of Navarre as king. Four sorts of violations were particularly frequently alleged: (1) fines or threats of legal action made against the Reformed for failing to attend processions, drape their houses on feast days, or otherwise participate in or show due respect for Catholic ceremonies, even though the law did not require them to do this; (2) attempts to block them from municipal offices; (3) attempts to stop them from worshipping in places where they believed that the terms of the Peace of Bergerac allowed them to do so; and (4) 'scandals' arising out of Catholic attacks on their funeral processions or the desecration of burial sites.[42] In the seventeenth century, reports of foreign travellers make it clear that the Reformed openly sold

---

[42] *Plaintes des Eglises réformées de France, sur les violences et injustices qui leur sont faites en plusieurs endrois du Royaume* (n.p., 1597), reprinted in [Simon Goulart], *Mémoires de la Ligue* (Amsterdam, 1758), VI, 428–86.

and served meat on *jours maigres* in many of the communities in southern France in which they were strong. According to the Protestant historian of the Edict of Nantes, Elie Benoist, the habit of working on feast days became so deeply entrenched in such places that even Catholic artisans followed suit.[43] Parish register evidence shows that the royal edict of 1662 requiring the Reformed to respect the prohibitions against celebrating marriages during certain periods was followed by a sharp drop in the number of Protestant weddings in Lent in a few parts of the country where the authorities were particularly vigilant in their surveillance of Huguenot behaviour, especially Poitou and Saintonge, but that the edict was flouted in Languedoc, Provence and even parts of northern France, including Benoist's home Alençon.[44] It is thus clear that a gap always existed between the letter of the law on these issues and actual behaviour across the length and breadth of the realm. We are still far from being able to indicate the full contours of the gap or the extent to which it narrowed or widened over time.

Coexistence in practice: cooperation and conflict

Discussion of the extent to which the laws governing Catholic–Reformed coexistence were actually observed leads us from the legal history of toleration to the social history of inter-group interaction. Several outstanding recent studies have greatly enhanced our understanding of the aspect of that history that is at once most immediately visible in the sources of the period and most troubling to modern sensibilities: the numerous incidents of popular violence, often accompanied by appalling acts of ritual humiliation and dismemberment, that punctuated the era. Other recent historians, moved by an understandable desire to combat the impression that violence is a necessary consequence of religious diversity, have highlighted the many forms of peaceful interaction that marked much of the day-to-day coexistence of the two groups and the social ties that cut across the confessional divide. A full picture of Protestant–Catholic relations needs to make room at once for the evidence of frequent, cordial interaction between members of the two faiths and for the recognition that a continuing sense of difference set them apart – differences that could, in certain situations, spark violence or panic.

---

43 Benoist, III, 23–4, 40; Hans Bots, 'Voyages faits par de jeunes hollandais en France. Deux voyages types: Gysbert de With et Nicolas Heinsius', in *La découverte de la France au XVIIe siècle* (Paris, 1980), p. 475; Gregory Hanlon, *Confession and Community in Seventeenth-Century France: Catholic and Protestant Coexistence in Aquitaine* (Philadelphia, 1993), p. 22.

44 Above, Chapter 2, p. 102.

If the years between 1560 and 1598 burned themselves into the memory of subsequent generations as the 'temps des troubles de religion', this was not simply because of the eight formally declared civil wars, but also because of the numerous incidents of religious rioting that troubled even putative periods of peace. Natalie Zemon Davis and Denis Crouzet have offered particularly fruitful models for understanding this violence.[45] In community after community, Protestant crowd actions began with mockery of the processions, eucharistic rituals and other rites of the Catholic church, and with iconoclastic attacks on the statuary and altarpieces that decorated France's churches and streets. Initially scattered, such incidents became a vast wave between 1560 and 1562, as the churches now being organized across the country grew in strength and daring. Efforts to rescue imprisoned co-religionists and physical violence against the clergy soon followed, as, on rarer occasions, did attacks on Catholic laymen. Catholic crowd actions most commonly took the form of violent reactions to a Protestant provocation perceived as an act of sacrilege, of attacks on Huguenots gathered for or returning from worship, and of efforts to prevent their burial in hallowed ground. Often, they grew into larger bloodlettings in which dozens or even hundreds of heretics were hunted down, dismembered and hurled into nearby bodies of water. In each case, the violence expressed powerful and widely shared attitudes that were fundamental to each group's religious outlook. On the Protestant side, the violence was part of the fundamental drive of the Reformation to purify society of the false forms of worship that had infected divine service, to proclaim a new understanding of the Gospel and to insist upon the rights of those who embraced it to assemble for worship, and to do away with an overgrown and unnecessary clerical establishment. On the Catholic side, it expressed the view that heretics were a dangerous threat to the moral and political order who properly deserved punishment and even eradication, overlain in many instances with fears that they threatened the natural order as well, for an angry God might scourge the kingdom with plagues and earthquakes if the blot of heresy were not removed. In other words, most of the crowd actions were the expression through extra-legal means of the principles that in other circumstances justified the legal proscription of one faith or the other.

---

45 Davis, 'The Rites of Violence: Religious Riot in Sixteenth Century France', *Past and Present* 59 (1973), 51–91, reprinted in her *Society and Culture in Early Modern France* (Stanford, 1975); Crouzet, *Les guerriers de Dieu. La violence au temps des troubles de religion, vers 1525–vers 1610* (Seyssel, 1990). Also extremely commendable on Huguenot iconoclasm is Olivier Christin, *Une révolution symbolique. L'iconoclasme huguenot et la reconstruction catholique* (Paris, 1991), and see further the pioneering Janine Estèbe, *Tocsin pour un massacre. La saison des Saint-Barthélemy* (Paris, 1968); Benedict, *Rouen*; Diefendorf, *Beneath the Cross*; Mark Greengrass, 'The Anatomy of a Religious Riot in Toulouse in May 1562', *Journal of Ecclesiastical History* 34 (1983), 367–91.

After reaching its paroxysm in the Saint Bartholomew's Massacre, the spontaneous religious violence that was so common between 1560 and 1572 diminished in frequency. Crouzet has explored the psychology of this decline: as the Huguenots rallied from the demoralization and shock of the event to mount a successful defence of their key strongholds from La Rochelle to Montauban, the initial Catholic euphoria at the apparently mortal blow delivered to their enemies gave way to guilt at the sheer horror of the event itself and a shift toward enterprises of penance and personal reform that now came to be believed to be the way to rid the country of the evils that afflicted it.[46] My own research has highlighted the local political causes of the decline: within most communities, the balance of power between the two faiths, often uneasy between 1562 and 1572, had tipped clearly in favour of one party or the other after the latter date, reducing the tensions between them. In most localities in northern France and parts of the South, the ranks of the Reformed underwent massive attrition through flight, massacre and abjuration, leaving them a far smaller and less politically threatening minority than they had been at the beginning of this period. In certain of the communities in which the Reformed were in the majority, they established their firm political control by the early 1570s. In either event, tension ebbed and intra-community violence declined, even if warfare continued between strongholds committed to each side.[47]

Religious violence in the years after 1572 has been little studied, but it would be wrong to think that it ever entirely disappeared. A preliminary inventory of religious riots from 1600 to 1685 reveals the irregular recurrence of violent episodes across these years.[48] Incidents were particularly frequent in the decade of renewed religious warfare in the 1620s and in the period immediately preceding the Revocation, but no decade was spared. Many of the flashpoints for trouble were the same as in the early years of the Wars of Religion, but a few new ones also appeared. Thus, with the construction of more permanent Reformed temples, attacks upon the physical structure of the temple itself became a favoured method for Catholics to demonstrate their hostility to the presence of Reformed

[46] Crouzet, *Guerriers de Dieu*, II, 112ff; *idem*, 'Le règne de Henri III et la violence collective', in Robert Sauzet, ed., *Henri III et son temps* (Paris, 1992), pp. 211–25.

[47] Benedict, *Rouen*, pp. 95–163, 240–42.

[48] My inventory of such incidents is based primarily on the numerous episodes of violence mentioned in Benoist. Other incidents are revealed by Dompnier, *Venin de l'hérésie*, pp. 166–8; Alain Croix, *La Bretagne aux 16e et 17e siècles: La vie, la mort, la foi* (Paris, 1981), p. 94; René Favier, *Les villes du Dauphiné aux XVIIe et XVIIIe siècles* (Grenoble, 1993), p. 88; Henry Ronot, 'Une famille de peintres protestants à Langres au début du XVIIe siècle: les Michelin', *B.S.H.P.F.* 96 (1949), pp. 71–2; Alfred Leroux, 'L'Eglise Réformée de Bordeaux de 1660 à 1670', *B.S.H.P.F.* 69 (1920), 178; Frank Puaux, 'Ephémérides de l'année de la révocation de l'édit de Nantes', *B.S.H.P.F.* 34 (1885), 87.

worship in their community.[49] As aggressively missionizing Catholic religious orders established themselves under the umbrella of royal protection in towns that had previously been Protestant strongholds, they became a focus of Huguenot anger. These incidents of religious violence were generally minor, but fears of a recurrence of events comparable to the worst episodes of the sixteenth century continued to haunt both sides. In 1645, a rumour swept through the Parisian congregation at Charenton that bands of Catholics had gathered in the nearby woods to slaughter all present. Shrieks of terror and a scramble to secure the temple door ensued.[50] In 1690, comparable rumours that the Huguenots were about to burn their way across two predominantly Catholic regions in the Midi led the authorities of these areas, Bigorre and the Agenais, to put the militia on full alert.[51] The establishment of a measure of peace between the two confessions had clearly not eliminated the memory of past horrors and the suspicion of the other faith that this engendered. A measure of friction continued to be attached to Catholic–Reformed relations.

As has already been suggested, the history of popular violence forms just one part of the story of Catholic–Reformed relations. In the initial years of the Reformed churches' growth, the decision to embrace or reject the new faith often cut right through individual families. While those who drafted the edicts of pacification felt compelled to prohibit parents from disinheriting their children strictly 'from hatred of their religion', relations between family members who chose different faiths frequently remained cooperative and cordial.[52] Local studies of religious life in the seventeenth century have revealed numerous instances of amicable relations between members of the two faiths, even between their spiritual leaders. In Besse (Dauphiné), an episcopal visitation found in 1672 that the parish curé 'plays boules with the huguenots, often eats with them, and had close contacts and friendship with the minister'. In Pontacq (Béarn), the two faiths shared the same church building and even, despite an episcopal prohibition, the same church bells.[53] Detailed community studies have

---

49 On this phenomenon, see Solange Deyon, 'La destruction des temples', in Zuber and Theis, eds, *Révocation de l'Edit de Nantes*, pp. 239–58.

50 Charenton en 1645. Récit d'un voyageur alsacien', *B.S.H.P.F.* 67 (1921), 155, cited in Dompnier, *Venin de l'hérésie*, p. 164. For another Protestant panic in 1621, see Daval and Daval, *Histoire de la Reformation à Dieppe*, I, 214–17; Ferdinand de Schickler, *Les Eglises du Refuge en Angleterre* (2 vols, Paris, 1892), I, 390–91.

51 Jean-François Soulet, *Traditions et réformes religieuses dans les Pyrénées centrales au XVIIe siècle (le diocèse de Tarbes de 1602 à 1716)* (Pau, 1974), 299; Hanlon, *Confession and Community*, p. 255.

52 Barbara B. Diefendorf, 'Les divisions religieuses dans les familles parisiennes avant la Saint-Barthélemy', *Histoire, Economie et Société* 7 (1988), 55–77.

53 Dompnier, *Venin de l'hérésie*, p. 140; Soulet, *Traditions et réformes*, p. 300. Similar reports from other regions in Robert Sauzet, *Les visites pastorales dans le diocèse de Chartres*

shown that Catholics and Protestants did business with one another, served as godparents for one another's children, placed their children as apprentices or servants in the households of members of the other faith, and even intermarried – the acid test of the strength of social barriers between different groups within a community. Of 482 marriages celebrated in the Catholic churches of Nîmes between 1609 and 1621, 117 involved one partner (typically, the woman) who had recently converted to the faith to allow the marriage to be celebrated.[54]

Although the character of everyday Catholic–Reformed social interaction in the localities has begun to be illuminated, again much remains to be done. To begin with, it must be observed that work to date has been content to underscore the fact of Catholic–Protestant cooperation, rather than trying to measure its precise frequency. The 24 per cent of Catholic marriages in Nîmes that involved a partner who had until recently been of the opposite faith takes on different significance when it is realized that the city was approximately 80 per cent Protestant at the time. Had no tendency existed toward religious endogamy within the city's population, fully four-fifths of all Catholic marriages would have been mixed marriages. The considerable interaction that marked everyday social relations between Catholics and Protestants should not obscure the strong tendency toward group endogamy.

Historians also need to address possible changes over time. It might be expected that with the achievement of a relatively stable political equilibrium in different local communities, everyday interaction between the members of the two faiths would gradually eradicate the mistrust between them and produce a lowering of social barriers. At the same time, however, elements within both churches worked through the seventeenth century to limit or eliminate certain social practices that blurred the boundaries between the two groups. Reformed consistories reprimanded church members who sent their children to Jesuit schools or attended Roman ceremonies. The Catholic hierarchy, and occasionally even lay churchwardens, admonished parish priests who socialized too convivially

---

pendant la première moitié du XVIIe siècle (Rome, 1975), pp. 226–7; 'Les paroissiens de Sainte-Cathérine de Honfleur: Leur curé et le pasteur en 1659', B.S.H.P.F. 46 (1897), 90–93.

54 Robert Sauzet, Contre-Réforme et Réforme catholique en Bas-Languedoc: Le diocèse de Nîmes au XVIIe siècle (Louvain, 1979), p. 166. The extent of good relations between most members of the two confessions in religiously divided communities has been highlighted particularly effectively by the detailed community studies of Gregory Hanlon on Layrac (Hanlon, Confession and Community) and Elisabeth Labrousse on Mauvezin. Labrousse indicates some of her findings in her 'Une foi, une loi, un roi?', pp. 81–9. For further evidence of ties of godparentage and domestic service across the confessional divide, see Miriam U. Chrisman, 'Family and Religion in Two Noble Families', Journal of Family History 8 (1983), 205; G.E. de Falguerolles, 'Les paroissiens de l'Eglise Réformée à Puylaurens (1630–1650)', B.S.H.P.F. 111 (1965), 100.

with Huguenots. By the fourth decade of the century, the authorities of both churches no longer permitted members of the other faith to act as godparents. Meanwhile, champions of the two faiths engaged one another in numerous public debates, whose result was rarely to win converts for either side, but which did have the effect of reinforcing the pre-existing convictions of those attending and deepening their awareness of the points of doctrine that separated them from their neighbours.[55] Even while ongoing social and commercial interactions may have knitted members of the two faiths more tightly together, a powerful cultural dynamic thus worked to heighten awareness of confessional differences.

Time softened but little the fundamentally hostile images that intellectuals of each party maintained of the other. Such late seventeenth-century Catholic historians as Bossuet, Maimbourg and Meurisse no longer suggested that Luther and Calvin were fathered by the devil or likened their followers to apes in the manner of certain anti-Protestant polemics of the later sixteenth century, but their depiction of the reformers as headstrong individuals who bucked at legitimate authority and of Protestantism as the religion of republicanism repeated with only modest variation the charges of sedition and immorality most commonly levelled against the faith in the early years of the Wars of Religion.[56] The mocking satire of clerical fraud and popular superstition found in much sixteenth-century Reformed propaganda disappeared from Huguenot publications by the mid-seventeenth century, but this is largely attributable to changing tastes and to governmental repression, for Protestant pastors faced expulsion from the kingdom if they expressed opinions that royal administrators deemed slanderous of the Roman church. When, on the eve of the Revocation, Huguenot ministers began to publish outspoken defences of their cause from the safety of exile, they drew amply on the stock bogeymen of seventeenth-century European anti-Catholicism: the Inquisition, the mistreatment of the Indians, and the claim that Catholics could never be loyal subjects since they always owed a share of their political fealty to the Pope in Rome.[57] Faced with increasingly intense

---

55 Dompnier, *Venin de l'hérésie*, chs 7–8; Falguerolles, 'Paroissiens de l'Eglise Réformée à Puylaurens', p. 100; Sauzet, *Contre-Réforme et Réforme catholique*, p. 173–8.

56 Dompnier, *Venin de l'hérésie*, chs 2–4, provides an excellent account of the image of Protestantism in the militant Catholic literature of the seventeenth century. This may be usefully compared with G. Wylie Sypher, ' "Faisant ce qu'il leur vient à plaisir": The Image of Protestantism in French Catholic Polemics on the Eve of the Religious Wars', *The Sixteenth Century Journal* 11 (1980), 59–84; Benedict, 'Of Marmites and Martyrs'.

57 [Claude Brousson], *Estat des Reformez en France* (Cologne, 1684); Jacques Solé, *Le débat entre protestants et catholiques français de 1598 à 1685* (Paris, 1985), pp. 175–94, 1364–5; Guy Howard Dodge, *The Political Theory of the Huguenots of the Dispersion, With Special Reference to the Thought and Influence of Pierre Jurieu* (New York, 1947; repr. New York, 1972), p. 14.

Catholic proselytization, the Reformed also revised their catechisms to spell out more clearly the reasons why theirs was the true faith and the Roman church was in error.[58]

The extent to which such views were shared by the less well educated or more broad-minded members of each faith may well be questioned.[59] When, in the wake of the Revocation, a Protestant from the Cévenol market town of Saint-Hippolyte-du-Fort set out an 'abrégé très sincère' of his beliefs so that his children would remember the faith into which they were baptized, the document was anything but prolix in its explanation of the points of difference with the church of Rome. The author, Pierre Lézan, listed only three items: (1) 'we' worship one God in three persons and address our prayers to God with the sole intercession of Christ, while the Roman church believes that one should also pray to the saints; (2) we say our prayers in a language understood by all, while the Roman church uses a language people cannot understand to keep them ignorant; and (3) our communion service conforms to the model of the Bible and the practice of the church until the Council of Constance, while the Roman church's does not. Still, the very fact that Lézan sought in this manner to keep alive within his family a sense of his ancestral faith's differences from Rome is a telling sign of the importance he placed upon remaining true to that faith, as is his claim that the conversion of one of his sons to Catholicism 'nearly killed' him and his wife.[60] With the growth over time of literacy and the efforts of the opinion makers of both confessions to underscore the flaws of the other, it seems probable that the strength of confessional identity was stronger in 1685 than in 1600.

Despite the fact that the intense interconfessional violence of the years 1560 to 1572 gave way to generally more peaceful, although by no means entirely untroubled, Catholic–Reformed interaction over the subsequent century, the two confessions thus remained divided by mutually hostile visions of one another and a strong tendency toward group endogamy. In such a situation, the failure of the Revocation of the Edict of Nantes to reunite all Frenchmen in a single church becomes anything but surprising. Rather than remain within the Roman church in the wake of the forced abjurations of 1685, the majority of Nouveaux Catholiques preferred to flee the country or to abstain from worship. Soon, they would begin to organize the clandestine assemblies of the 'Desert', bringing the history of

---

58 Kathleen L.M. Faust, 'A Beleaguered Society: Protestant Families in La Rochelle, 1628–1685' (Ph.D. dissertation, Northwestern University, 1980), 353.

59 Elisabeth Labrousse, 'Conversions dans les deux sens', in *La conversion au XVIIe siècle* (Marseilles, 1983), pp. 161–72, does just this.

60 'Pierre Lézan, secrétaire du consistoire de Saint-Hippolyte 1663–1700: Extraits de ses mémoires', in Clément Ribard, *Notes d'histoire cévenole* (Cazillac, 1898), pp. 57–61.

Reformed worship full circle to the situation of the years between 1555 and the Edict of January.

With the chief parameters for the history of Catholic–Reformed coexistence between 1555 and 1685 now sketched, it can be seen that it was anything but paradoxical that France should have been in the 1560s at once one of the first countries in Western Europe to grant rights of worship to a Protestant minority and the site of the bloodiest interconfessional violence of the era. Both were part of the difficult adjustment to the sudden emergence of a situation of religious pluralism for which little in the country's traditions prepared it. Catholic intolerance was encouraged by France's most deeply rooted political myths, which linked the nation's existence to its historic success in combating heresy; Reformed intolerance was encouraged by Calvin's insistence that Christian magistrates were obliged to uphold the true faith, and by the hopes that took root amid the surge of Protestant sentiment around 1560 that the established church might soon be swept away. Since the advance of the Reformed was accompanied by provocative gestures of rupture with the established church order, violence between the two groups soon followed. While the dominant outlook on both sides of the religious divide was hostile to the toleration of more than one faith, the country's cultural traditions none the less contained intellectual resources that could be deployed to justify a policy of toleration, especially as a temporary concession to urgent political necessity. The very strength of the Reformed movement's growth created such a necessity – or at least so it seemed to a ruling queen regent who was a stranger to the country's political traditions. But toleration initially proved impossible to implement. Recurring civil wars and violence led to constant alterations in the royal legislation governing the rights and privileges granted the Reformed, while in nearly all religiously divided localities, the adherents of whichever faith was politically the weaker were forced to interrupt public worship and then to struggle to resume it time and again.

After the great bloodbath of Saint Bartholomew, spontaneous interconfessional violence declined significantly. By 1598, the elements of an enduring legal regime to govern the coexistence of the two faiths had been defined, and the succession crisis that troubled the country after 1584 had been resolved. Even the worst periods of confessional tension had never eliminated all neighbourly relations between members of the two groups. Now, the retreat of confessional violence and the establishment of a successful legal framework for their mutual coexistence allowed their generally peaceful character to come to the fore.

Yet again it is no paradox that the achievement of more peaceful coexistence between the two religions was followed three generations later by the revocation of the rights of worship granted the Reformed. Continuing interconfessional competition for souls and the efforts of rigorists on both sides to combat certain practices that linked people together across the religious divide fuelled an ongoing process of boundary demarcation and group reinforcement. Mutual suspicion, continued skirmishing over the precise extent of the legal privileges granted the Reformed, and intermittent violence continued to mark relations between the groups. Once the realization set in among the Huguenots that their original dream of the complete transformation of the Gallican church along Reformed lines would never be realized, the ever-present threat of the repeal of their legal privileges moved certain of their theorists to articulate broad arguments in favour of the principle of freedom of conscience. The majority of their spokesmen defended their rights of worship on far narrower grounds, however, while the impetus that pushed the 95 per cent of the population that remained Catholic to embrace the general principle of toleration was far weaker yet. For the vast majority of the population, the granting of rights of worship to heretics remained, as it had been at the outset, a political concession to a group whose eradication, although perhaps desirable, carried too high a cost in lives to be practicable. In an era of growing state power, that was a weak foundation for enduring rights of worship, for as the power of the monarchy grew, the political calculus changed. In the absence of a widely shared belief in the principles of freedom of conscience or freedom of worship for all, a regime of toleration extracted essentially as a political concession to some always remained vulnerable to repeal by royal fiat. At the same time, the strength of group identity among both confessions guaranteed that, when royal fiat undid the regime of coexistence worked out with so much bloodshed between 1562 and 1598, the religious division of the kingdom would prove beyond repeal.

CHAPTER TEN

Confessionalization in France? Critical Reflections and New Evidence

In the past decade, the concept of 'confessionalization' that German historians first began to forge nearly fifty years ago has spread through the international literature on the European Reformation. The word's semantic fortunes received an initial boost outside Germany when R. Po-chia Hsia introduced it to an English-language audience in his 1989 *Social Discipline in the Reformation: Central Europe, 1550–1750*. Its international visibility grew when the authoritative *Handbook of European History 1400–1600* included in 1995 a forceful chapter on 'Confessional Europe' by one of the leading proponents of the confessionalization thesis, Heinz Schilling.[1] In that same year, English-language studies of the Netherlands by Benjamin Kaplan and Jonathan Israel used the theme of confessionalization and its limits to illuminate Dutch religious history in the generations following the Reformation.[2] In France, an ambitious multi-volume history of Christianity involving numerous leading scholars of the subject entitled the volume dealing with the period 1530–1620 *Le temps des confessions*.[3] By 1997, if not before, Italian scholars were also writing of '*confessionalizzazione*'.[4]

This is hardly the first time that the terminology and preoccupations of German Reformation scholarship have spread through the international community of those who study the religious history of the early modern centuries. In preceding decades, the theme of 'the Reformation in the cities' pioneered by Bernd Moeller enjoyed still greater influence; Peter Blickle's idea of 'the communal Reformation', although harder to apply to the Reformation beyond Germany, has also recently sparked international

---

1 Thomas A. Brady Jr, Heiko Oberman and James D. Tracy, eds, *Handbook of European History 1400–1600: Late Middle Ages, Renaissance and Reformation* (2 vols, Leiden, 1994–95), II, ch. 21.

2 Benjamin J. Kaplan, *Calvinists and Libertines: Confession and Community in Utrecht, 1578–1620* (Oxford, 1995); Jonathan I. Israel, *The Dutch Republic: Its Rise, Greatness, and Fall 1477–1806* (Oxford, 1995), ch. 16: 'Protestantization, Catholicization, Confessionalization'.

3 Jean-Marie Mayeur et al., *Histoire du Christianisme des origines à nos jours*, vol. 8, *Le temps des confessions (1530–1620/30)*, ed. Marc Venard (Paris, 1992). See esp. p. 9.

4 Oscar Di Simplicio, 'Confessionalizzazione e identità collettiva – Il caso italiano: Siena 1575–1800', *A.R.* 88 (1997), 380–411.

discussion. Nor is it surprising that the history of the European Reformation should so often be written in terms forged in Bielefeld, Göttingen, or Bern. Beyond the evident factors of Germany's demographic and economic weight within Europe and its longstanding investment in university research, German scholarship occupies a particularly important place within the international study of the Reformation because the Reformation itself has occupied a particularly central place within German national and historical consciousness since at least the time of Ranke.[5] The venerable Verein für Reformationgeschichte and Germany's many Protestant theological faculties provide strong institutional underpinnings for research in the field, while the ties that connect the Verein to the American Society for Reformation Research extend the reach of German scholarship across the Atlantic, as does the larger tendency for Reformation scholarship in America to be dominated numerically by specialists in German history.[6] The undeniable inventiveness of German historians in forging ideal-typical interpretative constructs, as well as their high degree of theoretical self-consciousness, also contributes to their strength as exporters of ideas in this field.

Those interested in the Reformation in national contexts other than Germany may wonder if the influence of German historical scholarship is always a blessing. Since the Reformation developed in Germany with a speed and under circumstances that have few parallels elsewhere in Europe, models that illuminate German developments may apply poorly to other national histories. Historians of the French, Dutch, Italian, or Scottish Reformations may have more to learn from one another than from looking to the historiography of the German Reformation for inspiration. The current German social history of the Reformation would also appear to be particularly vulnerable to Silvana Seidel Menchi's criticism that the social history of the Reformation is too often a secularized historiography addressed to an audience of agnostics that misses the *coeur religieux* of its subject.[7] Yet it would be as foolish to reject out of hand the *Begriffen* of *Deutsche geschichte* as it would be to accept them uncritically. The fertility of German historiography offers historians of other countries interpretative models and a conceptual vocabulary with an undeniable potential to generate new questions and insights, as long as these models and concepts

---

5 Thomas A. Brady Jr, 'The Protestant Reformation in German History', Occasional Paper 22 of the German Historical Institute (Washington, 1998).

6 Philip Benedict, 'Between Whig Traditions and New Histories: American Historical Writing about Reformation and Early Modern Europe', in Anthony Molho and Gordon Wood, eds, *Imagined Histories: American Historians Interpret the Past* (Princeton, 1998), p. 301.

7 Seidel Menchi, 'Italy', in Bob Scribner, Roy Porter and Mikulás Teich, eds, *The Reformation in National Context* (Cambridge, 1994), p. 183.

are first scrutinized with care. The first part of this chapter will attempt to do just that by examining the various ways in which German historians have used the idea of confessionalization, the assumptions associated with their theories, and the reception their work has received. The goal here will be to define how confessionalization might most usefully be applied to the religious history of early modern France. Part two is a little archival exercise intended to suggest how one kind of document found in abundance in French archives, marriage contracts, can be used to shed light on whether or not France in fact experienced a degree of confessionalization as defined in the manner that appears most appropriate.

Critical reflections

E.W. Zeeden was the first to articulate the theme of confessionalization. Along with Jean Delumeau in France and H.O. Evennett and John Bossy in England, Zeeden was part of the postwar generation of Catholic historians who recognized the ways in which Tridentine Catholicism promoted changes in lay behaviour similar to those long attributed to Protestantism, and who consequently emphasized the parallel consequences of the 'two Reformations'. Attentive to religious life at the parish level as well as to the history of theology, Zeeden also observed in studying the Rhineland that during the later sixteenth century worship in many areas still loyal to Rome contained significant 'Protestant' elements, and that Tridentine orthodoxy often required generations to establish. Like so many other historians of that ecumenical generation, he studied religious traditions beyond his own, which led him to observe numerous Catholic survivals in post-Reformation Lutheran church orders. An important 1958 article first called attention to the similar process whereby orthodox, self-conscious Catholic, Reformed and Lutheran religious communities all emerged from the confused mixture of the early Reformation and deemed this process one of the central historical developments of the early modern centuries. Zeeden explored the process in greater detail in his 1965 book *Die Entstehung der Konfessionen*. The label he affixed to it, *Konfessionsbildung*, also served as the title of a 1985 collection of his essays.[8]

During the same decades when Zeeden was first exploring *Konfessionsbildung*, Gerhard Oestreich's investigation of early modern

8 Ernst Walter Zeeden, 'Grundlagen und Wege der Konfessionsbildung in Deutschland im Zeitalter des Glaubenskämpfe', *Historische Zeitschrift* 185 (1958), 249–99; *Die Entstehung der Konfessionen: Grundlagen und Formen der Konfessionsbildung im Zeitalter der Glaubenskämpfe* (Munich–Vienna 1965); *Konfessionsbildung: Studien zur Reformation, Gegenreformation und katholischen Reform* (Stuttgart, 1985).

political thought led him to emphasize the importance of 'social disciplining' ('*Sozialdisziplinierung*') for early modern state-building.[9] In Oestreich's view, the Stoic intellectual legacy was particularly important in teaching Europeans to master their passions and dedicate themselves to the interests of the state. His ideas inspired two younger historians of the Reformation era, Wolfgang Reinhard and Heinz Schilling, to see that confessionalization also contained a good measure of social disciplining and might thus be said to have served the same function. In a series of books and articles published between 1980 and 1996, Reinhard and Schilling argued that it was not simply the establishment of Lutheran state churches that abetted the power of the territorial princes, as an old truism of German history asserted.[10] Rulers of all religions embraced the role of protector of the faith pressed upon them by their theologians, obliged their subjects to participate regularly in church services, imposed tests of doctrinal loyalty on the territorial clergy, issued ordinances regulating ever-widening forms of behaviour, and otherwise extended their reach and increased their authority. At the same time, the various churches also reinforced their oversight of the belief and behaviour of the faithful, whether by visitations, inquisitions, or consistories, in so doing moulding disciplined subjects far more powerfully than the writings of a Justus

---

9 Oestreich's most important ideas are usefully collected for English-language readers in *Neostoicism and the Early Modern State* (Cambridge, 1982).

10 Schilling's *Habilitationschrift* was a case study of how one German territorial prince augmented his power by pressing a Reformed state church on Lutheran communities that sought to resist, a situation that reversed the standard associations of Lutheranism with territorial absolutism and Calvinism with democracy. Schilling, *Konfessionskonflikt und Staatsbildung: Eine Fallstudie über das Verhältnis von religiösem und sozialem Wandel in der Frühneuzeit am Beispiel der Grafschaft Lippe* (Gütersloh, 1981). For other important statements of these two men's evolving ideas, see Reinhard, 'Gegenreformation als Modernisierung? Prolegomena zu einer Theorie des konfessionellen Zeitalters', *A.R.* 68 (1977), 226–52, French trans. in Reinhard, *Papauté, confessions, modernité* (Paris, 1998), pp. 155–69, English trans. in C. Scott Dixon, ed., *The German Reformation: The Essential Readings* (Oxford, 1999), pp. 169–92; 'Konfession und Konfessionalisierung in Europa', in Reinhard, ed., *Bekenntnis und Geschichte. Die Confessio Augustana im historischen Zusammenhang* (Munich, 1981), pp. 165–89; 'Zwang zur Konfessionalisierung? Prolegomena zu einer Theorie des konfessionellen Zeitalters', *Zeitschrift für historische Forschung* 10 (1983), 257–77; 'Reformation, Counter-Reformation, and the Early Modern State: A Reassessment', *Catholic Historical Review* 75 (1989), 383–404; 'Was ist katholische Konfessionalisierung?', in Reinhard and Schilling, eds, *Die katholische Konfessionalisierung* (Gütersloh and Münster, 1995), pp. 419–52; Schilling, 'Die Konfessionalisierung im Reich – religiöser und gesellschaftlicher Wandel in Deutschland zwischen 1555 und 1620', *Historische Zeitschrift* 246 (1988), 1–25; 'Confessional Europe', in Brady, Oberman and Tracy, eds, *Handbook*, II, 641–81; 'Die Konfessionalisierung von Kirche, Staat und Gesellschaft – Profil, Leistung, Defizite und Perspektiven eines geschichtswissenschaftlichen Paradigmas', in Reinhard and Schilling, eds, *Die katholische Konfessionalisierung*, pp. 1–49.

Lipsius could ever hope to do. In thus linking the themes of confessionalization, social disciplining and the growth of the state, Reinhard and Schilling drew inspiration from both Norbert Elias's influential theory of the 'civilizing process' and the older theories of Weber and Troeltsch, shorn of their confession-specific elements. The manner in which their ideas echoed the preoccupations and language of Michel Foucault further facilitated their reception. Three conferences of the Verein für Reformationsgeschichte, devoted respectively to Reformed, Lutheran and Catholic confessionalization, were landmarks in their dissemination.[11]

In the passage from the generation of Zeeden to that of Reinhard and Schilling, confessionalization thus took on additional meanings and implications. For analytical purposes, it is helpful to distinguish between two different versions of the concept. The view formulated by Schilling and Reinhard that links the development of confessional identities to social disciplining and state-building may be called the 'strong theory of confessionalization'. The position first articulated by Zeeden, but also embraced by such recent authors as Gregory Hanlon, may be called the 'weak theory of confessionalization'. This latter view simply defines confessionalization as the process of rivalry and emulation by which the religions that emerged from the upheavals of the Reformation defined and enforced their particular versions of orthodoxy and orthopraxy, demonized their rivals, and built group cohesion and identity. As Hanlon puts it, 'confessionalization can be regarded as the process whereby barricades were erected around each church group'.[12]

Are either of these theories illuminating for the historian of France?

An answer to this question might begin by investigating how historians of German-speaking Europe have received the arguments of these historians. The strong theory of confessionalization has never been exempt from criticism. Just as enthusiasm for this theory was building in Germany and first spilling over to America, Paula Sutter Fichtner's 1989 *Protestantism and Primogeniture in Early Modern Germany* pointed out one counter-argument to the claim that the Reformation and Counter-Reformation stimulated the emergence of the German territorial state. This slender volume elegantly demonstrated that Luther's criticism of princes who so avidly pursued worldly aggrandizement that they deprived their younger sons of their rightful inheritance slowed the tendency that had begun to develop before 1517 for Germany's dukes and counts to

---

11 Schilling, ed., *Die reformierte Konfessionalisierung in Deutschland – Das Problem der 'Zweiten Reformation'* (Gütersloh, 1986); Hans-Christoph Rublack, ed., *Die lutherische Konfessionalisierung in Deutschland* (Gütersloh, 1992); and Reinhard and Schilling, eds, *Die katholische Konfessionalisierung.*

12 Gregory Hanlon, *Confession and Community in Seventeenth-Century France: Catholic and Protestant Coexistence in Aquitaine* (Philadelphia, 1993), p. 193.

turn their possessions into more permanent territorial entities by establishing rules of succession through primogeniture.[13] Several archival studies of church discipline in German-speaking Switzerland then struck at the claim that the Reformation's reinforcement of church discipline abetted the process of state-building. Heinrich Richard Schmidt's study of the discipline exercised by the morals court established in Bernese territory at the moment of the Reformation suggested that this was best understood as an instrument controlled by parish-level notables and used to reinforce pre-existing moral norms, not as an instrument employed by the canton's governors to promote behaviour that enhanced their power.[14] Ulrich Pfister's study of the spread of consistorial discipline throughout the politically decentralized Grisons found that this was promoted more by church synods than by either the communal elites or the political authorities.[15] A 1997 article by Schmidt in the *Historische Zeitschrift* brought together these findings into a frontal attack on the strong theory of confessionalization.[16] Just as the strong theory was gaining wide international visibility, in other words, it was coming under attack within Germany itself. Indeed, Schilling's own recent statements on the question have expressed an open-minded recognition of limitations of the theory.[17] Historians who uncritically embrace it thus run the risk of repeating the experience of so many historians who have attempted interdisciplinary borrowings in the past: that of latching enthusiastically on to a concept developed by practitioners of another field of study, just as specialists in that field turn away from the idea or recognize its limitations.

The rather heavy-handed functionalism evident in Reinhard and Schilling's linkage of confessionalization with social discipline and state-building provides another reason to be sceptical of the strong theory. Historians of France are particularly likely to think that the association of confessionalization with the growth of the state oversimplifies the extremely unpredictable political consequences that confessional rivalry and religious reform movements could have for state power in early modern Europe. France's Wars of Religion, after all, illustrate how the division of

---

13 Fichtner, *Protestantism and Primogeniture in Early Modern Germany* (New Haven, 1989).

14 Schmidt, *Dorf und Religion: reformierte Sittenzucht in Berner Landgemeinden der frühen Neuzeit* (Stuttgart, 1995).

15 Pfister, 'Reformierte Sittenzucht zwischen kommunaler und territorialer Organisation: Graubünden, 16.–18. Jahrhundert', *A.R.* 87 (1996), 287–333.

16 Heinrich Richard Schmidt, 'Sozialdisziplinierung? Ein Plädoyer für das Ende des Etatismus in der Konfessionalisierungforschung', *Historische Zeitschrift* 265 (1997), 639–82.

17 Schilling, 'Konfessionalisierung von Kirche, Staat und Gesellschaft', pp. 16–40.

Christendom into rival confessions could bring even the era's strongest states to the very brink of dissolution. In direct opposition to the Reinhard–Schilling paradigm, recent French historiography has viewed the road to absolutism as passing through the separation of politics from religion, not their association.[18] Where one national historiography views confessionalization as an instrument of state-building and another ties the reinforcement of the state to the secularization of politics, it is legitimate to ask if both are not excessively concerned to relate all developments of the early modern era to the metanarrative of the growth of the modern state. In any event, the strong theory of confessionalization seems to hold little promise of illuminating French historical experience.

The weak theory of confessionalization is another story. To begin with, it has proven more illuminating and less controversial when applied to German history. Several excellent local studies of German religious life have confirmed and extended Zeeden's insight that the process of building attachment to the practices codified as orthodox by the various churches extended over several generations. Hsia's excellent study of Münster after the fall of the Anabaptist kingdom revealed a city ruled by a prince–bishop whose inhabitants incorporated such Protestant practices as communion in both kinds and the singing of German hymns into nominally Catholic worship, and who simply defined themselves as 'good Christians' in wills devoid of invocations of the saints or anniversary masses. With time, however, religious life increasingly evolved toward post-Tridentine Catholic orthopraxy, thanks less to political pressure from above than to the Jesuit-led introduction of a new culture.[19] Etienne François's model study of Augsburg after 1648 showed how high the barricades between the Catholics and Lutherans of that religiously divided city had become by the second half of the seventeenth century. Although the members of the two churches lived peacefully enough with one another, they were so rigidly separated by the 'invisible border' of different religious sensibilities, rituals and historical memories that they virtually never intermarried, changed faith, or explored some middle ground between the two orthodoxies.[20] Few historians taking the long view not simply of German history, but of the history of Europe as a whole, would deny that the

18 'In accelerating the relative distinction between the spheres of religion and politics, the Wars of Religion facilitated the progress of absolute monarchy.' Arlette Jouanna, quoted in Olivier Christin, 'L'édit de Nantes. Bilan historiographique', *Revue Historique* 301 (1999), 134. Christin's own *La paix de religion. L'autonomisation de la raison politique au XVIe siècle* (Paris, 1997) advances the same argument.

19 Hsia, *Society and Religion in Münster, 1535–1618* (New Haven, 1984).

20 François, *Die Unsichtbare Grenze: Protestanten und Katholiken in Augsburg, 1648–1806* (Sigmaringen, 1991), French edn *Protestants et catholiques en Allemagne: Identités et pluralisme, Augsbourg 1648–1806* (Paris, 1993).

creation of strong loyalties to confessional communities had consequences for political affiliation and personal identity among ordinary Europeans that endured deep into the twentieth century, making this perhaps the most durable long-term consequence of the Reformation.

While the weak theory of confessionalization undoubtedly calls attention to a fundamental set of changes in European culture and society, the historian of France might still question the applicability of one important aspect of this theory to the French case: the corollary that confessionalization was a gradual process extending over several generations. If confessionalization is to be something more than a multisyllabic label for the well-worn observation that the 'magnificent anarchy' of the early Reformation soon gave way to the formulation of creeds, this aspect of *longue durée* would appear to be fundamental. But is it appropriate to speak of a confessionalization *process* in France, where during just twenty years between 1543 and 1562 the Sorbonne drafted a series of articles that were taken by the law to define Catholic orthodoxy, the proliferation of Reformed churches after 1555 gave structure and doctrinal definition to previously unorganized currents of evangelical dissent, and the rivalry between these two camps precipitated a civil war that so polarized the country that attempts to restore the peace would fail time and again for the next 36 years? By the later 1560s, the rival groups of Huguenots and Papists were already so sharply defined in many cities that even when Protestantism was outlawed between 1568 and 1570 and former members of the Reformed church brought their infants to the Catholic church for baptism, the parish clergy placed a little 'H' or 'huot' in the margin, indicating that the family continued to be seen, and closely watched, as Huguenot.[21] Choices made for one side or another in a few critical years durably marked people's public identity.

Rather than highlighting a gradual process of confessionalization, an alternative view of France's religious history could envision a brief moment of confessional polarization, followed by a gradual movement toward confessional reconciliation. One might further hypothesize that the situation of relatively stable confessional coexistence established under the provisions of the Edict of Nantes diminished the barriers between Huguenots and Catholics by promoting greater everyday interaction and the slow accumulation of trust.

For all of the plausibility of this scenario, however, two recent books have offered reasons for thinking that the weak theory of confessionalization

---

[21] A.C. Rouen, Registre Paroissiaux 172; A.D. Seine-Maritime, E, parish registers of Saint Godard and Saint Vivien, Rouen (unclassified at the time I consulted them); David L. Rosenberg, 'Les registres paroissiaux et les incidences de la réaction à la Saint-Barthélémy', *Revue du Nord* 70 (1988), 505.

could apply to France in this period. The first of these is Hanlon's detailed study of the network of social relationships in a single confessionally divided town in Gascony, *Confession and Community in Seventeenth-Century France*. The second is Bernard Dompnier's wide-angle depiction of the Gallican church's image of Protestantism and its battle to reclaim the lost heretics for the faith, *Le Venin de l'hérésie*.[22] Despite their different approaches, both books call attention to corners of early seventeenth-century France, notably the small towns of regions such as Dauphiné and Aquitaine, where a fairly casual everyday coexistence governed relations between Protestants and Catholics at the beginning of the seventeenth century. Both show how, over the course of successive generations, rigorist elements within both churches mounted an ongoing campaign against the customs and social practices that facilitated this trans-confessional cooperation, forbidding the members of one faith from choosing a godparent of the other, and warning them against sending their youngsters to the other's schools. Far from lessening with time, the degree of suspicion and walls of separation between the two confessions may thus have increased in France over the course of the seventeenth century under the steady drumbeat of controversial polemics and legal battles over the rights and prerogatives of the Reformed churches. In the current state of our knowledge, it is an open question whether the ongoing process of confessional rivalry raised ever higher barriers between the two confessions, or whether the situation of stable *convivencia* created by the Edict of Nantes bred closer interaction with those of the other religion. The weak theory of confessionalization thus poses a very interesting question for historians of France.

New evidence

While many sources could undoubtedly be used to explore confessional identity and possible changes in the pattern of interaction between Catholics and Protestants in seventeenth-century France, I will use here a single corpus of material, the 1554 marriage contracts involving at least one resident of Montpellier that survive in that city's archives from the periods 1605–9, 1635–39 and 1665–69.[23] I initially looked at these contracts to explore very different questions about the relative status and wealth of the city's two faiths. To my surprise, it turned out that they

---

[22] Hanlon, *Confession and Community*; Bernard Dompnier, *Le venin de l'hérésie. Image du protestantisme et combat catholique au XVIIe siècle* (Paris, 1985).

[23] For full archival references to the sources consulted and a discussion of the nature and limits of the sample, see above, Chapter 3, pp. 129–30.

also shed useful light on confessional identity and interconfessional relations.

Montpellier passed from one camp to the other during the Religious Wars and was more evenly divided in the seventeenth century between Protestants and Catholics than any other major city in France. The Reformed faith grew so rapidly after the first church was organized in 1560 that the Protestants were able to drive out the mass in October 1561, six months before the outbreak of the First Civil War. Catholic worship was restored at the end of that conflict, only to suffer again during the Second Civil War in 1567–68. Thereafter, the king's lieutenants reasserted crown control over the city and pursued the restoration of Catholic worship with such vigour that many Protestants thought it safest to flee; during the Third Civil War of 1568–70 and again after the Saint Bartholomew's Massacre in 1572, it was Reformed worship's turn to cease. An uneasy toleration of both faiths reigned between 1570 and 1572 and again during the years between 1574 and 1577, when the duke of Montmorency-Damville sought to reinforce his power in the region by forging a political alliance between Huguenots and moderate Catholics. When this effort collapsed, the Protestants once again asserted a domination over the city that would endure for the remainder of the Wars of Religion, although the last decades of the civil wars were less troubled in this corner of Languedoc than elsewhere in the country, and Catholic worship was allowed to resume in the 1580s and to continue through the period of the League with only a brief interruption. Around 1610, Catholics comprised approximately 40 per cent of the population. When civil war flared up anew in 1621, the Protestants again took control and outlawed Catholicism, but the crown recaptured the city in the following year and restored Catholic worship. Over the subsequent decades, control of the municipality was increasingly transferred to the city's Catholics, while shifting patterns of immigration brought growing numbers of Roman worshippers into the city. In the later 1630s, 60 per cent of all marriages celebrated in the city took place in its Catholic churches. By the 1660s the Catholic share of the population was up to 70 per cent.[24]

The long struggle to control the city produced a sharp sense of division between the two religious camps that even affected the outlook of relative moderates, such as the local chronicler, Jean Philippi. Philippi initially joined the Reformed church, but he opposed the more zealous members of the church by seeking to arrange a negotiated peace during the First

---

[24] Jean Philippi, 'Histoire des troubles de Languedoc', in Louise Guiraud, ed., *La Réforme à Montpellier. Preuves* (Montpellier, 1918), *passim*; A.C. Montpellier, GG 1–3; Gérard Cholvy et al., *Histoire de Montpellier* (Toulouse, 1984), pp. 147–94; above, Chapter 2, p. 79, Chapter 3, p. 127.

Civil War, and he abjured the faith in 1568 in order to retain his seat in the Cour des Aides. Still, he remained sufficiently well intentioned to those of both faiths to include in his 1602 will a bequest of 50 *livres* to the city's poor 'without difference of religion'. Despite this, he unambiguously referred to the Protestants as 'the enemies' in the portions of his history written after his return to the Catholic church. He also went back over the early portions of the text to insert the phrase 'so-called' into all passages where he had previously spoken of the 'Reformed religion', so that he now called it the 'so-called Reformed religion' (*'religion pretendue réformée'*).[25] This was the label that the 1576 Edict of Beaulieu ordered to be applied to the faith in all public acts and documents, but members of the church naturally detested it and sought to avoid it whenever possible.[26]

The first way in which Montpellier's marriage contracts illuminate confessional consciousness is by revealing how the two faiths were labelled. During the first decade of the seventeenth century, Montpellier's largely Protestant corps of notaries affixed a surprisingly wide range of designations to the Reformed church. Not only did just one – a probable Catholic – use the hated label 'so-called Reformed religion'; only three others employed the terms 'Reformed church' or 'Reformed religion'. Instead, Isaac Durand, *notaire royal héréditaire*, wrote that his clients intended to marry in 'the Catholic, Apostolic, Reformed church' (*'l'eglise catholique, apostolique et reformee'*), a phrase that claimed for his church the adjectives 'catholic' and 'apostolic' enshrined in the Apostles' Creed. Maître Noel Planque, of uncertain religious affiliation, variously called this church 'the congregation and assembly of those of the religion' or 'the church of God'. Three other notaries also used this latter phrase, whose dissemination may have been fairly broad.[27] Still other documents employed the formulas 'the Christian Reformed church' or 'the Reformed church of God'. Virtually all notaries in this era referred to the Catholic church by the phrase 'Catholic Apostolic and Roman church', but even here some notaries were so inconsistent in the labels they used that it is impossible to determine in which church several dozen marriages were to be celebrated. The very labels attached to the different churches turn out to have been fluid in this period.[28]

Over the subsequent two generations, this fluidity disappeared, as militant voices within the Catholic church gained the backing of the courts

---

[25] Philippi, 'Histoire des troubles', pp. 11, 441, and *passim*.

[26] André Stegmann, ed., *Edits des guerres de religion* (Paris, 1979), p. 101; Benoist, I, 400, II, 91, 114, 176.

[27] See Benoist, III, 133.

[28] As they also were in Les Baux (Provence) in the same era. Céline Borello, 'Les Protestants de la vallée des Baux sous le régime de l'édit de Nantes (1598–1685)', *Provence Historique* 49 (1999), 625.

and the crown in imposing use of the phrase 'so-called Reformed religion'
– on pain of a fine for failure to do so in at least certain regions.[29] Between
1635 and 1639, just two notaries wrote that their clients intended to be
married before 'the Christian Reformed church', while twelve used the
formula '*religion pretendue reformee*', occasionally shortened to '*religion
P.R*' or '*R.P.R*'. Between 1665 and 1669, ten used a variant of this latter
formula, while only one supple notary, probably a Catholic, found a way
to allow his Protestant clients to avoid using the term by recording that
they intended to be married 'in the religion that they profess'. A new
consistency of confessional labelling thus triumphed, as the Protestants
were forced to include in their legal documents a phrase that expressed
the state's disqualification of the fundamental claim of their church.

It is, of course, a sociological truism that the frequency of intermarriage
between members of different social groups reveals perhaps more reliably
than any other indicator the rigidity or porosity of the barriers between
them. Hardly surprisingly, marriage contracts can also illuminate this aspect
of the question of confessionalization, although they are harder to use to
study the frequency of Catholic–Protestant marriage in seventeenth-century
France than might initially be thought. This is because authorities of both
churches forbade their members from marrying somebody who was not a
member of the same church. As a result, mixed marriages in seventeenth-
century France were generally preceded by the formal conversion of one
party or the other, generally the woman, so that both halves of the future
couple could qualify as members of the same church at the time of their
marriage. This conversion was often purely strategic, and was followed
by the convert's return to the church of her upbringing after a decent
interval of time had elapsed.[30] Since marriage contracts typically merely
specify the church in which the planned marriage was to be celebrated,
they provide no direct indication of most cases where the union in question
involved two people who had been raised in different faiths. The marriage
registers of the two churches likewise mask such cases. A fully reliable
statistical study of the frequency of intermarriage during this century
would thus require either the extraordinarily time-consuming establishment of complete genealogies for all families within a confessionally mixed
community, so that every case where a member of a Protestant family

---

[29] A fine of 500 *livres* was imposed throughout the jurisdiction of the Parlement of Paris
in 1634 on those who failed to use this phrase in marriage contracts. A probable native of
Languedoc urged a similar measure in 1648. I have not, however, been able to establish if
such fines were ever actually instituted in Languedoc. Benoist, II, 542, III, 133.

[30] Dompnier, *Venin de l'hérésie*, pp. 154–7; Hanlon, *Confession and Community*, pp. 102–
11; Robert Sauzet, *Contre-Réforme et Réforme catholique en Bas-Languedoc: Le diocèse de
Nîmes au XVIIe siècle* (Louvain, 1979), pp. 165–8; Elisabeth Labrousse, '*Une foi, une loi,
un roi?*' *La Révocation de l'édit de Nantes* (Geneva, 1985), pp. 83–4.

married a member of a Catholic family could be discerned despite the silence of the church registers or marriage contracts on this issue, or the existence for the same confessionally mixed locality of both a full run of marriage records and good registers of abjurations or church receptions that reveal when parties to a marriage had converted shortly before the ceremony, a rare combination of documents. As a result, published evidence about the changing frequency of mixed marriages in seventeenth-century France is scarce, although Dompnier asserts that these fell off sharply after 1663, when the crown made it illegal for Protestant converts to Catholicism to return to their original faith, while figures provided by Hanlon can be recalculated to show that mixed marriages fell from 12 per cent of a sample of 130 marriages in Layrac between 1606 and 1636, to 6 per cent of a sample of 86 marriages between 1672 and 1688.[31]

Despite the silence of many marriage contracts about whether or not they concern two individuals raised in different faiths, the sample of contracts examined here can be used to shed light on the changing frequency of mixed marriages in Montpellier in two ways. First, another surprise about Montpellier marriage contracts is that a few of them formally established a space for freedom of worship within the household that was about to be formed. After indicating that the marriage was to be celebrated in either the Catholic or the Reformed church, these contracts specify that the husband should subsequently allow his future wife to 'live following her conscience' according to the way of the other church 'which she professes'.

Tellingly, the frequency of such clauses diminished steadily across the three periods of time examined here. Clauses establishing this sort of contractual claim to freedom of worship within the household appear in ten of 534 contracts from 1605 to 1609, four of 420 contracts from 1635 to 1639, and just one of 600 contracts from 1665 to 1669. This would appear to suggest a declining frequency of mixed marriages, although it is impossible to be certain that it does not simply reflect instead a growing sense that such clauses were unnecessary or useless, since it seems that these 'religious-liberty clauses' were only written into a fraction of all marriage contracts between people of different religious backgrounds.

This last conclusion may be inferred from the second technique for discovering mixed marriages within our sample of marriage contracts. This involves linking together those contracts in the sample that concern the same nuclear family in order to catch instances where siblings or parents and children married in different churches. Of course, even where two siblings married in the same church, one may have made a mixed marriage

---

31 Dompnier, *Venin de l'hérésie*, p. 156; Hanlon, *Confession and Community*, Table 4.2, p. 113.

with a person of the other faith who converted for the purposes of the union. Conversely, cases where siblings or members of successive generations married in different churches may result from sincere conversions, not simply strategic ones made to allow a mixed marriage. None the less, instances where members of the same family married in different churches provide a rough proxy for the frequency of mixed marriages. Of 67 cases where marriage contracts for two or more siblings appear in the sample, totalling 144 marriages in all, brothers or sisters married in different churches seven times. For only one of these unions does the marriage contract stipulate the right of both spouses to live according to different faiths. The sample also yields 37 cases where marriage contracts appear for members of successive generations of the same family. Eliminating one case where the older generation had made a mixed marriage, three of the remaining 36 children married in a different church from that of their parents, none of them with religious-liberty clauses in their contract. With all due allowance for the approximate character of this measure, it would thus appear that mixed marriages represented something on the order of 5 to 10 per cent of all Montpellier marriages over the course of this period – not the 1 per cent of all marriages suggested by the frequency of religious-liberty clauses. This may be usefully compared with the situation in Layrac, where mixed marriages made up 10 per cent of all marriages in the years 1606–36, 1654–63 and 1672–88, and in the Luberon region of Provence, where the Huguenots were descended from a Waldensian population that had maintained its distinctiveness over centuries, and where mixed marriages accounted for 2 per cent of all marriages around 1630.[32]

If marriage across the confessional line was evidently more frequent than the number of religious-liberty clauses would suggest, it was still considerably less common than would be expected if the city's residents chose their spouses without regard to their religion. Given the nearly even distribution of Montpellier's population between the two faiths over the periods covered by the sample, it can be calculated that fully 45 per cent of all marriages would have been mixed had religion been of no significance in the choice of a spouse. Even if we set the number of mixed marriages at the upper bound of our estimate of 5 to 10 per cent of all marriages, this 10 per cent computes to just 23 per cent of the percentage of mixed marriages that would be expected if religious affiliation were of no significance. A powerful tendency toward confessional endogamy clearly marked seventeenth-century Montpellier.

---

[32] Hanlon, *Confession and Community*, p. 113; Gabriel Audisio, 'Se marier en Luberon: catholiques et protestants vers 1630', in *Mélanges Robert Mandrou: Histoire sociale, sensibilités collectives et mentalités* (Paris, 1985), p. 243.

Once again, this tendency also appears to have increased with time. Four of the cases of siblings who married in different churches come from 1605–9 (the sample contains 22 groups of siblings from this period), one from 1635–39 (of ten groups of siblings), and two from 1665–69 (of 29 groups of siblings). All three of the cases of children who celebrated their wedding in a church different from that of their parents involve parents married in 1605–9 and children married in 1635–39. The samples are small, but they agree in suggesting that the frequency of inter-religious marriages declined as the century advanced.

Marriage, of course, represents a particularly intimate and sustained form of interpersonal interaction. A final way in which Montpellier's marriage contracts can shed light on the extent of the gulf between the two faiths lies in the opportunity they also provide to observe a more casual kind of relationship that linked people across confessional lines – the business relationship between notaries and their clients. A variety of sources enable one to determine the religious affiliation of the majority of the notaries whose surviving registers provide our sample of marriage contracts.[33] Since the marriage contracts contain an indication of the religion of the couples intending to marry, they can be used to determine the frequency with which the city's inhabitants turned to a person of their own faith when seeking a trustworthy notary to handle their contractual affairs.

Just as the inhabitants of certain French villages spoke within living memory of 'the Protestant butcher' or 'the Catholic butcher', archivists and researchers will occasionally refer casually to certain notaries as 'Protestant notaries', as if economic transactions followed confessional lines and one could deduce a person's faith from his or her choice of notary. In fact, none of the 27 Montpellier notaries whose religious affiliation I was able to determine with confidence did business exclusively with members of his own faith. Since a majority of Montpellier's notaries were Protestant throughout the period examined here, a sizeable number of Catholics chose to employ the services of Protestant notaries. A smaller number of Protestants likewise opted for Catholic notaries. Still, a fairly clear tendency may be observed for the city's residents to choose notaries of their own religion. Only one notary in the sample, Antoine Comte, was able to win the confidence of so many clients of the other faith that the percentage of marriage contracts in his registers involving members of his

---

[33] Used for this purpose were: A.D.H., B 22662, 'Emprunt sur les Catholiques 1622/ Emprunt sur les habitans de la R Reformee 1622'; the city's Catholic and Protestant parish registers; the registers of the notaries themselves, which sometimes include pious formulas that provide an indication of the notary's faith; and the marriage contracts of notaries that appear in the sample. These sources permitted me to determine with confidence the religion of 27 of the 41 notaries represented in the sample.

own church fell below the percentage of his co-religionists within the larger universe of those signing marriage contracts during the five-year period in question. Most notaries did business disproportionately with members of their faith.

A simple index of integration can be used to gauge the strength of this preference for a notary of the same faith. The procedure utilized here involves first computing from the data collected the number of contracts that would have been drawn up by a notary of the same faith as the couple intending to marry if all city residents chose their notary without regard to religious affiliation. This has been labelled the 'hypothesis of perfect integration'. Next was computed the 'hypothesis of perfect segregation': the number of contracts that would have been drawn up by a notary of the couple's own faith if everybody did business only with co-religionists. Finally, the actually observed number of contracts written by notaries of the same religion was calculated as a percentage of the difference between these limit hypotheses. This yields what I have called the index of integration. For the first period this comes out to 56 per cent, for the second to 37 per cent, and for the third to 46 per cent.[34] Two conclusions emerge. First, the index of integration in all three periods exceeds the comparable index of 23 per cent that we have seen to be the upper bound for the strength of the tendency toward Catholic–Protestant intermarriage. As would be expected, people were considerably more likely to choose a notary of another religion than a spouse of another religion. Second, the index of integration declined between the first and the seventh decades of the century, albeit according to an irregular pattern. Once again, a modest tendency appears for the two confessions to become increasingly self-enclosed communities as the seventeenth century advanced.

More case studies involving other kinds of localities and additional means of observation will have to be attempted before it can be stated with assurance that confessionalization advanced across France as a whole over the seventeenth century. This admittedly exploratory study of a single source and a single city none the less clearly suggests that this is what happened in Montpellier. Even in this city, which had been unusually hotly

---

34 Because the sample contained the records of a few very active notaries whose religious affiliation could not be determined with confidence from other sources, but whose highly skewed clientele suggested that they were probably of one faith or the other, I calculated this index twice, once with the uncertain cases included and once with them excluded, to ensure that the decision to use only those cases where the notary's religion could be established on the basis of independent evidence about their faith did not affect the results obtained. Reassuringly, these two sets of calculations yielded virtually identical final results, although the pattern of individual cases looked very different when these uncertain cases were included. The figures provided here are for the sample of notaries whose religion was determined with confidence.

contested between Protestants and Catholics during the Wars of Religion, confessional labels were surprisingly fluid in the first decade of the seventeenth century, people frequently did business across confessional lines, and a fraction of the population contractually ensured at marriage that two different faiths could be simultaneously practised in the same household. Over time, increasingly tight confessional labels were imposed. Both intermarriage (always fairly rare) and cross-confessional economic interaction (more common) declined in frequency. The thrust toward the separation of the two religious communities generated by the ongoing rivalry between the leading spokesmen of each faith thus seems in the final analysis to have been more powerful than the forces working toward interconfessional cooperation fostered by the establishment of a more stable religious peace after 1598. In this sense, the weak theory of confessionalization would seem to apply fruitfully to France – or, at least, to this one city within it.

Index